HOLT

LITERATURE AND LANGUAGE ARTS

Warriner's Handbook

First Course

Grammar • Usage • Mechanics • Sentences

 Mastering the CALIFORNIA STANDARDS in English-Language Conventions

Instructional Framework by

John E. Warriner

HOLT, RINEHART AND WINSTON

AUTHOR **JOHN E. WARRINER** taught for thirty-two years in junior and senior high schools and in college. He was a high school English teacher when he developed the original organizational structure for his classic *English Grammar and Composition* series. The approach pioneered by Mr. Warriner was distinctive, and the editorial staff of Holt, Rinehart and Winston have worked diligently to retain the unique qualities of his pedagogy in the *Holt Handbook*. John Warriner also co-authored the *English Workshop* series and edited *Short Stories: Characters in Conflict.*

ISBN 978-0-03-099232-2

ISBN 0-03-099232-X

3 4 5 6   1083   11 10 09

CONTENTS IN BRIEF

CONTENTS

Parts of Speech Overview

Noun, Pronoun, Adjective **24**

 Standards Focus

Grammar 1.3 Identify parts of speech.

Parts of Speech Overview

Verb, Adverb, Preposition, Conjunction, Interjection

CHAPTER

3

Standards Focus

Grammar 1.3 Identify parts of speech.

Complements
Direct and Indirect Objects,
Subject Complements **72**

The Phrase
Prepositional, Verbal, and Appositive Phrases **88**

The Clause

CHAPTER

6

Independent and Subordinate Clauses **112**

 Standards Focus

Grammar 1.3 Identify structure of sentences.

Grammar 1.4 Demonstrate the mechanics of writing (e.g., commas at end of dependent clauses).

Kinds of Sentence Structure

Agreement

Grammar 1.2 Make clear references between pronouns and
antecedents.

Grammar 1.4 Demonstrate appropriate English usage (e.g., pronoun
reference).

Using Verbs Correctly
Principal Parts, Regular and Irregular Verbs,
Tense, Voice **174**

CHAPTER

9

Standards Focus

Sentence Structure 1.1 Use the active voice.

Grammar 1.4 Demonstrate appropriate English usage.

CHAPTER

10

Using Pronouns Correctly

Standards Focus

Grammar 1.2 Make clear references between pronouns and antecedents.

Grammar 1.4 Demonstrate appropriate English usage (e.g., pronoun reference).

Using Modifiers Correctly

CHAPTER 11

Comparison and Placement

Standards Focus

Sentence Structure 1.1 Place modifiers properly.

Grammar 1.4 Demonstrate appropriate English usage.

A Glossary of Usage

Capital Letters

Punctuation

End Marks, Commas, Semicolons, and Colons 288

CHAPTER

14

Standards Focus

Grammar 1.4 Demonstrate the mechanics of writing (e.g., commas at end of dependent clauses).

Punctuation 1.5 Identify semicolons and use them correctly.

Punctuation

Underlining (Italics), Quotation Marks, Apostrophes, Hyphens, Parentheses, Brackets, and Dashes 318

Standards Focus

Grammar 1.4 Demonstrate the mechanics of writing (e.g., quotation marks).

Punctuation 1.5 Identify hyphens, dashes, and brackets and use them correctly.

Spelling

Improving Your Spelling

Standards Focus

Spelling 1.7 Spell derivatives correctly by applying the spellings of bases and affixes.

Correcting Common Errors

Key Language Skills Review **376**

Standards Focus

Language Convention 1.0 Students write and speak with a command of standard English conventions appropriate to this grade level.

CHAPTER

Writing Effective Sentences 412

Standards Focus

Grammar 1.3 Identify types and structure of sentences.

Sentence Diagramming 444

Standards Focus

Grammar 1.3 Identify all parts of speech and types and structure of sentences.

TO OUR STUDENTS

Why should I study grammar, usage, and mechanics?

Many people would say that you should study grammar to learn to root out errors in your speech and writing. Certainly, *Warriner's Handbook* can help you learn to avoid making errors and to correct the errors you do make. More importantly, though, studying grammar, usage, and mechanics gives you the skills you need to take sentences and passages apart and to put them together, to learn which parts go together and which don't. Instead of writing sentences and passages that you hope sound good, you can craft your sentences to create just the meaning and style you want.

Knowing grammar, usage, and mechanics gives you the tools to understand and discuss your own language, to communicate clearly the things you want to communicate, and to develop your own communication style. Further, mastery of language skills can help you succeed in your other classes, in future classes, on standardized tests, and in the larger world, including, eventually, the workplace.

How do I use *Warriner's Handbook*?

Warriner's Handbook is part of the Holt Literature and Language Arts program. The skills taught in *Warriner's Handbook* are important to your success in the reading, writing, speaking, and listening components of this program.

Not only can you use this book as a complete grammar, usage, and mechanics textbook, but you can also use it as a reference guide when you work on any piece of writing. Whether you are writing a personal letter, a report for your social studies class, or some other piece of writing, you can use *Warriner's Handbook* to answer your questions about grammar, usage, capitalization, punctuation, and spelling.

How is *Warriner's Handbook* organized?

Warriner's Handbook is divided into three main parts:

● **PART 1** The **Grammar, Usage, and Mechanics** chapters provide instruction on and practice using the building blocks of language—words, phrases, clauses, capitalization, punctuation, and spelling. Use these chapters to discover how to take sentences apart and put them together. The last chapter, **Correcting Common Errors,** provides additional practice on key language skills as well as standardized test practice in grammar, usage, and mechanics.

● **PART 2** The **Sentences** chapters include Writing Effective Sentences and Sentence Diagramming. **Writing Effective Sentences** provides instruction on and practice with writing correct, clear, and interesting sentences. **Sentence Diagramming** teaches you to analyze and diagram sentences so you can see how the parts of a sentence relate to each other.

● **PART 3** The **Resources** section includes **History of English,** a concise history of the English language; **Test Smarts,** a handy guide to taking standardized tests in grammar, usage, and mechanics; and **Grammar at a Glance,** a glossary of grammatical terms.

How are the chapters organized?

Each chapter begins with a Diagnostic Preview, a short test that covers the whole chapter and alerts you to skills that need improvement, and ends with a Chapter Review, another short test that tells you how well you have mastered that chapter. In between, you'll see rules, which are basic statements of grammar, usage, and mechanics principles. The rules are illustrated with examples and followed by exercises and reviews that help you practice what you have learned.

What are some other features of this textbook?

■ **Oral Practice**—spoken practice and reinforcement of rules and concepts

■ **Writing Applications**—activities that let you apply grammar, usage, and mechanics concepts in your writing

■ **Tips & Tricks**—easy-to-use hints about grammar, usage, and mechanics

- **Meeting the Challenge**—questions or short activities that ask you to approach a concept from a new angle
- **Style Tips**—information about formal and informal uses of language
- **Help**—pointers to help you understand either key rules and concepts or exercise directions

Warriner's Handbook on the Internet

As you move through *Warriner's Handbook*, you will find the best online resources at **go.hrw.com**.

What are the California standards?

The California State Board of Education has adopted a set of standards for achievement in Written and Oral English Language Conventions. You will be expected to master these standards during the school year. Each chapter of *Warriner's Handbook* begins with a box listing the California standards that you will cover in that chapter.

1.0 Written and Oral English Language Conventions

Students write and speak with a command of standard English conventions appropriate to this grade level.

Sentence Structure

1.1 Place modifiers properly and use the active voice.

Grammar

1.2 Identify and use infinitives and participles and make clear references between pronouns and antecedents.

1.3 Identify all parts of speech and types and structure of sentences.

1.4 Demonstrate the mechanics of writing (e.g., quotation marks, commas at end of dependent clauses) and appropriate English usage (e.g., pronoun reference).

Punctuation

1.5 Identify hyphens, dashes, brackets, and semicolons and use them correctly.

Capitalization

1.6 Use correct capitalization.

Spelling

1.7 Spell derivatives correctly by applying the spellings of bases and affixes.

Grammar, Usage, and Mechanics

Grammar

Usage

Mechanics

GO TO: go.hrw.com
KEYWORD: HLLA

1.0 Written and Oral English Language Conventions
Students write and speak with a command of standard English conventions appropriate to this grade level.
1.3 Identify types of sentences.

The Parts of a Sentence

Subject and Predicate, Kinds of Sentences

Diagnostic Preview

A. Identifying Sentences

Identify each of the following word groups as a *sentence* or a *sentence fragment*. If a word group is a sentence fragment, rewrite it to make a complete sentence.

EXAMPLES   **1.** Having forgotten their lunches.

     1. sentence fragment—Having forgotten their lunches, the students bought sandwiches.

     2. How strong the wind is!

     2. sentence

1. After we visit the library and gather information for the research paper.
2. Are you ready for the big game next week?
3. Listen closely to our guest speaker.
4. Have written the first draft of my paper.
5. An excellent short story, "The Medicine Bag," is in that book.
6. That we helped Habitat for Humanity to build.
7. Mrs. Chin, our math teacher this year.
8. Be prepared to give your speech tomorrow.
9. Fishing, skiing, and swimming in the lake.
10. What a good idea you have, Amy!

B. Identifying Subjects and Predicates

Write the subject and the predicate in each of the following sentences. Then, underline the simple subject and the simple predicate.

EXAMPLE   **1.** A computer can be a wonderful tool for people with disabilities.

    1. *A <u>computer</u>; <u>can be</u> a wonderful tool for people with disabilities*

11. Specially designed machines have been developed in the past several years.
12. Have you ever seen a talking computer?
13. It is used mainly by people with visual impairments.
14. Most computers display writing on a screen.
15. However, these special models can give information by voice.
16. Closed-captioned television is another interesting and fairly recent invention.
17. Subtitles appear on the television screens of many hearing-impaired viewers.
18. These viewers can read the subtitles and enjoy their favorite television shows.
19. With a teletypewriter (TTY), people can type messages over phone lines.
20. Many new inventions and devices make life easier.

C. Punctuating and Classifying Sentences

Copy the last word of each of the following sentences, and then punctuate each sentence with the correct end mark. Classify each sentence as *declarative, interrogative, imperative,* or *exclamatory.*

EXAMPLE   **1.** Flowers and insects depend on one another for life

    1. *life.—declarative*

21. Have you ever watched a honeybee or a bumblebee in a garden
22. The bee flies busily from one flower to another, drinking nectar
23. Notice the yellow pollen that collects on the legs and body of the bee
24. The bee carries pollen from flower to flower, helping the plants to make seeds
25. What a remarkable insect the bee is

The Sentence

1a. A *sentence* is a word or word group that contains a subject and a verb and that expresses a complete thought.

A sentence begins with a capital letter and ends with a period, a question mark, or an exclamation point.

EXAMPLES   **S**he won a prize for her book**.**

Why did you stop running**?**

Wait**!** [The understood subject is *you*.]

Sentence or Sentence Fragment?

A *sentence fragment* is a group of words that looks like a sentence but does not contain both a subject and a verb or does not express a complete thought.

SENTENCE FRAGMENT	Sailing around the world. [The word group lacks a subject.]
SENTENCE	They are sailing around the world.
SENTENCE FRAGMENT	The hike through the Grand Canyon. [The word group lacks a verb.]
SENTENCE	The hike through the Grand Canyon was long and hard.
SENTENCE FRAGMENT	After they pitched the tent. [The word group contains a subject and a verb but does not express a complete thought.]
SENTENCE	After they pitched the tent, they rested.

Oral Practice **Identifying Sentences**

Read each of the following word groups aloud. Then, say whether each word group is a *sentence* or a *sentence fragment*. If a word group is a sentence fragment, add words to make it a complete sentence.

EXAMPLES   **1.** During her vacation last summer.

1. sentence fragment—During her vacation last summer, she hiked in the mountains.

2. My friend Michelle visited Colorado.

2. sentence

Reference Note

For information on the use of **capital letters**, see page 266. For information on **end marks**, see page 290.

Reference Note

For information on **the understood subject**, see page 19.

| STYLE   TIP |

Sentence fragments are common and acceptable in informal situations. However, in formal writing, you should avoid using sentence fragments.

| COMPUTER TIP

Many grammar-checking software programs can help you identify sentence fragments. If you have access to such a program, use it to help you evaluate your writing.

Reference Note

For information on **revising sentence fragments**, see pages 4 and 414.

---

1. Do you know what happened during Michelle's boat trip?
2. Down the rapids on the Colorado River.
3. At first her boat drifted calmly through the Grand Canyon.
4. Then the river dropped suddenly.
5. And became foaming rapids full of dangerous boulders.
6. Many of which can break a boat.
7. Michelle's boat was small.
8. With one guide and four passengers.
9. Some passengers prefer large inflatable boats with outboard motors.
10. Carrying eighteen people.

Subject and Predicate

Sentences consist of two basic parts: subjects and predicates.

The Subject

1b. The *subject* tells *whom* or *what* the sentence is about.

EXAMPLES **Nicholasa Mohr** is a writer and an artist.

The girls on the team were all good students.

He shared his lunch with the boy on the other team.

Swimming is good exercise.

Reference Note

A compound noun, such as *Nicholasa Mohr,* is considered one noun. For information about **compound nouns,** see page 25.

To find the subject, ask *who* or *what* is doing something or *whom* or *what* is being talked about. The subject may come at the beginning, middle, or end of a sentence.

EXAMPLES **The pitcher** struck Felicia out. [*Who* struck Felicia out? *The pitcher* struck Felicia out.]

After practicing for hours, **Tim** bowled five strikes. [*Who* bowled five strikes? *Tim* bowled five strikes.]

How kind **you** are! [*Who* is kind? *You* are kind.]

When will **the afternoon train** arrive? [*What* will arrive? *The afternoon train* will arrive.]

Hiding in the tall grass was **a baby rabbit.** [*What* was hiding? *A baby rabbit* was hiding.]

 Writing Subjects and Punctuating Sentences

Provide subjects to fill in the blanks in the following sentences. Use a different subject in each sentence.

EXAMPLE   **1.** ____ is very heavy.

          1. That box is very heavy.

1. ____ is an exciting game to play.
2. ____ works in the post office.
3. Luckily for me, ____ was easy to repair.
4. Tied to the end of the rope was ____.
5. Did ____ help you?
6. ____ eventually became President of the United States.
7. Have ____ always wanted to visit Peru?
8. Luis, ____ was the score?
9. Before the game, ____ will meet in the gym.
10. ____ has always been one of my favorite books.
11. What a great basketball player ____ is!
12. Has ____ called you yet?
13. In the afternoon ____ takes a nap.
14. ____ is playing at the theater this weekend?
15. When did ____ start making that sound?
16. In a minute ____ will feed you, Spot.
17. Under the pile of leaves in the front yard was ____.
18. ____ is the group's best-known song?
19. In my opinion, ____ is a better goalie than Alex.
20. Where in the world did ____ get that hat?

⌐ **TIPS** & **TRICKS** ⌐

Here is a test to find the simple subject of most sentences: If you leave out the simple subject, a sentence does not make sense.

EXAMPLE
The frisky cat chased its tail.
The frisky . . . chased its tail. [*Cat* is the simple subject.]

Simple Subject and Complete Subject

1c. The *simple subject* is the main word or word group that tells *whom* or *what* the sentence is about.

The *complete subject* consists of all the words that tell *whom* or *what* a sentence is about.

EXAMPLES   The four new students arrived early.

    Complete subject   **The four new students**
    Simple subject   **students**

Is the winner of the go-cart race present?

| *Complete subject* | the winner of the go-cart race |
| *Simple subject* | winner |

A round walnut table with five legs stood in the middle of the dining room.

| *Complete subject* | A round walnut table with five legs |
| *Simple subject* | table |

A simple subject may consist of one word or several words.

EXAMPLES   **Jets** often break the sound barrier. [one word]

Does **Aunt Carmen** own a grocery store? [two words]

On the library shelf was ***The Island of the Blue Dolphins.*** [six words]

NOTE   In this book, the simple subject is usually referred to as the *subject.*

Exercise 2 Identifying Subjects

Write the subject of each of the following sentences.

EXAMPLE   1. A book by N. Scott Momaday is on the table.

1. *book*

1. Born in 1934 in Oklahoma, Momaday lived on Navajo and Apache reservations in the Southwest.
2. Momaday's father was a Kiowa.
3. As a young man, Momaday attended the University of New Mexico and Stanford University.
4. In *The Way to Rainy Mountain,* he tells about the myths and history of the Kiowa people.
5. The book includes poems, an essay, and stories about the Kiowa people.
6. *The Way to Rainy Mountain* was published in 1969.
7. After Momaday's book came works by other modern American Indian writers.
8. William Least Heat-Moon traveled in a van across the United States and wrote about his journey.
9. Was he inspired to write by his travels?
10. Readers of this Osage writer enjoy his beautiful descriptions of nature.

Identifying Complete Subjects and Simple Subjects

Write the complete subject in each of the following sentences. Then, underline the simple subject.

EXAMPLES   1. Stories about time travel make exciting reading.
   1. *Stories* about time travel

   2. Samuel Delany writes great science fiction.
   2. *Samuel Delany*

   1. Ray Bradbury is also a writer of science fiction.
   2. *The Golden Apples of the Sun* is a collection of Bradbury's short stories.
   3. Is your favorite story in that book "A Sound of Thunder"?
   4. The main character in the story is called Mr. Eckels.
   5. For ten thousand dollars, Mr. Eckels joins Time Safari, Inc.
   6. He is looking for the dinosaur *Tyrannosaurus rex.*
   7. With four other men, Bradbury's hero travels more than sixty million years back in time.
   8. On the safari, trouble develops.
   9. Because of one mistake, the past is changed.
   10. Do the results of that mistake affect the future?

The Predicate

1d. The *predicate* of a sentence tells something about the subject.

EXAMPLES   The phone **rang.**

   Old Faithful **is a giant geyser in Yellowstone National Park.**

   Jade Snow Wong **wrote about growing up in San Francisco's Chinatown.**

   Like the subject, the predicate may be found anywhere in a sentence.

EXAMPLES   **Outside the tent was** a baby bear.

   Late in the night we **heard a noise.** [The predicate in this sentence is divided by the subject, *we.*]

Has the dough **risen enough**? [The predicate is divided by the subject, *the dough*.]

Stop right there! [The subject in this sentence is understood to be *you*.]

Exercise 4 Identifying Predicates

Write the predicate in each of the following sentences.

EXAMPLES   **1.** My favorite sports poster is this one of Roberto Clemente.
          1. is this one of Roberto Clemente

          2. Have you heard of this famous sports hero?
          2. Have heard of this famous sports hero

1. Also among my baseball treasures is a book about Clemente's life and career.
2. Clemente played right field for the Pittsburgh Pirates, my favorite team.
3. During his amazing career, he won four National League batting titles.
4. In 1966, he was named the league's Most Valuable Player.
5. Twice Clemente helped lead the Pirates to World Series victories.
6. In fourteen World Series games, Clemente never went without a hit.
7. Roberto Clemente died in a plane crash off the coast of his homeland, Puerto Rico.
8. The plane crash occurred during a flight to Nicaragua to aid earthquake victims.
9. After his death, Clemente was elected to the National Baseball Hall of Fame.
10. In New York, a park has been named for this beloved ballplayer.

Writing Predicates

Make a sentence out of each of the following word groups by adding a predicate to fill the blank or blanks.

EXAMPLES   **1.** A flock of geese _____

     1. A flock of geese flew high overhead.

     2. _____ a poster of Nelson Mandela.

     2. Over Kim's desk hung a poster of Nelson Mandela.

1. My favorite food _____.
2. A course in first aid _____.
3. _____ our car _____?
4. Rock climbing _____.
5. Spanish explorers in the Americas _____.
6. Several computers _____.
7. _____ a new pair of in-line skates.
8. The skyscrapers of New York City _____.
9. Some dogs _____.
10. _____ my family _____.
11. Victory in the championship _____.
12. _____ all sorts of birds _____.
13. The new store at the mall _____.
14. _____ a small, brown toad.
15. The flowers in Mr. Alvarez's garden _____.
16. _____ my chores _____.
17. Gerry's allowance _____.
18. _____ we _____?
19. The cool of the morning _____.
20. The tiny kittens _____.

Simple Predicate and Complete Predicate

1e. The *simple predicate,* or *verb,* is the main word or word group that tells something about the subject.

The *complete predicate* consists of a verb and all the words that describe the verb and complete its meaning.

EXAMPLES   The pilot broke the sound barrier.

     Complete predicate   **broke the sound barrier**

     Simple predicate (verb)   **broke**

We should have visited the diamond field in Arkansas.

Complete predicate   should have visited the
diamond field in Arkansas

Simple predicate (verb)   should have visited

The telephone on the table rang.

Complete predicate   rang

Simple predicate (verb)   rang

NOTE   In this book, the simple predicate is usually referred to as the *verb*.

Exercise 6   **Identifying Complete Predicates and Verbs**

Write the complete predicate of each of the following sentences. Then, underline the verb.

EXAMPLE   **1.** Who created the U.S. flag?

             1. <u>created</u> the U.S. flag

1. Many scholars are unsure about the history of the Stars and Stripes.
2. The Continental Congress approved a design for the flag.
3. The flag's design included thirteen red stripes and thirteen white stripes.
4. The top inner quarter of the flag was a blue field with thirteen white stars.
5. The name of the designer has remained a mystery.
6. During the American Revolution, the colonists needed a symbol of their independence.
7. George Washington wanted flags for the army.
8. Unfortunately, the flags did not arrive until the end of the Revolutionary War.
9. According to legend, Betsy Ross made the first flag.
10. However, most historians doubt the Betsy Ross story.

The Verb Phrase

Some simple predicates, or verbs, consist of more than one word. Such verbs are called *verb phrases* (verbs that include one or more helping verbs).

EXAMPLE   Kathy **is riding** the Ferris wheel.

Reference Note

For information about **helping verbs,** see page 49.

EXAMPLES   The carnival **has been** in town for two weeks.

Should Imelda **have gotten** here sooner?

Reference Note

For information on **adverbs,** see page 54.

NOTE   The words *not* and *never* are not verbs; they are adverbs. Adverbs are never part of a verb or verb phrase.

EXAMPLES   She **has** not **written** to me recently.

I **will** never **forget** her.

They **do**n't **know** my cousins. [*Don't* is the contraction of *do* and *not*. The *n't* is not part of the verb phrase *do know*.]

Exercise 7   Identifying Verbs and Verb Phrases

Write the verb or verb phrase in each of the following sentences.

EXAMPLES   1. Look at these beautiful pictures of Hawaii.
             1. *Look*

            2. They were taken by our science teacher.
             2. *were taken*

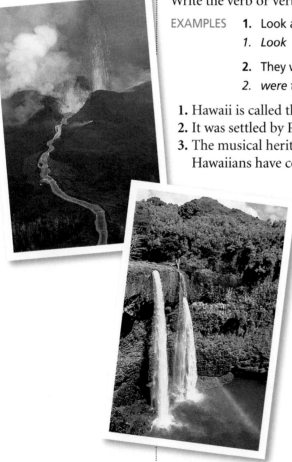

1. Hawaii is called the Aloha State.
2. It was settled by Polynesians about 2,000 years ago.
3. The musical heritage and rich culture of the original Hawaiians have contributed to the islands' popularity.
4. Have you ever seen a traditional Hawaiian dance, one with drums and chants?
5. The Hawaiian islands are also known for their lush, exotic scenery.
6. I can certainly not imagine anything more spectacular than an active volcano at night.
7. Would you like a helicopter ride over misty waterfalls like those in Hawaii?
8. What an incredible sight that surely is!
9. Those Hawaiian dancers must have been practicing for years.
10. Save me a place on the next flight!

Finding the Subject

To find the subject of a sentence, find the verb first. Then, ask *Who?* or *What?* before the verb.

EXAMPLES   In high school we will have more homework. [The verb is *will have. Who* will have? *We* will have. *We* is the subject of the sentence.]

Can you untie this knot? [*Can untie* is the verb. *Who* can untie? *You* can untie. *You* is the subject of the sentence.]

The peak of Mount Everest was first reached by Sir Edmund Hillary and Tenzing Norgay. [The verb is *was reached. What* was reached? *Peak* was reached. *Peak* is the subject of the sentence.]

Ahead of the explorers lay a vast wilderness. [The verb is *lay. What* lay? *Wilderness* lay. *Wilderness* is the subject of the sentence.]

Where are the Canary Islands located? [*Are located* is the verb. *What* are located? *Canary Islands* are located. *Canary Islands* is the subject of the sentence.]

Pass the salad, please. [*Pass* is the verb. *Who* should pass? *You* pass. Understood *you* is the subject of the sentence.]

┌HELP─

When you are looking for the subject of a sentence, remember that the subject is never part of a prepositional phrase. Cross through any prepositional phrases; the subject will be one of the remaining words.

EXAMPLE
Several ~~of the puzzle~~ ~~pieces are under the sofa.~~

SUBJECT
Several

VERB
are

Reference Note
For information on **prepositional phrases,** see page 59.

Compound Subjects and Compound Verbs

Compound Subjects

1f. A *compound subject* consists of two or more subjects that are joined by a conjunction and that have the same verb.

The conjunctions most commonly used to connect the words of a compound subject are *and* and *or.*

EXAMPLES   **Paris** and **London** remain favorite tourist attractions. [The two parts of the compound subject have the same verb, *remain.*]

Nelson Mandela or **Archbishop Desmond Tutu** will speak at the conference. [The two parts of the compound subject have the same verb, *will speak.*]

Among my hobbies are **reading, snorkeling,** and **painting.** [The three parts of the compound subject have the same verb, *are.*]

Reference Note
For information on **conjunctions,** see page 62.

In sentences with a compound subject joined by *or*, the verb agrees with the subject closest to it. Here is a quick test you can use. (1) Cover the part of the subject that is farther from the verb. (2) Decide whether the remaining part of the compound subject agrees with the verb.

EXAMPLE

The dog or the rabbits (*digs, dig*) holes in the garden. [*The rabbits digs* or *the rabbits dig*? *The rabbits dig* is correct.]

Exercise 8 Identifying Compound Subjects

Write the compound subject in each of the following sentences.

EXAMPLE 1. The shapes and sizes of sand dunes are determined by the wind.

1. *shapes, sizes*

1. The national parks and monuments of the United States include many of the world's most spectacular landforms.
2. The Grand Canyon and the waterfalls of Yosemite are examples of landforms shaped by erosion.
3. Water, wind, and other natural forces are continuing the age-old erosion of landforms.
4. On the Colorado Plateau, for example, natural bridges and arches, like the one in the photograph on the left, have been produced by erosion.
5. Likewise, Skyline Arch and Landscape Arch in Utah are two natural arches formed by erosion.
6. Underground, caves and immense caverns are created by rushing streams and waterfalls.
7. Stalagmites and stalactites, such as the ones in the photograph on the right, are formed by lime deposits from drops of water seeping into these caverns.

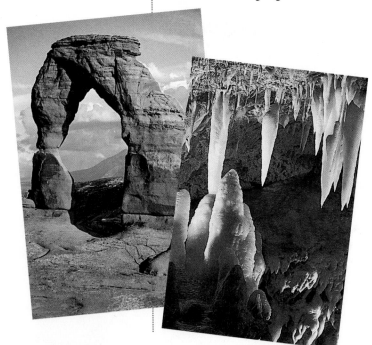

8. In river systems throughout the world, canyons and gorges are cut into the earth by erosion.
9. Many rapids and waterfalls have also originated through the process of erosion.
10. Do steep areas with heavy rainfall or dry regions with few trees suffer more from erosion?

Exercise 9 Writing Compound Subjects

Add a compound subject to each of the following predicates. Use *and* or *or* to join the parts of your compound subjects.

EXAMPLE   **1.** ____ were at the bottom of my locker.

         1. *My bus pass and a pair of gym socks were at the bottom of my locker.*

1. Yesterday ____ arrived in the mail.
2. ____ make loyal pets.
3. On the beach ____ spotted a dolphin.
4. ____ will present their report on the adventures of Álvar Núñez Cabeza de Vaca.
5. In the attic were piled ____ .
6. Ever since first grade, ____ have been friends and neighbors.
7. Is ____ coaching the tennis team this year?
8. For Indian food, ____ always go to the Bombay Cafe in the shopping center nearby.
9. To our great surprise, out of my little brother's pockets spilled ____ .
10. Both ____ may be seen on the African plains.

Compound Verbs

1g. A *compound verb* consists of two or more verbs that are joined by a conjunction and that have the same subject.

The conjunctions most commonly used to connect the words of a compound verb are *and, or,* and *but.*

EXAMPLES   The rain **has fallen** for days and **is** still **falling.**

           The team **played** well but **lost** the game anyway.

           Will Rolando **mop** the floor or **wash** the dishes?

A sentence may contain both a *compound subject* and a *compound verb*. Notice in the following example that both subjects carry out the action of both verbs.

EXAMPLE   A few **vegetables** and many **flowers sprouted** and **grew** in the rich soil. [The vegetables sprouted and grew, and the flowers sprouted and grew.]

| STYLE   TIP |

Using compound subjects and verbs, you can combine ideas to make your writing less wordy. Compare the examples below.

WORDY
Orville and Wilbur Wright built one of the first airplanes. Orville and Wilbur Wright flew it near Kitty Hawk, North Carolina.

REVISED
Orville and Wilbur Wright **built** one of the first airplanes and **flew** it near Kitty Hawk, North Carolina.

┌HELP─
Be sure to
include all parts of each
verb phrase in Exercise 10.

**MEETING THE
CHALLENGE**

You can use compound
subjects and compound
verbs to make your writing
smoother—less repetitive
and more concise. Find an
interesting picture or photograph that shows several
things or people. Then,
write a paragraph describing the picture, making sure
to use a compound subject
or compound verb in at
least four sentences.

┌HELP─
Some of the
subjects and verbs in
Exercise 11 are compound.

Exercise 10 **Identifying Compound Verbs**

Write each compound verb or verb phrase in the following
sentences.

EXAMPLE   **1.** Have you heard of the game Serpent or learned
the game Senet?

    1. have heard, learned

1. Just like children today, children in ancient Egypt played
games and enjoyed toys.
2. For the Egyptian board game Serpent, players found or
carved a serpent-shaped stone.
3. Players placed the serpent in the center of the board and then
began the game.
4. They used place markers and threw bones or sticks as dice.
5. The players took turns and competed with one another in a
race to the center.
6. Senet was another ancient Egyptian board game and was
played by children and adults alike.
7. Senet looked like an easy game but was actually difficult.
8. Players moved their playing pieces toward the ends of three
rows of squares but sometimes were stopped by their
opponents.
9. Senet boards were complex and had certain squares for good
luck and bad luck.
10. These squares could help players or could block their pieces.

Exercise 11 **Identifying Subjects and Verbs**

Identify the subject and verb in each of the following sentences.

EXAMPLE   **1.** American pioneers left their homes and traveled
to the West.

    1. pioneers—subject; left, traveled—verbs

1. Settlers faced and overcame many dangers.
2. Mount McKinley and Mount Whitney are two very high
mountains.
3. Sacagawea of the Shoshone people helped open the West to
explorers and settlers.
4. Every winter many skiers rush to the Grand Tetons.

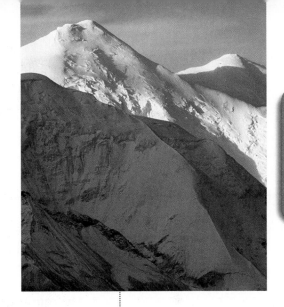

5. Did all of the mountaineers successfully ascend and descend Mount Everest?

6. Valleys and dense forests cool and refresh travelers in the Appalachian Mountains.

7. On Beartooth Highway in Montana, excellent campgrounds and scenic overlooks provide many views of distant glaciers.

8. Mount Evans is west of Denver and can be reached by the highest paved road in the United States.

9. Is the view from the top slopes of Mount Evans breathtaking?

10. Thick forests cover the Great Smoky Mountains and help form the peaks' smoky mist.

Review A   **Identifying Subjects and Predicates**

Write the simple subject and the verb or verb phrase in each of the following sentences.

HELP

Some of the subjects and verbs in Review A are compound.

EXAMPLE   1. Even the ancient Incas and the Aztecs paid and collected taxes.

1. *Incas, Aztecs; paid, collected*

1. Among the obligations of citizens in large cities is the prompt payment of taxes.

2. The ancient citizens of Mesoamerica were no exception to this rule.

3. Are some of these taxes also known today as "tribute"?

4. Bowls, blankets, honey, or even warriors' shields were given and accepted as tribute.

5. High officials and the sick did not, however, pay taxes.

6. In the interest of fairness, taxes must be counted and recorded in some way by accountants.

7. As a record, Incas knotted a string or cord and counted the number of knots.

8. The Codex Mendoza is a formal record of the Aztecs' taxes.

9. Both the Incas and the Aztecs used the number *20* as the base of their mathematics.

10. Might roads, buildings, or emergency supplies have been paid for with the tribute, or taxes?

Subject and Predicate   **17**

─HELP─

Some of the subjects and verbs in Review B are compound.

Review B **Identifying Subjects and Predicates**

Write the following sentences. Underline the complete subjects once and the complete predicates twice. Then, circle each simple subject and each verb.

EXAMPLES   1. The entire continent of Australia is occupied by a single country.

1. The entire (continent) of Australia (is occupied) by a single country.

2. What do you know about this continent?

2. What (do) (you) (know) about this continent?

1. It is located within the Southern Hemisphere.
2. Can you name the capital of Australia?
3. Australia is a federation of six states and two territories.
4. The continent of Australia was claimed for Britain by Captain James Cook.
5. The native people of Australia live mainly in the desert regions and, traditionally, have a very close bond with their environment.
6. A large number of British colonists settled in cities and towns on the coast.
7. Many ranchers raise sheep and export wool.
8. In addition, large quantities of gold and uranium are mined in Australia.
9. The country is also highly industrialized and produces a variety of goods, ranging from shoes to airplanes.
10. Among Australia's most unusual animals are the platypus and the anteater.

Kinds of Sentences

Reference Note

For information about how **sentences can be classified according to their structure,** see Chapter 7.

1h. A *declarative sentence* makes a statement and ends with a period.

EXAMPLES   Amy Tan was born in Oakland, California.

I couldn't hear what Jason said.

1i. An *imperative sentence* gives a command or makes a request. Most imperative sentences end with a period. A strong command ends with an exclamation point.

EXAMPLES   Be quiet during the play. [command]

Please give me another piece of melon. [request]

Stop! [strong command]

The subject of a command or a request is always *you*, even if *you* doesn't appear in the sentence. In such cases, *you* is called the **understood subject.**

EXAMPLES   (You) Be quiet during the play.

(You) Please give me another piece of melon.

(You) Stop!

The word *you* is the understood subject even when the person spoken to is addressed by name.

EXAMPLE   Miguel, (you) please answer the phone.

1j. An *interrogative sentence* asks a question and ends with a question mark.

EXAMPLES   When did you return from your camping trip?

Did the surfboard cost much?

1k. An *exclamatory sentence* shows excitement or expresses strong feeling and ends with an exclamation point.

EXAMPLES   Gabriella won the match!

How terrifying that movie was!

Exercise 12 **Classifying Sentences by Purpose**

Label each of the following sentences *declarative, imperative, interrogative,* or *exclamatory.*

EXAMPLE   **1.** Ask Yoshiko for the address.

          1. imperative

1. Will your grandfather compete in the Kansas City Marathon again this year?
2. Our school's project, cleaning up the Silver River Nature Preserve, was a success.
3. Bring more sandbags over here now!
4. Is the Rig-Veda the oldest of the Hindu scriptures?
5. Read this poem by Naomi Shihab Nye.

6. How huge this library is!
7. Origami is the fascinating Japanese folk art of folding paper into shapes.
8. How did you make that paper crane?
9. Please line up alphabetically.
10. After we eat supper, we're going to my aunt's house down the block.

Review C **Classifying and Punctuating Sentences**

Write the last word of each of the following sentences, adding the correct end mark. Then, label each sentence as *declarative, imperative, interrogative,* or *exclamatory.*

EXAMPLE   **1.** Are prairie dogs social creatures
        1. *creatures?—interrogative*

1. Many of these small mammals live together in underground "towns" like the one shown below
2. Look at how prairie dogs dig family burrows
3. How large are the burrows
4. The burrows sometimes cover several acres
5. These creatures can usually be seen at night or in the early morning
6. What alert animals prairie dogs are
7. At least one prairie dog always keeps a lookout for threats to the community
8. Look at how it sits up to see better
9. It then dives headfirst into the burrow and alerts the colony
10. How shrill the prairie dog's whistle of alarm is

Chapter Review

A. Identifying Sentences

Identify each of the following groups of words as a *sentence* or a *sentence fragment.*

1. Trying a double somersault.

2. She barely caught her partner's hands!

3. As she began the triple.

4. She fell into the net.

5. The crowd gasped.

6. Even the clowns turned and looked.

7. Was she hurt?

8. Rolled off the net to the ground.

9. Smiling as she waved to the crowd.

10. She was fine!

B. Identifying Subjects

Identify the complete subject of the following sentences. Then, underline the simple subject. The simple subject may be compound.

—HELP—
Remember that the subject may be the understood *you*.

11. Foods and beverages with large amounts of sugar can contribute to tooth decay.

12. The lava from a volcano hardens when it cools.

13. The earthquake survivors camped on blankets in the rubble.

14. In Beijing, bicyclists weave through the busy streets.

15. By 1899, many gold prospectors had rushed to Alaska.

16. The weather during an Alaskan summer can be hot.

17. Have you read this collection of Claude McKay's poems?

18. In the center of the table was a huge bowl of fruit.

19. Linked forever in legend are Paul Bunyan and Babe the Blue Ox.

20. Have many famous racehorses been trained in Kentucky?

21. The bright lights and the tall buildings amaze and delight most visitors to New York City.

22. Are Lita and Marisa going to give their presentation?

23. After soccer practice tomorrow afternoon, please come to my house for dinner.

24. Inside the box were letters and postcards written around the turn of the century.

25. The book *Come a Stranger* was written by the award-winning author Cynthia Voigt.

C. Identifying Predicates

Identify the complete predicate of the following sentences. Then, underline the simple predicate (verb or verb phrase). The simple predicate may be compound.

26. Teenagers need a balanced diet for good health.

27. A balanced diet improves student performance in school.

28. Students are sometimes in a hurry and skip breakfast.

29. For a nutritious breakfast, they can eat cereal and fruit.

30. Cheese and juice also provide good nutrition.

31. The cheese contains calcium, an important mineral.

32. People need protein as well.

33. Protein builds body tissue.

34. Protein can be supplied by eggs, dried beans, red meat, fish, and poultry.

35. Carbohydrates include whole grains, vegetables, and fruits.

36. Junk foods can ruin your appetite.

37. Sweets cause tooth decay and contain many calories.

38. According to nutritionists, sweets are low in nutrients and fill the body with "empty" calories.

39. Good eating habits keep you healthy and make you stronger.

40. Start eating right!

D. Classifying and Punctuating Sentences

Classify each of the following sentences as *declarative, interrogative, imperative,* or *exclamatory.* Then, write each sentence with the correct end punctuation.

41. In ancient times, the Julian calendar was used

42. Why was it called Julian

43. It was named after the Roman leader Julius Caesar

44. I thought so

45. Because the Julian calendar was not perfect, the Gregorian calendar was invented

46. In 1752, the calendar was changed in England

47. Tell me the result

48. Eleven days in September were lost

49. That's the strangest thing I've ever heard

50. Were those days lost forever

Writing Application
Writing a Letter

Using Complete Sentences   Think of a party or other interesting event you have attended. Write a letter describing the event to a friend or relative who lives far away. Include details about the activities you enjoyed and about the other people who were there. Use complete sentences to make sure your thoughts are clear.

Prewriting   Make a list of the details that you would like to include in your letter. At this stage, you do not have to use complete sentences. Simply jot down your thoughts.

Writing   Use your prewriting list of details as you write your rough draft. Choose details that would be interesting to your friend or relative. You might organize your letter chronologically (describing events in the order in which they occurred).

Revising   Read your letter aloud. As you read, mark any parts of the letter that seem unclear. Add, cut, or rearrange details to make your letter clear and interesting to your reader.

Publishing   Check your work to make sure you have used only complete sentences. Read your letter for any errors in spelling and punctuation. Then, send a copy of your letter to your friend or relative.

Parts of Speech Overview

Noun, Pronoun, Adjective

1.0 Written and Oral English Language Conventions
Students write and speak with a command of standard English conventions appropriate to this grade level.
1.3 Identify parts of speech.

Diagnostic Preview

Identifying Nouns, Pronouns, and Adjectives

Identify each italicized word in the following paragraphs as a *noun*, a *pronoun*, or an *adjective*.

EXAMPLES   The **[1]** *achievements* of the **[2]** *native* peoples of North America have sometimes been overlooked.

1. noun
2. adjective

Recent **[1]** *studies* show that the Winnebago people developed a **[2]** *calendar* based on careful observation of the **[3]** *heavens*. An **[4]** *archaeologist* has found that markings on an old **[5]** *calendar* stick are the precise records of a **[6]** *lunar* year and a solar year. These records are remarkably accurate, considering that at the time the **[7]** *Winnebagos* had neither a **[8]** *written* language nor a system of **[9]** *mathematics*.

   [10] *The* calendar stick is a carved **[11]** *hickory* branch with **[12]** *four* sides. **[13]** *It* is worn along the **[14]** *edges* and shows other signs of frequent use. A **[15]** *similar* stick appears in a portrait of an early chief of the Winnebagos. In the portrait, the chief holds a calendar stick in **[16]** *his* right hand. **[17]** *One* current theory is that the chief went out at **[18]** *sunrise* and sunset to observe the sun and the moon. [19] *He* then marked on the stick what he saw. According to one researcher, this calendar is the [20] *oldest* indication we have that native North American peoples recorded the year day by day.

The Noun

2a. A *noun* is a word or word group that is used to name a person, a place, a thing, or an idea.

Persons	Jessye Norman, teacher, chef, Dr. Ling
Places	Grand Canyon, city, Namibia, kitchen
Things	lamp, granite, Nobel Prize, Golden Gate Bridge
Ideas	happiness, self-control, liberty, bravery

Notice that some nouns are made up of more than one word. A *compound noun* is a single noun made up of two or more words used together. The compound noun may be written as one word, as a hyphenated word, or as two or more words.

One Word	grandmother, basketball
Hyphenated Word	mother-in-law, light-year
Two Words	grand piano, jumping jack

TIPS & TRICKS

To find the correct spelling of a compound noun, look it up in a recent dictionary.

Exercise 1 Identifying Nouns

Identify the nouns in the following sentences.

EXAMPLE 1. We have been reading about patriotic heroines in our textbook.
1. *heroines, textbook*

HELP

In Exercise 1, some nouns are used more than once.

1. Rebecca Motte was a great patriot.
2. During the Revolutionary War, British soldiers seized her mansion in South Carolina.
3. The American officer Henry Lee told Motte that the Americans would have to burn her home to smoke out the British.

4. Motte supported the plan and was glad to help her country.
5. She even supplied flaming arrows and a bow for the attack.
›6. Other people might not have been so generous or patriotic.
7. The house was saved after the enemy raised the white flag of surrender.
8. Afterward, Motte invited soldiers from both sides to dinner.
9. This gesture showed that Motte had a generous heart.
·10. The colonies and all citizens of the United States are in her debt.

Proper Nouns and Common Nouns

Reference Note

For more information about **capitalizing proper nouns,** see page 266.

A *proper noun* names a particular person, place, thing, or idea and begins with a capital letter. A *common noun* names any one of a group of persons, places, things, or ideas and is generally not capitalized.

Common Nouns	Proper Nouns
girl	Kay O'Neill
writer	Octavio Paz
country	Morocco
monument	Eiffel Tower
compact disc	*A Long Way Home*
book	*The Blue Sword*
religion	Buddhism
language	Arabic
city	Ottawa

Exercise 2 **Identifying Common Nouns and Proper Nouns**

Write the nouns in each of the following sentences. Then, identify each noun as a *common noun* or *proper noun*.

┌HELP┐

In Exercise 2, some nouns are used more than once.

EXAMPLE   1. <u>Mark</u> visited an interesting <u>museum</u> in <u>Colorado</u> last <u>month</u>.

1. *Mark—proper; museum—common; Colorado—proper; month—common*

1. Mark and his parents went to the Black American West Museum and Heritage Center in Denver.
2. The museum displays many items that cowboys used.
3. These items are from the collection of Paul Stewart, the man who founded the museum.
4. Mark saw saddles, knives, hats, and lariats.
5. He also saw many pictures of African American cowboys.
6. The museum is located in an old house that is listed in the National Register of Historic Places.
7. The house once belonged to Dr. Justina L. Ford.
8. She was the first black female physician in Colorado.
9. Mark was amazed by all of the old medical instruments in one display.
10. He said he was glad doctors don't use equipment like that anymore.

Exercise 3 **Revising Sentences by Using Proper Nouns**

Revise the following sentences by substituting a proper noun for each common noun. You might have to change some other words in each sentence. You may make up proper names.

EXAMPLE
1. An ambassador visited a local school and spoke about his country.
1. *Ambassador Rios visited Jackson High School and spoke about Brazil.*

1. That painting is in a famous museum.
2. The police officer cheerfully directed us to the building on that street.
3. My relatives, who are originally from a small town, now live in a large city.
4. The librarian asked my classmate to return the book as soon as possible.
5. That newspaper is published daily; this magazine is published weekly.
6. The girl read a poem for the teacher.
7. That state borders the ocean.
8. The owner of that store visited two countries during a spring month.
9. A man flew to a northern city one day.
10. Last week the mayor visited our school and talked about the history of our city.

Identifying and Classifying Nouns

Identify the nouns in the following sentences, and label each noun as a *common noun* or a *proper noun*.

EXAMPLE **[1]** Lillian Evanti performed in Europe, Latin America, and Africa.

  1. *Lillian Evanti—proper noun; Europe—proper noun; Latin America—proper noun; Africa—proper noun*

[1] Evanti was the first African American woman to sing opera professionally. [2] Her talent was recognized early; when she was a child, she gave a solo concert in Washington, D.C. [3] As an adult, she performed in a special concert at the White House for President Franklin Roosevelt and his wife, Eleanor. [4] Evanti also composed a musical piece titled "Himno Panamericano," which was a great success. [5] Her career inspired many other African American singers.

[6] A few years later Marian Anderson stepped into the limelight. [7] Always a champion of the arts, Mrs. Roosevelt again aided a great performer. [8] With the assistance and encouragement of the former First Lady, Anderson sang at a most appropriate site—the Lincoln Memorial. [9] Like Evanti, Anderson broke barriers, for before her, no other African American had sung at the famous Metropolitan Opera House in New York City. [10] One honor that Anderson earned was a place in the National Arts Hall of Fame.

Concrete Nouns and Abstract Nouns

A *concrete noun* names a person, place, or thing that can be perceived by one or more of the senses (sight, hearing, taste, touch, smell). An *abstract noun* names an idea, a feeling, a quality, or a characteristic.

Concrete Nouns	photograph, music, pears, filmmaker, sandpaper, rose, Brooklyn Bridge
Abstract Nouns	love, fun, freedom, self-esteem, beauty, honor, wisdom, Buddhism

Exercise 5 — Writing Sentences with Concrete and Abstract Nouns

Identify each noun in the following list as *concrete* or *abstract*. Then, use each noun in an original sentence.

EXAMPLE   **1.** truth

   1. abstract—People should always tell the truth.

1. soy sauce   **4.** ice   **7.** motor   **9.** pillow
2. brotherhood   **5.** excitement   **8.** health   **10.** honor
3. laughter   **6.** kindness

Collective Nouns

A ***collective noun*** is a word that names a group.

audience	committee	herd	quartet
batch	crew	jury	swarm
class	family	litter	team

Reference Note

For more information about **collective nouns,** see pages 158 and 167.

Review A — Using the Different Kinds of Nouns

Complete the following poem, which is based on this painting. Add common, proper, concrete, abstract, or collective nouns as directed. For proper nouns, you'll need to make up names of people and places. Be sure you capitalize all proper nouns.

Meet my [1] (*common*), the really amazing,
Truly tremendous [2] (*proper*), that's who.
You can see what [3] (*abstract*) he gives
The [4] (*collective*) of fans who hang on him
   like glue.

The walls of his gym on [5] (*proper*)
Are covered with [6] (*concrete*) that show
The muscled, tussled [7] (*common*) aplenty,
Who work out there, come rain or come snow.

Eduardo, [8] (*proper*), and I really enjoy
The [9] (*abstract*) of hanging on tight
Way above the [10] (*concrete*) and swinging,
Held up by the muscleman's might.

Jacob Lawrence, *Strong Man*. Gouache on paper, 22" x 17". Photo by Chris Eden, Francine Seders Gallery.

The Pronoun

2b. A *pronoun* is a word that is used in place of one or more nouns or pronouns.

EXAMPLES   Ask Dan if Dan has done Dan's homework.

Ask Dan if **he** has done **his** homework.

Both of Lois's friends said both would help Lois find Lois's missing books.

Both of Lois's friends said **they** would help **her** find **her** missing books.

The word or word group that a pronoun stands for (or refers to) is called its ***antecedent.***

            antecedent   pronoun   pronoun
EXAMPLES   **Frederick,** have **you** turned in **your** report?

              antecedent   pronoun
            Walking the dog is fun, and **it** is good exercise.

Sometimes the antecedent is not stated.

EXAMPLES   **Who** asked that question?

I did not understand what **you** said.

Someone will have to clean up the mess.

Personal Pronouns

A *personal pronoun* refers to the one speaking (*first person*), the one spoken to (*second person*), or the one spoken about (*third person*).

Personal Pronouns		
	Singular	**Plural**
First Person	I, me, my, mine	we, us, our, ours
Second Person	you, your, yours	you, your, yours
Third Person	he, him, his, she, her, hers, it, its	they, them, their, theirs

Reference Note

For information about choosing **pronouns that agree with their antecedents,** see page 165.

—HELP—

Some authorities prefer to call possessive pronouns (such as *my, your,* and *their*) possessive adjectives. Follow your teacher's directions when you are labeling these words.

Reflexive and Intensive Pronouns

A *reflexive pronoun* refers to the subject and is necessary to the meaning of the sentence. An *intensive pronoun* emphasizes a noun or another pronoun and is unnecessary to the meaning of the sentence.

Reflexive and Intensive Pronouns	
First Person	myself, ourselves
Second Person	yourself, yourselves
Third Person	himself, herself, itself, themselves

REFLEXIVE   Tara enjoyed **herself** at the party.
                     The team prided **themselves** on their victory.

INTENSIVE   I **myself** cooked that delicious dinner.
                     Did you redecorate the room **yourself**?

┌─HELP─

If you are not sure whether a pronoun is reflexive or intensive, use this test: Read the sentence aloud, omitting the pronoun. If the basic meaning of the sentence stays the same, the pronoun is intensive. If the meaning changes, the pronoun is reflexive.

EXAMPLES

Mark repaired the car **himself.** [Without *himself,* the meaning stays the same. The pronoun is intensive.]

The children amused **themselves** all morning. [Without *themselves,* the sentence doesn't make sense. The pronoun is reflexive.]

Demonstrative Pronouns

A *demonstrative pronoun* points out a person, a place, a thing, or an idea.

Demonstrative Pronouns			
this	that	these	those

EXAMPLES   **This** is the book I bought for my sister.

                     Are **those** the kinds of plants that bloom at night?

NOTE   *This, that, these,* and *those* can also be used as adjectives. When they are used in this way, they are called *demonstrative adjectives.*

DEMONSTRATIVE PRONOUN   **Those** are very sturdy shoes.
DEMONSTRATIVE ADJECTIVE   **Those** shoes are very sturdy.

DEMONSTRATIVE PRONOUN   Did you order **this**?
DEMONSTRATIVE ADJECTIVE   Did you order **this** salad?

Reference Note

For more about **demonstrative adjectives,** see page 36.

Interrogative Pronouns

An *interrogative pronoun* introduces a question.

Interrogative Pronouns				
what	which	who	whom	whose

EXAMPLES **What** is the best brand of frozen yogurt?

Who wrote *Barrio Boy*?

Indefinite Pronouns

TIPS & TRICKS

The indefinite pronouns *some, any, none, all, more,* and *most* may be singular or plural. Look closely at any prepositional phrase that follows these pronouns. The object of the preposition determines whether the pronoun is singular or plural.

SINGULAR
None of the milk **is** sour. [*Milk* is singular.]

PLURAL
None of the grapes **are** sweet. [*Grapes* is plural.]

Reference Note
For information on **indefinite pronouns and subject-verb agreement,** see page 153.

An *indefinite pronoun* refers to a person, a place, a thing, or an idea that may or may not be specifically named.

Common Indefinite Pronouns				
all	each	many	nobody	other
any	either	more	none	several
anyone	everything	most	no one	some
both	few	much	one	somebody

EXAMPLES **Both** of the girls forgot their lines.

I would like **some** of that chow mein.

NOTE Most indefinite pronouns can also be used as adjectives.

PRONOUN **Some** are bored by this movie.
ADJECTIVE **Some** people are bored by this movie.

Relative Pronouns

Reference Note
For information on **subordinate clauses,** see page 114.

A *relative pronoun* introduces an adjective clause.

Common Relative Pronouns				
that	which	who	whom	whose

EXAMPLES Thomas Jefferson, **who** wrote the Declaration of Independence, was our country's third president.

Exercise is something **that** many people enjoy.

Exercise 6 Identifying Pronouns

Identify each pronoun in the following sentences. Then, tell what type of pronoun each one is.

┌HELP┐
Some sentences
in Exercise 6 have more
than one pronoun.

EXAMPLES   **1.** The drama coach said he would postpone the rehearsal.

     1. he—personal

     2. Does Pamela, who is traveling to Thailand, have her passport and ticket?

     2. who—relative; her—personal

 1. "I want you to study," Ms. Gaines said to the class.
 2. The firefighter carefully adjusted her oxygen mask.
 3. The children made lunch themselves.
 4. Jenny and Rosa decided they would get popcorn, but Amy didn't want any.
 5. Who will be the next president of the school board?
 6. Mr. Yoshira, this is Mrs. Volt, a neighbor of yours.
 7. Ralph Bunche, who was awarded the Nobel Peace Prize, was a diplomat for his country at the United Nations.
 8. Of all United States Olympic victories, perhaps none were more satisfying than Jesse Owens's 1936 triumphs in the 200-meter dash and broad jump.
 9. Oh, yes, the puppy taught itself how to open the gate.
10. Only one of seventy-five qualified boys and girls will win the grand prize.

Oral Practice Adding Appropriate Pronouns to Sentences

Read each of the following sentences aloud. Then, re-read each sentence, replacing the italicized words with an appropriate pronoun.

EXAMPLE   **1.** The boy forgot *the boy's* homework.

     1. The boy forgot his homework.

 1. Put the flowers in water before *the flowers'* petals droop.
 2. The canoe capsized as *the canoe* neared the shore.
 3. The players convinced *the players* that *the players* would win the game.
 4. Lori oiled the bike before *Lori* put *the bike* in the garage.
 5. Tim said, "*Tim* answered all six questions on the quiz."
 6. Ben folded the newspapers for Ms. Luke, and then *Ben* stuffed *the newspapers* in plastic bags for *Ms. Luke*.

7. Sarah, Keith, and I arrived early so that *Sarah, Keith, and I* could get good seats.

8. Her wheelchair was amazingly fast, and *her wheelchair* was lightweight, too.

9. My sister just graduated from college, and *my sister* is now working as a computer programmer.

• 10. Because Japan fascinates Ron and *Ron's* brother, this film will interest *Ron and Ron's brother.*

The Adjective

2c. An *adjective* is a word that is used to modify a noun or a pronoun.

To *modify* a word means to describe the word or to make its meaning more definite. An adjective modifies a noun or a pronoun by telling *what kind, which one, how much,* or *how many.*

What Kind?	Which One or Ones?	How Much or How Many?
Korean children	**seventh** grade	**several** days
busy dentist	**these** countries	**five** dollars
braided hair	**any** book	**no** marbles

Sometimes an adjective comes after the word it modifies.

EXAMPLES   A woman, **kind** and **helpful,** gave us directions.
[The adjectives *kind* and *helpful* modify *woman.*]

The box is **empty.** [The predicate adjective *empty* modifies *box.*]

COMPUTER TIP

Using a software program's thesaurus can help you choose appropriate adjectives. To make sure that an adjective has exactly the connotation you intend, check the word in a dictionary.

Reference Note

For more about **predicate adjectives,** see page 81.

Articles

The most commonly used adjectives are *a*, *an*, and *the*. These adjectives are called **articles.** *A* and *an* are called **indefinite articles** because they refer to any member of a general group. *A* is used before a word beginning with a consonant sound. *An* is used before a word beginning with a vowel sound.

EXAMPLES   **A** frog croaked.

An orange is **a** good source of vitamin C.

My cousin Jimmy wears **a** uniform to school. [Even though *u* is a vowel, the word *uniform* begins with a consonant sound.]

This is **an** honor. [Even though *h* is a consonant, the word *honor* begins with a vowel sound. The *h* is not pronounced.]

The is called the **definite article** because it refers to someone or something in particular.

EXAMPLES   **The** frog croaked.

Where is **the** orange?

Nouns or Adjectives?

Many words that can stand alone as nouns can also be used as adjectives modifying nouns or pronouns.

Nouns	Adjectives
bean	**bean** soup
spring	**spring** weather
gold	**gold** coin
football	**football** game
Labor Day	**Labor Day** weekend
Super Bowl	**Super Bowl** party
Milan	**Milan** fashions
White House	**White House** security
Persian Gulf	**Persian Gulf** pearls

Reference Note

For more about **words used as different parts of speech,** see pages 39 and 67.

Demonstrative Adjectives

This, that, these, and *those* can be used both as adjectives and as pronouns. When they modify a noun or pronoun, they are called *demonstrative adjectives.* When they are used alone, they are called *demonstrative pronouns.*

Reference Note

For more about **demonstrative pronouns,** see page 31.

DEMONSTRATIVE ADJECTIVES	**This** drawing is mine, and **that** drawing is his.
	These soccer balls are much more expensive than **those** soccer balls are.
DEMONSTRATIVE PRONOUNS	**This** is mine and **that** is his.
	These are much more expensive than **those** are.

Exercise 7 Identifying Adjectives

Identify the adjectives in the following sentences, and give the noun or pronoun each modifies. Do not include the articles *a, an,* and *the.*

EXAMPLE   1. Why don't you take the local bus home from school on cold days?

1. *local—bus; cold—days*

˙ 1. On winter afternoons, I sometimes walk home after band practice rather than ride on a crowded, noisy bus.
 2. I hardly even notice the heavy traffic that streams past me on the street.
 3. The wet sidewalk glistens in the bright lights from the windows of stores.
 4. The stoplights throw green, yellow, and red splashes on the pavement.
 5. After I turn the corner away from the busy avenue, I am on a quiet street, where a jolly snowman often stands next to one of the neighborhood houses.
˙ 6. At last, I reach my peaceful home.
 7. There I am often greeted by my older brother, Kenny, and my sister, Natalie.
 8. I know they are glad to see me.
 9. Delicious smells come from the kitchen where Mom and Dad are cooking dinner.
˙ 10. This quiet, private walk always makes me feel a little tired but also happy.

Exercise 8 **Writing Appropriate Adjectives**

Complete the following story by writing an appropriate adjective to fill each blank.

EXAMPLES **[1]** ____ parks have **[2]** ____ trails for hikers.

1. *Many*

2. *wooded*

The hikers went exploring in the **[1]** ____ forest. Sometimes they had difficulty getting through the **[2]** ____ undergrowth. On **[3]** ____ occasions they almost turned back. They kept going and were rewarded for their **[4]** ____ effort. During the **[5]** ____ hike through the woods, they discovered **[6]** ____ kinds of **[7]** ____ animals. In the afternoon the **[8]** ____ hikers pitched camp in a **[9]** ____ clearing. They were **[10]** ____ for supper and rest.

Proper Adjectives

A *proper adjective* is formed from a proper noun.

Proper Nouns	Proper Adjectives
Thanksgiving	**Thanksgiving** dinner
Catholicism	**Catholic** priest
Middle East	**Middle Eastern** country
Africa	**African** continent

Notice that a proper adjective, like a proper noun, is capitalized. Common adjectives are generally not capitalized.

NOTE Some proper nouns, such as *Thanksgiving,* do not change spelling when they are used as adjectives.

Exercise 9 **Identifying Common and Proper Adjectives**

Identify the adjectives in the sentences on the next page. Then, tell whether each is a *common* or *proper* adjective. Do not include the articles *a, an,* and *the.*

Reference Note

For more information about **capitalizing proper adjectives,** see page 276.

MEETING THE CHALLENGE

Make a list of at least five nouns and five adjectives that describe you. Use your list to write a short personal description. Underline the nouns and adjectives you picked.

EXAMPLE 1. We have been studying how various animals protect themselves.

1. *various—common*

1. Many small animals defend themselves in unusual ways.
2. For example, South American armadillos wear suits of armor that consist of small, bony scales.
3. Armadillos seem delicate, with their narrow faces.
4. However, their tough armor protects them well.
5. Likewise, the Asian anteater has scales that overlap like the shingles on a roof.
6. Anteaters and armadillos have strong claws and long tongues.
7. *Armadillo* is a Spanish word that can be translated as "little armor."
8. Texas and Florida residents as well as Mexican citizens are familiar with these shy creatures.
9. At early twilight, look for armadillos, energetic and ready for a meal of unlucky spiders or insects.
10. Like tortoises, armadillos can pull in their noses and all four of their feet for better protection.

Exercise 10 Writing Proper Adjectives

Change the following proper nouns into proper adjectives.

EXAMPLE 1. Spain

1. *Spanish*

HELP

Use a dictionary to help you spell the adjectives in Exercise 10.

1. Rome
2. Victoria
3. Memorial Day
4. Korea
5. Congress

6. New Year's Day
7. Inca
8. Shakespeare
9. Judaism
10. Celt

Review B Identifying Nouns, Pronouns, and Adjectives

Identify each italicized word in the following paragraph as a *noun*, a *pronoun*, or an *adjective*.

EXAMPLE Four [1] *forces* govern the flight of an aircraft.

1. *noun*

Lift and thrust must overcome [1] *drag* and weight. If an airplane is very [2] *heavy,* it cannot lift off unless it has great thrust or speed. If the craft is slow, [3] *it* may not have enough thrust to achieve lift. By 1783, the [4] *French* Montgolfiers had learned how to beat gravity and achieve lift in their hot-air balloon. However, it had little thrust and didn't steer well. Nevertheless, [5] *Parisians* didn't mind the unpredictability. In fact, everybody [6] *who* was anybody wanted to hitch a ride on a balloon. With a rudder and propellers, airships (also known as blimps, dirigibles, and Zeppelins) achieved enough thrust to be steered but became unpopular after the [7] *Hindenburg* met [8] *its* fiery fate. Not until Orville and [9] *Wilbur Wright* put an engine on their famous craft and made its wings slightly [10] *movable* was the quest for thrust and lift achieved. As you know, the rest is history.

Determining Parts of Speech

Remember, the way a word is used in a sentence determines what part of speech it is. Some words may be used as nouns or as adjectives.

| NOUN | The helmet is made of **steel.** |
| ADJECTIVE | It is a **steel** helmet. |

Some words may be used as pronouns or as adjectives.

| PRONOUN | **That** is a surprise. |
| ADJECTIVE | **That** problem is difficult. |

Review C · Identifying Nouns, Pronouns, and Adjectives

Identify the nouns, pronouns, and adjectives in the following sentences. Do not include the articles *a, an,* and *the.*

EXAMPLE   **1.** We walked along the sandy beach at sundown.

   1. We—pronoun; sandy—adjective; beach—noun; sundown—noun

1. When the tide comes in, it brings a variety of interesting items from the sea.

2. When the tide ebbs, it leaves behind wonderful treasures for watchful beachcombers.

3. Few large creatures live here, but you almost certainly will find several small animals if you try.

4. Some live in shallow burrows under the wet sand and emerge in the cool evening to eat plants and other matter.

5. A number of different species of beetle like this part of the beach.

6. Around them you can find bristly flies and tiny worms.

7. You might also come across old pieces of wood with round holes and tunnels in them.

8. These holes are produced by shipworms.

9. If you watch the shoreline carefully, you will see many signs of life that casual strollers miss.

10. Low tide is a marvelous time to search along the shore.

Chapter Review

A. Identifying Types of Nouns

For each of the following sentences, identify the noun of the type indicated in parentheses. There may be more than one type of noun in each sentence.

1. No one understands why whales sometimes strand themselves. (*common*)
2. Since 1985, people in a group called Project Jonah have used an inflatable pontoon to rescue stranded whales and other marine mammals. (*proper*)
3. The people in Project Jonah find fulfillment in helping stranded mammals. (*abstract*)
4. More than two thousand marine mammals have been helped in recent years. (*concrete*)
5. The group has rescued mammals ranging in size from dolphins to whales. (*collective*)

B. Identifying Types of Pronouns

For each of the following sentences, identify the pronoun of the type indicated in parentheses. There may be more than one type of pronoun in each sentence.

6. Which of all the animals do you think has the worst reputation? (*interrogative*)
7. I believe the skunk is the animal that most people want to avoid. (*relative*)
8. The skunk can easily protect itself from others. (*reflexive*)
9. It can spray those nearby with a bad-smelling liquid. (*personal*)
10. This is a repellant that drives away predators. (*demonstrative*)
11. What do you think a skunk uses as its warning? (*interrogative*)
12. It warns possible predators by stamping its feet, which is intended to frighten the predator. (*relative*)
13. When the skunk needs to attack some other animal, it sprays in the direction of that animal. (*personal*)

14. Anyone who has ever been sprayed by a skunk will never forget the smell. (*indefinite*)

15. I myself would prefer never to upset a skunk. (*intensive*)

C. Identifying Adjectives

Identify the adjectives in each of the following sentences. Then, write the word the adjective modifies. Do not include the articles *a, an,* and *the.* A sentence may have more than one adjective.

16. Chapultepec is the name of a historic castle on a hill in Mexico City.

17. This word means "hill of the grasshopper" in the language of the early Aztecs.

18. Aztec emperors used the park area for hunting and relaxation.

19. In 1783, the hilltop was chosen as the location for the castle of the Spanish viceroy.

20. Even though the castle was never finished, it was used as a fortress during the colonial period of Mexican history.

21. After several decades of neglect, the unfinished castle became the home of the National Military Academy in 1842.

22. In 1847, during a war against the United States, this castle was captured by invading troops.

23. Almost twenty years later, the emperor of Mexico, Maximilian, converted the castle into an imperial residence.

24. After the downfall of Maximilian in 1867, the castle became the summer residence of Mexican presidents.

25. In 1937, the property was converted into a national museum.

D. Identifying Nouns, Pronouns, and Adjectives

The following paragraph contains twenty numbered, italicized words. Identify each italicized word as a *noun,* a *pronoun,* or an *adjective.*

In [**26**] *this* country [**27**] *mangroves* grow along the coasts of [**28**] *Florida.* [**29**] *They* form a [**30**] *wonderland* where land, water, and [**31**] *sky* blend. [**32**] *The* lush, green [**33**] *mangrove* islands and [**34**] *shoreline* are both beautiful and valuable. Mangroves are important to [**35**] *our* [**36**] *environment.* They produce [37] *tons* of valuable [38] *vegetable* matter and are an [39] *essential* part of [40] *tropical* biology. So far as [41] *we* know, the [42] *first* reference to mangroves dates back to [43] *Egyptian* times. A [44] *South African* expert has also discovered evidence of mangrove islands along the [45] *Red Sea*.

Writing Application
Using Pronouns in a Report

Clear Pronoun Reference Your class is creating a bulletin board display to honor exceptional people. For the display, write a brief report about someone you know and admire. Be sure that the pronouns you use refer clearly to their antecedents.

Prewriting   First, you will need to select your subject. Make a list of the different people you know. Which of these people do you find really remarkable? After you choose a subject, jot down notes about this person. Tell what this person has done to earn your respect and admiration.

Writing   As you write your first draft, refer to your notes. Your thesis statement should briefly state what is exceptional about your subject. In the rest of your paragraphs, give specific examples that illustrate why the person is exceptional.

Revising   Now, read through your report and imagine that you do not know the subject. What do you think about him or her? Does the person sound remarkable? If not, you may want to add or cut details or rearrange your report. Read your report aloud. Combine short, related sentences into longer, smoother sentences.

Publishing   Look closely at your use of pronouns. Be sure that each pronoun has a clear antecedent. You may need to correct some sentences to make the antecedents clear. You and your classmates may want to use your reports to make a classroom bulletin board display. If possible, include pictures or drawings of your subjects. You may also wish to send a copy of your report to your exceptional subject.

Reference Note
For more about **combining sentences,** see page 418.

Parts of Speech Overview

Verb, Adverb, Preposition, Conjunction, Interjection

1.0 Written and Oral English Language Conventions

Students write and speak with a command of standard English conventions appropriate to this grade level.

1.3 Identify parts of speech.

Diagnostic Preview

Identifying Verbs, Adverbs, Prepositions, Conjunctions, and Interjections

Identify each italicized word or word group in the following paragraphs as a *verb*, an *adverb*, a *preposition*, a *conjunction*, or an *interjection*.

EXAMPLES   Some [**1**] *very* unusual words [**2**] *are used* [**3**] *in* crossword puzzles.

    1. adverb

    2. verb

    3. preposition

       The first crossword puzzle was published [**1**] *in* 1913. It [**2**] *appeared* on the Fun Page [**3**] *of* a New York City newspaper, [**4**] *and* readers [**5**] *immediately* [**6**] *asked* the editors [**7**] *for* more. [**8**] *Almost* every daily newspaper in the United States [**9**] *now* publishes crossword puzzles.

       Every day, millions of Americans [**10**] *faithfully* work crossword puzzles. Many people take puzzles [**11**] *quite* seriously. For many, solving puzzles [**12**] *is* a competitive game.

I [13] *do* puzzles [14] *strictly* for fun. Best of all, I can work on them [15] *by* myself. That way, no one knows whether I succeed [16] *or* fail. I [17] *occasionally* [18] *brag* about my successes. [19] "*Aha*!" I exclaim. "That was a tough one, [20] *but* I filled in every space."

The Verb

3a. A *verb* is a word that expresses action or a state of being.

EXAMPLES   We **celebrated** the Chinese New Year yesterday.

The holiday **is** usually in February.

NOTE   In this book, verbs are classified as action or linking verbs, as helping or main verbs, and as transitive or intransitive verbs.

Action Verbs

3b. An *action verb* is a verb that expresses either physical or mental activity.

EXAMPLES   The owls **hooted** all night. [physical action]

Gloria **plays** volleyball. [physical action]

She **thought** about the problem. [mental action]

I **believe** you. [mental action]

NOTE   Action verbs may be transitive or intransitive.

Reference Note

For more information about **transitive and intransitive verbs,** see page 52.

Exercise 1   Classifying Verbs

Tell whether each of the following action verbs expresses physical or mental action.

EXAMPLE   **1.** visualize

1. mental

1. pounce	**5.** rest	**9.** shout
2. consider	**6.** remember	**10.** nibble
3. wish	**7.** dash	
4. want	**8.** anticipate	

Exercise 2 Identifying Action Verbs

Identify each action verb in the following sentences.

EXAMPLE   **1.** I saw that movie last week.

　　　　　　1. saw

┌ H E L P ─

Sentences in
Exercise 2 may contain
more than one action verb.

1. For a science project, Elena built a sundial.
2. Mr. Santos carefully explained the word problem to each of the students.
3. I enjoy soccer more than any other sport.
4. This waterfall drops two hundred feet.
5. Mike's bicycle suddenly skidded and fell hard on the wet pavement.
6. Mrs. Karras showed us the way to Johnson City.
7. Mix the ingredients slowly.
8. The heavy traffic delayed us.
9. For the Jewish holiday of Purim, Rachel and her sister Elizabeth gave a party.
10. The early Aztecs worshiped the sun.

Linking Verbs

3c. A *linking verb* is a verb that expresses a state of being. A linking verb connects, or links, the subject to a word or word group that identifies or describes the subject.

EXAMPLES   Denzel Washington **is** an actor. [The verb *is* connects *actor* with the subject *Denzel Washington*.]

　　　　　　The children **remained** quiet. [The verb *remained* links *quiet* with the subject *children*.]

Reference Note

┌ For more information
about **transitive and
intransitive verbs,** see
page 52.

NOTE   Linking verbs never have objects (words that tell who or what receives the action of the verb). Therefore, linking verbs are always intransitive.

Some Forms of the Verb *Be*			
am	were	will be	can be
is	has been	shall be	should be
are	have been	may be	would have
was	had been	might be	been

Other Linking Verbs			
appear	grow	seem	stay
become	look	smell	taste
feel	remain	sound	turn

NOTE *Be* is not always a linking verb. *Be* can express a state of being without having a complement (a word or word group that identifies or describes the subject). In the following sentences, forms of *be* are followed by words or word groups that tell *where*.

EXAMPLES   We **will be** there.

The apples **are** in the bowl.

Reference Note

For information about **complements,** see Chapter 4.

Some words may be either action verbs or linking verbs, depending on how they are used.

ACTION   Amy **looked** through the telescope.

LINKING   Amy **looked** pale. [The verb *looked* links *pale* with the subject *Amy.*]

ACTION   **Stay** in your seats until the bell rings.

LINKING   **Stay** calm. [The verb *stay* links *calm* with the understood subject *you.*]

Reference Note

For more about **understood subjects** in imperative sentences, see page 19.

Exercise 3 **Identifying Linking Verbs**

Identify the linking verb in each of the following sentences.

EXAMPLE   1. A radio station can be the voice of a community.

1. *can be*

1. This is Roberto Martínez, your weather forecaster.
2. Unfortunately, the forecast looks bad today.
3. Outside the window here at Station WOLF, the skies appear cloudy.
4. It certainly felt rainy earlier this morning.
5. According to the latest information, it should be a damp, drizzly day with an 85 percent chance of rainfall.
6. Our sportscaster this morning is Marta Segal.
7. Things have been quiet here around Arlington for the past few days.

MEETING THE CHALLENGE

A metaphor is an imaginative comparison that states directly that one thing is another thing. Metaphors often use linking verbs to connect two unlike things, as in "The stars **are** glittering jewels."

Write a descriptive paragraph that includes one or more metaphors. Then, underline all the linking verbs in your paragraph.

8. Stay alert for sports action tonight.
9. It should be an exciting game between our own Arlington Angels and the visiting Jackson City Dodgers.
10. The team looked great at practice today, and I predict a hometown victory.

Review A Identifying Action Verbs and Linking Verbs

Identify the verbs in the following sentences. Then, label each verb as either an *action verb* or a *linking verb*.

EXAMPLE   **1.** I always enjoy field trips.

       1. enjoy—action verb

1. Last spring, our earth science class visited the Hayden Planetarium.
2. It is a wonderful place, full of fabulous sights.
3. We wandered slowly through the various displays and saw a collection of fine exhibits.
4. One space vehicle seemed like something from a science fiction movie.
5. Another display showed a thirty-four-ton meteorite.
6. When this meteorite fell to earth many years ago, it made a huge crater.
7. After a delicious lunch, we stayed for the show in the observatory.
8. As the room became darker, the picture of a galaxy appeared on the ceiling of the dome above us.
9. The lecturer said that the galaxy is so far away from here that its light reaches us centuries after its first appearance.
10. When we look at such stars, we actually see the ancient past!

┌HELP┐

Sentences in Review A may contain more than one verb.

Exercise 4 **Identifying Action Verbs and Linking Verbs**

Exercise 4 **Identifying Action Verbs and Linking Verbs**

Identify the verb in each of the following sentences. Then, label each verb as either an *action verb* or a *linking verb*. If the verb is a linking verb, give the words that it connects.

EXAMPLES
1. We sent our dog to obedience school.
   1. *sent—action verb*

2. Some breeds are extremely nervous.
   2. *are—linking verb; breeds, nervous*

1. Everyone felt sorry about the misunderstanding.
2. In daylight, we looked for the lost ring.
3. The temperature plunged to ten degrees below zero.
4. The local museum exhibited beautiful Inuit sculptures.
5. Loretta felt her way carefully through the dark, quiet room.
6. The city almost always smells musty after a heavy summer thunderstorm.
7. Dakar is the capital of Senegal.
8. The firefighter cautiously smelled the burned rags.
9. Antonia Novello was the first female surgeon general of the United States.
10. They looked handsome in their party clothes.

Helping Verbs and Main Verbs

3d. A *helping verb* (*auxiliary verb*) helps the main verb express action or a state of being.

EXAMPLES
can speak   **has been** named

were sent   **should have been** caught

A *verb phrase* contains one main verb and one or more helping verbs.

EXAMPLES
Many people in Africa **can speak** more than one language.

The packages **were sent** to 401 Maple Street.

Kansas **has been named** the Sunflower State.

The ball **should have been caught** by the nearest player.

Commonly Used Helping Verbs			
Forms of *Be*	am	been	was
	are	being	were
	be	is	
Forms of *Do*	do	does	did
Forms of *Have*	have	has	had
Other Helping Verbs	can	might	would
	could	must	shall
	may	will	should

Some verbs can be used as either helping verbs or main verbs.

HELPING VERB   **Do** you like green beans?

  MAIN VERB   Did you **do** this math problem?

HELPING VERB   She **had** left early.

  MAIN VERB   She has **had** a cold.

HELPING VERB   **Have** they arrived yet?

  MAIN VERB   They will **have** another chance.

HELPING VERB   Where **can** he be?

  MAIN VERB   My grandparents will **can** green beans.

Sometimes a verb phrase is interrupted by another part of speech. Often the interrupter is an adverb. In a question, however, the subject often interrupts the verb phrase.

EXAMPLES   Our school **has** always **held** a victory celebration when our team wins.

Did you **hear** Jimmy Smits's speech?

Should Anita **bring** her layout design to class?

Ken **does** not [*or* **doesn**'t] **have** a new desk.

Notice in the last example that the adverb *not* (or its contraction *–n't*) is not included in the verb phrase.

Exercise 5 Identifying Verb Phrases and Helping Verbs

Identify the verb phrases in the following sentences. Underline the helping verbs.

EXAMPLE   **1.** You can recognize redwoods and sequoias by their bark.

   1. can recognize

1. Have you ever visited Redwood National Park?
2. The giant trees there can be an awesome sight.
3. For centuries, these trees have been an important part of the environment of the northwest United States.
4. Surely, these rare trees must be saved for future generations.
5. More than 85 percent of the original redwood forest has been destroyed over the years.
6. Because of this destruction, the survival of the redwood forest is being threatened.
7. With better planning years ago, more of the forest might already have been saved.
8. Unfortunately, redwood forests are still shrinking rapidly.
9. According to some scientists, redwood forests outside the park will disappear within our lifetime.
10. However, according to other experts, the redwood forests can still be saved!

Review B Identifying Action Verbs and Linking Verbs

Identify the verbs in the following sentences. Then, label each verb as an *action verb* or a *linking verb*.

EXAMPLE   **1.** Have you ever seen a play in Spanish?

   1. Have seen—action verb

1. The Puerto Rican Traveling Theatre performs plays about Hispanic life in the United States.
2. Over the past twenty years, this group has grown into a famous Hispanic theater group.
3. Sometimes, a production has two casts—one that speaks in English and one that speaks in Spanish.
4. In this way, speakers of both languages can enjoy the play.
5. In recent years many young Hispanic playwrights, directors, and actors have begun their careers at the Traveling Theatre.

┌─HELP─
Some sentences in Review B contain more than one verb. Also, be sure to include all parts of each verb phrase.

6. Some became well-known at the Puerto Rican Traveling Theatre and then moved on to Broadway or Hollywood.
7. Others remain happy at the Traveling Theatre, where they enjoy the warm, supportive atmosphere.
8. Each production by the Traveling Theatre has its own style.
9. Some shows are musicals, full of song and dance, while other plays seem more serious.
10. Light or serious, Puerto Rican Traveling Theatre productions present a lively picture of Hispanic life today.

Transitive and Intransitive Verbs

3e. A *transitive verb* is a verb that expresses an action directed toward a person, a place, a thing, or an idea.

With transitive verbs, the action passes from the doer—the subject—to the receiver of the action. Words that receive the action of a transitive verb are called *objects.*

Reference Note

For more about **objects** and their uses in **sentences,** see page 74.

EXAMPLES   Derrick **greeted** the visitors. [The action of the verb *greeted* is directed toward the object *visitors.*]

When **will** Felicia **paint** her room? [The action of the verb *will paint* is directed toward the object *room.*]

3f. An *intransitive verb* expresses action (or tells something about the subject) without the action passing to a receiver, or object.

EXAMPLES   The train **stopped.**

Last night we **ate** on the patio.

A verb may be transitive in one sentence and intransitive in another.

EXAMPLES   The children **play** checkers. [transitive]
The children **play** quietly. [intransitive]

Mr. Lopez **is baking** bread. [transitive]
Mr. Lopez **is baking** this afternoon. [intransitive]

Have Roland and Tracy **left** their coats? [transitive]
Have Roland and Tracy **left** yet? [intransitive]

Oral Practice **Identifying Transitive and Intransitive Verbs**

Read aloud each of the following sentences. Then, identify the italicized verb in each sentence as either *transitive* or *intransitive*.

EXAMPLE   **1.** She *runs* early in the morning.

     1. runs—intransitive

┌─HELP─┐
Ask yourself
whether the sentence
contains a person or thing
that receives the action of
the italicized verb. If so, the
verb is transitive.

1. If you do different kinds of exercises, you *are exercising* in the correct way.
2. When you exercise to improve endurance, flexibility, and strength, your body *develops*.
3. Aerobic exercise *builds* endurance and strengthens the heart and lungs.
4. When you *walk* quickly, you exercise aerobically.
5. Many active people in the United States *attend* classes in aerobics.
6. They *enjoy* the fun of exercising to popular music.
7. Exercises that *improve* flexibility require you to bend and stretch.
8. *Perform* these exercises slowly to gain the maximum benefit from them.
9. Through isometric and isotonic exercises, your muscle strength *increases*.
10. These exercises *contract* your muscles.

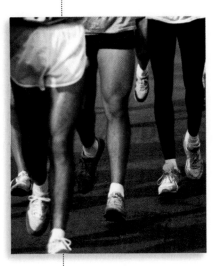

Exercise 6 **Writing Sentences with Transitive and Intransitive Verbs**

For each verb given below, write two sentences. In one sentence, use the verb as a *transitive* verb and underline its object. In the other sentence, use the verb as an *intransitive* verb. You may use different tenses of the verb.

EXAMPLE   **1.** write

     1. Alex is writing a research <u>report</u>. (transitive)

     Alex writes in his journal every day. (intransitive)

1. fly	**5.** drive	**9.** climb	**13.** turn	**17.** skip
2. leave	**6.** jump	**10.** watch	**14.** pay	**18.** read
3. return	**7.** hear	**11.** visit	**15.** row	**19.** help
4. draw	**8.** answer	**12.** shout	**16.** run	**20.** sing

The Adverb

3g. An **adverb** is a word that modifies a verb, an adjective, or another adverb.

Just as an adjective makes the meaning of a noun or a pronoun more definite, an adverb makes the meaning of a verb, an adjective, or another adverb more definite.

Adverbs answer the following questions:

Where?	How often? *or* How long?
When?	To what extent?
How?	*or* How much?

EXAMPLES   The sprinter ran **swiftly.** [The adverb *swiftly* modifies the verb *ran* and tells *how.*]

I read the funny pages **early** on Sunday morning. [The adverb *early* modifies the verb *read* and tells *when.*]

Jolene was comforting a **very** small child. [The adverb *very* modifies the adjective *small* and tells *to what extent.*]

The fire blazed **too wildly** for anyone to enter. [The adverb *too* modifies the adverb *wildly* and tells *to what extent.* The adverb *wildly* modifies the verb *blazed* and tells *how.*]

Dad will **sometimes** quote from Archbishop Desmond Tutu's speech. [The adverb *sometimes* modifies the verb *will quote* and tells *how often.*]

Put the apples **there,** and we will eat them **later.** [The adverb *there* modifies the verb *put* and tells *where.* The adverb *later* modifies the verb *will eat* and tells *when.*]

Words Often Used as Adverbs	
Where?	away, here, inside, there, up
When?	later, now, soon, then, tomorrow
How?	clearly, easily, quietly, slowly

Words Often Used as Adverbs	
How often? or *How long?*	always, usually, continuously, never, forever, briefly
To what extent? or *How much?*	almost, so, too, more, least, extremely, quite, very, not

NOTE The word *not* is nearly always used as an adverb modifying a verb. When *not* is part of a contraction, as in *hadn't, aren't,* and *didn't,* the *–n't* is still an adverb and is not part of the verb.

Reference Note

For more about **contractions,** see page 333.

Adverb or Adjective?

Many adverbs end in *–ly.* These adverbs are generally formed by adding *–ly* to adjectives.

Adjective	+	*–ly*	=	Adverb
clear	+	*–ly*	=	clearly
quiet	+	*–ly*	=	quietly
convincing	+	*–ly*	=	convincingly

However, some words ending in *–ly* are used as adjectives.

Adjectives Ending in *–ly*		
daily	friendly	lonely
early	kindly	timely

NOTE The adverb *very* is often overused. In your writing, try to use adverbs other than *very* to modify adjectives. You can also revise sentences so that other words carry more of the descriptive meaning.

EXAMPLE   Chloe is very tall.
REVISED   Chloe is **amazingly** tall.
                    or
              Chloe is **5'11" tall** and **is a guard on the varsity basketball team.**

HELP

If you aren't sure whether a word is an adjective or an adverb, ask yourself what it modifies. If a word modifies a noun or a pronoun, it is an adjective.

EXAMPLE
She gave us a **friendly** hello. [*Friendly* modifies the noun *hello* and is used as an adjective.]

If a word modifies a verb, an adjective, or an adverb, then it is an adverb.

EXAMPLE
People from many nations have come to the United States **recently.** [The adverb *recently* modifies the verb *have come.*]

Reference Note

For more about **adjectives,** see page 34.

Exercise 7 Identifying Adverbs

Identify each adverb and the word or words it modifies in each of the following sentences.

EXAMPLE   **1.** Today, many Cherokee people make their homes in Oklahoma.

1. *Today—make*

1. Oklahoma is not the Cherokees' original home.
2. The Cherokees once lived in Georgia, North Carolina, Alabama, and Tennessee.
3. A number of Cherokees still live in the Great Smoky Mountains of North Carolina.
4. Settlers often ignored the Cherokees' right to the land.
5. Feeling threatened by the settlers, the Cherokees readily supported the British during the Revolutionary War.
6. In 1829, people hurried excitedly to northern Georgia for the first gold rush in the United States.
7. Many white settlers of the region were extremely eager to find gold.
8. Later, the Cherokees were forced by the United States government to leave their land.
9. The Cherokee people were hardly given a chance to collect their belongings.
10. Many Cherokees will never forget the Trail of Tears, which led their ancestors to Oklahoma.

Statue of Cherokee mourning those who died on the Trail of Tears.

The Position of Adverbs

One of the characteristics of adverbs is that they may appear at various places in a sentence. Adverbs may come before, after, or between the words they modify.

EXAMPLES   We **often** study together.

We study together **often.**

Often we study together.

When an adverb modifies a verb phrase, it frequently comes in the middle of the phrase.

EXAMPLE   We have **often** studied together.

An adverb that introduces a question, however, appears at the beginning of a sentence.

EXAMPLES   **When** does your school start? [The adverb *When* modifies the verb phrase *does start.*]

How did you spend your vacation? [The adverb *How* modifies the verb phrase *did spend.*]

Exercise 8 **Identifying Adverbs**

Identify the adverbs and the words they modify in the following sentences.

EXAMPLE   1. "To Build a Fire" is a dramatically suspenseful short story.

    1. *dramatically—suspenseful*

┌ **H E L P** ──

Some sentences in Exercise 8 contain more than one adverb.

1. In this story, a nameless character goes outdoors on a terribly cold day in the Yukon.
2. Except for a dog, he is traveling completely alone.
3. Soon both the dog's muzzle and the man's beard are frosted with ice.
4. Along the way, the man accidentally falls into a stream.
5. Soaked and chilled, he desperately builds a fire under a tree.
6. The flames slowly grow stronger.
7. Unfortunately, he has built his fire in the wrong place.
8. A pile of snow suddenly falls from a tree limb and kills the small fire.
9. Unable to relight the fire, the man again finds himself in serious trouble.
10. Based on what you now know about the story, what kind of ending would you write for "To Build a Fire"?

Exercise 9 **Writing Adverbs**

Write ten different adverbs to fill the blanks in the following sentences.

EXAMPLE   I have **[1]** _____ been a music lover.

    1. *always*

Every Friday I **[1]** _____ go to the music store. I can **[2]** _____ wait to see what new music has arrived. As soon as school is out, I bicycle [3] ___ to the store and join the other [4] ___ enthusiastic customers. [5] ___ I stroll through the aisles and [6] ___ study the selections. I listen [7] ___ as the loudspeaker announces the day's specials. When I have decided what I want, I [8] ___ figure out which items I can afford. Then I walk [9] ___ to the cash register. I grin [10] ___ as I think of how much I will enjoy the music.

The Preposition

3h. A *preposition* is a word that shows the relationship of a noun or pronoun to another word.

Notice how changing the preposition in these sentences changes the relationship of *walked* to *door* and *kite* to *tree*.

> The cat walked **through** the door.
> The cat walked **toward** the door.
> The cat walked **past** the door.

> The kite **in** the tree is mine.
> The kite **beside** the tree is mine.
> The kite **in front of** the tree is mine. [Notice that a preposition may be made up of more than one word. Such a preposition is called a *compound preposition*.]

Commonly Used Prepositions

aboard	before	for	off	toward
about	behind	from	on	under
above	below	in	out	underneath
across	beneath	in front of	out of	unlike
after	beside	inside	over	until
against	between	instead	past	up
along	beyond	into	since	up to
among	by	like	through	upon
around	down	near	throughout	with
as	during	next to	till	within
at	except	of	to	without

GRAMMAR

Exercise 10 · Writing Prepositions

Write two prepositions for each blank in the following sentences. Be prepared to tell how the meanings of the two resulting sentences differ.

EXAMPLE
   1. The car raced _____ the highway.

     1. along, across

1. We practiced karate _____ dinner.

2. She jumped up and ran _____ the park.

3. A boat with red sails sailed _____ the river.

4. The hungry dog crawled _____ the fence.

5. The marathon runner jogged easily _____ the track at the stadium.

6. Put the speakers _____ the stage, Cody.

7. Brightly colored confetti streamed _____ the piñata when it burst open.

8. Why does Roseanne always sit _____ the door?

9. Excuse me, but the blue fountain pen _____ your chair is mine, I believe.

10. Parrots _____ the South American jungle squawked all through the hot afternoon.

The Prepositional Phrase

A *prepositional phrase* includes a preposition, a noun or pronoun called the *object of the preposition,* and any modifiers of that object.

EXAMPLES
   You can press those leaves **under glass.** [The noun *glass* is the object of the preposition *under.*]

   Fred stood **in front of us.** [The pronoun *us* is the object of the compound preposition *in front of.*]

   The books **in my new pack** are heavy. [The noun *pack* is the object of the preposition *in.* The words *my* and *new* modify *pack.*]

A preposition may have more than one object.

EXAMPLE
   Thelma's letter to **Nina** and **Ralph** contained good news. [The preposition *to* relates its objects, *Nina* and *Ralph,* to *letter.*]

DOWN THE CIRCULAR STAIRCASE..

AND DOWN THE CIRCULAR STAIRCASE

AND DOWN THE CIRCULAR STAIRCASE, AND—

OVERBOARD © 1993 Universal Press Syndicate. Reprinted with permission. All rights reserved.

The objects of prepositions may have modifiers.

EXAMPLE   It happened during **the last** examination. [*The* and *last* are adjectives modifying *examination,* which is the object of the preposition *during.*]

Reference Note
For more about **infinitives,** see page 102.

NOTE   Be careful not to confuse a prepositional phrase beginning with *to* (*to the park, to him*) with an infinitive beginning with *to* (*to sing, to be heard*).

---HELP---

Some sentences in Exercise 11 contain more than one prepositional phrase.

Exercise 11 Identifying Prepositional Phrases

Identify the prepositional phrases in the following sentences. Underline the preposition once and its object twice.

EXAMPLES   1. Commander Robert Peary claimed that he reached the North Pole in 1909.
1. *in 1909*

2. Peary and Matthew Henson searched for the North Pole for many years.
2. *for the North Pole, for many years*

1. Henson traveled with Peary on every expedition except the first one.
2. However, for a long time, Henson received no credit for his role.
3. Peary had hired Henson as an assistant on a trip Peary made to Nicaragua.
4. There, Peary discovered that Henson had sailing experience and could also chart a path through the jungle.
5. As a result, Peary asked Henson to join his Arctic expedition shown in the photograph on this page.
6. The two explorers became friends during their travels in the North.
7. On the last three miles to the North Pole, Henson did not go with Peary.
8. Because he was the leader of the trip, Peary received the credit for the achievement.
9. Finally, after many years, Henson was honored by Congress, Maryland's state government, and two U.S. presidents.
10. Both Peary and Henson wrote books about their experiences.

Preposition or Adverb?

Some words may be used either as prepositions or as adverbs. Remember that a preposition always has an object. An adverb never does. If you can't tell whether a word is used as an adverb or a preposition, look for an object.

ADVERB	I haven't seen him **since.**
PREPOSITION	I haven't seen him **since** Thursday. [*Thursday* is the object of the preposition *since.*]

ADVERBS	The bear walked **around** and then went **inside.**
PREPOSITIONS	The bear walked **around** the yard and then went **inside** the cabin. [*Yard* is the object of the preposition *around. Cabin* is the object of *inside.*]

TIPS & TRICKS

When you are looking for the object of a preposition, be careful. Sometimes the object comes before, not after, the preposition.

EXAMPLES
Here is the CD **that** I was looking for yesterday. [*That* is the object of the preposition *for.*]

She is the speaker **whom** we enjoyed listening to so much. [*Whom* is the object of the preposition *to.*]

GRAMMAR

Exercise 12 Identifying Adverbs and Prepositions

Identify the italicized word in each of the following sentences as either an *adverb* or a *preposition.*

EXAMPLE   1. He watches uneasily as the hunter slowly brings the pistol *up.*

1. *up—adverb*

1. "The Most Dangerous Game" is the story of Rainsford, a famous hunter who falls *off* a boat and comes ashore on a strange island.
2. Rainsford knows that this island is feared by every sailor who passes *by.*
3. In fact, *among* sailors, the place is known as Ship-Trap Island.
4. After looking *around* for several hours, Rainsford can't understand why the island is considered so dangerous.
5. Finally, he discovers a big house *on* a high bluff.
6. A man with a pistol *in* his hand answers the door.
7. Putting his pistol *down,* the man introduces Rainsford to the famous hunter General Zaroff.
8. Zaroff invites Rainsford *inside.*
9. Soon, however, Rainsford wishes he could get *out* and never see Zaroff again.
10. Rainsford has finally discovered the secret *about* the island— Zaroff likes to hunt human beings!

STYLE **TIP**

The conjunction *so* is often overused. In your writing, revise sentences as needed to avoid overusing *so*.

EXAMPLE
Traffic is bad, so we'll probably be late.

REVISED
Because traffic is bad, we'll probably be late.

TIPS & TRICKS

You can remember the seven coordinating conjunctions as FANBOYS:

For
And
Nor
But
Or
Yet
So

Reference Note

For more about **using commas between independent clauses,** see page 297.

The Conjunction

3i. A *conjunction* is a word that joins words or word groups.

(1) *Coordinating conjunctions* join words or word groups that are used in the same way.

Coordinating Conjunctions						
and	but	for	nor	or	so	yet

EXAMPLES   Josie, Han, Jill, **or** Anna [*Or* joins four nouns.]

strict **but** fair [*But* joins two adjectives.]

across town, over the river, **and** through the woods [*And* joins three prepositional phrases.]

Alice Walker wrote the book, **yet** she did not write the movie script. [*Yet* joins two independent clauses.]

The word *for* may be used either as a conjunction or as a preposition. When *for* joins word groups that are independent clauses, it is used as a conjunction. Otherwise, *for* is used as a preposition.

CONJUNCTION   He waited patiently, **for** he knew his ride would be along soon.

PREPOSITION   He waited patiently **for** his ride.

NOTE   Coordinating conjunctions that join independent clauses are almost always preceded by a comma. When *for* is used as a conjunction, there should always be a comma in front of it.

EXAMPLES   She has read the book, **but** she has not seen the movie.

We can bathe the dog, **or** you can do it when you get home from school.

Did Nazir call her, **and** has she called him back?

We asked Jim to be on time, **yet** he isn't here.

I'll be home late, **for** I have basketball practice until 4:30 or 5:00 today.

(2) *Correlative conjunctions* are pairs of conjunctions that join words or word groups that are used in the same way.

Correlative Conjunctions	
both . . . . and	not only . . . . but also
either . . . . or	whether . . . . or
neither . . . . nor	

EXAMPLES   **Both** Bill Russell **and** Larry Bird played for the team. [The pair of conjunctions joins two nouns.]

She looked **neither** to the left **nor** to the right. [The pair of conjunctions joins two prepositional phrases.]

Not only did Wilma Rudolph overcome her illness, **but** she **also** became an Olympic athlete. [The pair of conjunctions joins two independent clauses.]

NOTE   A third kind of conjunction—the *subordinating conjunction*—introduces an adverb clause.

EXAMPLES   Meet me in the park **after** the bell chimes.

Before I washed the dishes, I let them soak in the sudsy water.

Reference Note
For more information about **subordinating conjunctions,** see page 121. For more on **adverb clauses,** see page 120.

Exercise 13   **Identifying Conjunctions**

Identify the conjunction or conjunctions in each of the following sentences. Be prepared to tell what words or word groups each conjunction or pair of conjunctions joins.

EXAMPLE   **1.** Both she and her mother enjoy sailing.

     1. *Both . . . and*

1. I wanted to go to the beach, but it rained all weekend.
2. Our class is recycling not only newspapers but also glass bottles and aluminum cans.
3. He set the table with chopsticks and rice bowls.
4. Have you seen either LeAnn Rimes or George Strait in concert?

HELP
In the example in Exercise 13, the conjunction joins *she* and *her mother.*

5. We learned to use neither too many adjectives nor too few in descriptive writing.
6. That diet is dangerous, for it does not adequately meet the body's needs.
7. Both the Mohawk and the Oneida are part of the famous Iroquois Confederacy.
8. It snowed most of the day, yet we still enjoyed cross-country skiing.
9. Shall we walk home or take the bus?
10. Revise your paper, and proofread it carefully.

Exercise 14 Writing Conjunctions

Provide an appropriate conjunction for each blank in the following sentences.

EXAMPLES   1. ____ solve the problem yourself, ____ ask your teacher for help.
    1. *Either . . . or*

    2. Would she prefer juice ____ iced tea?
    2. *or*

1. We will visit ____ the Johnson Space Center ____ the Museum of Fine Arts in Houston, Texas.
2. Alaska ____ Hawaii were the last two states admitted to the Union.
3. Those two students are twin sisters, ____ they do not dress alike.
4. They were ____ hungry ____ thirsty.
5. ____ turn that radio down, ____ take it into your room while I'm studying.
6. These nails aren't long enough, ____ I'm going to buy some others.
7. You could put the chair in the living room, in your bedroom, ____ even in the dining room.
8. Their weather forecaster isn't sure ____ it will rain ____ not.
9. In the delicate ecosystem of the river, ____ motorboats ____ personal watercraft are allowed.
10. His bike is old, ____ it takes him anywhere he needs to go.

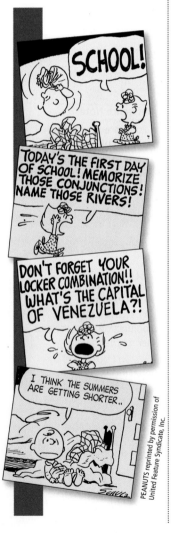

PEANUTS reprinted by permission of United Feature Syndicate, Inc.

Exercise 15 **Writing Sentences with Conjunctions**

Follow the directions given below to write sentences using conjunctions.

EXAMPLE   **1.** Use *and* to join two verbs.
                1. *The cast smiled at the audience and bowed.*

1. Use *and* to join two adverbs.
2. Use *or* to join two prepositional phrases.
3. Use *for* to join word groups that are sentences.
4. Use *but* to join two linking verbs.
5. Use *either . . . or* in an imperative sentence.
6. Use *or* to join two nouns.
7. Use *both . . . and* to join two subjects.
8. Use *neither . . . nor* to join two adverbs.
9. Use *yet* to join two adjectives.
10. Use *whether . . . or* in an interrogative sentence.

The Interjection

3j. An *interjection* is a word that expresses emotion.

Commonly Used Interjections			
aha	my	ouch	wow
hey	oh	rats	yikes
hurray	oops	well	yippee

An interjection has no grammatical relationship to the rest of the sentence.

Usually an interjection is followed by an exclamation point.

EXAMPLES   **Ouch!** That hurts!

                Goodness! What a haircut!

                Aha! I know the answer.

Sometimes an interjection is set off by a comma.

EXAMPLES   **Oh,** I wish it were Friday.

                Well, what have you been doing?

Interjections are common in casual conversation. In writing, however, they're usually used only in dialogue meant to represent such conversation. When you use interjections in dialogue, use exclamation points to indicate strong emotion and commas to indicate mild emotion.

EXAMPLES

Hey! Watch out for that jogger!

I like that outfit, but, **wow,** it's really expensive.

Notice in the second example above that commas are used both before and after an interjection that interrupts a sentence.

Exercise 16 Writing Interjections

Choose an appropriate interjection for each blank in the following sentences. Use a variety of interjections.

EXAMPLE   1. _____ , I'd love to go to your party.

   1. *Hey, I'd love to go to your party.*

   1. _____! The heel just fell off my shoe.
   2. There's, _____, about seven dollars in my wallet.
   3. _____, finally we're finished raking those leaves.
   4. _____! You squirrels, stop eating the birds' food!
   5. Young Eric, _____, you certainly have grown!
   6. _____! I sprained my ankle during the obstacle course!
   7. Weren't the special effects in the movie amazing? _____!
   8. _____, there's only one round left in the tournament.
   9. _____! I knew you were planning a surprise!
   10. _____, what a relief it is to have that term paper finished.

Review C Identifying Parts of Speech

Label each italicized word or word group in the following sentences as a *verb,* an *adverb,* a *preposition,* a *conjunction,* or an *interjection.*

EXAMPLE   **1.** *Both* otters *and* owls hunt *from* dusk to dawn.

   1. *Both . . . and—conjunction; from—preposition*

   1. *Oh*! I *just* spilled tomato soup on the new white tablecloth!
   2. Luis Alvarez *closely* studied atomic particles *for* many years.
   3. *Hey,* did Toni Morrison *or* Toni Cade Bambara write the book that you are reading?
   4. The Inuit hunters *ate* their meal *inside* the igloo.
   5. They were tired, *yet* they did *not* quit working.
   6. I *like* Persian carpets, *for* they are beautiful and wear well.
   7. The plane from Venezuela *nears* the terminal and taxis *down* the runway.
   8. *Either* geraniums *or* daisies would grow *well* in that sunny corner of the garden.
   9. Put your pencils *down,* class, *during* the instructions for this test.
   10. Computers and, *oh,* all that electronic stuff seem *so* easy for you, Brittany.

Determining Parts of Speech

3k. The way a word is used in a sentence determines what part of speech the word is.

The same word may be used as different parts of speech.

NOUN	The **play** had a happy ending.
VERB	The actors **play** their roles well.

NOUN	The **outside** of the house needs paint.
ADVERB	Let's go **outside** for a while.
PREPOSITION	I saw the birds' nest **outside** my window.

NOUN	The **well** has run dry.
ADVERB	Did you do **well** on the quiz?
ADJECTIVE	I don't feel **well** today.
INTERJECTION	**Well,** that's a relief.

Review D Identifying Verbs, Adverbs, Prepositions, Conjunctions, and Interjections

For each of the following sentences, identify the italicized, numbered word or word group as a *verb*, an *adverb*, a *preposition*, a *conjunction*, or an *interjection*.

EXAMPLE   **[1]** *Hey,* I recognize that place!

1. interjection

Though you might recognize the scene at right from the movies, it is **[1]** *not* a fake movie set. Khasneh al Faroun, or the "Pharaoh's Treasury," is the name of this magnificent structure, and it is **[2]** *quite* real. Located south of Jerusalem **[3]** *and* west of the Jordan River, the Pharaoh's Treasury is one of many sites in the ancient city of Petra. The word *Petra* **[4]** *means* "rock," and the city is carved out of solid sandstone. Petra served as a busy center of trade, and thousands of people strolled its streets **[5]** *or* sat in its outdoor theater. The theater seats **[6]** *about* four thousand people and is so old that the Romans had to repair it in A.D. 106. After a short occupation by Crusaders, the city was forbidden to Europeans **[7]** *for* about seven hundred years.

[8] *Well,* you're probably wondering about the "treasury" part of the name. For many years, the large urn atop the dome over the statue [9] *was believed* to be full of gold. However, as Bedouin treasure hunters [10] *discovered* long ago, the urn is just rock.

Review E **Writing Sentences**

Write ten sentences, following the directions given below. Underline the given word in each sentence, and identify how it is used.

EXAMPLE 1. Use *yet* as an adverb and as a conjunction.

1. *Are we there yet?—adverb*

The sky grew somewhat brighter, yet the rain continued falling.—conjunction

1. Use *walk* as a verb and as a noun.
2. Use *like* as a preposition and as a verb.
3. Use *well* as a noun and as an adjective.
4. Use *inside* as an adverb and as a preposition.
5. Use *fast* as an adjective and as an adverb.

Chapter Review

A. Identifying Types of Verbs

Identify each italicized verb in the following sentences as a *linking verb*, a *transitive action verb*, or an *intransitive action verb*.

1. A land survey *is* a method of measuring land.
2. When he was cutting lumber, my father *used* a table saw.
3. Each concert in the series *was* an hour long.
4. The water *became* ice when the temperature dropped.
5. *Hang* the banner from the ceiling.
6. The astronomer *calculated* the distance to the galaxy.
7. Mr. Lurie and Ms. Modeski *stroll* in the park.
8. The cook *multiplied* the ingredients of the stew by three.
9. Substitute teachers *work* hard!
10. *Are* they weary at the end of the day?

B. Identifying Verb Phrases

Identify the verb phrase in each of the following sentences, and underline the helping verb.

11. Have you ever heard of a mongoose?
12. Do these small carnivores inhabit parts of Africa and Asia?
13. In captivity they have lived for more than twenty years.
14. They will attack even the largest snakes.
15. The mongoose was made famous by a Rudyard Kipling story.

┌─HELP─
There may be
more than one adverb
in each sentence in
Chapter Review C.

C. Identifying Adverbs

Identify the adverb in each of the following sentences. Then, write the word it modifies.

16. The lonely boy looked longingly across the street.
17. "I'm going there after I've graduated," Rochelle said decisively, as she pointed to a map of Malaysia.
18. It is always easier for a child than for an adult to learn a second language.

19. I unfailingly read the newspaper at breakfast.

20. Did Joni remember the details of the accident later?

D. Identifying Prepositions and Prepositional Phrases

Identify the prepositional phrases in each of the following sentences. Underline the preposition once and its object twice. A sentence may have more than one prepositional phrase.

21. Will I find the broom beside the refrigerator?

22. My cat Sam likes to sit upon the television.

23. Mr. Takei used tofu in the recipe instead of chicken.

24. My mom gets upset when people talk throughout the film.

25. During the storm the windowpane streamed with rain.

E. Identifying Conjunctions

Identify the conjunctions in each of the following sentences.

26. Are you coming to the party, or are you staying home?

27. Not only did he produce the film, but he also wrote it.

28. I didn't finish the *Odyssey,* but I enjoyed what I did read.

29. We will have red beans and rice for dinner.

30. Both Taj Mahal and B. B. King performed at the blues festival.

F. Identifying Verbs, Adverbs, Prepositions, Conjunctions, and Interjections

The following paragraphs contain twenty numbered, italicized words and word groups. Identify each of these italicized words as a *verb*, an *adverb*, a *preposition*, a *conjunction*, or an *interjection*.

Have you ever [**31**] *hiked* into the wilderness [**32**] *with* a pack on your back? Have you ever [**33**] *camped* under the stars? Backpacking [**34**] *was* once popular only with mountaineers, [**35**] *but* now almost anyone who loves the outdoors [**36**] *can become* a backpacker.

First, however, you [**37**] *must be* able to carry a heavy pack long distances [**38**] *over* mountain trails. To get in shape, start with short walks and [**39**] *gradually* increase them to several miles. Exercising [40] *and* going on practice hikes can [41] *further* build your strength. [42] *After* a few short hikes, you [43] *should* be ready for a longer one.

[44] *Oh,* you [45] *may be thinking,* what equipment and food should I take? Write [46] *to* the International Backpackers Association [47] *for* a checklist. The first item on the list will [48] *usually* be shoes with rubber [49] *or* synthetic soles. The second item on the list will [50] *certainly* be a sturdy backpack.

Writing Application
Using Prepositions in Directions

Prepositional Phrases   Your class has decided to provide a "how-to" manual for seventh-graders. The manual will have chapters on crafts and hobbies, personal skills, school skills, and other topics. Write an entry for the manual, telling someone how to do a particular activity. In your entry, be sure to use prepositional phrases to make your directions clear and complete. Underline the prepositional phrases that you use.

Prewriting   First, picture yourself doing the activity you are describing. As you imagine doing the activity, jot down each step. Then, put each step in the order it is done.

Writing   Refer to your prewriting notes as you write your first draft. You may find it necessary to add or rearrange steps to make your directions clear and complete.

Revising   Ask a friend or a classmate to read your paragraph. Then, have your reader repeat the directions in his or her own words. If any part of the directions is unclear, revise your work. Make sure you have used prepositional phrases correctly.

Publishing   Read your entry again to check your spelling, grammar, and punctuation. You may want to share your "how-to" hints with other students.

Reference Note

See page 232 for more about the **correct placement of phrase modifiers.**

Complements

Direct and Indirect Objects, Subject Complements

1.0 Written and Oral English Language Conventions

Students write and speak with a command of standard English conventions appropriate to this grade level.

1.3 Identify structure of sentences.

Diagnostic Preview

Identifying Complements

Identify the complement or complements in each of the following sentences. Then, label each complement as a *direct object*, an *indirect object*, a *predicate nominative*, or a *predicate adjective*.

EXAMPLE **1.** I gave Marcy a tangerine.

1. *Marcy—indirect object; tangerine—direct object*

1. Our cat avoids skunks and raccoons.
2. Jim Thorpe was an American Indian athlete.
3. The teacher showed us a film about the Revolutionary War.
4. The television commercials for that new product sound silly.
5. Who put the tangerines in that basket?
6. I sent my grandparents a gift for their anniversary.
7. During her interview on television, the actress appeared relaxed and confident.
8. At first the colt seemed frightened.
9. Mrs. Constantine offered us olives and grapes.
10. The DJ played songs by some of my favorite singers.
11. The newspaper story prompted an investigation by the mayor's office.
12. My sister has become a computer-repair technician.
13. Write your name and address on the envelope.

14. The weather forecasters haven't issued a tornado warning.
15. Before long, the mistake became obvious to nearly everyone.
16. The sky looked gray and stormy.
17. The Irish poet Seamus Heaney won the Nobel Prize in literature in 1995.
18. The consumer group wrote the senator a letter about this type of airbag.
19. *Red Azalea* is the autobiography of Anchee Min.
20. The presidential candidate and his running-mate seem ambitious and sincere.

Recognizing Complements

4a. A *complement* is a word or word group that completes the meaning of a verb.

Every sentence has a subject and a verb. In addition, the verb often needs a complement to complete its meaning. A complement may be a noun, a pronoun, or an adjective.

	S V
INCOMPLETE	Dr. Charles Drew made [what?]
	S V C
COMPLETE	Dr. Charles Drew made **advances** in the study of blood plasma.
	S V
INCOMPLETE	Medical societies honored [whom?]
	S V C
COMPLETE	Medical societies honored **him.**
	S V
INCOMPLETE	Dr. Drew's research was [what?]
	S V C
COMPLETE	Dr. Drew's research was **important.**

An adverb is never a complement.

ADVERB	The package is **here.** [*Here* modifies the verb *is* by telling where the package is.]
COMPLEMENT	The package is **heavy.** [The adjective *heavy* modifies the subject *package* by telling what kind of package.]

Reference Note

For information on **adverbs,** see page 54.

Reference Note

For information on **prepositional phrases,** see page 59.

A complement is never in a prepositional phrase.

PREPOSITIONAL PHRASE
Erin is painting **in the garage.** [The prepositional phrase *in the garage* is an adverb phrase telling where Erin is painting.]

COMPLEMENT
Erin is painting her **room.** [The noun *room* completes the verb by telling what she is painting.]

Direct Objects

4b. A *direct object* is a noun, pronoun, or word group that tells *who* or *what* receives the action of the verb.

A direct object answers the question *Whom?* or *What?* after a transitive verb.

Reference Note

For information on **transitive verbs,** see page 52.

EXAMPLES
I met **Dr. Mason.** [I met *whom*? I met *Dr. Mason. Dr. Mason* receives the action of the verb *met.*]

Did Bill hit a **home run**? [Bill did hit *what*? Bill did hit a *home run. Home run* receives the action of the verb *hit.*]

Please buy **fruit, bread,** and **milk.** [Please buy *what*? Please buy *fruit, bread,* and *milk. Fruit, bread,* and *milk* receive the action of the verb *buy.*]

My uncle repairs **engines** and sells **them.** [My uncle repairs *what*? My uncle repairs *engines. Engines* receives the action of the verb *repairs.* My uncle sells *what*? He sells *them. Them* receives the action of the verb *sells.*]

Reference Note

For information on **linking verbs,** see page 46.

Because a linking verb does not express action, it cannot have a direct object.

LINKING VERB
Augusta Savage **was** a sculptor during the Harlem Renaissance. [The verb *was* does not express action; therefore, it has no direct object.]

A direct object is never in a prepositional phrase.

PREPOSITIONAL PHRASE
She worked **with clay.** [*Clay* is not the direct object of the verb *worked;* it is the object of the preposition *with.*]

DIRECT OBJECT
She worked the **clay** with her hands. [She worked *what*? She worked the *clay. Clay* receives the action of the verb *worked.*]

A direct object may be a compound of two or more objects.

EXAMPLE   We bought **ribbon, wrapping paper,** and **tape.** [The compound direct object *ribbon, wrapping paper,* and *tape* receives the action of the verb *bought.*]

Oral Practice **Identifying Direct Objects**

Say each of the following sentences aloud. Then, identify the direct object.

EXAMPLE   **1.** Many sports test an athlete's speed and agility.
           1. speed, agility

┌HELP─
Remember, direct objects may be compound.

1. Long-distance, or marathon, swimming requires strength and endurance.
2. A swimmer in training may swim five or six miles every day.
3. Marathon swimmers smear grease on their legs and arms for protection against the cold water.
4. During a marathon, some swimmers may lose several pounds.
5. Fatigue, pain, and huge waves challenge marathon swimmers.
6. As they swim, they endure extreme isolation.
7. Toward the end of the marathon, swimmers hear the loud applause and shouts of encouragement from their fans.
8. Spectators generally watch only the finish of a marathon.
9. Nevertheless, they know the long distance traveled by the accomplished athletes.
10. Emerging from the cold water, the exhausted swimmers have successfully completed another marathon.

┌HELP─

Remember, objects follow action verbs only. Also, direct objects in Exercise 1 may be compound.

Exercise 1 **Identifying Direct Objects**

Identify each direct object in the following sentences. If a sentence does not contain a direct object, write *no direct object.*

EXAMPLES
1. Have you ever flown a hang glider?
1. *hang glider*

2. Hang gliding has become a popular sport.
2. *no direct object*

1. Many adventurous people enjoy the thrill of gliding through the air.
2. As you can see, a hang glider can carry a full-grown person in its harness.
3. The hang glider has a lightweight sail with a triangular control bar underneath.
4. At takeoff, the pilot lifts the glider shoulder-high and runs hard down a slope into the wind.
5. The wind lifts the hang glider and the pilot off the ground.
6. Because of wind currents, takeoffs from a hilltop or a cliff are the easiest.
7. Once airborne, the glider pilot directs the path of flight.
8. He or she also controls the glider's speed by either pushing or pulling on the control bar.
9. For example, a gentle pull increases speed.
10. To land, the pilot stalls the glider near the ground and drops lightly to his or her feet.

Indirect Objects

┌HELP─

Indirect objects almost always come between a verb and its direct object.

4c. An ***indirect object*** is a noun, pronoun, or word group that sometimes appears in sentences containing direct objects.

Indirect objects tell *to whom* or *to what,* or *for whom* or *for what,* the action of the verb is done. If a sentence has an indirect object, it always has a direct object also.

EXAMPLES
The waiter gave **her** the bill. [The pronoun *her* is the indirect object of the verb *gave.* It answers the question "To whom did the waiter give the bill?"]

Pam left the **waiter** a tip. [The noun *waiter* is the indirect object of the verb *left*. It answers the question "For whom did she leave a tip?"]

Did she tip **him** five dollars? [The pronoun *him* is the indirect object of the verb *Did tip*. It answers the question "For whom did she tip five dollars?"]

If the word *to* or *for* is used, the noun or pronoun following it is part of a prepositional phrase and cannot be an indirect object.

Reference Note

For information on **prepositional phrases** and **objects of prepositions,** see page 59.

OBJECTS OF PREPOSITIONS	The ship's captain gave orders to the **crew.**
	Vinnie made some lasagna for **us.**
INDIRECT OBJECTS	The ship's captain gave the **crew** orders.
	Vinnie made **us** some lasagna.

Like a direct object, an indirect object can be a compound of two or more objects.

EXAMPLE   Felicia threw **David, Jane,** and **Paula** slow curveballs. [The compound indirect object *David, Jane,* and *Paula* tells to whom Felicia threw curveballs.]

MOTHER GOOSE & GRIMM © Tribune Media Services, Inc. All rights reserved. Reprinted with permission.

Exercise 2 Identifying Direct Objects and Indirect Objects

Identify and label the direct objects and the indirect objects in the following sentences. Make sure that you include all parts of compound objects.

EXAMPLE   1. Did you buy Mom a calculator for her birthday?
             1. *Mom—indirect object; calculator—direct object*

1. The usher found us seats near the stage.
2. I'll gladly lend you my new CD.

┌HELP─

In Exercise 2, you may find it easier to identify the direct object first and then to look for the indirect object.

3. The Nobel Foundation awarded Octavio Paz the Nobel Prize in literature.
4. Please show me your beaded moccasins.
5. They owe you and me an apology.
6. Our teacher taught us some English words of American Indian origin.
7. After the ride to Laramie, I fed the horse and the mule some hay and oats.
8. My secret pal sent me a birthday card.
9. Mai told the children stories about her family's escape from Vietnam.
10. Will you please save Ricardo a seat?

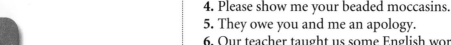

Review A **Identifying Objects of Verbs**

Identify and label the direct objects and the indirect objects in the following sentences. Make sure that you include all parts of compound objects.

EXAMPLES **1.** Did you bring the map?
1. *map—direct object*

2. My parents gave me a choice of places to go on our camping vacation.
2. *me—indirect object; choice—direct object*

1. I told them my answer quickly.
2. I had recently read a magazine article about the Flathead Reservation in Montana.
3. A Salishan people known as the Flatheads governs the huge reservation.
4. We spent five days of our vacation there.
5. We liked the friendly people and the rugged land.
6. I especially liked the beautiful mountains and twenty-eight-mile-long Flathead Lake.
7. My sister and I made camp beside the lake.
8. Someone gave my father a map and some directions to the National Bison Range, and we went there one day.
9. We also attended the Standing Arrow Pow Wow, which was the highlight of our stay.
10. The performers showed visitors traditional Flathead dances and games.

Subject Complements

4d. A *subject complement* is a word or word group in the predicate that identifies or describes the subject.

EXAMPLES   Julio has been **president** of his class since October. [*President* identifies the subject *Julio.*]

Was the masked stranger **you**? [*You* identifies the subject *stranger.*]

The racetrack looks **slippery.** [*Slippery* describes the subject *racetrack.*]

A subject complement is connected to the subject by a linking verb.

Common Linking Verbs					
appear	become	grow	remain	smell	stay
be	feel	look	seem	sound	taste

There are two kinds of subject complements—*predicate nominatives* and *predicate adjectives.*

Predicate Nominatives

4e. A *predicate nominative* is a word or word group that is in the predicate and that identifies the subject.

A predicate nominative may be a noun, a pronoun, or a word group that functions as a noun. A predicate nominative is connected to its subject by a linking verb.

EXAMPLES   A dictionary is a valuable **tool.** [*Tool* is a predicate nominative that identifies the subject *dictionary.*]

This piece of flint could be an old **arrowhead.** [*Arrowhead* is a predicate nominative that identifies the subject *piece.*]

The winner of the race was **she.** [*She* is a predicate nominative that identifies the subject *winner.*]

Is that **what you ordered**? [*What you ordered* is a predicate nominative that identifies the subject *that.*]

| TIPS & TRICKS |

To find a subject complement in a question, rearrange the sentence to make a statement.

EXAMPLE
Is Reagan the drummer in the band?

Reagan is the **drummer** in the band.

Reference Note
For more about **linking verbs,** see page 46.

| STYLE TIP |

Expressions such as *It is I* and *That was he* may sound awkward even though they are correct. In conversation, many people say *It's me* and *That was him.* Such expressions may one day become acceptable in formal writing and speaking as well as in informal situations. For now, however, it is best to follow the rules of standard, formal English, especially in your writing.

Like other sentence complements, a predicate nominative may be compound.

EXAMPLES The discoverers of radium were **Pierre Curie** and **Marie Sklodowska Curie.**

The yearbook editors will be **Maggie, Imelda,** and **Clay.**

Be careful not to confuse a predicate nominative with a direct object. A predicate nominative always completes a linking verb. A direct object always completes an action verb.

PREDICATE We are the **delegates** from our school.
NOMINATIVE

DIRECT OBJECT We elected the **delegates** from our school.

A predicate nominative is never part of a prepositional phrase.

PREPOSITIONAL Bill Russell became famous **as a basketball player.**
PHRASE

PREDICATE Bill Russell became a famous basketball **player.**
NOMINATIVE

Reference Note

For more information about **prepositional phrases,** see page 59.

Exercise 3 Identifying Predicate Nominatives

Identify the linking verb and the predicate nominative in each of the following sentences.

EXAMPLE 1. Are whales mammals?

1. *Are—mammals*

HELP

Sentences in Exercise 3 may contain a compound predicate nominative.

1. Kilimanjaro is the tallest mountain in Africa.
2. The kingdom of Siam became modern-day Thailand.
3. Dandelions can be a problem for gardeners.
4. Sue Mishima should be a lawyer or a stockbroker when she grows up.
5. When will a woman be president of the United States?
6. Reuben has become a fine pianist.
7. The team captains are Daniel, Mark, and Hannah.
8. At the moment, she remains our choice as candidate for mayor.
9. Is Alaska the largest state in the United States?
10. According to my teacher, *philately* is another name for stamp collecting.

Predicate Adjectives

4f. A *predicate adjective* is an adjective that is in the predicate and that describes the subject.

A predicate adjective is connected to the subject by a linking verb.

EXAMPLES   Cold milk tastes **good** on a hot day. [*Good* is a predicate adjective that describes the subject *milk*.]

The pita bread was **light** and **delicious**. [*Light* and *delicious* form a compound predicate adjective that describes the subject *bread*.]

How **kind** you are! [*Kind* is a predicate adjective that describes the subject *you*.]

Exercise 4 **Identifying Predicate Adjectives**

Identify the linking verbs and the predicate adjectives in the following sentences.

EXAMPLES   **1.** The crowd became restless.

1. became—restless

2. Do the waves seem high and rough today?

2. Do seem—high, rough

1. Everyone felt good about the decision.
2. The milk in this container smells sour.
3. From my seat in the stadium, I thought the big bass drums sounded too loud.
4. The situation appears dangerous and complicated.
5. Everyone remained calm during the emergency.
6. Why does the water in that pond look green?
7. During Annie Dillard's speech, the audience grew thoughtful and then enthusiastic.
8. Jan stays cheerful most of the time.
9. She must be happy with her excellent results on the science midterm.
10. Don't the black beans mixed with rice and onions taste delicious?

MEETING THE CHALLENGE

As you review your writing, you may get the feeling that nothing is *happening*, that nobody is *doing* anything. That feeling is one sign that your writing may contain too many *be* verbs. In the following sentences, replace each dull *be* verb with a verb that expresses action.

1. Behind the door was a hideous monster.

2. What is under the bed?

┌**HELP**──

Sentences in Exercise 4 may contain a compound predicate adjective.

Review B Identifying Predicate Nominatives and Predicate Adjectives

Identify each subject complement in the following sentences. Then, label each complement as a *predicate nominative* or a *predicate adjective.*

EXAMPLE **1.** Are these your shoes, Janelle?

   1. shoes—predicate nominative

1. This tasty eggplant dish is a favorite in Greece.
2. The twins are tired after the long flight.
3. How beautiful that kimono is, Keiko!
4. This perfume smells sweet and almost lemony.
5. When will the piñata be ready?
6. The winners of the race are Don, Shelby, and she.
7. Vijay Singh is a professional golfer.
8. What good dogs they are!
9. Why is your little brother acting so shy?
10. Loyal and true are the royal bodyguards.

Review C Writing Predicate Nominatives and Predicate Adjectives

Choose an appropriate predicate nominative or predicate adjective for each blank in the following sentences. Then, label each answer as a *predicate adjective* or *predicate nominative.*

EXAMPLES **1.** The currents looked ＿＿＿ than they were.

   1. slower—predicate adjective

   2. Should I become a ＿＿＿?

   2. veterinarian—predicate nominative

1. He remained a ＿＿＿ in the army for more than twenty years.
2. My sister became a ＿＿＿ after many years of study.
3. In the night air, the jasmine smelled ＿＿＿.
4. The Navajo way of life was sometimes ＿＿＿.
5. Peggy seemed ＿＿＿ with her new kitten.
6. For many travelers, a popular vacation spot is ＿＿＿.
7. My favorite season has been ＿＿＿ ever since I was five.
8. Don't these Japanese plums taste ＿＿＿, Alex?
9. How ＿＿＿ Grandpa will be to see us!
10. One of the most dangerous animals in the ocean is the ＿＿＿.

Review D   Identifying Complements

Identify the complement or complements in each of the following sentences. Then, label each complement as a *direct object,* an *indirect object,* a *predicate nominative,* or a *predicate adjective.*

┌HELP┐
Complements in Review D may be compound.

EXAMPLES   1. Our teacher read us stories from *The Leather-Stocking Tales.*

1. *us—indirect object; stories—direct object*

2. James Fenimore Cooper is the author of these tales.

2. *author—predicate nominative*

1. Leather-Stocking is a fictional scout in Cooper's popular novels.
2. He is also a woodsman and a trapper.
3. He cannot read, but he understands the lore of the woods.
4. To generations of readers, this character has been a hero.
5. He can face any emergency.
6. He always remains faithful and fearless.
7. Leather-Stocking loves the forest and the open country.
8. In later years he grows miserable.
9. The destruction of the wilderness by settlers and others greatly disturbs him.
10. He tells no one his views and retreats from civilization.

Review E   Identifying Complements

Identify the complement or complements in each of the following sentences. Then, label each complement as a *direct object,* an *indirect object,* a *predicate nominative,* or a *predicate adjective.*

EXAMPLES   1. Sean, my brother, won three medals at the Special Olympics.

1. *medals—direct object*

2. Are the Special Olympics an annual event?

2. *event—predicate nominative*

┌HELP┐
Complements in Review E may be compound.

1. Sean was one of more than one hundred special-education students who competed in the regional Special Olympics.

2. The games brought students from many schools to our city.
3. The highlights of the games included track events such as sprints and relay races.
4. These were the closest contests.
5. Sean's excellent performance in the relays gave him confidence.
6. The softball throw and high jump were especially challenging events.
7. Sean looked relaxed but determined as he prepared for the broad jump.
8. He certainly felt great after his winning jump, shown in the top photograph.
9. Mrs. Duffy, one of the coaches, told us the history of the Special Olympics.
10. Eunice Kennedy Shriver founded the program in 1968.
11. To begin with, the program was a five-week camp.
12. Several years later, the camp became an international sports event with contestants from twenty-six states and Canada.
13. Today, the organizers of the Special Olympics sponsor regional and international games.
14. The Special Olympics are exciting and inspiring.
15. Many of the contestants have physical impairments; some cannot walk or see.
16. Teachers and volunteers train contestants in the different events.
17. However, the young athletes themselves are the force behind the program.
18. The pictures on the left give you a glimpse of the excitement at the Special Olympics.
19. In the middle photograph, a volunteer guides a runner.
20. In the photo on the left, this determined boy prepares himself for the wheelchair race.

Chapter Review

A. Classifying Complements

Classify each underlined complement in the following sentences as a *direct object*, an *indirect object*, a *predicate adjective*, or a *predicate nominative*.

 1. Pamela was the <u>star</u> of the play.
 2. The guidebook gave the lost <u>tourists</u> the wrong directions.
 3. Monet is <u>famous</u> for the way his paintings captured light.
 4. Manuel offered <u>Anita</u> some good advice.
 5. Ms. Benton is our next-door <u>neighbor</u>.
 6. Bring <u>me</u> the cutting board, please.
 7. The box was <u>big</u> and awkward to handle.
 8. The library receives many new <u>books</u> each week.
 9. Mexico celebrates its <u>independence</u> on September 16.
10. The new president of the bank will be <u>Ms. Morales</u>.
11. Angel became a professional jai alai <u>player</u>.
12. Amelia Earhart flew her <u>plane</u> across the Atlantic in 1932.
13. The glow from the diamond is <u>dazzling</u>!
14. Thomas Edison provided <u>people</u> with electric light bulbs.
15. New York City was briefly the <u>capital</u> of the United States.
16. The Simpsons showed <u>him</u> slides of China.
17. My chair was hard and <u>uncomfortable</u>.
18. The machine can produce two <u>crates</u> a day.
19. Have you seen Akiho's yellow <u>sweater</u>?
20. The house appeared <u>empty</u>.

B. Identifying Complements

Write the complement or complements in each sentence. Then, identify each complement as a *direct object*, an *indirect object*, a *predicate adjective*, or a *predicate nominative*. Write *none* if the sentence does not contain a complement.

21. American Indian peoples taught the English colonists many useful skills for survival.

22. Steven Spielberg is a famous director and producer of motion pictures.
23. A hurricane of immense power lashed the Florida coast a few years ago.
24. The fans became very anxious during the final minutes of the game.
25. This winter was colder and drier than most.
26. Nora sent postcards from Argentina to her friends.
27. The new homeowners found some rare photographs in the back of the attic.
28. Although many eggshells are white, others are brown, and still others are light green.
29. Lita and Trenell studied until seven o'clock.
30. During this month, Mars is too close to the sun to be seen easily from Earth.
31. Both the House and the Senate gave the President their support on the bill.
32. The movers carried the sofa and dining room table up the front stairs.
33. Armand worked all day with his grandfather.
34. That gigantic reflector may be the world's most powerful telescope.
35. Our dog Spike is both a good watchdog and an affectionate family pet.
36. *A Raisin in the Sun* was certainly Lorraine Hansberry's most successful play.
37. Why do some animals seem nervous during a storm?
38. The theater manager will pay each usher an extra five dollars this week.
39. Luis Alvarez won a Nobel Prize for his important research in nuclear power.
40. Our neighbor has offered my mother and father a good price for their car.

Writing Application
Using Subject Complements to Write Riddles

Predicate Nominatives and Predicate Adjectives

A magazine for young people is sponsoring a riddle-writing contest. Whoever writes the best riddle will win the most advanced computer game on the market. You are determined to write the best riddle and win. Write two riddles to enter in the contest. In each one, use at least two subject complements.

Prewriting   The best way to make up a riddle is to begin with the answer. List some animals, places, and things that suggest funny or hidden meanings. For each animal, place, or thing, jot down a description based on the funny or hidden meaning. Then, choose the two topics that you think will make the best riddles.

Writing   Use your prewriting notes as you write your first draft. In each riddle, make sure that your clues will help your audience guess the answer. Be sure that you use a subject complement (a predicate nominative or a predicate adjective) in the riddle.

Revising   Ask a friend to read your riddles. If the riddles are too difficult or too simple, revise them. You may want to add details that appeal to the senses. Linking verbs such as *appear, feel, smell, sound,* and *taste* can help you add such details.

Reference Note

For a longer **list of linking verbs,** see page 79.

Publishing   Read through your riddles again to check for errors in spelling, punctuation, and capitalization. Pay special attention to the capitalization of proper nouns. You and your classmates may want to publish a book of riddles. Collect your riddles, and draw or cut out pictures as illustrations. Make photocopies for all the members of the class.

The Phrase
Prepositional, Verbal, and Appositive Phrases

1.0 Written and Oral English Language Conventions
Students write and speak with a command of standard English conventions appropriate to this grade level.
1.2 Identify and use infinitives and participles.

Diagnostic Preview

A. Identifying and Classifying Prepositional Phrases

Identify the prepositional phrase in each of the following sentences. Then, classify each phrase as an *adjective phrase* or an *adverb phrase*, and write the word that the phrase modifies.

EXAMPLE   **1.** The chairs in the kitchen need new cushions.
     1. in the kitchen—adjective phrase—chairs

1. I wish I were better at tennis.
2. The Rio Grande is the boundary between Texas and Mexico.
3. Those apples come from Washington State.
4. The most popular name for the United States flag is the Stars and Stripes.
5. The pony with a white forelock is Sally's.
6. Through the window crashed the baseball.
7. Cathy Guisewite is the creator of that comic strip.
8. During the last presidential election, we watched the national news often.
9. The first United States space shuttle was launched in 1981.
10. Outside the door the hungry cat waited patiently.

B. Identifying and Classifying Verbal Phrases and Appositive Phrases

Identify the verbal phrase or appositive phrase in each of the following sentences. Then, classify each phrase as a *participial phrase*, an *infinitive phrase*, or an *appositive phrase*.

EXAMPLE   **1.** The snow, falling steadily, formed huge drifts.

     1. *falling steadily—participial phrase*

11. Kevin, my cousin, was born in May.
12. The bus, slowed by heavy traffic, arrived at our stop later than it usually does.
13. Breaking the eggs into the wok, he made egg foo yong.
14. To remain calm is not always easy.
15. She wants to study Japanese in high school.
16. Maggie's favorite time of year, late spring, soon arrived.
17. Chilled to the bone, the children finally went inside.
18. Who are the candidates that they plan to support in the election?
19. Bethune-Cookman College, founded by Mary McLeod Bethune, is in Daytona Beach, Florida.
20. Teresa called Kam, her best friend, to ask about the assignment.

What Is a Phrase?

5a. A *phrase* is a group of related words that is used as a single part of speech and that does not contain both a verb and its subject.

VERB PHRASE	could have been hiding [no subject]
PREPOSITIONAL PHRASE	in the kitchen [no subject or verb]
INFINITIVE PHRASE	to go with them [no subject or verb]

NOTE If a word group has both a subject and a verb, it is called a *clause.*

EXAMPLES   The wind howled. [*Wind* is the subject of the verb *howled.*]

         when the Wilsons left [*Wilsons* is the subject of the verb *left.*]

Reference Note
For information on **clauses,** see Chapter 6.

Reference Note

For a list of commonly used **prepositions,** see page 58.

Reference Note

For more about the **object of a preposition,** see page 59.

Exercise 1 **Identifying Phrases**

Identify each of the following word groups as a *phrase* or *not a phrase.*

EXAMPLES 1. on the paper
          1. *phrase*

          2. after we eat
          2. *not a phrase*

 1. when you know
 2. as they walked in
 3. in the garden
 4. is sleeping
 5. how she remembered
 6. smiling brightly
 7. to the supermarket
 8. where the car is
 9. to laugh at myself
10. if he says so

Prepositional Phrases

5b. A *prepositional phrase* includes a preposition, the object of the preposition, and any modifiers of that object.

EXAMPLES   under the umbrella   for ourselves
           among good friends   next to them

Notice that an article or another modifier may appear in a prepositional phrase. The first example above contains the article *the.* In the second example, *good* modifies *friends.*

The noun or pronoun that completes a prepositional phrase is called the ***object of the preposition.***

EXAMPLES   Linh Phan has the lead in the school **play.** [The noun *play* is the object of the preposition *in.*]

           Standing between **them** was the Russian chess champion. [The pronoun *them* is the object of the preposition *between.*]

Any modifier that comes between the preposition and its object is part of the prepositional phrase.

EXAMPLE   **Into the thick mist** vanished the carriage. [The adjectives *the* and *thick* modify the object *mist.*]

An object of a preposition may be compound.

EXAMPLE   Come with **Rick** and **me** to the concert. [Both *Rick* and *me* are objects of the preposition *with.*]

NOTE Be careful not to confuse an infinitive with a prepositional phrase beginning with *to*. A prepositional phrase always has an object that is a noun or a pronoun. An infinitive is a verbal that usually begins with *to*.

PREPOSITIONAL PHRASE   Send the package **to them.**

INFINITIVE   Are you ready **to go**?

Reference Note

For more information about **infinitives,** see page 102.

GRAMMAR

Exercise 2 Identifying Prepositional Phrases

Identify the prepositional phrases in each of the following sentences.

EXAMPLE   1. Many soldiers fought bravely during the Vietnam War.

1. *during the Vietnam War*

┌HELP─

The sentences in Exercise 2 may contain more than one prepositional phrase apiece.

1. One of these soldiers was Jan C. Scruggs.
2. When the war was over, he and other veterans wondered why there was no national memorial honoring those who had served in Vietnam.
3. Scruggs decided he would raise funds for a Vietnam Veterans Memorial.
4. The memorial would include the names of all American men and women who were missing in action or who had died.
5. Organizing the project took years of great effort.
6. Many different people contributed their talents to the project.
7. Maya Ying Lin, a college student, designed the memorial that now stands in Washington, D.C.
8. This picture shows the V-shaped, black granite wall that was built from Lin's design.
9. A glass company from Memphis, Tennessee, engraved each name on the shiny granite.
10. Now the names of those who died in Vietnam will never be forgotten by the American people.

Adjective Phrases

A prepositional phrase used as an adjective is called an *adjective phrase.*

ADJECTIVE	Rosa chose the **blue** one.
ADJECTIVE PHRASE	Rosa chose the one **with blue stripes.**

5c. An *adjective phrase* modifies a noun or a pronoun.

Adjective phrases generally come after the words they modify and answer the same questions that single-word adjectives answer.

What kind?	Which one?
How many?	How much?

EXAMPLES   The store **with the neon sign** is open. [The prepositional phrase *with the neon sign* is used as an adjective
modifying the noun *store.* The phrase answers the question *Which one?*]

We saw a performance **by a street magician.** [*By a
street magician* is used as an adjective modifying the
noun *performance.* The phrase answers the question
What kind?]

More than one adjective phrase may modify the same noun
or pronoun.

EXAMPLE   Here's a gift **for you from Uncle Steve.** [The
prepositional phrases *for you* and *from Uncle Steve*
both modify the noun *gift.*]

An adjective phrase may also modify the object in another
adjective phrase.

EXAMPLE   A majority **of the mammals in the world** sleep
during the day. [The adjective phrase *of the mammals*
modifies the noun *majority.* The adjective phrase *in the
world* modifies the noun *mammals,* which is the object
of the preposition in the first phrase.]

Exercise 3   Identifying Adjective Phrases

Identify the adjective phrase in each of the following sentences,
and write the word that each phrase modifies.

EXAMPLE   1. Marie Sklodowska Curie, a scientist from Poland, was awarded the Nobel Prize in 1911.

    1. from Poland—scientist

1. While she was a student in France, Marie met Pierre Curie.
2. Pierre had already gained fame as a scientist.
3. Paris was where the two of them became friends.
4. Their enthusiasm for science brought them together.
5. The marriage between the two scientists was a true partnership.
6. The year after their marriage another scientist discovered natural radioactivity.
7. The Curies began researching the radioactivity of certain substances.
8. Their theories about a new element were proved to be true.
9. Their research on the mineral pitchblende uncovered a new radioactive element, radium.
10. In 1903, the Curies and another scientist shared a Nobel Prize for their discovery.

Exercise 4   Identifying Adjective Phrases

Identify the adjective phrases in the following sentences. Then, write the word that each phrase modifies.

EXAMPLE   1. R.I.C.E. is the recommended treatment for minor sports injuries.

    1. for minor sports injuries—treatment

1. The first letters of the words *Rest, Ice, Compression,* and *Elevation* form the abbreviation *R.I.C.E.*
2. Total bed rest is not necessary, just rest for the injured part of the body.
3. Ice helps because it deadens pain and slows the loss of blood.
4. Ice also reduces swelling of the injured area.
5. Compression with a tight bandage of elastic cloth prevents further strain on the injury.
6. This photograph shows an ice pack treating the injured knee of the athlete Robert Horry.
7. The last step in the treatment is elevation of the injured area.
8. The effect of gravity helps fluid drain away.

GRAMMAR

9. If pain continues, someone with medical training should be called to examine the injured person.

10. Even injuries of a minor nature need proper attention.

Oral Practice Using Adjective Phrases

Read each of the following sentences aloud, providing an adjective phrase for the blank. Then, say which word the phrase modifies.

EXAMPLE **1.** A flock _____ flew overhead.

     1. A flock of small gray birds flew overhead.—flock

1. The sound _____ suddenly filled the air.

2. The theater _____ often shows kung-fu movies.

3. May I have some more _____?

4. Our vacation _____ was relaxing.

5. Her photograph _____ looks like a prizewinner.

6. Andrea found the answer _____.

7. He put the flowers in a vase _____.

8. A boy _____ hung a piñata in the tree.

9. The nest is in the top branch _____.

10. Someone _____ shouted for quiet.

Adverb Phrases

A prepositional phrase used as an adverb is called an *adverb phrase.*

     ADVERB   The cavalry will reach the fort **soon.**

    ADVERB PHRASE   The cavalry will reach the fort **by noon.**

5d. An *adverb phrase* modifies a verb, an adjective, or an adverb.

Adverb phrases answer the same questions that single-word adverbs answer: *When? Where? How? Why? How often? How long? To what extent?*

EXAMPLES   We got our new puppy **at the animal shelter.** [The adverb phrase *at the animal shelter* modifies the verb *got,* telling *where.*]

    A puppy is always ready **for a game.** [The adverb phrase *for a game* modifies the adjective *ready,* telling *how.*]

    He barks loudly **for a puppy.** [The adverb phrase *for a puppy* modifies the adverb *loudly,* telling *to what extent.*]

┌HELP┐

Remember, an adjective phrase must modify a noun or a pronoun.

GRAMMAR

Unlike adjective phrases, which generally follow the word or words they modify, adverb phrases may appear at various places in sentences.

EXAMPLES   **At dusk,** we went inside to eat dinner.

We went inside **at dusk** to eat dinner.

We went inside to eat dinner **at dusk.**

Like adjective phrases, more than one adverb phrase may modify the same word.

EXAMPLES   She drove **for hours through the storm.** [Both adverb phrases, *for hours* and *through the storm,* modify the verb *drove.*]

The library is open **during the day on weekends.** [Both adverb phrases, *during the day* and *on weekends,* modify the adjective *open.*]

On Saturday we will rehearse our drill routine **before the game.** [Both adverb phrases, *On Saturday* and *before the game,* modify the verb phrase *will rehearse.*]

NOTE An adverb phrase may be followed by an adjective phrase that modifies the object in the adverb phrase.

EXAMPLE   The boat landed **on an island near the coast.** [The adverb phrase *on an island* modifies the verb *landed.* The adjective phrase *near the coast* modifies the noun *island.*]

5
d

TIPS & TRICKS

If you are not sure whether a prepositional phrase is an adjective phrase or an adverb phrase, remember that an adjective phrase almost always follows the word it modifies. If you can move the phrase without changing the meaning of the sentence, the phrase is probably an adverb phrase.

GRAMMAR

Exercise 5 **Identifying Adverb Phrases**

Identify the adverb phrase in each of the following sentences. Then, write the word that each phrase modifies. Do not list adjective phrases.

EXAMPLE   1. Pecos Bill will live forever in the many legends about him.

      1. *in the many legends—will live*

1. When he was only a baby, Pecos Bill fell into the Pecos River.
2. His parents searched for him but couldn't find him.
3. He was saved by coyotes, who raised him.
4. He thought for many years that he was a coyote.
5. After a long argument, a cowboy convinced Bill that he was not a coyote.

6. During a drought, Bill dug the bed of the Rio Grande.
7. On one occasion he rode a cyclone.
8. A mountain lion once leaped from a ledge above Bill's head.
9. Bill was always ready for trouble and soon had the mountain lion tamed.
10. Stories like these about Pecos Bill are common in the West.

Exercise 6 **Identifying Adverb Phrases**

Identify the adverb phrases in the following sentences. Then, write the word or words that each phrase modifies. Do not list adjective phrases.

┌HELP──
The sentences in Exercise 6 may contain more than one adverb phrase apiece.

EXAMPLE   1. Never before had a blizzard struck the coastal area with such force.

        1. *with such force—had struck*

1. Andrea saw the dark clouds and turned toward home.
2. The raging wind blew the eleven-year-old over a sea wall near the shore.
3. She found herself trapped in a deep snowdrift.
4. No one could hear her shouts over the howling wind.
5. Andrea's dog charged through the snow toward the beach.
6. He plunged into the snow around Andrea and licked her face, warming the skin.
7. Then the huge dog walked around Andrea until the snow was packed down.
8. The dog pulled her to an open area on the beach.
9. With great effort, Andrea and her dog made their way home.
10. Grateful to their dog, Andrea's family served him a special steak dinner.

Review A **Identifying and Classifying Prepositional Phrases**

Identify the prepositional phrase in each of the following sentences, and classify it as an *adjective phrase* or an *adverb phrase*. Then, write the word or words the phrase modifies.

EXAMPLE   1. Here is some information about sharks.

        1. *about sharks—adjective phrase; information*

1. Did you know that there are hundreds of shark species?
2. Scientists group these species into twenty-eight families.
3. Sharks within the same family share many traits.
4. The body shape, tail shape, and teeth determine the differences among families.
5. Sharks are found throughout the world's oceans.
6. As the map shows, some sharks prefer cold waters, and others live mostly in warm tropical oceans.
7. Only thirty kinds of sharks are dangerous.
8. The huge whale shark, however, falls under the "not dangerous" category.
9. Divers can even hitch a ride on its fins.
10. Beautiful yet frightening to most people, sharks are perhaps the world's most awesome creatures.

Review B **Writing Sentences with Prepositional Phrases**

For each of the following items, write a sentence using the given prepositional phrase. Then, tell whether you have used each phrase as an *adjective phrase* or an *adverb phrase*.

EXAMPLE   1. through the tollbooth
          1. *A car passed through the tollbooth.—adverb phrase*

1. in the movie theater
2. for the party
3. along the water's edge
4. about Madeleine
5. into the department store
6. underneath the bed
7. with chopsticks
8. of the equipment
9. in front of city hall
10. at the campsite

Verbals and Verbal Phrases

A *verbal* is a word that is formed from a verb but is used as a noun, an adjective, or an adverb.

The Participle

5e. A *participle* is a verb form that can be used as an adjective.

Two kinds of participles are *present participles* and *past participles.*

(1) Present participles end in *–ing.*

EXAMPLES   Mr. Sanchez rescued three people from the **burning** building. [*Burning* is the present participle of the verb *burn.* The participle modifies the noun *building.*]

              Chasing the cat, the dog ran down the street. [*Chasing* is the present participle of the verb *chase.* The participle modifies the noun *dog.*]

Reference Note

For a list of **irregular past participles,** see page 179.

(2) Past participles usually end in *–d* or *–ed.* Some past participles are formed irregularly.

EXAMPLES   Well **trained,** the soldier successfully carried out her mission. [The past participle *trained* modifies the noun *soldier.*]

              We skated on the **frozen** pond. [The irregular past participle *frozen* modifies the noun *pond.*]

NOTE   Be careful not to confuse participles used as adjectives with participles used in verb phrases. Remember that the participle in a verb phrase is part of the verb.

ADJECTIVE   **Discouraged,** the fans went home.
VERB PHRASE   The fans **were discouraged** by the string of losses.

ADJECTIVE   **Singing** cheerfully, the birds perched among the branches of the trees.
VERB PHRASE   The birds **were singing** cheerfully among the branches of the trees.

Identifying Participles and the Nouns They Modify

Identify the participles used as adjectives in the following sentences. Then, write the noun that each participle modifies.

EXAMPLE   **1.** The deserted cities of the Anasazi are found in the Four Corners area of the United States.

     1. deserted—cities

1. Utah, Colorado, New Mexico, and Arizona are the bordering states that make up the Four Corners.
2. Because of its natural beauty, Chaco Canyon is one of the most visited sights in this region of the Southwest.
3. Among the remaining ruins in Chaco Canyon are the houses, public buildings, and plazas of the Anasazi.
4. What alarming event may have caused these people to leave their valley?
5. Historians are studying the scattered remains of the Anasazi culture to learn more about these mysterious people.
6. Woven baskets were important to the earliest Anasazi people, who were excellent basket weavers.
7. On the floors of some caves are pits for stored food and other vital supplies.
8. Surviving descendants of the Anasazi include today's Zuni, Hopi, and some of the Pueblo peoples.
9. Programs protecting archaeological sites help ensure the preservation of our nation's heritage.
10. There are several national parks and monuments commemorating the Pueblo's past.

Identifying Participles and the Words They Modify

Identify the participles used as adjectives in the following sentences. Then, write the noun or pronoun each participle modifies.

EXAMPLE   **1.** Buzzing mosquitoes swarmed around me.

     1. Buzzing—mosquitoes

1. Annoyed, I went inside to watch TV.
2. I woke my sleeping father to ask about mosquitoes.
3. Irritated, he directed me to an encyclopedia.

4. I learned that some flying insects carry diseases.
5. Biting mosquitoes can spread malaria.
6. Bites make the skin swell, and the swollen skin itches.
7. Sucking blood for food, mosquitoes survive in many different climates.
8. Sometimes you can hear mosquitoes buzzing.
9. Their beating wings make the sound.
10. Mosquitoes, living only a few weeks, may go through as many as twelve generations in a year.

The Participial Phrase

5f. A *participial phrase* consists of a participle together with its modifiers and complements. The entire phrase is used as an adjective.

Reference Note

For information on **modifiers,** see Chapter 11. For information on **complements,** see Chapter 4.

EXAMPLES   **Stretching slowly,** the cat jumped down from the windowsill. [The participle *Stretching* is modified by the adverb *slowly*. The phrase modifies *cat.*]

The tornado **predicted by the meteorologist** did not hit our area. [The participle *predicted* is modified by the prepositional phrase *by the meteorologist*. The whole participial phrase modifies *tornado.*]

Reading the assignment, she took notes carefully. [The participle *Reading* has the direct object *assignment*. The phrase modifies *she.*]

Reference Note

For information on **how to place participial phrases correctly,** see page 236.

A participial phrase should be placed close to the word it modifies. Otherwise, the phrase may appear to modify another word, and the sentence may not make sense.

MISPLACED   Hopping along the fence, I saw a rabbit. [Was *I* hopping along the fence?]

CORRECTED   I saw a rabbit **hopping along the fence.**

(Exercise 9)   **Identifying Participial Phrases and the Words They Modify**

Identify the participial phrases in the following sentences. Then, write the word or words each phrase modifies.

EXAMPLE   1. Living over four hundred years ago, Leonardo da Vinci kept journals of his ideas and inventions.

1. *Living over four hundred years ago—Leonardo da Vinci*

1. The journals, written backwards in "mirror writing," are more than five thousand pages long.
2. Leonardo drew many pictures showing birds in flight.
3. He hoped that machines based on his sketches of birds would enable humans to fly.
4. Shown here, his design for a helicopter was the first one in history.
5. Studying the eye, Leonardo understood the sense of sight.
6. He worked hard, filling his journals with sketches like the ones on this page for a movable bridge.
7. The solutions reached in his journals often helped Leonardo when he created his artworks.
8. He used the hands sketched in the journals as models when he painted the hands in the *Mona Lisa*.
9. Painting on a large wall, Leonardo created *The Last Supper*.
10. Leonardo, experimenting continually, had little time to paint in his later years.

The Granger Collection, New York.

Exercise 10 **Writing Sentences with Participial Phrases**

For each of the following items, write a sentence using the given participial phrase. Make sure the participial phrase modifies a noun or pronoun.

EXAMPLE   1. cheering for the team

1. *Cheering for the team, we celebrated the victory.*

1. confused by the directions
2. gathering information on the Hopi
3. practicing my part in the play
4. followed closely by my younger brother

HELP

In Exercise 10, place a comma after a participial phrase that begins a sentence.

Reference Note

For more information about **punctuating participial phrases,** see pages 299 and 305.

5. searching through the crowd
6. shaped by wind and water
7. freshly painted at the shop
8. born in Tahiti
9. reading a book by the window
10. holding the Ming vase

The Infinitive

5g. An *infinitive* is a verb form that can be used as a noun, an adjective, or an adverb. Most infinitives begin with *to*.

Infinitives	
Used as	**Examples**
Nouns	**To succeed** is my goal. [*To succeed* is the subject of the sentence.]
	My ambition is **to teach** Spanish. [*To teach* is a predicate nominative.]
	She tried **to win.** [*To win* is the direct object of the verb *tried*.]
Adjectives	The place **to meet** tomorrow is the library. [*To meet* modifies the noun *place*.]
	She is the one **to call.** [*To call* modifies the pronoun *one*.]
Adverbs	Tamara claims she was born **to surf.** [*To surf* modifies the verb *was born*.]
	This math problem will be hard **to solve** without a calculator. [*To solve* modifies the adjective *hard*.]

NOTE *To* plus a noun or a pronoun (*to Washington, to her*) is a prepositional phrase, not an infinitive.

| PREPOSITIONAL PHRASE | I am going **to the mall** today. |
| INFINITIVE | I am going **to shop** for new shoes. |

Reference Note

For more information about **prepositional phrases,** see page 90.

Identify the infinitives in the following sentences. If a sentence does not contain an infinitive, write *none.*

EXAMPLE   1.   I would like to go to New York City someday.

              1. *to go*

1. My first stop would be to visit the Statue of Liberty.
2. Thousands of people go to see the statue every day.
3. They take a boat to Liberty Island.
4. The statue holds a torch to symbolize freedom.
5. The idea of a statue to represent freedom came from a French historian.
6. France gave the statue to the United States in 1884.
7. The statue was shipped to this country in 214 cases.
8. It was a gift to express the friendship between the two nations.
9. In the 1980s, many people helped to raise money for repairs to the statue.
10. The repairs were completed in time to celebrate the statue's hundredth anniversary on October 28, 1986.

The Infinitive Phrase

5h. An *infinitive phrase* consists of an infinitive together with its modifiers and complements. The entire phrase may be used as a noun, an adjective, or an adverb.

EXAMPLES   **To be a good gymnast** takes hard work. [The infinitive phrase is used as a noun. The infinitive *To be* has a complement, *a good gymnast.*]

                The first person **to fly over both the North Pole and the South Pole** was Richard Byrd. [The infinitive phrase is used as an adjective modifying the noun *person.* The infinitive *to fly* is modified by the prepositional phrase *over both the North Pole and the South Pole.*]

                Are you ready **to go to the gym now**? [The infinitive phrase is used as an adverb modifying the adjective *ready.* The infinitive *to go* is modified by the prepositional phrase *to the gym* and by the adverb *now.*]

Reference Note

For information on **modifiers,** see Chapter 11. For information on **complements,** see Chapter 4.

Exercise 12 Identifying Infinitive Phrases

Identify the infinitive phrase in each of the following sentences.

EXAMPLE 1. We went to the park to watch birds.

1. *to watch birds*

1. A bird is able to control many of its feathers individually.
2. Birds use their feathers to push their bodies through the air.
3. Human beings learned to build aircraft by carefully studying the way birds fly.
4. A bird sings to claim its territory.
5. To recognize the songs of different birds takes many hours of practice.
6. By molting (or gradual shedding), birds are able to replace their feathers.
7. Eagles use their feet to catch small animals.
8. Since they have no teeth, many birds have to swallow their food whole.
9. In many cases both parents help to build a nest.
10. Most birds feed their young until the young are ready to fly from the nest.

Exercise 13 Writing Sentences with Infinitive Phrases

For each of the following items, write a sentence using the given infinitive phrase. Try to vary your sentences as much as possible.

EXAMPLE 1. to see the carved masks of the Haida people

1. *Terry wants to see the carved masks of the Haida people.*

1. to sing with the Boys Choir of Harlem
2. to ask a question about the test
3. to write a poem to his girlfriend
4. to understand the assignment
5. to give a report on the Spanish exploration of California
6. to learn a little Japanese over the summer
7. to predict accurately the weather patterns
8. to imitate that style
9. to be the best at everything
10. to dry in the sun

Identifying and Classifying Participial Phrases and Infinitive Phrases

Identify the participial phrase or the infinitive phrase in each sentence of the following paragraph. Classify each phrase as a *participial phrase* or an *infinitive phrase.*

EXAMPLES

[1] My family is proud to celebrate our Jewish holidays.

1. *to celebrate our Jewish holidays—infinitive phrase*

[2] Observing Jewish traditions, we celebrate each holiday in a special way.

2. *Observing Jewish traditions—participial phrase*

[1] During Rosh Hashana we hear writings from the Torah read in our synagogue. [2] Celebrated in September or October, Rosh Hashana is the Jewish New Year. [3] On this holiday, our rabbi chooses to wear white robes instead of the usual black robes. [4] Representing newness and purity, the white robes symbolize the new year. [5] My favorite food of Rosh Hashana is the honey cake baked by my grandmother. [6] During this holiday everyone eats a lot, knowing that Yom Kippur, a day of fasting, is only ten days away. [7] Yom Kippur, considered the holiest day of the Jewish year, is a serious holiday. [8] To attend services like the one you see here is part of my family's Yom Kippur tradition. [9] I am always pleased to see many of my friends and neighbors there. [10] Sunset, marking the end of the day, brings Yom Kippur to a peaceful close.

Appositives and Appositive Phrases

5i. An *appositive* is a noun or pronoun placed beside another noun or pronoun to identify or describe it.

EXAMPLES   My teacher **Mr. Craig** enjoys books by Jane Austen. [The appositive *Mr. Craig* identifies the noun *teacher.*]

Mr. Craig wishes he could go back in time to talk to one author, **her.** [The appositive *her* identifies the noun *author.*]

5j. An *appositive phrase* consists of an appositive and its modifiers.

EXAMPLES   I recently saw the movie version of *Persuasion,* **a novel by Jane Austen.** [The noun *novel* is the appositive; *a* and *by Jane Austen* modify *novel.*]

Amanda Root, **the female lead in the movie,** plays Anne Elliot. [The noun *lead* is the appositive; *the, female,* and *in the movie* modify *lead.*]

Appositives and appositive phrases that are not essential to the meaning of a sentence are set off by commas. If the appositive is essential to the meaning, it is generally not set off by commas.

EXAMPLES   Anne, **a goodhearted and intelligent woman,** must learn not to be too easily persuaded by others. [The appositive phrase *a goodhearted and intelligent woman* adds descriptive information that is unnecessary to the sentence's basic meaning, so it is set off by commas.]

Anne's friend **Lady Russell** sometimes gives Anne poor advice. [Anne has more than one friend. The appositive *Lady Russell* tells you which friend is meant, so it is not set off by commas.]

> **Exercise 14**   **Identifying Appositives and Appositive Phrases**

Identify the appositives and appositive phrases in the following sentences. Then, give the word or words each appositive or appositive phrase identifies or describes.

EXAMPLE   **1.** My sister Roseanne is a software support specialist.

    1. Roseanne—sister

1. John, a carpenter, lives across the street from us.
2. Will your cousin Charlene visit you this fall?
3. That book, *The White Mountains,* is my favorite.
4. Janey is playing with her favorite toy, a stuffed horse named Dapples.
5. I asked for a volunteer, anyone, to lead the program.
6. Al, the security guard at Mom's office, always says hello to me.
7. Noel sent Tony's son Ethan a birthday present.
8. The shortstop on our softball team, Deanna, broke her toe last Wednesday.
9. Jackson Square, a landmark in New Orleans, has a statue of Andrew Jackson in it.
10. The beach was covered with sargassum, a seaweed that is made up of brown algae.

MEETING THE
CHALLENGE

To make your writing more interesting, you can vary your sentence beginnings. Rather than beginning each sentence with the subject of a clause, you can begin with a prepositional, verbal, or appositive phrase.

Rearrange the following sentences so that they begin with a phrase.

1. The daisies bloomed in the window box.

2. I will need a calculator to work those problems.

3. The children gasped, frightened by the noise.

4. Mr. Jaenz, a clever inventor, has several patents.

Review D **Identifying Verbal Phrases and Appositive Phrases**

Write the verbal phrase or appositive phrase in each of the following sentences. Then, label it as a *participial phrase,* an *infinitive phrase,* or an *appositive phrase.*

EXAMPLE   1. Startled by the noise, I looked up.

        1. Startled by the noise—participial phrase

1. Josie wants to visit Thailand someday.
2. I found Clive, my cat, on top of the refrigerator.
3. A job baby-sitting for a nice family is what I want.
4. The newspaper, an unreadable blob of wet paper, had been outside in the gutter during the storm.
5. A boy playing basketball asked Chris and Laney whether you rode our bus.
6. Monique would like that sweater, the green one.
7. Launched into the atmosphere, the spaceship turned in the direction of the moon.
8. To leave the place neat and clean was our goal.
9. Do you want to play kickball, Jason?
10. Laughing hard, Derrick could barely catch his breath.

Reference Note

For more information on **varying sentence beginnings,** see page 432.

Review E Writing Phrases for Sentences

For each of the following sentences, write the kind of phrase that is called for in parentheses.

EXAMPLE   1. _____, the audience cheered Yo-Yo Ma's performance. (participial phrase)

1. *Clapping loudly, the audience cheered Yo-Yo Ma's performance.*

1. We walked slowly _____. (adverb phrase)
2. The people _____ applauded Mayor Garza's speech. (adjective phrase)
3. Dennis, _____, is afraid of fire ants. (appositive phrase)
4. The water _____ dripped steadily. (adjective phrase)
5. _____ we saw many beautiful Navajo rugs. (adverb phrase)
6. _____, the principal entered the classroom. (participial phrase)
7. Suddenly, _____, the lion pounced. (participial phrase)
8. My friends and I like _____. (infinitive phrase)
9. _____ is my greatest ambition. (infinitive phrase)
10. I gave Stephen a present, _____, for his birthday. (appositive phrase)

GRAMMAR

Chapter Review

A. Identifying Prepositional Phrases

Identify each prepositional phrase in the following sentences. Then, write the word or words each phrase modifies. There may be more than one prepositional phrase in a sentence.

1. The view from Mount Fuji is spectacular.
2. Boulder Dam was the original name of Hoover Dam.
3. Eat something before the game.
4. We heard stories about our Cherokee ancestors.
5. The coach paced nervously on the sidelines.
6. The second-longest river in Africa is the Congo.
7. For the costume party, Jody dressed as a lion tamer.
8. Has the hiking party returned to the campsite?
9. The Hudson River was once the chief trading route for the western frontier.
10. Hearing a loud noise, Rita stopped the car and looked underneath it.

B. Identifying Adjective and Adverb Phrases

Classify each italicized prepositional phrase in the following sentences as an *adjective phrase* or an *adverb phrase*. Then, write the word or words the phrase modifies.

11. The jacket *with the gray stripes* is mine.
12. The man *across the aisle* is sleeping.
13. Mai spoke *with confidence* at the leadership conference.
14. A young woman *in a blue uniform* answered the phone.
15. Nobody *except Alicia* was amazed at the sudden downpour.
16. Were you upset *about the delay*?
17. Does your doctor work *at Emerson Hospital*?
18. *Along the Appalachian National Scenic Trail,* you will find painted rocks that indicate the route.
19. Masud's friends *from New Jersey* are coming to visit.
20. He is tall *for his age.*

C. Classifying Verbal Phrases

Identify each italicized verbal phrase in the following sentences as an *infinitive phrase* or a *participial phrase.*

21. *Returning her library books,* Janelle chose two more.
22. Scott, *chilled by the brisk wind,* pulled on his gloves.
23. *To become a park ranger* is Keisha's dream.
24. The awards dinner *planned for this evening* was canceled.
25. A soufflé can be difficult *to prepare properly.*
26. *Organized in 1884,* the first African American professional baseball team was the Cuban Giants.
27. Guillermo hopes *to visit us soon.*
28. My brother was the first person *to see a meteor* last evening.
29. Stella did not disturb the cat *sleeping in the window.*
30. How do you plan *to tell the story*?

D. Identifying Verbal Phrases

Identify the verbal phrase in each of the following sentences. Then, classify each phrase as an *infinitive phrase* or a *participial phrase.*

31. To skate around the neighborhood was Lee's favorite pastime.
32. Racing around on his in-line skates, he felt as if he were flying.
33. Then one afternoon, prevented from skating by the rain, Lee wondered about the history of skates.
34. He decided to search the Internet for information.
35. Lee learned that Joseph Merlin, an eighteenth-century Dutchman, was the first person to adapt ice skates for use on dry land.
36. Merlin's idea was to attach wooden spools to a plate that supported them.
37. First fashioned in 1763, skates with metal wheels were in use for a century.
38. Appearing in 1863, the first modern skates were invented by an American.
39. Skates with more durable ball-bearing wheels, introduced later in the nineteenth century, popularized roller skating.
40. At the end of the afternoon, Lee exclaimed, "It's fun to know the history of skates!"

E. Identifying Appositive Phrases

Identify the appositive phrase in each of the following sentences.

41. Bamboo, a kind of grass, may reach a height of 120 feet.

42. My favorite author is Truman Capote, an American writer.

43. The capybara, the world's largest rodent, can grow to 4 feet in length.

44. *Centigrade,* another word for *Celsius,* comes from the Latin for *100 degrees.*

45. Mom, an avid bird watcher, enjoyed visiting the state park.

46. Are you familiar with okra, a vegetable used in gumbo?

47. I bought a protractor, an instrument for measuring and plotting angles.

48. Provence, a region of France, is on the Mediterranean.

49. His best move, the jump shot, earned the team twenty points.

50. Spaghetti, my favorite dish, is on the menu.

Writing Application
Using Prepositional Phrases in a Note

Adjective and Adverb Phrases   Write a note to a friend to explain how to care for your pet while you are away. In your note, use a combined total of at least ten adjective phrases and adverb phrases to give detailed instructions to your friend.

Prewriting   Begin by thinking about a pet you have or would like to have. Then, make a chart or list of the pet's needs. If you need more information about a particular kind of pet, ask a friend or someone else who owns such a pet.

Writing   As you write your first draft, focus on giving information about each of your pet's needs. Tell your friend everything he or she needs to know to care for your pet properly.

Revising   Ask a family member or friend to read your note. Add any missing information and take out any unnecessary instructions. Be sure that you have used at least ten adjective and adverb phrases.

Publishing   Check the grammar, punctuation, and spelling of your note. You and your classmates may wish to create a pet care guide by organizing your notes in a three-ring binder.

The Clause
Independent and Subordinate Clauses

1.0 Written and Oral English Language Conventions

Students write and speak with a command of standard English conventions appropriate to this grade level.

1.3 Identify structure of sentences.

1.4 Demonstrate the mechanics of writing (e.g., commas at end of dependent clauses).

Diagnostic Preview

A. Identifying and Classifying Independent and Subordinate Clauses

Identify each of the following clauses as either *independent* or *subordinate.*

EXAMPLE   **1.** when I was eleven years old

            1. subordinate

1. because I have lived in Chile and Ecuador
2. his writing has improved
3. although Gullah is still spoken on South Carolina's Sea Islands
4. when that baseball team won the National League pennant
5. she served as secretary of labor
6. which we brought to the Juneteenth picnic
7. everyone laughed
8. whose mother you met yesterday
9. during the storm the power failed
10. to whom his mother explained the reason for the delay

B. Identifying and Classifying Subordinate Clauses

Identify the subordinate clause in each of the following sentences. Then, classify each as either an *adjective clause* or an *adverb clause*.

EXAMPLES   **1.** Today is the day that you are eating at my house.
         1. that you are eating at my house—adjective clause

         2. I will give you a map so that you can find my house.
         2. so that you can find my house—adverb clause

11. If you have never had Caribbean food, you are in for a treat.
12. My mother, who was born and raised in Jamaica, really knows how to cook.
13. Whenever I have a chance, I try to learn her secrets.
14. My grandmother, whose cooking is spectacular, is making her special sweet potato pone for dessert.
15. Some of the fruits and vegetables that grow in Jamaica are hard to find in the markets around here.
16. Today we are shopping for coconuts, avocados, and callaloo greens, which were introduced to the Caribbean by Africans.
17. We must also remember to buy the fresh hot peppers, onions, and spices that are needed for seasoning the meat.
18. Although my mother never uses measuring spoons, she seems to know just how much of each spice to add.
19. As soon as we pay for these items, let's take them home.
20. Part of your treat will be to smell the delicious aroma from the kitchen before you even begin eating.

What Is a Clause?

6a. A *clause* is a word group that contains a verb and its subject and that is used as a sentence or as part of a sentence.

Every clause contains a subject and a verb. However, not all clauses express complete thoughts. A clause that does express a complete thought is called an *independent clause*. A clause that does not express a complete thought is called a *subordinate clause*.

> NOTE   A subordinate clause that is capitalized and punctuated as if it were a sentence is a **sentence fragment**.

Reference Note
For information about **correcting sentence fragments,** see page 414.

The Independent Clause

6b. An *independent* (or *main*) *clause* expresses a complete thought and can stand by itself as a sentence.

EXAMPLES   I woke up late this morning.

Do you know Joseph?

When an independent clause stands alone, it is called a sentence. Usually, the term *independent clause* is used only when such a clause is joined with another clause.

EXAMPLES   **My mother drove me to school.** [This entire sentence is an independent clause.]

My mother drove me to school, but **my brother rode his bicycle.** [This sentence contains two independent clauses.]

Since I missed the bus, **my mother drove me to school.** [This sentence contains one subordinate clause and one independent clause.]

The Subordinate Clause

6c. A *subordinate* (or *dependent*) *clause* does not express a complete thought and cannot stand by itself as a complete sentence.

Words such as *because, if, since, that, until, which,* and *whom* signal that the clauses following them may be subordinate. *Subordinate* means "lesser in rank or importance." A subordinate clause must be joined with at least one independent clause to make a sentence and express a complete thought.

SUBORDINATE   **if** the dress is too long
     CLAUSES
          that the veterinarian recommended

SENTENCES   **If the dress is too long,** we will hem it.

The new food **that the veterinarian recommended** is good for our hamster.

Subordinate clauses may appear at the beginning, in the middle, or at the end of a sentence.

Reference Note

For information on using **commas and coordinating conjunctions to join two independent clauses,** see page 297. For information about **using commas to join independent and subordinate clauses,** see page 299.

COMPUTER TIP

A computer can help you proofread your writing for subordinate clauses that are sentence fragments. Most grammar checkers point out sentences that seem incomplete. Grammar checkers are not perfect, though. Be sure to check your work for fragments yourself, and double-check any word group that the computer says is incomplete.

GRAMMAR

Exercise 1 **Identifying Independent and Subordinate Clauses**

Identify the italicized clause in each of the following sentences as *independent* or *subordinate*.

EXAMPLE **1.** *If you know any modern music history,* then you are probably familiar with the Motown sound.

    1. subordinate

1. Do you recognize the entertainers *who are shown in the photographs on this page and the next*?

2. These performers had hit records in the 1950s and 1960s *when the music business in Detroit (the Motor City, or "Motown") was booming.*

3. Berry Gordy, *who founded the Motown record label,* began his business in a small office in Detroit.

4. He was a songwriter and producer, and *he was able to spot talent.*

5. Gordy went to clubs to hear local groups *whose sound he liked.*

6. The Miracles, *which was the first group discovered by Gordy,* had a lead singer named Smokey Robinson.

7. *Robinson was also a songwriter,* and Gordy included him in the Motown team of writers and musicians.

8. Gordy carefully managed all aspects of the Motown sound, *which is a special combination of rhythm and blues and soul.*
9. Diana Ross and the Supremes, Stevie Wonder, Marvin Gaye, the Four Tops, the Temptations, Gladys Knight and the Pips, and Michael Jackson are just some of the performers *that Gordy discovered.*
10. As you look carefully at the photographs again, *can you and your classmates recognize these music legends?*

<table>
<tr><td>

MEETING THE CHALLENGE

To make your writing smoother, you can combine short, choppy sentences by changing some into subordinate clauses.
  Combine the following sentences.

  Our dog, Skippy, is five years old. He is a Yorkshire terrier.

  I visit my aunt in June. I will get to swim in a nearby lake.

</td></tr>
</table>

Exercise 2 Identifying Subordinate Clauses

Identify the subordinate clause in each of the following sentences.

EXAMPLE   1. When you get up in the morning, do you look at your sleepy face in a mirror?
          1. When you get up in the morning

1. A mirror is a piece of polished metal or glass that is coated with a substance such as silver.
2. The most common type of mirror is the plane mirror, which is flat.
3. The image that is reflected in a plane mirror is reversed.
4. As you look into a mirror, your left hand seems to be the image's right hand.
5. When an image is reversed, it is called a mirror image.
6. A sailor who looks through the periscope of a submarine is using a system of lenses and mirrors in a tube to see above the water's surface.
7. Right-hand rearview mirrors on cars, which show a wide area of the road behind, are usually convex, or curved outward.
8. Drivers must be careful because convex mirrors make reflected objects appear far away.
9. Because the mirror in a flashlight is concave, or curved inward, it strengthens the light from a small lightbulb.
10. When you look in a concave mirror, you sometimes see a magnified reflection of yourself.

Reference Note

For information about **using subordinate clauses to combine sentences,** see page 425.

Oral Practice **Writing Sentences with
Subordinate Clauses**

Read each of the following subordinate clauses aloud. Then, add
an independent clause to make a complete sentence. Make your
sentences interesting by using a variety of independent clauses.

EXAMPLES   **1.** who lives next door to us
         1. *Have you or Peggy met the woman who lives next
            door to us?*

         2. that Alexander bought
         2. *The sleeping bag that Alexander bought was
            on sale.*

1. when I bought the CD
2. who won the contest
3. if my parents agree
4. as Jessye Norman began to sing
5. because we are going to a concert
6. that you made
7. who built the pyramids
8. for which this musician is famous
9. since the telephone was invented
10. whose paintings are now in the museum

The Adjective Clause

6d. An *adjective clause* is a subordinate clause that
modifies a noun or a pronoun.

Like an adjective or an adjective phrase, an adjective clause may
modify a noun or a pronoun. Unlike an adjective phrase, an
adjective clause contains both a verb and its subject.

ADJECTIVE   a **blue** flower

ADJECTIVE   a flower **with blue petals** [The phrase does not
    PHRASE   have a verb and its subject.]

ADJECTIVE   a flower **that has blue petals** [The clause does
    CLAUSE   have a verb, *has,* and its subject, *that.*]

An adjective clause usually follows the word or words it
modifies and tells *which one* or *what kind.*

EXAMPLES　Emma Willard was the one **who founded the first women's college in the United States.** [The adjective clause modifies the pronoun *one*, telling *which one*.]

I want a bicycle **that I can ride over rough ground.** [The adjective clause modifies the noun *bicycle*, telling *what kind*.]

The Relative Pronoun

An adjective clause is usually introduced by a *relative pronoun*.

Commonly Used Relative Pronouns				
that	which	who	whom	whose

These words are called **relative pronouns** because they *relate* an adjective clause to the noun or pronoun that the clause modifies.

EXAMPLES　A snorkel is a hollow tube **that lets a diver breathe underwater.** [The relative pronoun *that* begins the adjective clause and relates it to the noun *tube*.]

The team's mascot, **which is a horse,** is called Renegade. [The relative pronoun *which* begins the adjective clause and relates it to the noun *mascot*.]

Gwendolyn Brooks is the writer **who wrote *Annie Allen*.** [The relative pronoun *who* begins the adjective clause and relates it to the noun *writer*.]

Those **whose library books are overdue** must pay fines. [The relative pronoun *whose* begins the adjective clause and relates it to the pronoun *Those*.]

NOTE In some cases, the relative pronoun can be omitted.

EXAMPLE　The person [**that** *or* **whom**] **we met at the market** was Mrs. Herrera.

Exercise 3 **Identifying Adjective Clauses**

Identify the adjective clause in each of the sentences on the next page. Underline the relative pronoun that begins the clause.

┌HELP─

The relative pronoun *that* is used to refer both to people and to things. The relative pronoun *which* is used to refer to things.

EXAMPLES
She is the person **that** I met yesterday.

This is the CD **that** you should buy.

The bus, **which** is behind schedule, stops at the next corner.

Reference Note

For information about **when to use commas to set off adjective clauses,** see page 299.

EXAMPLE **1.** The person who wrote the Declaration of Independence was Thomas Jefferson.

    1. *who wrote the Declaration of Independence*

1. In his later years, Jefferson lived at his home, Monticello, which he designed.

2. Jefferson planned a daily schedule that kept him busy all day.

3. He began each day by writing himself a note that recorded the morning temperature.

4. Then he did his writing, which included letters to friends and businesspeople.

5. Afterward, he ate breakfast, which was served around 9:00 A.M.

6. Jefferson, whose property included stables as well as farm fields, went horseback riding at noon.

7. Dinner, which began about 4:00 P.M., was a big meal.

8. From dinner until dark, he talked to friends and neighbors who came to visit.

9. His large family, whom he often spent time with, included twelve grandchildren.

10. Jefferson, whose interests ranged from art and architecture to biology and mathematics, read each night.

Exercise 4 **Writing Appropriate Adjective Clauses**

Complete each of the following sentences with an adjective clause. Then, underline the relative pronoun.

EXAMPLE **1.** We read the Greek legend ____.

    1. *We read the Greek legend that tells the story of the Trojan horse.*

1. You should proofread every composition ____.

2. My best friend, ____, is a good student.

3. Mrs. Rivera, ____, was my fifth-grade teacher.

4. We heard a sound ____.

5. Our neighbors ____ are from Fez, Morocco.

6. The ship, ____, carried bananas.

7. Anyone ____ is excused from the final exam.

8. Carmen, can you tell us about the scientist ____?

9. Is Victor Hugo the author ____?

10. Wow! I didn't know you had a dog ____.

—HELP—

Remember, to be a clause, a word group must contain both a verb and its subject.

The Adverb Clause

6e. An *adverb clause* is a subordinate clause that modifies a verb, an adjective, or an adverb.

Like an adverb or an adverb phrase, an adverb clause can modify a verb, an adjective, or an adverb. Unlike an adverb phrase, an adverb clause contains both a verb and its subject.

ADVERB	**Bravely,** Jason battled the fierce dragon.
ADVERB PHRASE	**With great bravery,** Jason battled the fierce dragon. [The phrase does not have both a verb and its subject.]
ADVERB CLAUSE	**Because Jason was brave,** he battled the fierce dragon. [The clause does have a verb and its subject.]

Adverb clauses answer the following questions: *How? When? Where? Why? To what extent? How much? How long?* and *Under what condition?*

EXAMPLES   I feel **as though I will never catch up.** [The adverb clause tells *how* I feel.]

After I finish painting my bookcases, I will call you. [The adverb clause tells *when* I will call you.]

I paint **where there is plenty of fresh air.** [The adverb clause tells *where* I paint.]

I have more work to do today **because I didn't paint yesterday.** [The adverb clause tells *why* I have more work to do.]

Jennifer can paint better **than Victor can.** [The adverb clause tells *to what extent* Jennifer can paint better.]

I will paint **until Mom comes home;** then I will clean my brushes and set the table for supper. [The adverb clause tells *how long* I will paint.]

If I paint for two more hours, I should be able to finish. [The adverb clause tells *under what condition* I should be able to finish.]

Reference Note

For more information on **punctuating introductory adverb clauses,** see page 305.

Notice in the preceding examples that adverb clauses may be placed in various positions in sentences. When an adverb clause comes at the beginning, it is usually followed by a comma.

Subordinating Conjunctions

Adverb clauses begin with *subordinating conjunctions.*

Common Subordinating Conjunctions		
after	because	though
although	before	unless
as	how	until
as if	if	when
as long as	in order that	whenever
as much as	since	where
as soon as	so that	wherever
as though	than	while

Some words that are used as subordinating conjunctions, such as *after, as, before, since,* and *until,* can also be used as prepositions.

PREPOSITION **Before** sunrise, we left for the cabin.

SUBORDINATING **Before** the sun had risen, we left for
CONJUNCTION the cabin.

PREPOSITION In the nineteenth century, buffalo skins were used **as** blankets and clothing.

SUBORDINATING Around 1900, **as** the buffalo became nearly
CONJUNCTION extinct, conservationists fought for its protection.

Exercise 5 Identifying Adverb Clauses

Identify the adverb clause in each of the following sentences.

EXAMPLE 1. As long as they have been a people, the Chinese have been making kites.

1. *As long as they have been a people*

1. Although the following story is only a legend, many people believe that a kite like the one pictured on the next page may have saved the people of China's Han dynasty.
2. The Chinese were about to be attacked by an enemy army when an advisor to the emperor came up with a plan.
3. As the advisor stood beside an open window, his hat was lifted off by a strong wind.
4. He immediately called for a number of kites to be made so that they might be used to frighten the enemy.

5. The kite makers had no trouble finding lightweight bamboo for their kite frames because bamboo grows widely in China.
6. As each frame was completed, silk was stretched over it.
7. The emperor's advisor attached noisemakers to the kites so that they would produce an eerie sound.
8. He ordered his men to fly the kites in the darkest hour of night because then the enemy would hear the kites but would not be able to see them.
9. Unless the advisor was wrong, the enemy would think that the kites were gods warning them to retreat.
10. According to the legend, the enemy retreated as if they were being chased by a fire-breathing dragon.

┌HELP┐

Remember, a clause contains both a verb and its subject.

Exercise 6 Writing Adverb Clauses

Complete each of the following sentences with an adverb clause. Then, underline the subordinating conjunction.

EXAMPLE 1. ____, Jesse will win the dance contest.

1. *If I'm right, Jesse will win the dance contest.*

1. ____, everything seemed fresh and new.
2. The gears jammed ____.
3. ____, the African dancers began their routine.

4. From the trees, a Bengal tiger watched the herd ____.

5. ____, maybe he'll help you clean your room.

6. Call us ____.

7. ____, the cement mixer backed up to the wooden frame.

8. The buses have been running on time ____.

9. ____, street sweepers rolled slowly next to the curb.

10. His map looked ____.

GRAMMAR

Review A **Identifying and Classifying Subordinate Clauses**

Identify the subordinate clause in each of the following sentences. Then, classify each clause as an *adjective clause* or an *adverb clause*.

EXAMPLES   **1.** American history is filled with stories of people who performed heroic deeds.

    1. who performed heroic deeds—adjective clause

    2. As the American colonists struggled for independence, women played important roles.

    2. As the American colonists struggled for independence—adverb clause

1. When you study the American Revolution, you may learn about the adventures of a woman known as Molly Pitcher.

2. Molly Pitcher, whose real name was Mary, was the daughter of farmers.

3. Although she was born in New Jersey, she moved to the Pennsylvania colony.

4. There she married William Hays, who was a barber.

5. Hays joined the colonial army when the Revolution began.

6. Mary Hays went to be with her husband in Monmouth, New Jersey, which was the site of a battle on a hot June day in 1778.

7. At first, she carried water to the soldiers so that they would not be overcome by the intense heat.

8. The soldiers nicknamed her "Molly Pitcher" because she carried the water in pitchers.

9. Later, when her husband collapsed from the heat, she took over his cannon.

10. George Washington, who was the commander of the Continental Army, made Molly an honorary sergeant.

Write twenty different sentences of your own. In each sentence, include a subordinate clause that begins with one of the following words or word groups. Underline the subordinate clause. After the sentence, classify the subordinate clause as an *adjective clause* or an *adverb clause.*

EXAMPLES
1. so that
1. We hurried <u>so that we wouldn't miss the bus going downtown.</u>—adverb clause

2. whom
2. Jim Nakamura, <u>whom I met at summer camp</u>, is now my pen pal.—adjective clause

1. which
2. before
3. since
4. who
5. than
6. whose
7. as though
8. although
9. that
10. if
11. because
12. unless
13. as soon as
14. whom
15. while
16. whenever
17. after
18. where
19. as much as
20. wherever

Chapter Review

A. Identifying Independent and Subordinate Clauses

Identify the italicized clause in each of the following sentences as an *independent* or a *subordinate clause.*

1. As Jawan walked to school, *he saw a strange sight.*
2. *If you go to the library,* you should take a look at the young adult section.
3. The book *that I read last night* was very scary!
4. Long after the rain had stopped, *the ground was still wet.*
5. If the trip is cancelled, *we can play tennis.*
6. *When the spin cycle stops,* please take the laundry out of the washing machine.
7. The shells *that they found* are still in the closet.
8. *Most people are asleep* when the morning newspaper is delivered.
9. Was the movie *that the reviewers liked* sold out?
10. Since we moved here from Chile, *we have met many people.*

B. Identifying Adjective and Adverb Clauses

Identify each italicized clause in the following sentences as an *adjective clause* or an *adverb clause.* Then, write the word each clause modifies.

11. We camped near Lake Arrowhead *when we went fishing last year.*
12. *Because the weather was cold,* I wore a sweater under my jacket.
13. The coat *that my mother bought for me* was blue.
14. *As she left her office,* Cletha heard the phone.
15. Vince hit the home run *that won the game*!
16. Everyone *who signed up for the marathon* should meet at 8:00 A.M. tomorrow in the school parking lot.
17. On Tuesday the Chavez family went to the Rex parade, *which is held every year in New Orleans during Mardi Gras.*

18. Larry is a little taller *than Dana is.*

19. The CD *that Rita wanted to buy* was out of stock.

20. Louise stayed home today *because she has a bad case of the flu.*

21. Play soccer *if you need more exercise.*

22. The turtle moves faster *than I expected.*

23. My older sister, *who is on the varsity basketball team,* practices after school every day.

24. *Since it was such a beautiful evening,* we decided to take a long walk.

25. Will the students *whose families observe the Jewish Sabbath* be excused early on Friday?

C. Identifying Subordinate Clauses

Identify the subordinate clause in each sentence. Then, classify the clause as an *adjective clause* or an *adverb clause.* Write *none* if the sentence does not contain a subordinate clause.

26. The denim blue jeans that are known as Levi's have an interesting history.

27. They were created in 1873 by Levi Strauss.

28. Strauss, who had immigrated to the United States from Bavaria, founded a clothing company called Levi Strauss & Co.

29. Six years after his arrival in the United States, he sailed to San Francisco because his sister and brother-in-law had a dry goods business there.

30. In 1872, Strauss had received a letter from Jacob Davis, a tailor in Nevada who was one of his regular customers.

31. Davis told Strauss about riveting the pocket corners of work pants so that the pants would be more durable.

32. Since Davis lacked the money to patent this invention, he asked Strauss to be his partner.

33. Both men were named as patent holders in 1873.

34. The copper-riveted overalls were popular with working people who needed tough but comfortable pants.

35. In 1880, the company, whose sales had reached $2.4 million, was selling denim pants to retailers for about $1.50 a pair.

36. Strauss died in 1902, four years before an earthquake and fire in San Francisco destroyed his company's factories.

37. After the earthquake, the company built a new factory that is still operating today.

38. The company suffered financially, as did many other businesses, during the Great Depression of the 1930s.

39. Since the 1940s, the pants have become increasingly fashionable among young people.

40. In the 1950s, when actors such as James Dean wore them in film roles, the jeans skyrocketed in popularity.

Writing Application
Using Clauses in a Manual

Subordinate Clauses   Your class project for National Safety Week is to write a safety manual. Each class member will write one page of instructions telling what to do in a particular emergency. Use subordinating conjunctions to show the relationships between your ideas.

Prewriting   Think of a specific emergency that you know how to handle. List the steps that someone should follow in this emergency. Number the steps in order. If you aren't sure of the order or don't know a particular step, stop writing and get the information you need.

Writing   Use your prewriting list to begin your first draft. As you write, make your instructions as clear as possible. Define or explain terms that might be unfamiliar to your readers. Be sure that your instructions are in the right order.

Revising   Read over your instructions to be sure that you've included all necessary information. Add, cut, or rearrange steps to make the instructions easy to follow. Be sure to use appropriate subordinating conjunctions to make the order of the steps clear.

Publishing   Check your work carefully for any errors in grammar, punctuation, and spelling. To publish your class safety manual, gather all the pages and make booklets out of printouts or photocopies. Organize your topics alphabetically, or group them by kinds of emergencies.

┌HELP──

A health teacher, the school nurse, or an organization such as the Red Cross should be able to provide information.

Reference Note

For information about **punctuating introductory adverb clauses,** see page 305.

Kinds of Sentence Structure

Simple, Compound, Complex, and Compound-Complex Sentences

1.0 Written and Oral English Language Conventions

Students write and speak with a command of standard English conventions appropriate to this grade level.

1.3 Identify structure of sentences.

┌HELP─

You may wish to review Chapter 6 before completing this part of the Diagnostic Preview.

Diagnostic Preview

A. Identifying and Classifying Clauses

Identify each clause in the following sentences. Then, classify each clause as an *independent clause* or a *subordinate clause*.

EXAMPLE   **1.** Students who are interested in attending the science fair at the community college should sign up now.

1. *Students should sign up now—independent clause; who are interested in attending the science fair at the community college—subordinate clause*

1. We did warm-up exercises before we practiced the routine.
2. The musical *West Side Story* is a modern version of the story of Romeo and Juliet.
3. The first poem in the book is about spring, and the second one is about autumn.
4. Molasses, which is made from sugar cane, is a thick brown liquid used for human food and animal feed.
5. Before the test we studied the chapter and did the chapter review exercises.
6. While our teacher discussed the formation of the African nation of Liberia, we took notes.

7. It rained Saturday morning, but the sun came out in time for the opening of the Special Olympics.

8. The player whose performance is judged the best receives the Most Valuable Player Award.

9. Not all stringed instruments sound alike, for their shapes and the number of their strings vary.

10. The tourists that we saw wandering up Esplanade Avenue went to the Japanese ceramics exhibit after they had reached the museum.

B. Identifying Simple, Compound, Complex, and Compound-Complex Sentences

Identify each of the following sentences as *simple, compound, complex,* or *compound-complex.*

EXAMPLE 1. The Museum of Science and Industry, which is in Chicago, features a German submarine captured during World War II.

  1. *complex*

11. Either Ana or Lee will sing the opening song for the fair.

12. We visit the Liberty Bell whenever we go to Philadelphia.

13. Have you chosen a topic for your report yet, or are you still making your decision?

14. When George Washington Carver was working on soil improvement and plant diseases, the South was recovering from the Civil War, and his discoveries gave planters a competitive edge.

15. *A Tree Grows in Brooklyn,* which was written by Betty Smith, is one of my favorite books.

16. The call of a peacock sounds very much like that of a person in distress.

17. Although it was warm enough to go swimming on Monday, snow fell the next day.

18. The student whose photographs of American Indian cliff dwellings won the contest was interviewed on the local news.

19. The house looked completely empty when I first saw it, yet a party was going on in the backyard.

20. The game was tied at the top of the ninth inning, but then Earlene hit a home run.

┌HELP─
Remember
that an independent clause
contains a subject and a
verb, expresses a complete
thought, and can stand by
itself as a sentence. A subordinate clause also con-
tains a subject and a verb,
but it does not express a
complete thought and
cannot stand alone.

INDEPENDENT CLAUSE
  Dr. Martin has a successful
  medical practice in Cedar
  Park.

SUBORDINATE CLAUSE
  that she has built during
  the last ten years

Reference Note
For information on
**independent and
subordinate clauses,**
see Chapter 6.

Reference Note
For information on the
understood subject,
see page 19.

┌HELP─
Some sentences
in Exercise 1 have a
compound subject, a
compound verb, or both.

The Simple Sentence

7a. A *simple sentence* contains one independent clause and no subordinate clauses.

EXAMPLES

        S   V
A good rain will help the farmers.

              V   S
Up for the rebound leaped Reggie.

      V   S
Where are my keys?

      V
Please put that down near the table in the corner.
[The understood subject is *you*.]

A simple sentence may have a compound subject, a compound verb, or both.

EXAMPLES

      S   S V
Chalupas and **fajitas are** two popular Mexican dishes.
[compound subject]

      S   V   V
Kelly read The Planet of Junior Brown and **reported** on it last week. [compound verb]

      S   S V   V
The **dog** and the **kitten lay** there and **napped.**
[compound subject and compound verb]

> **Exercise 1** Identifying Subjects and Verbs in Simple Sentences

Identify the subjects and the verbs in each of the following sentences.

EXAMPLE

1. I enjoy urban life but need to escape from the city once in a while.
1. *I—subject; enjoy, need—verbs*

1. My favorite escape from city life is the green world of Central Park in New York City.
2. Its beautiful woods and relaxing outdoor activities are just a few minutes from our apartment.

3. The enormous size of the park, however, can sometimes be a problem.
4. Often, I take this map with me for guidance.
5. Using the map, I can easily find the zoo, the band shell, and the Lost Waterfall.
6. In the summertime my brothers and I row boats on the lake, climb huge rock slabs, and have picnics in the Sheep Meadow.
7. I also watch birds and often wander around the park in search of my favorite species.
8. Last month a pair of purple finches followed me along the pond.
9. Near Heckscher Playground, the birds tired of the game and flew off.
10. In Central Park my family and I can enjoy a little bit of nature in the middle of a bustling city.

- ▭ Bridge
- ● Monument
- ▪ Building
- F Food
- R Restroom
- P Playground

The Compound Sentence

7b. A *compound sentence* contains two or more independent clauses and no subordinate clauses.

INDEPENDENT CLAUSE	Melvina wrote about her mother's aunt
INDEPENDENT CLAUSE	Leroy wrote about his cousin from Jamaica
COMPOUND SENTENCE	Melvina wrote about her mother's aunt, and Leroy wrote about his cousin from Jamaica.

The independent clauses of a compound sentence are usually joined by a comma and a coordinating conjunction (*and, but, for, nor, or, so,* or *yet*).

EXAMPLES   A variety of fruits and vegetables should be a part of everyone's diet, **for** they supply many important vitamins.

Kathryn's scene is in the last act of the play, **so** she must wait in the wings for her cue.

No one was injured in the fire, **but** several homes were destroyed, **and** many trees burned down.

Reference Note

For more about using **commas in compound sentences,** see page 297.

The Compound Sentence   **131**

Reference Note

For more about using **semicolons in compound sentences,** see page 310.

The independent clauses of a compound sentence may be joined by a semicolon.

EXAMPLES   Pedro Menéndez de Avilés founded St. Augustine, the first permanent European settlement in the United States; he also established six other colonies in the Southeast.

My favorite places are Miami, Florida, and Aspen, Colorado; Bernie's favorites are San Diego, California, and Seattle, Washington.

Exercise 2   Identifying Subjects and Verbs in Compound Sentences

Identify the subject and verb in each independent clause. Then, give the punctuation mark and coordinating conjunction (if there is one) that join the clauses.

EXAMPLE   1. A newspaper reporter will speak to our class next week, and we will learn about careers in journalism.

     1. *reporter—subject; will speak—verb; we—subject; will learn—verb; comma + and*

1. Ruth Benedict was a respected anthropologist, and Margaret Mead was one of her students.
2. An area's weather may change rapidly, but its climate changes very slowly.
3. Linh Phan lived in Vietnam for many years, so he could tell us about Vietnamese foods such as *nuoc mam.*
4. Students may prepare their reports on the computer, or they may write them neatly.
5. Our apartment manager is kind, yet she will not allow pets in the building.
6. Daniel Boone had no formal education, but he could read and write.
7. Sofia's favorite dance is the samba; Elena enjoys the merengue.
8. Benjamin Franklin is known for his inventions, and he should also be remembered for his work during the Constitutional Convention.
9. Sheena did not play soccer; she had sprained her ankle.
10. They did not watch the shuttle take off, nor did they watch it land.

Simple Sentence or Compound Sentence?

A simple sentence has only one independent clause. It may have a compound subject or a compound verb or both.

A compound sentence has two or more independent clauses. Each independent clause has its own subject and verb. Any of the independent clauses in a compound sentence may have a compound subject, a compound verb, or both.

SIMPLE SENTENCE	**S** **S** **V** Kim and Maureen read each other's short stories **V** and made many suggestions for improvements. [compound subject and compound verb]

COMPOUND SENTENCE	**S** **S** **V** Kim and Maureen read each other's stories, **S** **V** and they gave each other suggestions for improvements. [The first independent clause has a compound subject and a single verb. The second independent clause has a single subject and a single verb.]

NOTE When a subject is repeated after a coordinating conjunction, the sentence is not simple.

SIMPLE SENTENCE	**S** **V** **We studied** the artist Romare Bearden **and** **V** **went** to an exhibit of his paintings.

COMPOUND SENTENCE	**S** **V** **We studied** the artist Romare Bearden, **and** **S** **V** **we went** to an exhibit of his paintings.

Exercise 3 **Distinguishing Compound Sentences from Sentences with Compound Subjects or Compound Verbs**

Identify the subjects and verbs in each of the sentences on the following page. Then, identify each sentence as either *simple* or *compound*.

EXAMPLES 1. A rain forest is a tropical evergreen forest and has heavy rains throughout the year.

1. *rain forest—subject; is, has—verbs; simple*

2. The trees and other plants in a rain forest grow close together, and they rise to different heights.

2. *trees, plants—subjects; grow—verb; they—subject; rise—verb; compound*

1. The Amazon River is located in South America and is one of the longest rivers in the world.
2. The Amazon begins in Peru, and it flows across Brazil to the Atlantic Ocean.
3. This river carries more water than any other river and drains about one fifth of the earth's entire freshwater supply.

4. The Amazon is actually a network of several rivers, but most people think of these combined rivers as only one river.
5. These rivers drain the largest rainy area in the world, and during the flood season, the main river often overflows its banks.
6. In the photo at the left, the Amazon does twist and curve.
7. Generally, it follows a fairly straight course and flows at an average rate of about one and one-half miles an hour during the dry season.
8. The Amazon rain forest is only two hundred miles wide along the Atlantic, but it stretches to twelve hundred miles wide at the foot of the Andes Mountains in Peru.
9. The variety of plant life in the Amazon rain forest is remarkable; in fact, of all rain forests in the world, this area may contain the greatest number of plant species.
10. Raw materials are shipped directly from ports deep in the rain forest, for oceangoing ships can sail more than two thousand miles up the Amazon.

The Complex Sentence

7c. A *complex sentence* contains one independent clause and at least one subordinate clause.

Two kinds of subordinate clauses are adjective clauses and adverb clauses. Adjective clauses usually begin with relative pronouns such as *who, whom, whose, which,* and *that.* Adverb clauses begin with subordinating conjunctions such as *after, as, because, if, since,* and *when.*

EXAMPLES The boy **who left** is my cousin. [complex sentence with adjective clause]

When I hear classical music, I think of Aunt Sofia. [complex sentence with adverb clause]

One interesting annual event **that is held in the Southwest** is the Inter-Tribal Indian Ceremonial, **which involves many different American Indian peoples.** [complex sentence with two adjective clauses]

Reference Note

For more information about **adjective clauses,** see page 117. For more about **adverb clauses,** see page 120. For more about **relative pronouns,** see page 118. For more about **subordinating conjunctions,** see page 121.

Reference Note

For information on using **commas with subordinate clauses,** see page 299.

Oral Practice **Identifying Subordinate Clauses**

Read each of the following sentences aloud, and identify the subordinate clause. Finally, identify the relative pronoun or subordinating conjunction that begins the subordinate clause.

EXAMPLES **1.** Helen Keller, who overcame severe physical impairments, showed great determination.
1. who overcame severe physical impairments—who

2. Keller was fortunate because she had such a skillful and loving teacher.
2. because she had such a skillful and loving teacher—because

1. Helen Keller, who is shown in the photograph at right, became very ill as a small child.
2. After she recovered from the illness, she could no longer see or hear.
3. Because she could not hear, she also lost her ability to speak.

4. Helen's parents asked Alexander Graham Bell, who trained teachers of people with hearing impairments, for his advice about the child's education.
5. Upon Bell's suggestion, a special teacher, whose name was Anne Sullivan, stayed at the Kellers' home to teach Helen.
6. Sullivan spelled words into Helen's hand as the child touched the object represented by the word.
7. From this basic understanding of language, Helen went on to learn Braille, which is the alphabet used by people with visual impairments.
8. Sullivan, whose own vision had been partly restored by surgery, remained with Helen for many years.
9. Because she had triumphed over her impairments, Helen Keller was awarded the Medal of Freedom.
10. Keller's autobiography, which is titled *The Story of My Life,* tells about her remarkable achievements.

Review A **Classifying Simple, Compound, and Complex Sentences**

Classify each of the following sentences as *simple, compound,* or *complex.*

EXAMPLE   1. The Mississippi River, which begins in the town of Lake Itasca, Minnesota, is the setting for many of Mark Twain's stories.

    1. *complex*

1. I drew an illustration for a poem that was written by Robert Hayden.
2. The Olympic skaters felt anxious, but they still performed their routine perfectly.
3. Kamehameha Day is an American holiday that honors the king who united the islands of Hawaii.
4. For the first time in his life, Luke saw the ocean.
5. If you had a choice, would you rather visit China or Japan?
6. The bull was donated to the children's zoo by the people who bought it at the auction.
7. Lookout Mountain was the site of a battle during the Civil War.
8. The guide led us through Mammoth Cave; she explained the difference between stalactites and stalagmites.
9. Wilhelm Steinitz of Austria became famous after he was officially recognized as the first world champion of chess.
10. Amy Tan is the author of the book *The Joy Luck Club*; it was published in 1989.

MEETING THE CHALLENGE

Simple sentences are best used to express single ideas. To describe more complicated ideas and to show how the ideas fit together, use compound and complex sentences.

Revise the sentences below to include at least one compound or complex sentence.

We went camping in the national park. Darla saw a snake. At first she was afraid. Then she looked more closely at it.

The Compound-Complex Sentence

7d. A *compound-complex sentence* contains two or more independent clauses and at least one subordinate clause.

In the examples below, independent clauses are underlined once. Subordinate clauses are underlined twice.

EXAMPLES

       S   V   S   V

The band began to play, and Clarissa was pulled onto

                 S   V

the floor for a dance that was starting. [compound-complex sentence with adjective clause]

          S V   S   V

Whenever we go on vacation, our neighbors mow our

         S   V

yard, and they collect our mail. [compound-complex sentence with adverb clause]

Reference Note

For more about **adjective and adverb clauses,** see pages 117 and 120.

Exercise 4 Identifying Compound, Complex, and Compound-Complex Sentences

Identify each of the following sentences as either *compound,* *complex,* or *compound-complex.*

EXAMPLE 1. I'll sweep the porch, and Ben will start supper before Mom gets home.

   1. *compound-complex*

1. If you've never tried Indian curry, try some of Usha's.
2. The disk drive light went on, and the drive motor whirred, but the computer would not read the disk.
3. Although the river appeared calm, crocodiles lay motionless beneath the surface.
4. Several small herds of mustangs roam these hills; we're going to find them.
5. An antique wagon, whose wheels once rolled along the Chisholm Trail, stood next to the barn.
6. You can talk to me whenever you have a problem, or you can talk to your mom.
7. Since daylight saving time started, the sky doesn't get dark until late, and that just doesn't seem right to me.
8. The plaster, which had been given a rough texture, cast shadows on itself.
9. They don't have the book that we need, so let's go to the library.
10. Did you really live in Nairobi, or are you just kidding?

COMPUTER TIP

A computer can help you focus on sentence length and structure in your writing. Programs are now available that can tell you the average number of words in your sentences. Such programs can also tell you how many different kinds of sentences you used. You can compare your numbers with the averages for students at your grade level. Using these programs, you can easily see which sentence structures you have mastered and which ones need work.

Review B Classifying Simple, Compound, Complex, and Compound-Complex Sentences

Classify each of the following sentences as *simple, compound, complex,* or *compound-complex.*

EXAMPLE 1. The Iroquois people traditionally held a Green Corn Festival in August when their crops were ready for harvesting.

   1. *complex*

1. For the early Iroquois, the Green Corn Festival was a celebration that included many events, so it often lasted several days.
2. During the celebration, all children who had been born since midwinter received their names.

3. Iroquois leaders made speeches, and adults and children listened to them carefully.

4. In one traditional speech, the leader would give thanks for the harvest.

5. After they had heard the speeches, the people sang and danced.

6. On the second day of the festival, the people performed a special dance; during the dance they gave thanks for the sun, the moon, and the stars.

7. On the third day, the Iroquois gave thanks for the helpfulness of their neighbors and for good luck.

8. The festival ended on the fourth day when teams of young people would play a bowling game.

9. During the festival the people renewed their friendships, and they rejoiced in their harmony with nature.

10. This Iroquois festival resembles the U.S. Thanksgiving holiday, which has its roots in similar American Indian celebrations.

The Corn Dance

Review C **Writing Simple, Compound, Complex, and Compound-Complex Sentences**

Write ten sentences of your own, following the guidelines given below.

EXAMPLE   **1.** Write a simple sentence with a compound subject.

       1. Jorge and Pilar gave me their recipe for guacamole.

1. Write a simple sentence with a compound verb.

2. Write a simple sentence with a compound subject and a compound verb.
3. Write a compound sentence with two independent clauses joined by a comma and the coordinating conjunction *and*.
4. Write a compound sentence with two independent clauses joined by a comma and the coordinating conjunction *but*.
5. Write a compound sentence with two independent clauses joined by a semicolon.
6. Write a compound sentence with three independent clauses.
7. Write a complex sentence with an adjective clause.
8. Write a complex sentence with an adverb clause.
9. Write a compound-complex sentence with an adjective clause.
10. Write a compound-complex sentence with an adverb clause.

Chapter Review

A. Identifying Independent and Subordinate Clauses

Identify each clause in the following sentences. Then, classify each clause as an *independent clause* or a *subordinate clause.*

1. Yvette raked the leaves, and Tito mowed the lawn.
2. Lupe and Ben went to the park so that they could watch the fireworks display.
3. Carl and I chose enchiladas instead of sandwiches from the cafeteria's menu.
4. The new camp that offers instruction in computer programming will be in session from August 17 through August 28.
5. The rain changed to snow that was mixed with sleet.
6. Practice your tai chi exercises when you go to the beach.
7. My grandparents, who enjoy exciting vacations, visited Nepal last year.
8. Since last year Simone has grown three inches, but she still can't reach the top shelf in the kitchen.
9. Will Martin lend me this book by Jamaica Kincaid when he is through with it?
10. Aretha hopes to be a veterinarian because she likes to be around animals.

B. Identifying Simple and Compound Sentences

Classify each of the following sentences as *simple* or *compound.*

11. Do Nathan and Shenille read only science fiction or fantasy short stories?
12. My sister and brother-in-law live in Colorado, and they raise sheep and grow fruit trees.
13. Chai wants to walk to the theater, but I want to take the bus.
14. Aunt Evelyn and Uncle Michael are both surgeons and work at Riverside Hospital.
15. The good queen pardoned the jester, for he had meant no real harm.

16. Taking the train, Mei-Ling and her parents can be in Chicago in two hours.

17. Blair is interested in becoming an astronaut, so she wrote to NASA for information.

18. Tate laid out the patio and built it himself.

19. After eating, Marcia's cat Bartinka likes to take a long nap.

20. Mike designed and constructed the sets for the play, and Mary Anne designed the costumes and makeup.

C. Identifying Compound and Complex Sentences

Identify each of the following sentences as *compound* or *complex*. If the sentence is compound, write the comma and coordinating conjunction or the semicolon that joins the clauses. If the sentence is complex, write the relative pronoun or subordinating conjunction that joins the clauses.

21. Nineteenth-century shopkeepers often attracted customers by placing a carved wooden figure, which was called a shop figure, outside their shops.

22. The shop figures were usually carved by ship carvers, who had learned to carve figures by creating ship figureheads.

23. The figures cost a great deal to make, and they were expensive to maintain.

24. Many shopkeepers were upset because the figures were so very costly.

25. Many of the wooden figures were of politicians and baseball players; others represented American Indians.

26. One surviving figure represents Father Time, and another one represents a New York City firefighter.

27. The firefighter, which commemorates Columbian Engine Company 14, now stands in the New York City Fire Museum.

28. The figures were popular between the 1840s and the 1890s, and during that time they actually became a fad.

29. By the end of the century, the carved shop figure was no longer widely used since new types of advertising had become available.

30. People saw shop figures as old-fashioned, so shopkeepers stopped using them.

D. Classifying Compound, Complex, and Compound-Complex Sentences

Classify each of the following sentences as *compound, complex,* or *compound-complex.*

31. Islam, which originated in Arabia, is the religion of the Muslims, and it is based on a belief in one God.

32. Most Muslims live in Africa, the Middle East, and Malaysia; in recent years many have come to the United States and have brought their religion with them.

33. Some American Muslims are members of the Nation of Islam, which was founded in the United States after World War II.

34. When a mosque was opened in New York in May 1991, religious leaders and other Muslims went there to pray.

35. Some worshipers wore the traditional clothing of their homelands; others were dressed in typical American clothes.

36. Muslims were particularly pleased that the new mosque opened in the spring.

37. The Muslim month of fasting, which is called Ramadan, had just ended, so the holiday after Ramadan could be celebrated in the new house of worship.

38. Although Muslims share a common religion, their languages differ.

39. Many Muslims speak Arabic, but those in Iran, Turkey, and neighboring countries, for example, speak other languages.

40. Of course, Muslims who were born in the United States generally speak English, and many Muslims who are recent immigrants are learning it as a new language.

E. Classifying Sentences by Structure

Classify each of the following sentences as *simple, compound, complex,* or *compound-complex.*

41. Easter Island, which is also known as Rapa Nui, is a small Polynesian island in the South Pacific.

42. The island is the most remote inhabited place on the planet.

43. The Polynesians were among the most accomplished sailors in the world; they are especially known for their skill at navigation.

44. The earliest evidence of people on Easter Island dates from around A.D. 700, but the island may have been inhabited earlier than that.

45. The island is best known for its giant stone statues with long noses and pursed lips.

46. The statues, which are called *moai,* were carved out of volcanic rock, and some of them were placed upright on platforms called *ahu.*

47. The *moai* that were set up on platforms were transported as far as six miles from the quarry, but no one knows for certain how.

48. Several theories have been proposed, yet no single theory explains all the evidence.

49. When the British explorer Captain Cook visited the island in 1774, he noticed that many of the statues had been overturned.

50. The oral tradition of the islanders speaks of a civil war that broke out between two peoples on the island, the Hanau Eepe and the Hanau Momko.

Writing Application
Writing a Letter

Using a Variety of Sentence Structures   Anyone can enter the "Win Your Dream House" Contest. All you have to do is describe your ideal house. Write a letter to the contest judges, describing where your dream house would be and what it would look like. Use a variety of sentence structures to make your letter interesting for the judges to read.

Prewriting   Make a list of the special features of the house you want to describe. To help you think of ideas, you may want to look through magazines or books to find pictures of interesting homes. You may also find it helpful to draw a rough diagram of the rooms, yard, and other features you would want to add. Take notes on the details you want to include.

Writing   As you write your first draft, use your notes to include vivid details that will give the contest judges a clear picture of your dream house.

Revising   Read your letter to make sure it is interesting and clear. Also, check to see whether you can combine similar ideas by using either compound or complex sentences. Ask an adult to read your letter. Does he or she think your description would impress the contest judges?

Publishing   Check the grammar and spelling in your letter. Also, make sure that you have used commas correctly in compound sentences and complex sentences. You and your classmates may want to create a bulletin board display of the pictures or diagrams you used in designing your dream house and to post your descriptions next to the display.

Reference Note

For information on **using commas,** see pages 297 and 299.

1.0 Written and Oral English Language Conventions

Students write and speak with a command of standard English conventions appropriate to this grade level.

1.2 Make clear references between pronouns and antecedents.

1.4 Demonstrate appropriate English usage (e.g., pronoun reference).

Agreement
Subject and Verb, Pronoun and Antecedent

Diagnostic Preview

A. Identifying Correct Subject-Verb Agreement and Pronoun-Antecedent Agreement

Choose the correct word or word group in parentheses in each of the following sentences.

EXAMPLE   **1.** Some of the paintings (*is, are*) dry now.

       1. are

1. Three hours of work (*is, are*) needed to finish the charcoal drawing for art class.
2. Everybody has offered (*his or her, their*) advice.
3. *Harlem Shadows* (*is, are*) a collection of poems by the writer Claude McKay.
4. Either Stu or Ryan can volunteer (*his, their*) skill in the kitchen.
5. Black beans, rice, and onions (*tastes, taste*) good together.
6. Not one of them has offered (*his or her, their*) help.
7. Sometimes my family (*disagrees, disagree*) with one another, but usually we all get along fairly well.
8. Five dollars (*is, are*) all you will need for the matinee.
9. (*Doesn't, Don't*) too many cooks spoil the broth?
10. One of my aunts gave me (*her, their*) silk kimono.

B. Proofreading for Subject-Verb Agreement and Pronoun-Antecedent Agreement

Most of the following sentences contain an agreement error. Write the incorrect verb or pronoun. Then, write the correct form. If the sentence is already correct, write *C*.

EXAMPLE   **1.** Most stargazers has seen points of light shooting across the night sky.

   1. has—have

11. These points of light is commonly called shooting stars.
12. Scientists who study our solar system calls these points of light *meteors.*
13. Some meteors are pieces of asteroids that exploded long ago.
14. Each of these pieces are still flying through space on the path of the original asteroid.
15. Most nights, a person is lucky if they can see a single meteor now and then.
16. Throughout the year, however, there is meteor "showers."
17. None of these showers are as big as the ones that come each year in August and November.
18. Either Katie or Carla once saw a spectacular meteor shower on their birthday.
19. In November 1833, one of the largest meteor showers in history were recorded.
20. Two hundred forty thousand meteors observed in just a few hours are a record that has never been matched!

Number

Number is the form a word takes to indicate whether the word is singular or plural.

8a. When a word refers to one person, place, thing, or idea, it is *singular* in number. When a word refers to more than one, it is *plural* in number.

Reference Note

For more about **forming plurals,** see page 355.

Singular	igloo	she	one	child	class
Plural	igloos	they	many	children	classes

USAGE

Exercise 1 Classifying Nouns and Pronouns by Number

Classify each of the following words as *singular* or *plural*.

EXAMPLES   **1.** girl   **2.** rivers

           1. singular   *2. plural*

1. evening	**6.** teeth	**11.** hoof	**16.** magazine
2. wolves	**7.** tacos	**12.** mice	**17.** oxen
3. women	**8.** we	**13.** I	**18.** he
4. leaf	**9.** thief	**14.** shelf	**19.** cities
5. they	**10.** armies	**15.** geese	**20.** cargo

TIPS & TRICKS

Most nouns ending in *s* are plural (*cheetahs, families*). Most verbs that end in *s* are singular (*fills, begins*). However, verbs used with the singular pronouns *I* and *you* do not end in *s*.

EXAMPLES
Ed takes the bus.

I take the train.

You ride your bike.

Reference Note

The plurals of some nouns do not end in *s* (*mice, teeth, deer*). For more about **irregularly formed plurals**, see page 356.

Agreement of Subject and Verb

8b. A verb should agree in number with its subject.

Two words *agree* when they have the same number. The number of a verb should agree with the number of its subject.

(1) Singular subjects take singular verbs.

EXAMPLES   The **lightning fills** the sky. [The singular verb *fills* agrees with the singular subject *lightning.*]

             Jan begins her vacation today. [The singular verb *begins* agrees with the singular subject *Jan.*]

(2) Plural subjects take plural verbs.

EXAMPLES   **Cheetahs run** fast. [The plural verb *run* agrees with the plural subject *Cheetahs.*]

             New **families move** into our neighborhood often. [The plural verb *move* agrees with the plural subject *families.*]

When a sentence contains a verb phrase, the first helping verb in the verb phrase agrees with the subject.

EXAMPLES   The **motor is** running.
             The **motors are** running.

             The **girl has** been delayed.
             The **girls have** been delayed.

             Is anyone filling the aquarium?
             Are any **students** filling the aquarium?

Exercise 2 **Identifying Verbs That Agree in Number with Their Subjects**

Identify the form of the verb in parentheses that agrees with its subject.

EXAMPLE   **1.** wind (*howls, howl*)

    1. howls

1. people (*talks, talk*)
2. rain (*splashes, splash*)
3. birds (*flies, fly*)
4. we (*helps, help*)
5. it (*appears, appear*)
6. geese (*hisses, hiss*)
7. night (*falls, fall*)
8. roofs (*leaks, leak*)
9. baby (*smiles, smile*)
10. tooth (*aches, ache*)

Exercise 3 **Identifying Verbs That Agree in Number with Their Subjects**

Identify the form of the verb in parentheses that agrees with its subject.

EXAMPLE   **1.** Special tours (*is, are*) offered at the National Air and Space Museum in Washington, D.C.

    1. are

1. This museum (*has, have*) been called the best of all the Smithsonian museums.
2. This enormous building (*covers, cover*) three blocks.
3. Twenty-three galleries (*offers, offer*) visitors information and entertainment.
4. The different showrooms (*deals, deal*) with various aspects of air and space travel.
5. As you can see, the exhibits (*features, feature*) antique aircraft as well as modern spacecraft.
6. In another area, a theater (*shows, show*) films on a five-story-high screen.
7. A planetarium (*is, are*) located on the second floor.
8. Projectors (*casts, cast*) realistic images of stars on the ceiling.
9. Some tours (*is, are*) conducted by pilots.
10. In addition, the museum (*houses, house*) a large research library.

Exercise 4 **Proofreading for Errors in Subject-Verb Agreement**

Most of the following sentences contain errors in subject-verb agreement. If a verb does not agree with its subject, write the correct form of the verb. If a sentence is already correct, write *C*.

EXAMPLE 1. More than fifteen million people lives in and around Mexico's capital.

1. *live*

1. Located in an ancient lake bed, Mexico City have been built on Aztec ruins.
2. Visitors admire the colorful paintings of Diego Rivera at the National Palace.
3. In one of the city's many subway stations, an Aztec pyramid still stand.
4. Sculptures grace the Alameda, which is Mexico City's main park.
5. Atop the Latin American Tower, an observatory offer a great view on a clear day.
6. At the National Autonomous University of Mexico, the library's outer walls is famous as works of art.
7. Juan O'Gorman's huge mosaics shows the cultural history of Mexico.
8. Usually, tourists is quite fascinated by the Great Temple of the Aztecs.
9. Many fiestas fills Mexico City's social calendar.
10. In addition, the city has one of the largest soccer stadiums in the world.

Problems in Agreement
Phrases Between Subject and Verb

8c. The number of a subject is not changed by a phrase following the subject.

EXAMPLES The **hero** of those folk tales **is** Coyote. [The verb *is* agrees with the subject *hero,* not with *tales.*]

The successful **candidate,** along with two of her aides, **has entered** the auditorium. [The helping verb *has* agrees with the subject *candidate,* not with *aides.*]

Scientists from all over the world **have gathered** in Geneva. [The helping verb *have* agrees with the subject *Scientists,* not with *world.*]

The crystal **pitcher,** oozing water droplets, **was cracked** along the base. [The helping verb *was* agrees with the subject *pitcher,* not with *droplets.*]

8 c

NOTE   If the subject is the indefinite pronoun *all, any, more, most, none,* or *some,* its number may be determined by the object of a prepositional phrase that follows it.

Reference Note

For more about **indefinite pronouns,** see Rules 8d–8f on page 152.

EXAMPLES   **Most** of the essays **were** graded. [*Most* refers to the plural word *essays.*]

Most of this essay **is** illegible. [*Most* refers to the singular word *essay.*]

USAGE

Exercise 5 Identifying Verbs That Agree in Number with Their Subjects

Identify the form of the verb in parentheses that agrees with its subject.

EXAMPLE   1. The water in the earth's oceans (*cover, covers*) much of the planet's surface.
1. *covers*

1. A tidal wave, despite its name, (*is, are*) not caused by the tides.
2. Earthquakes beneath the sea (*causes, cause*) most tidal waves.
3. A network of warning signals (*alert, alerts*) people in coastal areas of an approaching tidal wave.
4. The tremendous force of tidal waves sometimes (*causes, cause*) great destruction.
5. Walls of earth and stone along the shore (*is, are*) often too weak to protect coastal villages.
6. Some tidal waves, according to this encyclopedia article, (*travel, travels*) more than five hundred miles an hour.
7. Tidal waves in the open ocean generally (*do, does*) not cause much interest.
8. The height of tidal waves there often (*remain, remains*) low.
9. However, waves up to one hundred feet high (*occur, occurs*) when tidal waves hit land.
10. The scientific name for tidal waves (*are, is*) *tsunamis.*

Indefinite Pronouns

You may recall that personal pronouns refer to specific people, places, things, or ideas. A pronoun that does not refer to a definite person, place, thing, or idea is called an **indefinite pronoun.**

Personal Pronouns	Indefinite Pronouns
she	anybody
them	both
we	either
you	everyone

8d. The following indefinite pronouns are singular: *anybody, anyone, anything, each, either, everybody, everyone, everything, neither, nobody, no one, nothing, one, somebody, someone,* and *something.*

EXAMPLES **Each** of the newcomers **was welcomed** to the city.

Neither of these papayas **is** ripe.

Does anybody on the bus **speak** Arabic?

Exercise 6 **Identify Verbs That Agree in Number with Their Subjects**

Choose the form of the verb in parentheses that agrees with its subject.

EXAMPLE 1. One of these books (*is, are*) yours.
    1. is

1. Neither of the movies (*were, was*) especially funny.
2. Everybody in those classes (*gets, get*) to research a historical person.
3. Someone among the store owners (*donates, donate*) the big trophy each year.
4. Each of the Jackson brothers (*study, studies*) dance.
5. No one on either team (*was, were*) ever in a playoff before.
6. Everyone with an interest in sports (*are, is*) at the tryouts.
7. Anybody with sewing skills (*are, is*) needed for the project.
8. Each of our neighbors (*have, has*) helped us plant the new community garden.

┌─HELP─

The words *one, thing,* and *body* are singular. The indefinite pronouns that contain these words are singular, too.

EXAMPLES
Was [every]**one** there?

[No]**thing works** better.

[Some]**body has** answered.

┌─HELP─

Remember that the subject is never part of a prepositional phrase.

9. One of the new Spanish teachers (*supervises, supervise*) the language lab.

10. Nobody in our family (*speak, speaks*) Greek well, but we all can speak a little bit.

8e. The following indefinite pronouns are plural: *both, few, many, several.*

EXAMPLES   **Few** of our neighbors **have** parakeets.

Many of them **keep** dogs as pets.

8f. The indefinite pronouns *all, any, more, most, none,* and *some* may be either singular or plural, depending on their meaning in a sentence.

The number of the pronouns *all, any, more, most, none,* and *some* is often determined by the number of the object in a prepositional phrase following the subject. These pronouns are singular when they refer to a singular word and are plural when they refer to a plural word.

EXAMPLES   **All** of the fruit **is** ripe. [*All* is singular because it refers to the singular word *fruit.* The verb *is* is singular to agree with the subject *All.*]

All of the pears **are** ripe. [*All* is plural because it refers to the plural word *pears.* The verb *are* is plural to agree with the subject *All.*]

Some of the harvest **has been sold.** [*Some* is singular because it refers to the singular word *harvest.* The helping verb *has* is singular to agree with the subject *Some.*]

Some of the apples **have been sold.** [*Some* is plural because it refers to the plural word *apples.* The helping verb *have* is plural to agree with the subject *Some.*]

NOTE   The pronouns listed in Rule 8f aren't always followed by prepositional phrases.

EXAMPLES   **All are** here.

Some has spilled.

In such cases you should look at the **context**—the sentences before and after the pronoun—to see if the pronoun refers to a singular or a plural word.

┌HELP─

Some indefinite pronouns, such as *both, each,* and *some,* can also be used as adjectives. When an indefinite adjective comes before the subject of a sentence, the verb agrees with the subject as it normally would.

USAGE

EXAMPLES
Children love playing in the park.
Both children love playing in the park.

The **child loves** playing in the park.
Each child loves playing in the park.

Exercise 7 **Identifying Verbs That Agree in Number with Their Subjects**

Identify the verb form in parentheses that agrees with its subject.

EXAMPLE   **1.** Somebody in the club (*want, wants*) the meetings held on a different day.

     1. wants

1. "Both of the songs (*sound, sounds*) good to me," Gregory said.
2. If anyone (*know, knows*) a better way to get to Washington Square, please tell me.
3. Each of the problems (*are, is*) easy to solve if you know the correct formulas.
4. Probably everyone in the class (*remember, remembers*) how to solve the equation.
5. All of the new research on dreams (*is, are*) fascinating.
6. Most of our dreams (*occur, occurs*) toward morning.
7. Few of us really (*understand, understands*) the four cycles of sleep.
8. Most of the research (*focus, focuses*) on the cycle known as rapid eye movement, or REM.
9. None of last night's dream (*is, are*) clear to me.
10. Many of our dreams at night (*is, are*) about that day's events.

Review A **Identifying Verbs That Agree in Number with Their Subjects**

Identify the verb form in parentheses that agrees with its subject.

EXAMPLE   **1.** The flying object shown on the next page probably (*look, looks*) familiar to you.

     1. looks

1. Many people throughout the world (*claims, claim*) to have seen objects like this.
2. However, no one (*know, knows*) for sure what they are.
3. They (*resembles, resemble*) huge plates or saucers.
4. Not surprisingly, people (*call, calls*) them flying saucers.
5. Since 1947, they (*has, have*) been officially called unidentified flying objects, or UFOs.
6. The U.S. government (*has, have*) investigated many unusual UFO sightings.

7. The U.S. Air Force (*was, were*) responsible for conducting these investigations.
8. Government records (*shows, show*) that more than twelve thousand sightings were reported between 1948 and 1969.
9. Most reported sightings (*has, have*) turned out to be fakes, but others remain unexplained.
10. None of the official reports positively (*proves, prove*) that UFOs come from outer space.

Compound Subjects

8g. Subjects joined by *and* usually take a plural verb.

EXAMPLES   Our **dog and cat get** baths in the summer.

Mr. Duffy and his **daughter have gone** fishing.

A compound subject that names only one person or thing takes a singular verb.

EXAMPLES   **A famous singer and dancer is going** to speak at our drama club meeting. [One person is meant.]

Macaroni and cheese is my favorite pasta dish. [One dish is meant.]

Exercise 8 Identifying Verbs That Agree in Number with Their Subjects

Identify the correct form of the verb in parentheses. If you choose a singular verb with any of these compound subjects, be prepared to explain why.

EXAMPLE   1. Chris and her sister (*is, are*) in the school band.

            1. *are*

1. (*Is, Are*) the brown bear and the polar bear related?
2. Wind and water (*erodes, erode*) valuable farmland through-out the United States.
3. My guide and companion in Bolivia (*was, were*) Pilar.
4. New words and new meanings for old words (*is, are*) included in a good dictionary.
5. Mrs. Chang and her daughter (*rents, rent*) an apartment.
6. Iron and calcium (*needs, need*) to be included in a good diet.
7. Mr. Marley and his class (*has, have*) painted a wall-size map.
8. A horse and buggy (*was, were*) once a common way to travel.
9. Tornadoes and hurricanes (*is, are*) dangerous storms.
10. Fruit and cheese (*tastes, taste*) good together.

8h. Singular subjects joined by *or* or *nor* take a singular verb.

EXAMPLES   The chief **geologist or** her **assistant is** due to arrive tonight. [Either one *is* due, not both.]

            Neither a **rabbit nor** a **mole does** that kind of damage. [Neither one *does* the damage.]

Plural subjects joined by *or* or *nor* take a plural verb.

EXAMPLES   Either **mice or squirrels are** living in our attic.

            Neither the **senators nor** the **representatives want** the bill to be vetoed by the President.

8i. When a singular subject and a plural subject are joined by *or* or *nor,* the verb agrees with the subject nearer the verb.

EXAMPLES   A **book or flowers** usually **make** an appropriate gift. [The verb agrees with the nearer subject, *flowers.*]

            Flowers or a **book** usually **makes** an appropriate gift. [The verb agrees with the nearer subject, *book.*]

STYLE TIP

Compound subjects that have both singular and plural parts can sound awkward even though they are correct. Whenever possible, revise sentences to avoid such constructions.

AWKWARD
Two small boards or one large one is what we need to patch that hole.

REVISED
We need two small boards or one large one to patch that hole.

Exercise 9 Identifying Verbs That Agree in Number with Their Subjects

Identify the correct form of the verb in parentheses in each of the following sentences. Be prepared to explain the reason for your choice.

─HELP─

In the example, the verb *meet* agrees with the nearer subject, *officers.*

EXAMPLE 1. The club president or the officers (*meets, meet*) regularly with the sponsors.
1. *meet*

1. Neither pens nor pencils (*is, are*) needed to mark the ballots.
2. Either my aunt or my uncle (*is, are*) going to drive us.
3. That table or this chair (*was, were*) made by hand in Portugal.
4. (*Has, Have*) the sandwiches or other refreshments been served yet?
5. Index cards or a small tablet (*is, are*) handy for taking notes.
6. Neither that clock nor my wristwatch (*shows, show*) the correct time.
7. One boy or girl (*takes, take*) the part of the narrator.
8. During our last visit to Jamaica, a map or a guidebook (*was, were*) my constant companion.
9. The dentist or her assistant (*checks, check*) my braces.
10. Either Japanese poetry or Inuit myths (*is, are*) going to be the focus of my report.

USAGE

Review B Proofreading for Subject-Verb Agreement

Identify each verb that does not agree with its subject in the following sentences. Then, write the correct form of each verb.

EXAMPLE 1. The players in the photograph on the next page is competing in the most popular sport in the world— soccer.
1. *is—are*

1. One expert in the field of sports have described soccer as the world's favorite type of football.
2. Some sports writers has estimated that there are over thirty million registered soccer players around the globe.
3. Youth leagues and coaching clinics has helped make amateur soccer the fastest-growing team sport in the United States.
4. In Dallas, Texas, neither baseball nor American football attract as many young players as soccer does.

5. Also, more colleges now has varsity soccer teams than have football teams.
6. This increase in soccer fans are a trend that started in 1967, when professional teams began playing in the United States.
7. Additional interest were generated when the U.S. Youth Soccer Association was formed.
8. Both males and females enjoys playing this sport.
9. In fact, by the 1980s, many of the soccer teams in the country was women's teams.
10. In the past, professional soccer were more popular abroad, but the United States hosted the World Cup in 1994.

Other Problems in Subject-Verb Agreement

Reference Note

For more information about **collective nouns,** see page 29.

8j. A collective noun may be either singular or plural, depending on its meaning in a sentence.

A *collective noun* is singular in form but names a group of persons, animals, or things.

Common Collective Nouns		
People	**Animals**	**Things**
audience	brood	batch
chorus	flock	bundle
committee	gaggle	cluster
crew	herd	collection
faculty	litter	fleet
family	pack	set
jury	pod	squadron

USAGE

A collective noun takes a singular verb when the noun refers to the group as a unit. A collective noun takes a plural verb when the noun refers to the individual parts or members of the group.

EXAMPLES   The **class has decided** to have a science fair in November. [The class as a unit has decided.]

The **class were divided** in their opinions of the play. [The members of the class were divided in their opinions.]

My **family plans** to attend Beth's graduation. [The family as a unit plans to attend.]

My **family are coming** from all over the state for the reunion. [The members of the family are coming.]

8k. When the subject follows the verb, find the subject and make sure that the verb agrees with it.

The subject usually follows the verb in questions and in sentences beginning with *here* or *there*.

EXAMPLES   Where **was** the **cat**?
Where **were** the **cats**?

Does Jim know the Chens?
Do the **Chens** know Jim?

Here **is** my **umbrella**.
Here **are** our **umbrellas**.

There **is** a scary **movie** on TV.
There **are** scary **movies** on TV.

MEETING THE CHALLENGE

Gaggle, pride, and *brood*—these words are examples of collective nouns. Choose five collective nouns, and look them up if you're not sure what they refer to. Then, for each word, write a pair of sentences. In the first sentence, use the collective noun as a singular subject that refers to the group as a unit. In the second sentence, use the collective noun as a plural subject that refers to the individual parts of the group. Be sure to check your sentences for correct subject-verb agreement.

NOTE When the subject of a sentence follows part or all of the verb, the word order is said to be ***inverted.*** To find the subject of a sentence with inverted order, restate the sentence in normal subject-verb word order.

INVERTED   Here **are** your **gloves.**
NORMAL   Your **gloves are** here.

INVERTED   **Were you arriving** late, too?
NORMAL   **You were arriving** late, too.

INVERTED   In the pond **swim** large **goldfish.**
NORMAL   Large **goldfish swim** in the pond.

Reference Note

For more information about **contractions,** see page 333.

The contractions *here's*, *there's*, and *where's* contain the verb *is* and should be used only with singular subjects.

NONSTANDARD   There's our new neighbors.
STANDARD   There**'s** our new **neighbor.**
STANDARD   There **are** our new **neighbors.**

Exercise 10 **Identifying Verbs That Agree in Number with Their Subjects**

Identify the subject in each of the following sentences. Then, write the correct form of the verb in parentheses.

EXAMPLE   1. That flock of geese (*migrates, migrate*) each year.
           1. *flock—migrates*

1. There (*is, are*) at least two solutions to this complicated Chinese puzzle.
2. The soccer team (*was, were*) all getting on different buses.
3. (*Is, Are*) both of your parents from Korea?
4. Here (*comes, come*) the six members of the prom decorations committee.
5. Here (*is, are*) some apples and bananas for the picnic basket.
6. There (*is, are*) neither time nor money for that project.
7. (*Here's, Here are*) the social studies notes I took.
8. At the press conference, there (*was, were*) several candidates for mayor and two for governor.

9. The family (*has, have*) invited us over for a dinner to celebrate Grandma's promotion.

10. Here (*is, are*) some masks carved by the Haida people.

8l. Some nouns that are plural in form take singular verbs.

EXAMPLES   **Electronics is** a branch of physics.

           Civics is being taught by Ms. Gutierrez.

           Gymnastics is my favorite Olympic sport.

           The **news was** not encouraging.

8m. An expression of an amount (a measurement, a percentage, or a fraction, for example) may be singular or plural, depending on how it is used.

A word or phrase stating an amount is singular when the amount is thought of as a unit.

EXAMPLES   Fifteen **dollars is** enough for that CD.

           Sixteen **ounces equals** one pound.

           Is two **weeks** long enough for a hiking trip?

Sometimes, however, the amount is thought of as individual pieces or parts. If so, a plural verb is used.

EXAMPLES   **Ten** of the dollars **were borrowed.**

           Two of the hours **were spent** at the theater.

A fraction or a percentage is singular when it refers to a singular word and plural when it refers to a plural word.

EXAMPLES   **One fourth** of the salad **is** gone.

           Forty percent of the students **are** new.

NOTE Expressions of measurement (such as length, weight, and area) are usually singular.

EXAMPLES   Ten **feet is** the height of a regulation basketball hoop.

           Seventy-five **pounds is** the maximum baggage weight for this airline.

USAGE

8n. Even when plural in form, the title of a creative work (such as a book, song, film, or painting), the name of an organization, or the name of a country or city generally takes a singular verb.

EXAMPLES   ***World Tales* is** a collection of folk tales retold by Idries Shah. [one book]

Tonya's painting ***Sunflowers* was inspired** by the natural beauty of rural Iowa. [one painting]

Friends of the Earth was founded in 1969. [one organization]

The **Philippines is** an island country in the southwest Pacific Ocean. [one country]

Is Marble Falls a city in central Texas? [one city]

Exercise 11   **Identifying Verbs That Agree in Number with Their Subjects**

Identify the correct form of the verb in parentheses in each of the following sentences.

EXAMPLE   **1.** Three inches in height (*is, are*) a great deal to grow in one year.

1. is

  1. *The Friends* (*is, are*) a book about a girl from the West Indies and a girl from Harlem.
  2. Two cups of broth (*seems, seem*) right for that recipe.
  3. Fifteen feet (*was, were*) the length of the winning long jump.
  4. Navarro and Company (*is, are*) selling those jackets.
  5. The National Council of Teachers of English (*is, are*) holding its convention in our city this year.
  6. Physics (*is, are*) the study of matter and energy.
  7. Three hours of practice (*is, are*) not unusual for the band.
  8. *Arctic Dreams* (*was, were*) written by Barry Lopez.
  9. Two weeks of preparation (*has, have*) been enough.
 10. A dollar and a half (*is, are*) the cost of a subway ride.

8o. *Don't* and *doesn't* should agree in number with their subjects.

The word *don't* is a contraction of *do not*. Use *don't* with plural subjects and with the pronouns *I* and *you*.

EXAMPLES The **children don't** seem nervous.

I don't understand.

Don't you remember?

The word *doesn't* is a contraction of *does not*. Use *doesn't* with singular subjects except the pronouns *I* and *you*.

EXAMPLES **Kim doesn't** ride the bus.

He doesn't play tennis.

It doesn't snow here.

Oral Practice Using *Don't* and *Doesn't*

Read the following sentences aloud, stressing the italicized words.

1. My friend *doesn't* understand the problem.
2. *Doesn't* she want to play soccer?
3. The tomatoes *don't* look ripe.
4. Our school *doesn't* have a gymnasium.
5. Italy *doesn't* border Germany.
6. The geese *don't* hiss at Mr. Waverly.
7. Our Muslim neighbors, the Nassers, *don't* eat pork.
8. He *doesn't* play chess.

Review C **Identifying Verbs That Agree in Number with Their Subjects**

Write the verb form in parentheses that agrees with its subject.

EXAMPLE 1. Wheelchairs with lifts (*help, helps*) many people.
        1. *help*

1. Twenty-five cents (*is, are*) not enough to buy the Sunday newspaper.
2. Everyone in her family (*prefers, prefer*) to drink water.
3. Allen and his parents (*enjoy, enjoys*) basketball.
4. Jan (*don't, doesn't*) know the rules of volleyball.
5. Neither the radio nor the speakers (*work, works*) as well as we had hoped.
6. There (*is, are*) 132 islands in the state of Hawaii.
7. Many California place names (*comes, come*) from Spanish.

8. The principal or her assistant (*is, are*) the one who can help you.

9. Home economics (*is, are*) a required course in many schools.

10. A flock of sheep (*was, were*) grazing on the hill.

Review D **Proofreading for Subject-Verb Agreement**

Most of the following sentences contain errors in subject-verb agreement. If a verb does not agree with its subject, write the correct form of the verb. If a sentence is already correct, write *C*.

EXAMPLE   **1.** The two pictures below shows Vera Wang and one of her dress designs.

      1. show

1. There is few names in fashion today as recognizable as Vera Wang.

2. Perhaps Ralph Lauren or *Vogue* are more familiar to you?

3. Well, Vera Wang has worked as a design director for Ralph Lauren and as a senior fashion editor for *Vogue* magazine.

4. Now, Wang run a company famous for its bridal gowns.

5. Retailers and the fashion press routinely praises Wang's innovative bridal offerings.

6. She don't just make one kind of dress, though.

7. Some of her designs has been seen at the Olympic games.

8. A former figure skater herself, Wang creates dazzling costumes for some of skating's biggest stars.

9. Skaters such as Michelle Kwan has performed in outfits Wang designed.

10. Vera Wang's diverse collection also include jewelry, shoes, and fragrances.

Agreement of Pronoun and Antecedent

A pronoun usually refers to a noun or another pronoun called its *antecedent.* Whenever you use a pronoun, make sure that it agrees with its antecedent.

8p. A pronoun should agree in number and gender with its antecedent.

Some singular pronouns have forms that indicate gender. Feminine pronouns refer to females. Masculine pronouns refer to males. Neuter pronouns refer to things (neither male nor female) and sometimes to animals.

Feminine	she	her	hers	herself
Masculine	he	him	his	himself
Neuter	it	it	its	itself

EXAMPLES   **Carlotta** said that **she** found **her** book.

Aaron brought **his** skates with **him.**

The **plant** with mold on **it** is losing **its** leaves.

The antecedent of a pronoun can be another kind of pronoun. In such cases, you may need to look in a phrase that follows the antecedent to determine which personal pronoun to use.

EXAMPLES   **Each** of the **girls** has offered **her** ideas. [*Each* is the antecedent of *her*. The word *girls* tells you to use the feminine pronoun *her* to refer to *Each*.]

One of the **men** lost **his** keys. [*One* is the antecedent of *his*. The word *men* tells you to use the masculine pronoun *his* to refer to *One*.]

Some antecedents may be either masculine or feminine. In such cases, use both the masculine and the feminine forms.

EXAMPLES   Every **one** of the parents praised **his or her** child's efforts that day.

No one in the senior play forgot **his or her** lines on opening night.

Reference Note

For more information on **antecedents,** see page 30.

STYLE   TIP

In conversation, people often use a plural personal pronoun to refer to a singular antecedent that may be either masculine or feminine. This nonstandard usage is becoming more common in writing, too.

NONSTANDARD
  Everybody brought their swimsuit.

For now, however, it is best to follow the rules of standard usage in formal situations.

STANDARD
  Everybody brought his or her swimsuit.

STYLE   TIP

To avoid the awkward use of *his or her,* try to rephrase the sentence.

EXAMPLE
  Everybody brought his or her swimsuit.
  Everybody brought **a** swimsuit.

USAGE

8q. Use a singular pronoun to refer to *anybody, anyone, anything, each, either, everybody, everyone, everything, neither, nobody, no one, nothing, one, somebody, someone,* or *something.*

EXAMPLES   **Each** of the snakes escaped from **its** cage.

           Someone in the class left behind **his or her** pencil.

8r. Use a plural pronoun to refer to *both, few, many,* or *several.*

EXAMPLES   **Both** of the sailors asked **their** captain for shore leave.

           Many among the others waiting below deck hoped that **they** could go, too.

8s. The indefinite pronouns *all, any, more, most, none,* and *some* may be singular or plural, depending on how they are used in a sentence.

EXAMPLES   **All** of the book is interesting, isn't **it**?
           All of the books are interesting, aren't **they**?

           None of the casserole is left; **it** was terrific!
           None of the casseroles are left; **they** were terrific!

8t. Use a singular pronoun to refer to two or more singular antecedents joined by *or* or *nor.*

EXAMPLES   Either **Ralph or Carlos** will display **his** baseball cards.

           Neither **Nina nor Mary** will bring **her** CD player.

8u. Use a plural pronoun to refer to two or more antecedents joined by *and.*

EXAMPLES   **Isaac and Jerome** told me that **they** were coming.

           Elena and Roberto sent letters to **their** cousin.

| STYLE   TIP |

Sentences with singular antecedents joined by *or* or *nor* can sound awkward if the antecedents are of different genders. If a sentence sounds awkward, revise it to avoid the problem.

AWKWARD
  Odessa or Raymond will bring her or his road map.

REVISED
  Odessa will bring **her** road map, or **Raymond** will bring **his.**

Exercise 12   **Using Pronouns in Sentences**

For each of the following sentences, write a pronoun or a pair of pronouns that will correctly complete the sentence.

EXAMPLE 　　**1.** David or Martin will show _____ slides.

　　　　　　1. his

1. A writer should proofread _____ work carefully.
2. One of the boys had finished _____ homework.
3. No, Joyce has not given me _____ answer.
4. The store sent Paula and Eric the posters that _____ had ordered.
5. Mark or Hector will arrive early so that _____ can help us.
6. Everyone will read one of _____ poems aloud.
7. One of the students raised _____ hand.
8. _____ of the tennis rackets were damaged by the water leak.
9. The hamsters had eaten none of _____ food.
10. Each of the dogs ate the scraps that we gave _____ .
11. The principal and the Spanish teacher announced _____ plans for the Cinco de Mayo fiesta.
12. All of the bowling pins were on _____ sides.
13. The movie made sense to _____ of the audience members.
14. Everyone in my class has _____ own writer's journal.
15. Neither recalled the name of _____ first-grade teacher.
16. _____ of the players, Sharon and P. J., agreed that the game was a draw.
17. Ms. Levine said _____ was proud of the students.
18. Frank had tried on all of the hats before _____ chose one.
19. Anyone may join if _____ collects stamps.
20. Either Vanessa or Marilyn was honored for _____ design.

COMPUTER TIP

Using indefinite pronouns correctly can be tricky. To help yourself, you may want to create an indefinite pronoun guide. First, summarize the information in Rules 8d–8f and 8q–8s.

Then, choose several examples to illustrate the rules. If you use a computer, you can create a Help file in which to store this information.

Call up your Help file whenever you run into difficulty with indefinite pronouns in your writing. If you don't use a computer, you can keep your guide in a writing notebook.

USAGE

8v. A pronoun that refers to a collective noun has the same number as the noun.

A collective noun is singular when it refers to the group as a unit and plural when it refers to the individual members of the group.

EXAMPLES 　　The **cast** is giving **its** final performance tonight. [The cast as a unit is giving its final performance.]

　　　　　　The **cast** are trying on **their** costumes. [The members of the cast are trying on their individual costumes.]

　　　　　　The **faculty** has prepared **its** report. [The faculty as a unit has prepared its report.]

　　　　　　The **faculty** are returning to **their** classrooms. [The members of the faculty are returning to their separate classrooms.]

8w. An expression of an amount may take a singular or plural pronoun, depending on how the expression is used.

EXAMPLES   **Five dollars** is all I need. I hope my sister will lend **it** to me. [The amount is thought of as a unit.]

                Two dollars are torn. The vending machine won't take **them.** [The amount is thought of as individual pieces or parts.]

8x. Even when plural in form, the title of a creative work (such as a book, song, film, or painting), the name of an organization, or the name of a country or city usually takes a singular pronoun.

EXAMPLES   Have you read **Great Expectations**? **It** is on our summer reading list.

                The **United Nations,** which has **its** headquarters in New York, also has offices in Geneva and Vienna.

                My grandmother, who is from the **Maldives,** told us of **its** coral reefs and lagoons.

Exercise 13   **Choosing Pronouns That Agree with Their Antecedents**

Choose the correct word or words in parentheses in the following sentences.

EXAMPLE   **1.** Even a trio can have a big sound if (*it, they*) can arrange the score properly.

          1. it

1. They are asking two hundred dollars, but (*it, they*) should be a lower price because there is no chair with the desk.
2. Darla, *The Hero and the Crown* has been checked out; however, (*it, they*) should be back next Wednesday.
3. If the high school band doesn't show up soon, (*it, they*) won't lead the parade.
4. These plans call for ten feet of African ebony, and although (*it, they*) would look great, I have no idea where we could even find ebony.
5. Seven points may not seem like much, but in jai alai, (*it, they*) can be enough to decide the game.
6. The cavalry unit took up (*its, their*) position on the hill.

7. "Sixteen Tons" has always been one of my favorite songs, and (*it, they*) always will be.
8. Six of the sales teams exceeded (*its, their*) goals.
9. Will the board of directors alter (*its, their*) decision?
10. Try Harper Brothers Appliances first; if (*it, they*) happens to be closed, go up the street to Smith's Hardware.

Review E **Proofreading Sentences for Correct Pronoun-Antecedent Agreement**

Most of the following sentences contain errors in pronoun-antecedent agreement. Identify each error, and write the correct pronoun or pronouns. If a sentence is already correct, write *C*.

EXAMPLE 1. At the meeting, each member of the Small Business Council spoke about their concerns.
   1. *their—his or her*

1. Everybody had a chance to express their opinion about the new shopping mall.
2. Mrs. Gomez and Mr. Franklin are happy about his or her new business locations at the mall.
3. Both said that his or her profits have increased significantly.
4. Neither Mr. Chen nor Mr. Cooper, however, feels that his or her customers can find convenient parking.
5. Anyone shopping at the mall has to park their car too far from the main shopping area.
6. Several members of the council said that the mall has taken away many of their customers.
7. One of the women on the council then presented their idea about creating a farmers' market on weekends.

8. Many members said he or she favored the plan, and a proposal was discussed.

9. Each farmer could have their own spot near the town hall.

10. The Small Business Council then agreed to take their proposal to the mayor.

Review F **Writing Sentences That Demonstrate Correct Subject-Verb and Pronoun-Antecedent Agreement**

Using the following words or word groups as subjects, write twenty sentences. In each sentence, underline the verb that agrees with the subject. Then, underline twice any pronoun that agrees with the subject.

EXAMPLE   **1.** all of the players

          1. All of the players <u>were tired</u>; <u><u>they</u></u> had had a long practice.

<table>
<tr><td>

1. both Jed and Bob

2. none of the puppies

3. Los Angeles

4. fifty cents

5. *Anne of Green Gables*

6. news

7. either the teacher or the students

8. the litter of kittens

9. neither Nancy nor Tim

10. everyone

</td><td>

11. *The Adventures of Tom Sawyer*

12. the football team

13. each of the chairs

14. athletics

15. the Masters tournament

16. few armadillos

17. most of the apple

18. several days

19. any of the orange juice

20. none of the pizza

</td></tr>
</table>

┌HELP┐

Not every sentence in Review F needs to have a pronoun that agrees with the subject.

USAGE

Chapter Review

A. Determining Subject and Verb Agreement

Identify the correct form of the verb given in parentheses in each of the following sentences. Base your answers on the rules of standard, formal usage.

1. Elephants (*has, have*) worked with people for centuries.
2. A blue vase (*is, are*) the only thing on the shelf.
3. (*Doesn't, Don't*) Midori come here every afternoon?
4. The exhibit of drawings by John James Audubon (*was, were*) fascinating, don't you think?
5. Civics (*was, were*) only one of the classes that challenged me.
6. Since Mom repaired them, both of the radios (*work, works*).
7. Everyone (*calls, call*) Latisha by her nickname, Tish.
8. Fifty cents (*was, were*) a lot of money in 1910!
9. Ms. Sakata's former neighbor and best friend, Ms. Chang, (*writes, write*) poetry.
10. (*Is, Are*) there any other blacksmiths in town?
11. I'm sorry, but somebody (*has, have*) checked out that book.
12. (*Was, Were*) the geese in the cornfield again?
13. All of the shells in my collection (*was, were*) displayed.
14. Neither Cindy nor her cousins (*knows, know*) how to sew.
15. Outside the back door (*is, are*) a few of your friends.
16. My brother and my uncles (*plays, play*) rugby.
17. The Netherlands (*has, have*) a coastline on the North Sea.
18. Here (*is, are*) several subjects for you to consider.
19. The team (*has, have*) all received their jerseys and hats.
20. Some of Ernest Hemingway's writings (*was, were*) autobiographical.
21. This news (*was, were*) just what Barb wanted to hear.
22. *Giants of Jazz* (*is, are*) an interesting book.
23. Everyone (*is, are*) expected to attend.
24. Most of our reading (*was, were*) done on weekends.
25. Either Gordon or Ruben (*knows, know*) the right answer.

B. Determining Pronoun and Antecedent Agreement

If the italicized pronoun in each of the following sentences does not agree with its antecedent, write the correct form of the pronoun. If the pronoun does agree with its antecedent, write *C*. Base your answers on the rules of standard, formal usage.

26. Everyone put *their* suitcases on the bus.
27. Either Marcia or Christina will bring *her* serving platter to the dinner party.
28. Both Sarah and Sue agreed with *her* counselor.
29. Several of my friends do *his or her* homework after school.
30. One of the boys used *their* bat in the game.
31. My grandfather's favorite television show is <u>The Honeymooners</u>. He watches *them* every night on cable.
32. All of the horses received *its* vaccinations.
33. Either Maria or Louise will receive *their* award today.
34. Everybody should know *their* ZIP Code.
35. Each student in the class has given *their* report on an African American folk tale.
36. Every one of the dogs obeyed *its* owner.
37. I found twenty dollars in my sock drawer. Do you think I should spend *them* on Christmas presents?
38. Will either Hector or Tony read *his* paper aloud?
39. Not one of the students had finished *their* science project on time this semester.
40. After Celia finished her solo, the audience roared *their* approval for five minutes.

Writing Application
Using Agreement in a Composition

Subject-Verb Agreement   If you could be any person in history, who would you be? Why? Answer these questions in a short composition. Be sure to use correct subject-verb agreement in explaining your choice.

Prewriting First, decide what historical person you would like to be, and freewrite about that person. As you write, think about why the person is noteworthy and why you would want to be him or her.

Writing Use your freewriting ideas to write your first draft. Begin with a sentence that states the purpose of your composition and identifies your historical figure. Then, give your main reasons for wanting to be that person. Summarize your main points in a conclusion.

Revising Read through your composition, and then answer these questions: (1) Is it clear what person from history I want to be? If not, revise your main idea statement. (2) Is it clear why I want to be that person? If not, explain your reasons in more detail.

Publishing Make sure that all subjects and verbs agree in number. Check your composition for errors in spelling, capitalization, and punctuation. Your class may want to create a display using the compositions and pictures of the historical figures chosen.

Using Verbs Correctly

Principal Parts, Regular and Irregular Verbs, Tense, Voice

1.0 Written and Oral English Language Conventions

Students write and speak with a command of standard English conventions appropriate to this grade level.

1.1 Use the active voice.

1.4 Demonstrate appropriate English usage.

Diagnostic Preview

Proofreading Sentences for Correct Verb Forms

If a sentence contains an incorrect past or past participle form of a verb, write the correct form. If a sentence is already correct, write *C.*

EXAMPLE **1.** Melissa drunk the medicine in one gulp.

  1. drank

1. We swum in the lake last weekend.

2. Carlos come from the Dominican Republic.

3. The crow just set there on the wire fence.

4. The balloon burst with a loud pop.

5. I seen that magician on television.

6. The leader raised his tambourine to begin the dance.

7. You should have went with Thomas to the game.

8. The ice cube has shrinked to half its original size.

9. Meanwhile, the water level has rose.

10. I would have wrote to you much sooner, but I lost your new address.

11. Sandra throwed the ball to the shortstop.

12. Ms. Lopez has spoke before many civic groups.

13. All of these photographs were taken in Florida's Everglades National Park.
14. The bell has rang for fourth period.
15. While visiting Los Angeles last August, I run into an old friend in the city's Little Tokyo district.
16. I laid down under a tree to rest.
17. I done everything asked of me.
18. It begun to rain shortly after dusk.
19. Some of the saucers were broken.
20. Sue lay her pen down and studied the question again.

Principal Parts of Verbs

The four basic forms of a verb are called the ***principal parts*** of the verb.

9a. The principal parts of a verb are the ***base form,*** the ***present participle,*** the ***past,*** and the ***past participle.***

When they are used to form tenses, the present participle and the past participle forms require helping verbs (forms of *be* and *have*).

Base Form	Present Participle	Past	Past Participle
talk	[is] talking	talked	[have] talked
draw	[is] drawing	drew	[have] drawn

Because *talk* forms its past and past participle by adding *–ed*, it is called a ***regular verb.*** *Draw* forms its past and past participle differently, so it is called an ***irregular verb.***

The principal parts of a verb are used to express time.

PRESENT TIME   He **draws** excellent pictures.
Susan **is drawing** one now.

PAST TIME   Last week they **drew** two maps.
She **has** often **drawn** cartoons.

FUTURE TIME   Perhaps she **will draw** one for you.
By Thursday, we **will have drawn** two more.

USAGE

┌HELP┐
Some teachers refer to the base form as the *infinitive.* Follow your teacher's directions when you are labeling this form.

Reference Note
For information on **participles used as adjectives,** see page 98. For information on **helping verbs,** see page 49.

Regular Verbs

9b. A *regular verb* forms its past and past participle by adding *–d* or *–ed* to the base form.

Base Form	Present Participle	Past	Past Participle
clean	[is] cleaning	cleaned	[have] cleaned
hope	[is] hoping	hoped	[have] hoped
inspect	[is] inspecting	inspected	[have] inspected
slip	[is] slipping	slipped	[have] slipped

One common error in forming the past or the past participle of a regular verb is to leave off the *–d* or *–ed* ending.

| NONSTANDARD | Our street use to be quieter. |
| STANDARD | Our street **used** to be quieter. |

Another common error is to add unnecessary letters.

| NONSTANDARD | The swimmer almost drownded in the riptide. |
| STANDARD | The swimmer almost **drowned** in the riptide. |

| NONSTANDARD | The kitten attackted that paper bag. |
| STANDARD | The kitten **attacked** that paper bag. |

Oral Practice 1 **Using Regular Verbs**

Read each of the following sentences aloud, stressing the italicized verbs.

1. We are *supposed* to meet at the track after school.
2. The twins *happened* to buy the same shirt.
3. They have already *called* me about the party.
4. Do you know who *used* to live in this house?
5. I had *hoped* they could go to the concert with us.

© 1992 by Sidney Harris.

USAGE

6. The chairs have been *moved* into the hall for the dance.

7. That salesclerk has *helped* my mother before.

8. Eli may not have *looked* under the table for the cat.

> **Exercise 1** **Writing the Forms of Regular Verbs**

Write the correct present participle, past, or past participle form of the italicized verb given before each of the following sentences.

EXAMPLES **1.** *learn*   Many people today are _____ folk dances from a variety of countries.

   1. *learning*

   2. *hope*   Dad and I had _____ to take lessons in folk dancing this summer.

   2. *hoped*

1. *practice* These Spanish folk dancers must have _____ for a long time.

2. *perform* Notice that they are _____ in their colorful native costumes.

3. *wish* Have you ever _____ that you knew how to do any folk dances?

4. *use* Virginia reels _____ to be popular dances in the United States.

5. *promise* Mrs. Stamos, who is from Greece, _____ to teach her daughter the Greek chain dance.

6. *lean* The young Jamaican dancer _____ backward before he went under the pole during the limbo dance competition.

7. *start* The group from Estonia is _____ a dance about a spinning wheel.

8. *request* Someone in the audience has _____ an Irish square dance called "Sweets of May."

9. *dance* During the Mexican hat dance, the woman _____ around the brim of the sombrero.

10. *fill* The Jewish wedding dance _____ the room with both music and movement.

USAGE

HELP

If you are not
sure about the principal
parts of a verb, look in a
dictionary. Entries for irregular verbs list the principal
parts of the verb. If the
principal parts are not
given, the verb is a
regular verb.

USAGE

Irregular Verbs

9c. An *irregular verb* forms its past and past participle in some way other than by adding *–d* or *–ed* to the base form.

Irregular verbs form their past and past participle in various ways:

- by changing vowels

Base Form	Past	Past Participle
sing	sang	[have] sung
become	became	[have] become
drink	drank	[have] drunk

- by changing consonants

Base Form	Past	Past Participle
make	made	[have] made
build	built	[have] built
lend	lent	[have] lent

- by changing vowels *and* consonants

Base Form	Past	Past Participle
do	did	[have] done
go	went	[have] gone
buy	bought	[have] bought

- by making no changes

Base Form	Past	Past Participle
hurt	hurt	[have] hurt
put	put	[have] put
let	let	[have] let

Common Irregular Verbs

Base Form	Present Participle	Past	Past Participle
begin	[is] beginning	began	[have] begun
bite	[is] biting	bit	[have] bitten *or* bit
blow	[is] blowing	blew	[have] blown
break	[is] breaking	broke	[have] broken
bring	[is] bringing	brought	[have] brought
build	[is] building	built	[have] built
burst	[is] bursting	burst	[have] burst
buy	[is] buying	bought	[have] bought
catch	[is] catching	caught	[have] caught
choose	[is] choosing	chose	[have] chosen
come	[is] coming	came	[have] come
cost	[is] costing	cost	[have] cost
cut	[is] cutting	cut	[have] cut
do	[is] doing	did	[have] done
draw	[is] drawing	drew	[have] drawn
drink	[is] drinking	drank	[have] drunk
drive	[is] driving	drove	[have] driven
eat	[is] eating	ate	[have] eaten
fall	[is] falling	fell	[have] fallen
feel	[is] feeling	felt	[have] felt
fight	[is] fighting	fought	[have] fought
find	[is] finding	found	[have] found
fly	[is] flying	flew	[have] flown
forgive	[is] forgiving	forgave	[have] forgiven
freeze	[is] freezing	froze	[have] frozen
get	[is] getting	got	[have] got *or* gotten
give	[is] giving	gave	[have] given
go	[is] going	went	[have] gone
grow	[is] growing	grew	[have] grown

(continued)

Common Irregular Verbs			
Base Form	Present Participle	Past	Past Participle
have	[is] having	had	[have] had
hear	[is] hearing	heard	[have] heard
hide	[is] hiding	hid	[have] hid or hidden
hit	[is] hitting	hit	[have] hit
hold	[is] holding	held	[have] held
know	[is] knowing	knew	[have] known
lead	[is] leading	led	[have] led

Oral Practice 2 Using Irregular Verbs

Read the following sentences aloud, stressing the italicized verbs.

1. Edward's sister *drove* him to the mall this afternoon.
2. My parents *came* to the spelling bee last year.
3. I should have *known* the test would be difficult.
4. He's *going* to Cape Canaveral this summer.
5. Maya has been *chosen* to play on our team.
6. The water pipe *burst* during the ice storm.
7. *Did* you see the northern lights last night?
8. Wyatt *brought* his new computer game to the party at Alexander's house.

Exercise 2 Writing the Past and Past Participle Forms of Irregular Verbs

Write the correct past or past participle form of the italicized verb given before each of the following sentences.

EXAMPLE   1. *choose*   Sara has _____ her song for next month's piano recital.

1. chosen

1. *drive*   Last summer we _____ to Denver, where we visited the U.S. Mint.
2. *begin*   The concert _____ an hour ago.

USAGE

3. *break*   Mike Powell ____ the world long-jump record by jumping 29 feet 4½ inches.

4. *blow*   The wind has ____ the tent down.

5. *get*   We ____ tickets to ride *The Silverton*.

6. *fall*   The leaves have ____ from the trees.

7. *do*   Kate ____ her best, and she got a promotion.

8. *drink*   According to legend, the Aztec emperor Montezuma ____ chocolate.

9. *build*   People in Africa ____ large cities hundreds, even thousands, of years ago.

10. *go*   You've never ____ to Puerto Rico, have you?

11. *bite*   I think that Roseanne ____ into a green chile!

12. *grow*   Well, nephew, you surely have ____!

13. *catch*   You look like you just ____ the brass ring!

14. *give*   Mom had already ____ us a color copy of her grandmother's journal.

15. *eat*   The Japanese have box lunches, too, but they call them *obentos*; we have ____ them several times.

16. *feel*   They ____ better after taking a short nap.

17. *cost*   Those tickets shouldn't have ____ so much.

18. *buy*   Have you ever ____ a Greek sandwich called a *gyro*?

19. *find*   My cousin said that she has ____ a new canyon trail.

20. *freeze*   The pond ____ last winter, and we went skating.

More Common Irregular Verbs			
Base Form	Present Participle	Past	Past Participle
leave	[is] leaving	left	[have] left
lend	[is] lending	lent	[have] lent
let	[is] letting	let	[have] let
light	[is] lighting	lighted *or* lit	[have] lighted *or* lit
lose	[is] losing	lost	[have] lost
make	[is] making	made	[have] made
meet	[is] meeting	met	[have] met
pay	[is] paying	paid	[have] paid

(continued)

┌HELP─

Some verbs have two correct past or past participle forms. However, these forms are not always interchangeable.

EXAMPLES

I **shone** the flashlight into the woods. [*Shined* also would be correct in this usage.]

I **shined** my shoes. [*Shone* would be incorrect in this usage.]

If you are unsure about which past participle form to use, check an up-to-date dictionary.

(continued)

More Common Irregular Verbs			
Base Form	Present Participle	Past	Past Participle
put	[is] putting	put	[have] put
read	[is] reading	read	[have] read
ride	[is] riding	rode	[have] ridden
ring	[is] ringing	rang	[have] rung
run	[is] running	ran	[have] run
say	[is] saying	said	[have] said
see	[is] seeing	saw	[have] seen
seek	[is] seeking	sought	[have] sought
sell	[is] selling	sold	[have] sold
send	[is] sending	sent	[have] sent
shrink	[is] shrinking	shrank or shrunk	[have] shrunk
sing	[is] singing	sang	[have] sung
sink	[is] sinking	sank or sunk	[have] sunk
speak	[is] speaking	spoke	[have] spoken
spend	[is] spending	spent	[have] spent
stand	[is] standing	stood	[have] stood
steal	[is] stealing	stole	[have] stolen
swim	[is] swimming	swam	[have] swum
swing	[is] swinging	swung	[have] swung
take	[is] taking	took	[have] taken
teach	[is] teaching	taught	[have] taught
tear	[is] tearing	tore	[have] torn
tell	[is] telling	told	[have] told
think	[is] thinking	thought	[have] thought
throw	[is] throwing	threw	[have] thrown
wear	[is] wearing	wore	[have] worn
win	[is] winning	won	[have] won
write	[is] writing	wrote	[have] written

USAGE

Oral Practice 3 Using Irregular Verbs

Read the following sentences aloud, stressing the italicized verbs.

1. When the bell *rang,* we hurried out of the building.
2. The audience was quiet as the acrobats *swung* from the trapeze.
3. That dress had already *shrunk* before I washed it.
4. Otherwise, Lily would have *worn* it to the dance.
5. Have you *met* the new foreign exchange student?
6. We were late to the picnic because I *lost* the map.
7. My father *lent* me the money to buy a new watch.
8. Did you know that Rachel *took* singing lessons?

Exercise 3 Writing the Past and Past Participle Forms of Irregular Verbs

Write the correct past or past participle form of the italicized verb given before each of the following sentences.

EXAMPLE **1.** *see*   I have ＿＿ that movie twice already.

          1. seen

  1. *run*   Michael ＿＿ the 100-meter dash in excellent time.
  2. *sell*   My aunt has ＿＿ more houses than any other real estate agent in the city.
  3. *speak* The director of the state health department ＿＿ to our class today.
  4. *win*   The Mexican poet Octavio Paz ＿＿ the Nobel Prize in literature.
  5. *write* I have ＿＿ some poems, but I am shy about showing them to anyone.
  6. *ride*   Tamisha's whole family ＿＿ mules to the bottom of the Grand Canyon.
  7. *sing*   At the concert, the group ＿＿ my favorite song.
  8. *throw* Someone must have ＿＿ this trash from a car.
  9. *swim* Within minutes, the two beautiful swans had ＿＿ across the lake.
10. *sink*   King Arthur's sword Excalibur had ＿＿ slowly to the bottom of the lake.
11. *send*   My aunt in South America ＿＿ me a fabulous sweater made from the wool of an alpaca, which is an animal similar to a llama.

12. *tell*   Mr. Noguchi ____ us that *R.S.V.P.* at the bottom of an invitation means that you should let the host know whether you are coming or not.

13. *lend*   Before the softball game, my friend Gabriela ____ me her glove.

14. *wear*   Shouldn't you have ____ a warmer jacket for the hike this morning?

15. *swim*   Soon-hee, who is training for a triathlon, ____ two miles on Saturday.

16. *ring*   I have ____ the doorbell several times, but no one has come to the door.

17. *lose*   The swan ____ many large feathers; Tony said it must be molting.

18. *take*   It has ____ over ten minutes to locate the missing glasses.

19. *sing*   Gerald, Annie, and Trish have ____ the national anthem at assembly.

20. *say*   The weather forecast this morning ____ to expect snow flurries.

Review A **Writing the Past and Past Participle Forms of Irregular Verbs**

Write the correct past or past participle form of the italicized verb given before each of the following sentences.

EXAMPLE   **1.** *tell*   Has Alameda ____ you about the book *The Indian Tipi: Its History, Construction, and Use*?

          1. told

1. *write*   Reginald and Gladys Laubin ____ that book and others about American Indian culture.

2. *build*   The Laubins ____ their own tepee.

3. *stand*   Tepees of various sizes once ____ all across the Great Plains.

4. *see*   I have ____ pictures of camps full of beautifully decorated tepees.

5. *make*   For many years, American Indians have ____ tepees out of cloth rather than buffalo hides.

6. *come*   The word *tepee*, or *tipi*, has ____ into English from the Sioux language.

7. *draw* On the outside of their tepees, the Sioux and Cheyenne peoples ____ designs like the ones shown on the previous page.

8. *take* Because the Plains Indians followed animal herds, they needed shelter that could be easily ____ from place to place.

9. *know* Even before reading the book, I ____ that the inside of a tepee cover was rarely painted.

10. *do* Traditionally, women ____ all the work of making tepees and putting them up.

Review B   **Writing the Past and Past Participle Forms of Irregular Verbs**

Write the correct past or past participle form of the italicized verb given before each of the following sentences.

EXAMPLE   **1.** *write*   I ____ a report on Jim Thorpe.

   1. wrote

1. *blow* Yesterday the wind ____ the leaves into our yard.

2. *break* My pen pal from Australia has never ____ his promise to write once a week.

3. *bring* I ____ the wrong book to class.

4. *burst* The children almost ____ with excitement.

5. *choose* The director ____ James Earl Jones for the role.

6. *come* My aunt and her friend ____ to dinner last night.

7. *do* I have always ____ my homework right after supper.

8. *drink* The guests ____ fruit punch and lemonade.

9. *fall* One of Julian's Russian nesting dolls has ____ off the shelf.

10. *freeze* Has the pond ____ yet?

11. *go* We have never ____ to see the Parthenon in Nashville.

12. *know* Had I ____, I would have called you sooner.

13. *ring* Suddenly the fire alarm ____.

14. *run* Joan Samuelson certainly ____ a good race.

15. *see* I ____ you in line at the movies.

16. *shrink* The apples we dried in the sun have ____.

17. *speak* After we had ____ to George and Marc, we decided to play dominoes.

18. *swim* We ____ out to the float and back.

19. *write*   She has ____ me several long letters.

20. *throw*   You shouldn't have ____ the ball to second base.

Tense

9d. The *tense* of a verb indicates the time of the action or of the state of being that is expressed by the verb.

EXAMPLES   Yesterday, Denise **served** lox and bagels for breakfast.

           Randy **has played** bass guitar for the band, but now he **plays** drums.

           Once they **have painted** the signs, Jill and Cody **will finish** the decorations for the dance.

Verbs in English have six tenses.

Present	Past	Future
Present Perfect	Past Perfect	Future Perfect

The following time line shows the relationship between the six tenses.

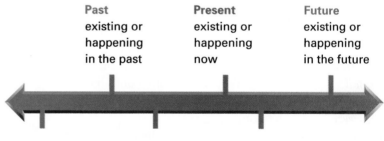

Past	Present	Future
existing or happening in the past	existing or happening now	existing or happening in the future

Past Perfect	Present Perfect	Future Perfect
existing or happening before a specific time in the past	existing or happening sometime before now; may be continuing now	existing or happening before a specific time in the future

Listing the different forms of a verb is called *conjugating* the verb.

Conjugation of the Verb *See*

Present Tense

Singular	Plural
I see	we see
you see	you see
he, she, *or* it sees	they see

Past Tense

Singular	Plural
I saw	we saw
you saw	you saw
he, she, *or* it saw	they saw

Future Tense

Singular	Plural
I will (shall) see	we will (shall) see
you will (shall) see	you will (shall) see
he, she, *or* it will (shall) see	they will (shall) see

Present Perfect Tense

Singular	Plural
I have seen	we have seen
you have seen	you have seen
he, she, *or* it has seen	they have seen

Past Perfect Tense

Singular	Plural
I had seen	we had seen
you had seen	you had seen
he, she, *or* it had seen	they had seen

Future Perfect Tense

Singular	Plural
I will (shall) have seen	we will (shall) have seen
you will (shall) have seen	you will (shall) have seen
he, she, *or* it will (shall) have seen	they will (shall) have seen

STYLE · TIP

Traditionally, the helping verbs *shall* and *will* were used to mean different things. Now, however, *shall* can be used almost interchangeably with *will*.

┌HELP┐

The progressive form is not a separate tense but an additional form of each of the six tenses.

NOTE Each tense has an additional form called the **progressive form,** which expresses continuing action or state of being. In each tense, the progressive form of a verb consists of the appropriate tense of *be* plus the verb's present participle.

Present Progressive	am, is, are seeing
Past Progressive	was, were seeing
Future Progressive	will (shall) be seeing
Present Perfect Progressive	has been seeing, have been seeing
Past Perfect Progressive	had been seeing
Future Perfect Progressive	will (shall) have been seeing

Consistency of Tense

9e. Do not change needlessly from one tense to another.

When writing about events that take place at the same time, use verbs that are in the same tense. When writing about events that occur at different times, use verbs that are in different tenses.

INCONSISTENT   When we go to the movies, we bought some popcorn. [The events occur at the same time, but *go* is in the present tense and *bought* is in the past tense.]

CONSISTENT   When we **go** to the movies, we **buy** some popcorn. [Both *go* and *buy* are in the present tense.]

CONSISTENT   When we **went** to the movies, we **bought** some popcorn. [Both *went* and *bought* are in the past tense.]

Exercise 4 Making Tenses of Verbs Consistent

┌HELP┐

When you rewrite Exercise 4, either tense is correct, as long as you are consistent.

Read the following sentences, and choose whether to rewrite them in the present or past tense. Then, rewrite the sentences, changing the verb forms to correct any needless changes.

EXAMPLE   **[1]** I picked up the telephone receiver quickly, but the line is still dead.

1. *I picked up the telephone receiver quickly, but the line was still dead.*

                          or

    I pick up the telephone receiver quickly, but the line is still dead.

[1] Lightning struck our house, and I run straight for cover. [2] "Oh, no!" I exclaim. [3] The electricity was out! [4] My parents get out the flashlights, and we played a game. [5] Later, since the stove, oven, and microwave didn't work without electricity, we have a cold supper in the living room—picnic style! [6] My younger brother asks me what lightning is. [7] "Lightning is a big spark of electricity from a thundercloud," I tell him. [8] He nods. [9] I started to tell him about positive and negative charges creating lightning, but he doesn't understand what I'm talking about and walks away. [10] In the morning, we were all glad when the sun shone and our electricity is on again.

Active and Passive Voice

A verb in the *active voice* expresses an action done *by* its subject. A verb in the *passive voice* expresses an action done *to* its subject. In passive voice, the verb phrase always includes a form of *be* and the past participle of the main verb. Other helping verbs may also be included. Compare the following sentences:

Reference Note

For more about **helping verbs,** see page 49.

ACTIVE VOICE   The pilot **instructed** us. [The subject, *pilot,* performs the action.]

PASSIVE VOICE   We **were instructed** by the pilot. [The subject, *We,* receives the action.]

ACTIVE VOICE   Alice **caught** a fly ball. [The subject, *Alice,* performs the action.]

PASSIVE VOICE   A fly ball **was caught** by Alice. [The subject, *ball,* receives the action.]

ACTIVE VOICE   The firefighters **have put** out the blaze. [The subject, *firefighters,* performs the action.]

PASSIVE VOICE   The blaze **has been put** out by the firefighters. [The subject, *blaze,* receives the action.]

STYLE TIP

In general, you should avoid using the passive voice because it can make your writing sound weak and awkward. Using the active voice helps make your writing direct and forceful.

PASSIVE VOICE
A no-hitter **was pitched** by Valerie, and the game **was won** by her team.

ACTIVE VOICE
Valerie **pitched** a no-hitter, and her team **won** the game.

Exercise 5 **Identifying Active and Passive Voice**

Tell whether the verb is in the *active voice* or *passive voice* in each of the following sentences.

EXAMPLE   **1.** The 10K race was won by Mikki.

1. *passive voice*

1. On Sunday afternoon we painted the den.
2. Brianne was elected to the student council.
3. The CD has been misplaced by my cousin.
4. The new animation software creates vivid images.
5. Many of the yearbook photos were taken by Adrienne.
6. Shoddy work was done on the building.
7. Mike and I don't understand this algebra problem.
8. I am unloading the food and supplies at the campsite.
9. The tickets had been sold months before the concert.
10. Andre was awarded the certificate for his service to the community.

Six Troublesome Verbs

Sit and *Set*

The verb *sit* means "to be seated" or "to rest." *Sit* seldom takes an object. The verb *set* usually means "to place (something somewhere)" or "to put (something somewhere)." *Set* usually takes an object. Notice that *set* has the same form for the base form, past, and past participle.

STYLE **TIP**

You may know that the word *set* has more meanings than the two given here. Check in a dictionary to see if the meaning you intend requires an object.

EXAMPLE
The sun **sets** in the West.
[Here, *sets* does not take an object.]

Base Form	Present Participle	Past	Past Participle
sit	[is] sitting	sat	[have] sat
set	[is] setting	set	[have] set

EXAMPLES   Who **is sitting** on the blanket by the pool? [no object]

Theresa **is setting** the lawn chairs by the pool. [Theresa is setting what? *Chairs* is the object.]

Three boys **sat** on the platform. [no object]

The boys **set** the instruments on the platform. [The boys set what? *Instruments* is the object.]

We **had sat** on the pier for an hour before Suzanne arrived with the bait. [no object]

I **had set** the bucket of bait on the pier. [I had set what? *Bucket* is the object.]

Oral Practice 4 Using the Forms of *Sit* and *Set* Correctly

Read each of the following sentences aloud, stressing the italicized verbs.

1. Darnell and I *sat* down to play a game of chess.
2. After we had been *sitting* for a while, he decided to make bread.
3. I *set* the pan on the table.
4. After Darnell had *set* out the ingredients, he mixed them.
5. We returned to our game but could not *sit* still for long.
6. We had not *set* the pan in the oven.
7. Then, we almost *sat* too long.
8. If the bread had *sat* in the oven much longer, it would have burned.

Exercise 6 Writing the Forms of *Sit* and *Set* Correctly

Write the correct form of *sit* or *set* for each blank in the following sentences.

EXAMPLE   **1.** I _____ my suitcase on the rack.
        1. set

1. On the train, I _____ next to a woman wearing a shawl.
2. She _____ a large covered basket on the floor by her feet.
3. When the conductor asked her if she would like to _____ it in the baggage rack, she refused.
4. She insisted that the basket must _____ by her feet.
5. As I _____ beside her, I wondered what was in the basket.
6. I _____ my book down and tried to see inside the tightly woven basket.
7. Perhaps I was _____ next to a woman with a picnic lunch.
8. Maybe she had _____ next to me because I looked hungry.
9. As the woman _____ her packages down, I watched the basket.
10. A sudden movement of the train caused the basket to open, and inside it _____ a small, white rabbit.

Rise and *Raise*

The verb *rise* means "to move upward" or "to go up." *Rise* does not take an object. The verb *raise* means "to lift (something) up." *Raise* usually takes an object.

USAGE

Base Form	Present Participle	Past	Past Participle
rise	[is] rising	rose	[have] risen
raise	[is] raising	raised	[have] raised

EXAMPLES The fans **were rising** to sing the national anthem. [no object]

Fans **were raising** signs and banners. [Fans were raising what? *Signs* and *banners* are the objects.]

The student **rose** to ask a question. [no object]
The student **raised** a good question. [The student raised what? *Question* is the object.]

Prices **had risen.** [no object]
The store **had raised** prices. [The store had raised what? *Prices* is the object.]

Oral Practice 5 Using Forms of *Rise* and *Raise* Correctly

Read the following sentences aloud, stressing the italicized verbs.

1. Mount Everest *rises* over 29,000 feet.
2. He *raises* the flag at sunrise.
3. The TV reporter *raised* her voice to be heard.
4. She *rose* from her seat and looked out the window.
5. The constellation Orion had not yet *risen* in the southern sky.
6. They had *raised* the piñata high in the tree.
7. I hope the bread is *rising*.
8. He will be *raising* the bucket from the well.

Exercise 7 Identifying the Correct Forms of *Rise* and *Raise*

Identify the correct verb of the two given in parentheses in each of the following sentences.

EXAMPLE 1. After the storm, Diana (*rose, raised*) the window.
1. *raised*

1. The entire audience quickly (*rose, raised*) to their feet to sing the "Hallelujah Chorus."

2. They used a jack to (*rise, raise*) the car so that they could change the tire.
3. The fire juggler is (*rising, raising*) two flaming batons over his head to signal the start of the show.
4. Some people have trouble remembering that the sun always (*rises, raises*) in the east.
5. He gently (*rose, raised*) the injured duckling from the lake.
6. Only half of Mauna Kea, a volcano on the island of Hawaii, (*rises, raises*) above the ocean.
7. The proud winner has (*risen, raised*) her trophy so that everyone can see it.
8. The wedding guests have (*risen, raised*) from their seats to see the bride enter.
9. Yeast makes the dough for pizza and other baked goods, such as bread and rolls, (*rise, raise*).
10. They will (*rise, raise*) the couch while I look under it.

Lie and *Lay*

The verb *lie* generally means "to recline," "to be in a place," or "to remain lying down." *Lie* does not take an object. The verb *lay* generally means "to put (something) down" or "to place (something somewhere)." *Lay* usually takes an object.

Base Form	Present Participle	Past	Past Participle
lie	[is] lying	lay	[have] lain
lay	[is] laying	laid	[have] laid

EXAMPLES   The silverware **is lying** on the table. [no object]
The waiter **is laying** silverware beside each plate.
[The waiter is laying what? *Silverware* is the object.]

The apple dolls **lay** drying in the sun. [no object]
Aunt Martha **laid** her apple dolls in the sun to dry. [Aunt Martha laid what? *Dolls* is the object.]

That bicycle **had lain** in the driveway for a week. [no object]
Bill **had laid** that bicycle in the driveway. [Bill had laid what? *Bicycle* is the object.]

MEETING THE CHALLENGE

Write a poem, correctly using each of the six troublesome verbs, *sit, set, rise, raise, lie,* and *lay*. Be sure to check your poem for correct usage of the troublesome verbs.

USAGE

STYLE   **TIP**

The verb *lie* can also mean "to tell an untruth." Used in this way, *lie* still does not take an object.

EXAMPLE
   Don't **lie** to her, Beth.

The past and past participle forms of this meaning of *lie* are *lied* and [*have*] *lied*.

Oral Practice 6 **Using Forms of *Lie* and *Lay* Correctly**

Read the following sentences aloud, stressing the italicized verbs.

1. If you are tired, *lie* down for a while.
2. *Lay* your pencils down, please.
3. Two huge dogs *lay* by the fire last night.
4. The cat has been *lying* on the new bedspread.
5. Mr. Cortez *laid* the map of Puerto Rico on the table.
6. In our state, snow usually *lies* on the ground until late March or the first weeks of April.
7. He had *laid* your coats on the bed in my room.
8. After the baby had *lain* down for a nap, she still wanted to play with her new toy.

Exercise 8 **Identifying the Correct Forms of *Lie* and *Lay***

Identify the correct verb of the two in parentheses for each of the following sentences.

EXAMPLE **1.** Marc (*lay, laid*) his new tennis shoes on the floor.
    1. laid

1. The islands of American Samoa (*lie, lay*) about 4,800 miles southwest of San Francisco.
2. Dad quickly (*lay, laid*) the hermit crab down when it began to pinch him.
3. I don't know where I have (*lain, laid*) my copy of *Chinese Proverbs* by Ruthanne Lum McCunn.
4. I have often (*lain, laid*) under the oak tree and napped.
5. Many visitors (*lie, lay*) flowers and wreaths at the Vietnam Veterans Memorial in Washington, D.C.
6. My brother, who is sick, has been (*lying, laying*) in bed all day.
7. The clerk (*lay, laid*) the small package on the scale.
8. (*Lie, Lay*) your backpack down, and come see the new comic books I bought yesterday.
9. Those clothes will (*lie, lay*) on the floor until you pick them up.
10. After he had circled several times, the puppy (*lay, laid*) down and slept.

Identify the correct verb of the two given in parentheses in each of the following sentences.

EXAMPLE   **1.** The bricklayer (*rose, raised*) from the patio floor and dusted himself off.

1. rose

1. These rocks have (*lain, laid*) here for centuries.
2. Please (*sit, set*) there until your name is called.
3. The nurse (*lay, laid*) her cool hand on the sick child's brow and decided to take his temperature.
4. The horses are (*lying, laying*) in the pasture.
5. The senator and her advisors had (*sat, set*) around the huge conference table.
6. After the picnic, everyone (*lay, laid*) on blankets to rest in the shade of the oak tree.
7. Smoke (*rose, raised*) from the chimney.
8. The farmhands (*sat, set*) their lunch boxes under a tree to shade them from the sun.
9. Have you been (*sitting, setting*) there all afternoon?
10. The sun has already (*risen, raised*).
11. Why has the stage manager (*rose, raised*) the curtains before the second act has begun?
12. A gust of hot air caused the enormous balloon to (*rise, raise*) out of sight of the spectators.
13. Be sure to (*lie, lay*) these windowpanes down carefully.
14. When the queen enters, each guest should (*rise, raise*) from his or her chair.
15. Who (*sat, set*) these glasses on my chair?
16. "(*Lie, Lay*) down!" the trainer sharply ordered the puppy, but the puppy didn't obey.
17. If we had a pulley, we could (*rise, raise*) that stone.
18. Just (*sit, set*) those green beans by the sink; I'll get to them in a minute.
19. Mom and Aunt Linda must have been (*lying, laying*) tile in the kitchen all afternoon.
20. You (*rise, raise*) the garage door, and I'll bring the bikes in out of the rain.

USAGE

Most of the following sentences contain incorrect verb forms. If a sentence contains the wrong form of a verb, write the correct form. If a sentence is already correct, write *C*.

EXAMPLE   1. During the 1800s, many German settlers choosed to live in the Hill Country of central Texas.

            1. *chose*

1. These hardy, determined pioneers builded towns and cleared land for farming.
2. I have went to the town of Fredericksburg several times with my family.
3. This interesting town lays about 80 miles west of Austin.
4. Fredericksburg use to be in Comanche territory.
5. Early on, German settlers made peace with neighboring Comanche chiefs.
6. The town then growed rapidly.
7. German-style churches, public buildings, and houses like the one shown here raised along the town's central street.
8. On one of our visits, my family set and talked about the town with a woman who had been born there.
9. She said that she had spoke German all her life.
10. When we left, she raised a hand and said, *"Auf Wiedersehen"* (until we meet again).

USAGE

Chapter Review

A. Using Irregular Verbs

Write the correct past or past participle form of the italicized irregular verb provided before each sentence.

1. *break*   The thunder ____ the silence.

2. *ring*   Who ____ the fire alarm so quickly?

3. *shrink*   This shirt must have ____ in the dryer.

4. *throw*   You've ____ the ball out of bounds!

5. *lead*   Julio ____ the parade last year, so now it's my turn.

6. *rise*   The sun ____ over the pyramids of Giza in Egypt.

7. *swim*   We have ____ only three laps.

8. *choose*   Vera was ____ as captain of the volleyball team.

9. *go*   I have ____ to visit the Grand Canyon twice.

10. *sit*   The tiny tree frog ____ motionless. ·

11. *write*   Joan has ____ a story about aliens from the Andromeda galaxy.

12. *do*   During class, Jorge ____ the first five problems of his homework assignment.

13. *steal*   Three runners ____ bases during the first inning.

14. *break*   This summer's heat wave has ____ all records.

15. *drink*   Have you ____ all of the tomato juice?

16. *sink*   The log had slowly ____ into the quicksand.

17. *lie*   The old postcards have ____ in the box for years.

18. *drive*   Have you ever ____ across the state of Texas?

19. *begin*   Our local PBS station ____ its fund-raising drive.

20. *set*   Have you ____ the paper plates and napkins on the picnic table?

21. *throw*   Who ____ the ball to first base?

22. *know*   I have ____ some of my classmates for six years.

23. *take*   Kadeem ____ the role of Frederick Douglass.

24. *tear*   My mother ____ the paper to make confetti.

25. *come*   We ____ close to winning the tournament.

USAGE

B. Changing Tenses of Verbs

Rewrite each of the following sentences to change the verb or verbs to the tense indicated in italics.

26. *present perfect*   Every time Roger comes to visit me, he brings his dog Zip with him.

27. *past perfect*   The dog will sleep on the kitchen floor for the entire visit.

28. *present*   Zip moved only if he heard the sounds of food being prepared.

29. *future perfect*   Zip has broken all records for a dog not moving a muscle.

30. *past*   We had known Zip before he had grown old.

C. Making Verb Tenses Consistent

Read the following sentences, and choose whether to rewrite them in the present or past tense. Then, rewrite the sentences, changing the verb forms to make the verb tense consistent.

31. My uncle comes back to Michigan for Christmas, and he drove his vintage sports car.

32. Ava finished her assignment, but she forgets to put a title page on it.

33. The stages of the booster rocket dropped away as the space shuttle climbs into the sky.

34. Aunt Maureen jumped to her feet and cheers when Mia made the winning basket.

35. When Barbara presents her science fair project, all the judges were very impressed.

D. Identifying Active and Passive Voice

Tell whether the italicized verb is in the *active voice* or the *passive voice* in each of the following sentences.

36. The grass clippings and the kitchen scraps *were placed* on the compost pile.

37. Most of the class *had* already *gone* to see that play.

38. All of the pencils *were sharpened* by Erica and Austin before the test began.

39. My father *was asked* for his advice on repairing the old playground equipment.

40. Every Friday night the Lopez family *invites* us to their house for dinner.

Writing Application
Using Verbs in a Story

Verb Forms and Tenses   A local writers' club is sponsoring a contest for the best "cliffhanger" opening of an adventure story. Write an exciting paragraph to enter in the contest. Your paragraph should leave readers wondering "What happens next?" In your paragraph, use at least five verbs from the lists of Common Irregular Verbs in this chapter.

Prewriting   First, you will need to imagine a suspenseful situation to describe. Jot down several ideas for your story opening. Then, choose the one you like best. With that situation in mind, scan the lists of irregular verbs. Note at least ten verbs you can use. Include some lively action verbs like *burst, swing,* and *throw.*

Writing   As you write your rough draft, think of your readers. Choose words that create a suspenseful, believable scene. Remember that you have only one paragraph to catch your readers' interest.

Revising   Ask a friend to read your paragraph. Does your friend find it interesting? Can he or she picture the scene clearly? If not, you may want to add, delete, or revise some details.

Publishing   Check your spelling, usage, punctuation, and grammar. Check to make sure the forms of verbs are correct and the tenses are consistent. You may want to exchange your cliffhanger with a partner, and complete each other's stories. With your teacher's permission, you can then read the completed stories aloud to the class.

Using Pronouns Correctly

Nominative and Objective Case Forms, Other Pronoun Problems

1.0 Written and Oral English Language Conventions

Students write and speak with a command of standard English conventions appropriate to this grade level.

1.2 Make clear references between pronouns and antecedents.

1.4 Demonstrate appropriate English usage (e.g., pronoun reference).

Diagnostic Preview

A. Correcting Errors in Pronoun Forms

Most of the following sentences contain errors in the use of pronoun forms. Identify the error, and give the correct pronoun form for each sentence. If a sentence is already correct, write *C*.

EXAMPLE   **1.** The Garcia children and them grew up together in East Texas.

     1. them—they

1. Us basketball players know the value of warming up.
2. The computer experts in our class are Rosalinda and her.
3. Pablo and me are planning to visit the Andes Mountains.
4. At Passover, my grandparents make gefilte fish and other traditional foods for my cousins and I.
5. Give Sue and him this invitation to the awards ceremony.
6. Josh made hisself a bookcase in industrial arts class.
7. Two angry hornets chased Earline and she all the way home.
8. The first actors on stage were Jesse and him.
9. Mr. Mendez and us organized a debate about student rights.
10. Will you attend the rally with Scott and me?
11. Jeannette and her know a great deal about Greek myths.

12. The hickory smoke smelled good to we campers.
13. Liang was telling them and me about his home in Hong Kong.
14. Julia and them learned how to make batik patterns on cloth.
15. Tom asked Mark and he if they wanted to join a gospel band.

B. Revising for Clear Pronoun Reference

Revise each of the following sentences, correcting each unclear pronoun reference.

EXAMPLE   1. Brad informed Luke that his brother was late.

       1. *Brad informed Luke that Luke's brother was late.*

16. Liz called Gail while she was doing her Spanish homework.
17. Ryan spotted John in the crowded theater when he stood up.
18. As soon as Mom and Aunt Sue arrived in Denver, she e-mailed me.
19. Julie saw Louise while she was in Paris.
20. Before Chad met Kyle, he had never water-skied.

┌HELP──
Sentences in Part B of the Diagnostic Preview may have more than one possible answer.

Case

10a. *Case* is the form that a noun or pronoun takes to show its relationship to other words in a sentence.

English has three cases for nouns and pronouns:

- nominative
- objective
- possessive

    The form of a noun is the same for both the nominative and the objective cases. For example, a noun used as a subject (nominative case) will have the same form when used as a direct object (objective case).

NOMINATIVE CASE   That Ming **vase** is very old. [subject]

OBJECTIVE CASE   Who bought the **vase**? [direct object]

    A noun changes its form only in the possessive case, usually by adding an apostrophe and an *s.*

POSSESSIVE CASE   The Ming **vase's** new owner is pleased.

┌HELP──
The nominative case is sometimes referred to as the subject form. The objective case is sometimes referred to as the object form. Follow your teacher's instructions when using these terms.

Reference Note
For more about **forming the possessive case of nouns,** see page 330.

USAGE

Unlike nouns, most personal pronouns have different forms for all three cases.

Personal Pronouns		
Nominative Case	Objective Case	Possessive Case
Singular		
I	me	my, mine
you	you	your, yours
he, she, it	him, her, it	his, her, hers, its
Plural		
we	us	our, ours
you	you	your, yours
they	them	their, theirs

NOTE The personal pronouns in the possessive case—*my, mine, your, yours, his, her, hers, its, our, ours, their, theirs*—are used to show ownership or relationship.

The possessive pronouns *mine, yours, his, hers, its, ours,* and *theirs* are used as parts of sentences in the same ways in which the pronouns in the nominative and the objective cases are used.

EXAMPLES   His book and **mine** are overdue.

This desk is **his.**

We completed **ours** this morning.

The possessive pronouns *my, your, his, her, its, our,* and *their* are used as adjectives before nouns.

EXAMPLES   **My** shoes need to be cleaned.

Have you proofread **her** report yet?

There goes **their** dog Rex.

NOTE Some authorities prefer to call these words adjectives. Follow your teacher's instructions regarding these possessive forms.

The Nominative Case

10b. The *subject* of a verb should be in the nominative case.

EXAMPLES   **He** and **I** mowed lawns. [*He* and *I* are used together as the compound subject of *mowed*.]

Did **they** craft candles from antique molds? [*They* is the subject of *Did craft*.]

She baked cranberry bread while **we** wrapped packages. [*She* is the subject of *baked*. *We* is the subject of *wrapped*.]

Oral Practice 1   **Using Pronouns as Subjects**

Read each of the following sentences aloud, stressing the italicized pronouns.

1. Dr. Chen and *they* discussed the usefulness of herbal medicines.
2. *He* and *I* live next door to each other.
3. *They* should try to get along better.
4. Yesterday *she* and *they* gave their reports on modern African American poets.
5. *You* and *she* left the party early.
6. Since the third grade, *we* have been friends.
7. *He* and his family are moving to Puerto Rico.
8. *I* will miss them.

Exercise 1   **Identifying Correct Pronoun Forms**

Choose the correct form of the pronoun in parentheses in each of the following sentences.

EXAMPLE   **1.** My friends and (*I, me*) like to spend time outdoors.

     1. I

1. Lou and (*me, I*) asked my mother to drive us to a nearby state park.
2. There (*he and I, him and me*) set out on a marked trail through the woods.
3. Before long, (*he and I, him and me*) were exploring a snowy area off the beaten track.
4. At midday Lou and (*me, I*) reluctantly followed our tracks back to the path.
5. (*Us, We*) had had the best time of our lives.

Reference Note

For more about **subjects**, see page 5.

TIPS & TRICKS

To help you choose the correct pronoun in a compound subject, try each form of the pronoun separately.

EXAMPLE
(*She, Her*) and (*I, me*) found them. [*She found* or *Her found*? *I found* or *Me found*?]

ANSWER
She and **I** found them.

USAGE

6. I told Mother that I thought (*she, her*) would enjoy the trail.

7. To my surprise, (*she, her*) wanted to walk part of the trail then.

8. Lou and (*she, her*) immediately started hiking down the trail.

9. (*They, Them*) knew that I would follow.

10. (*Us, We*) had fun but were ready to ride instead of walk home!

10c. A *predicate nominative* should be in the nominative case.

A ***predicate nominative*** is a word or word group that is in the predicate and that identifies or refers to the subject of the verb. A pronoun used as a predicate nominative completes the meaning of a linking verb, usually a form of the verb *be* (such as *am, are, is, was, were, be, been,* or *being*).

EXAMPLES   The candidates should have been **he** and **she.** [*He* and *she* follow the linking verb *should have been* and identify the subject *candidates.*]

The members of the team are **they.** [*They* follows the linking verb *are* and identifies the subject *members.*]

Oral Practice 2   Using Pronouns as Predicate Nominatives

Read each of the following sentences aloud, stressing the italicized pronouns.

1. Were the only Spanish-speaking people you and *they*?

2. The caller could have been *she.*

3. The leaders will be my mother and *he.*

4. The three candidates for class president are *she* and *we.*

5. That must be the pilot and *he* on the runway.

6. The three winners were Eduardo, Maya, and *I.*

7. The first ones on the scene were our neighbors and *they.*

8. The speakers at the rally were *she* and Jesse Jackson.

Exercise 2   Identifying Correct Pronoun Forms

Choose the correct form of the pronoun in parentheses in each of the following sentences.

EXAMPLE   **1.** Were the ones who left early (*they, them*)?

1. *they*

1. Two witnesses claimed that the burglar was (*him, he*).

STYLE   TIP

Expressions such as *It's me* and *That's her* are acceptable in everyday speaking. However, these expressions contain the objective case pronouns *me* and *her* used incorrectly as predicate nominatives. Such expressions should be avoided in formal writing and speaking.

Reference Note

For more about **predicate nominatives,** see page 79.

TIPS & TRICKS

To choose the correct form of a pronoun used as a predicate nominative, try reversing the order of the sentence.

EXAMPLE
The fastest runner is (*he, him*).

REVERSED
(*He, Him*) is the fastest runner.

ANSWER
The fastest runner is **he.**

2. The volunteers must be (*them, they*).
3. Is the last performer (*she, her*)?
4. The next speaker will be (*him, he*).
5. The guests of honor are Luther and (*us, we*).
6. I knew the one in red was (*she, her*), of course.
7. The hardest workers are Susan, Tranh, and (*me, I*).
8. Can that be (*she, her*) in the Indian sari?
9. The next batter should be (*she, her*).
10. Our newest neighbors are the Blumenthals and (*them, they*).

Review A **Writing Sentences That Contain Pronouns in the Nominative Case**

The busy scene you see on the next page was painted by the Mexican American artist Carmen Lomas Garza. It shows one of her childhood birthday parties. The fish-shaped object is a piñata, full of treats for the children. Carmen is getting ready to take a swing at the piñata. Answer each of the following questions by writing a sentence. Follow the directions after each question.

EXAMPLE 1. What are the kneeling boys in the lower right-hand corner doing? (*Use a plural personal pronoun as the subject.*)

1. *They are getting ready to play marbles.*

1. What is Carmen using to hit the piñata? (*Use a singular personal pronoun as the subject.*)
2. For whom are the presents on the table? (*Use a plural personal pronoun as the subject.*)
3. Who will get the gifts and treats inside the piñata? (*Use a person's name and a plural personal pronoun as the compound subject.*)
4. Have you and your classmates ever played a game that requires a blindfold? (*Use a plural and a singular personal pronoun as the compound subject.*)
5. Why does the boy at the far left have presents in his hands? (*Use a singular personal pronoun as the subject.*)
6. What would Carmen say if you asked her, "Who's the birthday girl?" (*Use a singular personal pronoun as a predicate nominative.*)
7. Did Carmen's parents and her grandmother plan the party? (*Use a plural and a singular personal pronoun as a compound predicate nominative.*)

8. Are the baby and his mother near the table having a good time? (*Use* the baby *and a singular personal pronoun as the compound subject.*)

9. Is Carmen's father the man holding the piñata rope? (*Use a singular personal pronoun as a predicate nominative.*)

10. Who is the one now looking at the picture of Carmen Lomas Garza's birthday party? (*Use a singular personal pronoun as a predicate nominative.*)

Reprinted by permission of GRM Associates, Inc., Agents for Children's Book Press, from the book *Family Pictures* by Carmen Lomas Garza, copyright 1990 by Carmen Lomas Garza.

The Objective Case

Reference Note

For more about **direct and indirect objects,** see pages 74 and 76.

10d. ***Direct objects*** **and** ***indirect objects*** **of verbs should be in the objective case.**

A ***direct object*** is a noun, pronoun, or word group that tells *who* or *what* receives the action of the verb.

EXAMPLES   Mom called **me** to the phone. [*Me* tells *whom* Mom called.]

Julia bought sweet potatoes and used **them** to make filling for the empanadas. [*Them* tells *what* she used.]

USAGE

An *indirect object* is a noun, pronoun, or word group that often appears in sentences containing direct objects. An indirect object tells *to whom* or *to what* or *for whom* or *for what* the action of the verb is done.

An indirect object generally comes between an action verb and its direct object.

EXAMPLES   The hostess handed **her** a name tag. [*Her* tells *to whom* the hostess handed the name tag.]

Mr. Tanaka raises large goldfish; he often feeds **them** rice. [*Them* tells *to what* Mr. Tanaka feeds rice.]

NOTE Indirect objects do not follow prepositions. If *to* or *for* precedes a pronoun, the pronoun is an object of a preposition, not an indirect object.

OBJECT OF A PREPOSITION   Send a letter to **me**.
INDIRECT OBJECT   Send **me** a letter.

10 d

TIPS & TRICKS

To help you choose the correct pronoun in a compound object, try each form of the pronoun separately in the sentence.

EXAMPLE
The teacher chose Luisa and (*I, me*). [The teacher chose *I* or The teacher chose *me*?]

ANSWER
The teacher chose Luisa and **me**.

USAGE

Oral Practice 3   **Using Pronouns as Direct Objects and Indirect Objects**

Read each of the following sentences aloud, stressing the italicized pronouns.

1. I took Joe and *her* to a performance by French mimes.
2. The bus driver let Melba, Joe, and *me* off at the corner.
3. An usher gave *us* programs.
4. Another usher showed *them* and *me* our seats.
5. The performers fascinated Melba and *me*.
6. Their costumes delighted the crowd and *her*.
7. No one else impressed Joe and *me* as much as the youngest mime did.
8. We watched *her* exploring the walls of an invisible room.

Exercise 3   **Writing Pronouns Used as Direct Objects and Indirect Objects**

Write an appropriate pronoun for each blank in the sentences on the following page. Use a variety of pronouns, but do not use *you* or *it*.

EXAMPLE   1. Have you seen Kim and _____?
    1. *her*

1. The manager hired Susana and ____.
2. Lana sent ____ and ____ invitations.
3. We gave Grandpa López and ____ round-trip tickets to Mexico City.
4. The firefighters rescued ____ and ____.
5. Aunt Coretta showed my cousins and ____ a carved mask from Nigeria.
6. The show entertained the children and ____.
7. The waiter served ____ and ____ a variety of dumplings.
8. Our team chose ____ and ____ as representatives.
9. The election committee nominated Gerry and ____.
10. The clerk gave Misako and ____ the receipt for the paper lanterns.

Review B Identifying Correct Pronoun Forms

Choose the correct form of each pronoun in parentheses in the following sentences.

EXAMPLE
1. Paul told Ms. Esteban that (*he, him*) and (*I, me*) need a topic for our report.

1. *he, I*

1. In our American history class, some of the other students and (*he, him*) thought that there should be more reports on women.
2. We were interested in Amelia Earhart and wanted to give (*she, her*) the recognition she deserves.
3. The picture on the left, showing Amelia Earhart looking relaxed and confident, interested Paul and (*I, me*).
4. Both (*he, him*) and (*I, me*) were eager to find out more about her contribution to aviation.
5. We learned that it was (*she, her*) who made the first solo flight by a woman across the Atlantic.
6. The fact that Amelia Earhart was the first pilot to fly from Hawaii to California surprised the rest of the class and (*we, us*), too.
7. In 1937, her navigator and (*she, her*) took off in a twin-engine plane for a trip around the world.
8. After (*they, them*) had completed two thirds of the trip, Earhart and her navigator lost contact with radio operators.

9. No one ever saw (*they, them*) or the airplane again.
10. Ms. Esteban and (*we, us*) are among the many people still puzzling over this mystery.

10e. The ***object of a preposition*** should be in the objective case.

A noun or pronoun that follows a preposition is called the ***object of a preposition.*** Together, the preposition, its object, and any modifiers of the object make a ***prepositional phrase.***

EXAMPLES   Before **us** lay rows of green cornstalks. [*Us* is the object of the preposition *Before.*]

The secret is between **him** and **me.** [*Him* and *me* are the compound object of the preposition *between.*]

Please stand next to **her.** [*Her* is the object of the compound preposition *next to.*]

Reference Note

For a list of commonly used **prepositions,** see page 58. For more about **prepositional phrases,** see page 90.

USAGE

Oral Practice 4   **Using Pronouns as Objects of Prepositions**

Read each of the following sentences aloud, stressing the italicized prepositions and pronouns.

1. Mr. Torres divided the burritos *among them* and *us.*
2. At the game Maria sat *near him* and *her.*
3. Rose walked *toward* Nell and *me.*
4. Sam stood *between him* and *me.*
5. Mom ordered sandwiches *for* Hannah and *her.*
6. "*Without* Squanto and *me,* the Pilgrims won't last another winter," thought Samoset.
7. I have read biographies *about him* and Martin Luther.
8. David's parents gave a bar mitzvah party *for him.*

┌ TIPS & TRICKS ┐

To determine the correct pronoun form when the object of a preposition is compound, use each pronoun separately in the prepositional phrase.

EXAMPLE
Maria sent a postcard to (*she, her*) and (*I, me*). [*To she* or *to her*? *To I* or *to me*?]

ANSWER
Maria sent a postcard to **her** and **me.**

Exercise 4   **Choosing Pronouns Used as Objects of Prepositions**

Choose the correct form of the pronoun in parentheses in each of the sentences on the following page.

EXAMPLE   1. Of all the people who traveled with Lewis and Clark, Sacagawea was particularly helpful to (*them, they*).

1. *them*

STYLE TIP

Sometimes pronouns such as *I, he, she, we,* and *they* sound awkward when used as parts of a compound subject. In such cases, it is a good idea to revise the sentence.

AWKWARD
She and we are going to the concert.
They and I will meet for lunch.

REVISED
We are going to the concert with her.
I will meet them for lunch.

USAGE

1. Sacagawea's husband, a guide named Toussaint Charbonneau, joined the expedition with (*her, she*) and their newborn baby.
2. The Shoshone were Sacagawea's people, and she longed to return to (*them, they*).
3. Captain Clark soon realized how important she would be to Lewis and (*he, him*).
4. The land they were exploring was familiar to (*she, her*).
5. Luckily for (*she, her*) and the expedition, they met a group of friendly Shoshone.
6. From (*them, they*), Sacagawea obtained the ponies that Lewis and Clark needed.
7. Sacagawea's baby boy delighted the expedition's leaders, and they took good care of (*he, him*).
8. In fact, Captain Clark made a promise to (*she, her*) and Charbonneau that he would give the boy a good education.
9. At the age of eighteen, the boy befriended a prince and traveled with (*him, he*) in Europe.
10. Although sources disagree about when Sacagawea died, a gravestone for (*she, her*) in Wyoming bears the date April 9, 1884.

STYLE TIP

Just as there are good manners in behavior, there are also good manners in language. In English it is considered polite to put first-person pronouns (*I, me, my, mine, we, us, our, ours*) last in compound constructions.

EXAMPLE
Please return the photos to **Bill, Ellen,** or **me** [not me, Bill, or Ellen].

Review C Identifying Correct Pronoun Forms

Choose the correct form of the pronoun in parentheses in each of the following sentences. Then, tell what part of the sentence each pronoun is: *subject, predicate nominative, direct object, indirect object,* or *object of a preposition.*

EXAMPLE   1. My brother Pete and (*I, me*) wanted to know more about Elizabeth Blackwell.
          1. *I—subject*

1. Mom told Pete and (*I, me*) the story of Elizabeth Blackwell, the first woman to graduate from medical school in the United States.
2. Geneva College granted (*she, her*) a degree in 1849.
3. At first, because she was a woman, no male doctor would let her work for (*he, him*).
4. Pete and (*I, me*) admire Elizabeth Blackwell for not giving up.
5. She wanted to help the poor and opened her own clinic for (*they, them*).

6. Wealthy citizens were soon supporting (*she, her*) and the clinic with donations.
7. Before long, one of the most talked-about topics in medical circles was (*she, her*) and the excellent work she was doing for the poor.
8. Mom and (*we, us*) read more about Dr. Blackwell, and we learned that she opened a medical school just for women.
9. Dr. Blackwell set high standards for students and gave (*they, them*) hard courses of study to complete.
10. Her teaching prepared (*they, them*) well, and many went on to become successful physicians.

Special Pronoun Problems

Who and *Whom*

The pronoun *who* has different forms in the nominative and objective cases. *Who* is the nominative form; *whom* is the objective form.

When you need to decide whether to use *who* or *whom* in a question, follow these steps:

STEP 1	Rephrase the question as a statement.
STEP 2	Decide how the pronoun is used in the statement—as a subject, a predicate nominative, a direct or an indirect object, or an object of a preposition.
STEP 3	Determine the case of the pronoun according to the rules of formal, standard English.
STEP 4	Select the correct form of the pronoun.

EXAMPLE	(*Who, Whom*) is she?
STEP 1	The statement is *She is* (*who, whom*).
STEP 2	The pronoun is a predicate nominative that refers to the subject *She.*
STEP 3	A pronoun used as a predicate nominative should be in the nominative case.
STEP 4	The nominative form is *who.*
ANSWER:	**Who** is she?

STYLE TIP

In informal English, the use of *whom* is becoming less common. In fact, in informal situations, you may correctly begin a question with *who* regardless of the grammar of the sentence. In formal English, however, you should distinguish between *who* and *whom*.

EXAMPLE   (*Who, Whom*) will you invite to the dance?

STEP 1   The statement is *You will invite (who, whom) to the dance.*

STEP 2   The pronoun is the direct object of the verb *will invite.*

STEP 3   A pronoun used as a direct object should be in the objective case.

STEP 4   The objective form is *whom.*

ANSWER: **Whom** will you invite to the dance?

Oral Practice 5 Using *Who* and *Whom*

Read each of the following sentences aloud, stressing the italicized pronouns.

1. *Who* is captain of the football team this year?
2. To *whom* did you give your old skateboard?
3. *Whom* will you call to come and pick us up after band practice?
4. *Who* were the first Americans?
5. In the last play of the game, *who* passed the ball to *whom*?
6. *Who*'s that woman in the green sari?
7. For *whom* did you buy those flowers?
8. *Who* painted that beautiful picture?

Exercise 5 Choosing *Who* or *Whom*

Choose the correct form of the pronoun in parentheses in each of the following sentences.

EXAMPLE   1. (*Who, Whom*) helped load the hay on the wagon this morning?

1. Who

2. To (*who, whom*) are you going to give the award?

2. whom

1. (*Who, Whom*) will your brother invite to his birthday party?
2. (*Who, Whom*) will be our substitute teacher while Mr. Chen is away?
3. (*Who, Whom*) has Ms. Spears appointed?
4. Of the three candidates, in (*who, whom*) do you have the most confidence?
5. To (*who, whom*) do you wish these balloons sent?
6. For (*who, whom*) is the package that was delivered?

7. (*Who, Whom*) is the architect of the new library building?
8. With (*who, whom*) would you most like to talk?
9. Among your friends, (*who, whom*) is the tallest?
10. (*Who, Whom*) have the students elected class president?

Pronouns with Appositives

Sometimes a pronoun is followed directly by a noun that identifies the pronoun. Such a noun is called an ***appositive.*** To help you choose which pronoun to use before an appositive, omit the appositive and try each form of the pronoun separately.

Reference Note

For more about **appositives,** see page 301.

EXAMPLE On Saturdays, (*we, us*) cyclists ride to Mount McCabe and back. [*Cyclists* is the appositive identifying the pronoun.]
We ride or *Us ride*?

ANSWER On Saturdays, **we** cyclists ride to Mount McCabe and back.

EXAMPLE The speaker praised (*we, us*) volunteers. [*Volunteers* is the appositive identifying the pronoun.]
The speaker praised we or *The speaker praised us*?

ANSWER The speaker praised **us** volunteers.

Exercise 6 Choosing Correct Pronouns

Choose the correct form of the pronoun in parentheses in each of the following sentences.

EXAMPLE 1. Hanukkah is always an exciting holiday for (*we, us*) Feldmans.

1. *us*

1. Tiger Woods is a role model for (*we, us*) golfers.
2. Miss Jefferson, (*we, us*) students want to thank you for all your help.
3. (*We, Us*) contestants shook hands warmly.
4. The woman gave (*we, us*) girls five dollars for shoveling the snow.
5. The attorneys politely answered the questions from (*we, us*) reporters.
6. For (*we, us*) volunteers, service is its own reward.
7. Frank loaned (*we, us*) fans two classical albums.

USAGE

8. The pilot flew (*we, us*) passengers to Chicago.

9. (*We, Us*) actors need to rehearse again before Friday night.

10. The new team members were (*we, us*) boys.

Reflexive Pronouns

┌HELP───

The pronouns *himself* and *themselves* can also be used as intensive pronouns.

EXAMPLES
Daniel **himself** will lead the parade.

They **themselves** traveled only twenty miles to get here.

Reference Note

For more about **reflexive and intensive pronouns,** see page 31.

Do not use the nonstandard forms *hisself* and *theirself* or *theirselves* in place of *himself* and *themselves*.

| NONSTANDARD | The secretary voted for hisself in the last election. |
| STANDARD | The secretary voted for **himself** in the last election. |

| NONSTANDARD | The cooks served theirselves some of the hot won-ton soup. |
| STANDARD | The cooks served **themselves** some of the hot won-ton soup. |

Exercise 7 Identifying Correct Pronoun Forms

Choose the correct form of the pronoun in parentheses in each of the following sentences.

EXAMPLE 1. The contestants promised (*theirselves, themselves*) it would be a friendly competition.

1. *themselves*

1. Before he started to read, Zack asked (*hisself, himself*) three questions to set his purpose.

2. My little brother often falls down, but he never seems to hurt (*himself, hisself*).

3. The guests helped (*theirselves, themselves*) to the nuts and raisins.

4. John Yellowtail enjoys (*himself, hisself*) when he is making fine silver jewelry.

5. When the early settlers wanted cloth, they had to spin it (*theirselves, themselves*).

6. My brother was upset with (*hisself, himself*) for being rude.

7. Andrew gave (*himself, hisself*) an early birthday present—a new CD.

8. The Sartens talked (*theirselves, themselves*) out of buying a second vehicle.

9. Uncle Allen took the last potatoes for (*hisself, himself*) and passed the broccoli to me.
10. Bart and Ana consider (*theirself, themselves*) authorities on stamp collecting.

DRABBLE reprinted by permission of United Feature Syndicate, Inc.

Review D **Identifying Correct Pronoun Forms**

Choose the correct form of the pronoun in parentheses in each of the following sentences.

EXAMPLE   **1.** To me, the two most interesting explorers are (*he, him*) and Vasco da Gama.

    1. *he*

1. The team captains will be Jack and (*he, him*).
2. The finalists in our school talent contest are Alexandra, Tomás, and (*I, me*).
3. We were praised by our parents and (*they, them*).
4. The Washington twins and (*I, me*) belong to the same club.
5. Both (*he and she, her and him*) promised to mail us postcards from Buenos Aires.
6. Pelé and (*he, him*) both played soccer for the New York Cosmos.
7. "What do you think of (*he and I, him and me*)?" I asked.
8. "You and (*he, him*) are improving," they replied.
9. When Miriam Makeba and the troupe of African musicians arrived, we gave (*she and they, her and them*) a party.
10. Do you remember my sister and (*I, me*)?
11. The coach spoke to (*we, us*) players before the game.
12. Was the joke played on you and (*he, him*)?
13. Are you and (*she, her*) going to celebrate Kwanzaa this year?
14. Madame Durand taught my brother and (*I, me*) several phrases in French.

15. Mom, Andy gave (*himself, hisself*) the biggest piece of banana bread.
16. Who are (*they, them*), Travis?
17. They congratulated (*themselves, theirselves*) on a difficult job well done.
18. Don't leave without (*he and I, him and me*).
19. (*We, Us*) skiers had a beautiful view from the lift.
20. (*Who, Whom*) were you expecting?
21. When we met at the auditions for the school play last year, (*he and I, him and me*) got along very well right away.
22. (*Who, Whom*) recommended that book about the history of Ireland to you?
23. When Sharon and (*I, me*) work on homework together, we always get through it faster and remember it better.
24. (*Who, Whom*) will you be tutoring from the elementary school, Margaret Tanaka or Billy Worthington?
25. Everyone agreed that the science project designed by Shannon and (*him, he*) was the best one in the show.

Clear Reference

A pronoun should refer clearly to its ***antecedent,*** the word or word group the pronoun stands for. If a pronoun could refer to more than one antecedent, revise the sentence to make the meaning clear.

UNCLEAR	Jeremy promised to meet Sean in front of his house. [To whom does *his* refer? Are Jeremy and Sean meeting in front of Jeremy's house or in front of Sean's house?]
CLEAR	Jeremy promised to meet Sean in front of Sean's house.
	or
CLEAR	Jeremy promised to meet Sean in front of Jeremy's house.

UNCLEAR	Mr. Cassner asked Todd to file the memo after he had read it. [To whom does *he* refer? Is Todd filing the memo after Mr. Cassner has read it or after Todd has read it?]
CLEAR	After Mr. Cassner had read the memo, he asked Todd to file it.
	or
CLEAR	Mr. Cassner asked Todd to file the memo after Todd had read it.

MEETING THE CHALLENGE

Unclear pronoun references may confuse your reader. Compose five sentences that each contain an unclear pronoun reference. Then, write a revision that clarifies the unclear reference for each sentence.

USAGE

Exercise 8 Revising for Clear Pronoun Reference

Revise each of the following sentences, correcting each unclear pronoun reference.

HELP—

Sentences in Exercise 8 may have more than one correct answer.

EXAMPLE   1. The dog and the cat were both eating out of its dish.

1. *The dog and the cat were both eating out of the dog's dish.*

1. Jessica waved to Betsy while she was riding the Ferris wheel.
2. Byron told Alec that his cousin was on the telephone.
3. After Tracey and Jen arrived home, their mom gave her a birthday bouquet.
4. Tabitha asked Jill whether she could help with the painting.
5. As soon as Brett saw Carlos, he said hello.
6. The beagle and the Dalmatian played with its old chew toy.
7. Jake helped Austin clean the kitchen after he had finished preparing the bread dough.
8. Mr. Lewis told Mr. Washington that he had won the award.
9. As soon as she completed the chores, Wendy and Lori left for the soccer game.
10. Kip didn't see Matt at the pep rally until he stood on the bleachers.

Review E Revising Sentences for Correct Pronoun
Forms and Clear Pronoun Reference

Revise each of the following sentences, correcting each incorrect
pronoun form and unclear pronoun reference. If a sentence is
already correct, write *C*.

EXAMPLE 1. The twins, Veronica and Caroline, were reading her
Caldecott Honor Book together.

1. *The twins, Veronica and Caroline, were reading
Veronica's Caldecott Honor Book together.*

1. Malcolm met Aaron at the branch library after he got
off work.
2. Peter and she were leaving the art museum.
3. The winner of the race is him.
4. Carnell spoke to Ed and I before hockey practice.
5. Who should I ask?
6. Joseph asked Matthew to wash his dirty dishes before their
mom came home from work.
7. Elizabeth gave miniature roses to Lee and they.
8. Lisa asked Terri whether she could bake bread for our fund-
raiser.
9. Katherine informed Theresa that she needed to change the
oil in the car.
10. He and Angela won trophies yesterday.

Chapter Review

A. Identifying Correct Pronoun Forms

Identify the correct form of the pronoun in parentheses in each of the following sentences.

1. The counselor chose (*we, us*) students to give the tour.

2. Don't worry; my stepmother will take you and (*I, me*) home.

3. Ms. Chavez sat between Kareem and (*I, me*) at the assembly.

4. It's a shame that the boys hurt (*themselves, theirselves*) last night.

5. Will you and (*I, me*) be able to reach them in time?

6. Mayor Petrakis asked my mom and (*she, her*) to help.

7. Is this (*she, her*) to whom we spoke yesterday?

8. Our coach e-mailed (*we, us*) sprinters about the next meet.

9. The fastest typists in class are Tamika and (*they, them*).

10. While we were at the store, we saw my cousin and (*she, her*).

11. Our dog Piper will bring the ball to (*he, him*) or (*she, her*).

12. Last night Dad told Carlyn and (*I, me*) a story.

13. (*Whom, Who*) wrote *The Wind in the Willows*?

14. (*We, Us*) students were not expecting the pop quiz.

15. The referee signaled (*we, us*) players to begin the game.

16. The best calligrapher in the school is (*she, her*).

17. (*Whom, Who*) is the better candidate?

18. To (*who, whom*) is the letter addressed?

19. Roger and (*I, me*) are studying for our lifeguard certificates.

20. Derek looked at (*hisself, himself*) in the mirror.

B. Correcting Errors in Pronoun Forms

Most of the following sentences contain an error in the use of pronoun forms. Identify the error, and give the correct form for each sentence. If a sentence is already correct, write *C*.

21. May us choir members leave science class early today?

22. To who are you sending the flowers?

23. The opening procession of the Olympics will be led by he.

24. Please give these copies of Consuela's report to her and the committee members.
25. Him and his best friend watched the World Cup finals.
26. Darnell enjoyed hisself at the African Heritage Festival.
27. The last tennis player to beat my sister in straight sets was her.
28. Who have you asked for help with your math homework?
29. Tell Jennifer and I what your science project will be this year.
30. Whom did you invite to the awards ceremony?
31. Us science fiction fans are going to the book signing.
32. Who will we see at the mosque?
33. Mario's mother will be driving Elena and we to the stadium.
34. Emilio and him volunteered to decorate the cafeteria.
35. The perfect person to play Lady Macbeth is she.
36. Neither Kevin nor I can decide which of Ray Bradbury's stories we like best.
37. Whom are the most famous inventors in history?
38. Last year, the best piñata was designed by the twins and she.
39. They really outdid theirselves!
40. You should hear the fight song written by us four fans this year!
41. My father and me watched *Amadeus* on video last night.
42. Between you and I, I think Ko will win the Web page contest.
43. The state trooper gave her a ticket for an illegal left turn.
44. The last people to arrive at the party were Cordelia and him.
45. Mom, will you take us tired yard workers out for dinner?

C. Revising for Clear Pronoun Reference

Revise each of the following sentences, correcting each unclear pronoun reference.

46. When she arrived, Sonia asked Liz for a pen.
47. As soon as Grant and Patrick paddled back to the dock, he lashed the boat securely.
48. The tabby cat and the beagle both curled up on its rug before the warm fireplace.
49. Sheila waved to Juliet as she biked along the trail.
50. Before Sara met Jan, she had never been kayaking.

┌HELP──

Sentences in Part C of the Chapter Review may have more than one possible answer.

Writing Application
Using Pronouns in a Letter

Nominative and Objective Case Your favorite radio station is having a "Create a Radio Show" contest. Write a letter to the manager of the station explaining what you would like to include in a half-hour weekly radio show. In your letter, use a variety of pronouns in the nominative case and the objective case. Be sure to include enough nouns so that the meaning of all your pronouns is clear.

Prewriting Discuss your ideas for a radio program with a group of your classmates. List the kinds of entertainment and information you could present. Above all, think about what you would like to hear on the radio.

Writing As you write your first draft, follow the format for a business letter. Give specific examples of what you want to do on the show, and give reasons for your choices. Remember that even though your ideas may be very creative, your writing must be formal.

Revising Ask the other group members to read your letter to see if your ideas sound interesting and are clearly stated. Ask them if the relationship between each pronoun and its antecedent is clear. If your meaning is not clear, revise your letter.

Publishing Re-read your letter, and correct any remaining errors in usage, spelling, punctuation, or capitalization. Be sure that you have followed the correct format for a business letter. Also, make sure that you have used all pronouns according to the rules for standard written English. With your teacher's permission, the class might vote on the best idea for a show and then produce and tape the pilot episode.

USAGE

Using Modifiers Correctly

Comparison and Placement

Diagnostic Preview

┌HELP─

Although two possible answers are shown, you need to give only one answer for each item in the Diagnostic Preview.

Revising Sentences by Correcting Errors in the Use of Modifiers

Most of the following sentences contain errors in the use, form, or placement of modifiers. Revise each incorrect sentence to eliminate the error. If a sentence is already correct, write *C*.

EXAMPLE **1.** There wasn't nothing missing.

1. *There wasn't anything missing.*

or

There was nothing missing.

1. Please weigh both packages to see which of them is heaviest.
2. Alarmed, the wildfire started to spread quickly to our camp.
3. Did you read that Eduardo Mata received an award in the newspaper?
4. The bean soup tasted good.
5. We pass my aunt and uncle's restaurant walking to school.
6. I think the play *Fiddler on the Roof* is better than the movie.
7. Reading a magazine, my cat jumped up in my lap.
8. Jason tried to push the huge desk but couldn't scarcely move it.
9. The balloons startled the young children when they burst.
10. A jet taking off can sound more noisier than a jackhammer.

11. Surprised, my coin collection interested a local coin dealer.
12. He examined two old Greek coins but couldn't see no date.
13. The shinier of those two coins looked newer.
14. That coin turned out to be the oldest of the two, however.
15. I showed one coin to the dealer valued at nearly twenty dollars.
16. He said he couldn't hardly pay more than fifteen dollars for it.
17. If I had bargained good, I might have gotten more for it.
18. Those two coins come from Ireland that have images of harps on them.
19. Collecting coins, my knowledge about other countries and peoples increases.
20. I polished my Saudi Arabian fifty-halala piece careful so that I could see the Arabic writing on it.

What Is a Modifier?

A *modifier* is a word, a phrase, or a clause that makes the meaning of a word or word group more specific. The two kinds of modifiers are *adjectives* and *adverbs*.

One-Word Modifiers

Adjectives

11a. *Adjectives* make the meanings of nouns and pronouns more specific.

ADJECTIVES   Andy gave a **loud** cheer. [The adjective *loud* tells *what kind* of cheer.]

The one I made is **blue**. [The adjective *blue* tells *which one*.]

Adverbs

11b. *Adverbs* make the meanings of verbs, adjectives, and other adverbs more specific.

ADVERBS   Andy cheered **loudly**. [The adverb *loudly* makes the meaning of the verb *cheered* more specific.]

Reference Note

For more about **adjectives,** see page 34. For more about **adverbs,** see page 54.

┌─────────────────────┐
│ T I P S & T R I C K S │
└─────────────────────┘

Many adverbs end in *–ly,* but many others do not. Furthermore, not all words with the *–ly* ending are adverbs. Some adjectives end in *–ly.*

ADVERBS
quickly   soon
calmly   not

ADJECTIVES
elderly   holy
curly   silly

To decide whether a word is an adjective or an adverb, look at how the word is used in the sentence.

What Is a Modifier?   **223**

The design is **very** modern. [The adverb *very* makes the meaning of the adjective *modern* more specific.]

The crocodile moved **surprisingly** quickly. [The adverb *surprisingly* makes the meaning of the adverb *quickly* more specific.]

Phrases Used as Modifiers

Like one-word modifiers, phrases can also be used as adjectives and adverbs.

Reference Note

For more about different kinds of **phrases,** see Chapter 5.

EXAMPLES   **Leaping from the step,** the toddler flapped his arms in the air. [The participial phrase *Leaping from the step* acts as an adjective that modifies the noun *toddler.*]

The Greek salad is the one **to try.** [The infinitive phrase *to try* acts as an adjective that modifies the pronoun *one.*]

Ms. Elizondo planted rosebushes **along the fence.** [The prepositional phrase *along the fence* acts as an adverb that modifies the verb *planted.*]

Clauses Used as Modifiers

Like words and phrases, clauses can also be used as modifiers.

Reference Note

For more about **clauses,** see Chapter 6.

EXAMPLES   Italian is the language **that I like best.** [The adjective clause *that I like best* modifies the noun *language.*]

Before Albert went to school, he took the trash to the curb. [The adverb clause *Before Albert went to school* modifies the verb *took.*]

Comparison of Adjectives and Adverbs

When adjectives and adverbs are used in comparisons, they take different forms. The specific form they take depends upon how many things are being compared. The different forms of comparison are called *degrees of comparison.*

USAGE

11c. The three degrees of comparison of modifiers are the *positive*, the *comparative*, and the *superlative*.

(1) The ***positive degree*** is used when at least one thing is being described.

EXAMPLES   This suitcase is **heavy.**

Luís **cheerfully** began the job.

Those murals are **colorful.**

(2) The ***comparative degree*** is used when two things or groups of things are being compared.

EXAMPLES   My suitcase is **heavier** than yours.

Luís talked **more cheerfully** than Albert.

Those murals are **more colorful** than these.

(3) The ***superlative degree*** is used when three or more things or groups of things are being compared.

EXAMPLES   Sylvia's suitcase is the **heaviest** of all.

Of the four boys, Luís worked at the task **most cheerfully.**

Those murals are the **most colorful** ones I've seen.

Regular Comparison

Most one-syllable modifiers form the comparative degree by adding *–er* and the superlative degree by adding *–est*.

Positive	Comparative	Superlative
close	clos**er**	clos**est**
slow	slow**er**	slow**est**
soon	soon**er**	soon**est**
straight	straight**er**	straight**est**

Notice that both adjectives and adverbs form their degrees of comparison in the same way.

USAGE

STYLE   TIP

In conversation, you may hear and use expressions such as *Put your best foot forward* and *May the best team win.* Such uses of the superlative are acceptable in spoken English. However, in your writing for school and other formal occasions, you should generally use superlatives only when three or more things are compared.

Reference Note

For guidelines on how to spell words when **adding –er or –est,** see page 353.

HELP

Here is a way to remember which form of a modifier to use. When comparing two things, use *–er* (the two-letter ending). When comparing three or more things, use *–est* (the three-letter ending).

Two-syllable modifiers form the comparative degree by adding –*er* or by using *more*. They form the superlative degree by adding –*est* or by using *most*.

Positive	Comparative	Superlative
simple	simpl**er**	simpl**est**
easy	easi**er**	easi**est**
jealous	**more** jealous	**most** jealous
swiftly	**more** swiftly	**most** swiftly

Modifiers that have three or more syllables form the comparative degree by using *more* and the superlative degree by using *most*.

Positive	Comparative	Superlative
powerful	**more** powerful	**most** powerful
illegible	**more** illegible	**most** illegible
joyfully	**more** joyfully	**most** joyfully
attractively	**more** attractively	**most** attractively

STYLE   TIP

Many two-syllable modifiers can correctly form the comparative and superlative degrees using either the suffixes –*er* and –*est* or the words *more* and *most*. If adding –*er* or –*est* sounds awkward, use *more* or *most*.

AWKWARD
  bitterer
  comicest

BETTER
  more bitter
  most comic

Exercise 1 **Forming the Degrees of Comparison of Modifiers**

Give the forms for the comparative and superlative degrees of the following modifiers.

EXAMPLE   **1.** light
              1. lighter; lightest

1. near	**6.** tiny	**11.** healthy	**16.** confident
2. proud	**7.** timidly	**12.** tall	**17.** enthusiastically
3. carefully	**8.** loyal	**13.** grateful	**18.** dry
4. honestly	**9.** safe	**14.** quick	**19.** tasty
5. small	**10.** shady	**15.** easy	**20.** generous

Decreasing Comparison

To show decreasing comparisons, modifiers form the comparative degree by using *less* and the superlative degree by using *least*.

Positive	Comparative	Superlative
sharp	**less** sharp	**least** sharp
costly	**less** costly	**least** costly
often	**less** often	**least** often
frequently	**less** frequently	**least** frequently

Irregular Comparison

The comparative and superlative degrees of some modifiers are irregular in form.

Positive	Comparative	Superlative
bad	worse	worst
far	farther *or* further	farthest *or* furthest
good	better	best
well	better	best
many	more	most
much	more	most

Review A **Writing Comparative and Superlative Forms of Modifiers**

Correctly complete each of the following sentences with the comparative or superlative form of the italicized adjective or adverb given.

EXAMPLE   **1.** *unusual*   The Corn Palace in Mitchell, South Dakota, is one of the _____ buildings in the United States.

    1. most unusual

1. *big*   The Corn Palace is _____ than I thought it would be.

2. *pretty*   People in Mitchell try to make each year's Corn Palace decorations _____ than the ones before.

3. *fresh*   The building looks the _____ in September after new corn and grasses are put on it.

4. *easy*   Some workers find it _____ to saw and nail the corn to panels, while others prefer to hang the finished panels on the building.

USAGE

5. *well*   I could not decide which of the many corn murals on the Corn Palace I liked ____.

6. *mysterious*   The mural of the dancing figure was the ____ one to me.

7. *famous*   Until his death in 1983, Mitchell's ____ artist, Oscar Howe, helped to design and paint these murals.

8. *interesting*   The life of this Sioux artist is the ____ story I've ever heard.

9. *slowly*   My parents walked ____ around the Corn Palace than I did and studied every design.

10. *often*   I met a family from Mexico who had traveled ____ than we had to see the Corn Palace.

Special Problems in Using Modifiers

11d. Use *good* to modify a noun or a pronoun in most cases. Use *well* to modify a verb.

Reference Note

For more about **using good and well**, see page 249.

EXAMPLES   The weather was **good** on the day of the match. [*Good* modifies the noun *weather.*]

If you want a pear, here is a **good** one. [*Good* modifies the pronoun *one.*]

The trees are producing **well** this fall. [*Well* modifies the verb phrase *are producing.*]

Good should not be used to modify a verb.

NONSTANDARD   Both teams played good.

STANDARD   Both teams played **well.**

Although *well* is usually used as an adverb, *well* may also be used as an adjective meaning "in good health" or "in good condition."

EXAMPLE   Mom feels quite **well** today. [Meaning "in good health," *well* modifies *Mom*.]

Reference Note
For a discussion of **standard and non-standard English,** see page 245.

11e. Use adjectives, not adverbs, after linking verbs.

Linking verbs are often followed by predicate adjectives modifying the subject.

EXAMPLES   Ingrid looked **sleepy** [not *sleepily*] this morning. [The predicate adjective *sleepy* modifies the subject *Ingrid*.]

Christina felt **uncertain** [not *uncertainly*] about running in the relay race. [The predicate adjective *uncertain* modifies the subject *Christina*.]

Reference Note
For a list of **linking verbs,** see page 46.

USAGE

NOTE   Some verbs can be used as either linking or action verbs. As action verbs, they may be modified by adverbs.

EXAMPLES   Ingrid looked **sleepily** at the clock. [*Sleepily* modifies the action verb *looked*.]

Christina **uncertainly** felt her way along the hall. [*Uncertainly* modifies the action verb *felt*.]

Exercise 2   **Using Adjectives and Adverbs Correctly**

Choose the adjective or adverb that will make each sentence correct.

EXAMPLE   **1.** John seems (*nervous, nervously*) about his speech.

   1. nervous

1. When we came into the house after ice-skating, the fire felt (*good, well*).
2. The wind sounds (*fierce, fiercely*) at night.
3. Tino looked (*good, well*) after recovering from his operation.
4. After all, it doesn't taste (*bad, badly*).
5. Venus looks (*beautiful, beautifully*) tonight.
6. Liang cooked a (*good, well*) meal of vegetables and shrimp.

7. Is the sick child feeling (*good, well*) enough to eat something?

8. We looked (*close, closely*) at the fragile cocoon.

9. A cup of soup tastes (*good, well*) on a cold day.

10. Kudzu grows (*rapid, rapidly*) in the South.

11f. Avoid using double comparisons.

A *double comparison* is the incorrect use of both *–er* and *more* (or *less*) or *–est* and *most* (or *least*) to form a comparison. When you make a comparison, use only one form, not both.

NONSTANDARD	This is Kathleen Battle's most finest performance.
STANDARD	This is Kathleen Battle's **finest** performance.

NONSTANDARD	His hair is more curlier than his sister's.
STANDARD	His hair is **curlier** than his sister's.

NONSTANDARD	The baby is less fussier in the morning than in the evening.
STANDARD	The baby is **less fussy** in the morning than in the evening.

Exercise 3 **Correcting Double Comparisons**

Identify the incorrect modifier in each of the following sentences. Then, give the correct form of the modifier.

EXAMPLES
1. I have been studying more harder lately.

1. more harder—harder

2. Frederick Douglass was one of the most brilliantest speakers against slavery.

2. most brilliantest—most brilliant

1. Sunday was less rainier than Saturday.

2. That is the most saddest story I have ever heard.

3. Are you exercising more oftener than you used to?

4. That evening was the least cloudiest one in weeks.

5. Native arctic peoples have learned to survive in the most coldest weather.

6. Please show me the most finest tennis racket in the shop.

7. It is more farther from New York to Montreal than from New York to Boston.

8. Grumpkins was less jollier than the other elves.

9. Your suitcase is more lighter since you took out the boots.
10. Is Venus the most brightest object in the sky tonight?

Double Negatives

11g. Avoid using double negatives.

A *double negative* is the use of two or more negative words to express one negative idea. Most of the negative words in the chart below are adjectives or adverbs.

Common Negative Words			
barely	never	none	nothing
hardly	no	no one	nowhere
neither	nobody	not (–n't)	scarcely

NONSTANDARD	We couldn't hardly move in the subway car.
STANDARD	We **could hardly** move in the subway car.

NONSTANDARD	Yolanda didn't eat no breakfast this morning.
STANDARD	Yolanda **didn't** eat **any** breakfast this morning.
STANDARD	Yolanda **ate no** breakfast this morning.

NONSTANDARD	Didn't she get you nothing for your birthday?
STANDARD	**Didn't** she get you **anything** for your birthday?
STANDARD	Did she get you **nothing** for your birthday?

Oral Practice **Correcting Double Negatives**

Read each of the following sentences aloud. Then, say each sentence again, correcting the double negative.

EXAMPLE   **1.** I couldn't find no one to go camping with me.
        1. I couldn't find anyone to go camping with me.
            or
        I could find no one to go camping with me.

1. I didn't see no one I knew at the game.
2. Early Spanish explorers searched that area of Florida for gold, but they didn't find none.

┌HELP─

Although two possible answers are given for the example in the Oral Practice, you need to give only one revision for each item.

3. We couldn't hardly hear the guest speaker.

4. The cafeteria didn't serve nothing I like today.

5. Double negatives don't have no place in standard English.

6. The bird-watchers saw scarcely no bald eagles this year.

7. The club officers never do none of the work themselves.

8. We wouldn't never need three tractors on our small farm.

9. Jesse couldn't barely see the top of the waterfalls.

10. The Paynes didn't go nowhere special during the three-day holiday weekend.

Review B **Using Modifiers Correctly**

Most of the following sentences contain errors in the use of modifiers. Revise each incorrect sentence to eliminate the error. If a sentence is already correct, write *C*.

EXAMPLES   **1.** My cold is worst today than it was yesterday.

   1. My cold is worse today than it was yesterday.

   2. There wasn't nobody willing to go into that house alone.

   2. There wasn't anybody willing to go into that house alone.

1. She is the funnier of the two comedians.

2. Kendo, a Japanese martial art, is more gracefuller than many other sports.

3. No one in our class can play volleyball as good as Sylvia Yee.

4. Time passes real slowly during the summer.

5. After a long swim, she felt good.

6. I wasn't scarcely able to hear you.

7. Which of the Rogers twins is strongest?

8. Some people don't seem to have no control over their tempers.

9. He hardly ever visits us.

10. Of all the folk dances my grandfather taught me, the polka is the most simplest.

Placement of Modifiers

11h. Place modifying words, phrases, and clauses as close as possible to the words they modify.

USAGE

Notice how the meaning of the following sentence changes when the position of the phrase *from Cincinnati* changes.

EXAMPLES   The basketball player **from Cincinnati** gave a TV interview for his fans. [The phrase modifies *player.*]

The basketball player gave a TV interview for his fans **from Cincinnati.** [The phrase modifies *fans.*]

From Cincinnati the basketball player gave a TV interview for his fans. [The phrase modifies *gave.*]

A modifier that seems to modify the wrong word in a sentence is called a *misplaced modifier.* A modifier that does not clearly modify another word in a sentence is called a *dangling modifier.*

MISPLACED   Ringing, everyone glared at the man with the cell phone.

CORRECT   Everyone glared at the man with the **ringing** cell phone.

DANGLING   Before moving to Philadelphia, Mexico City was their home.

CORRECT   **Before moving to Philadelphia,** they lived in Mexico City.

Prepositional Phrases

A *prepositional phrase* consists of a preposition, a noun or a pronoun called the *object of the preposition,* and any modifiers of that object.

A prepositional phrase used as an adjective generally should be placed directly after the word it modifies.

MISPLACED   The hat belongs to that girl with the feathers.

CLEAR   The hat **with the feathers** belongs to that girl.

A prepositional phrase used as an adverb should be placed near the word it modifies.

MISPLACED   She read that a new restaurant had opened in today's newspaper.

CLEAR   She read **in today's newspaper** that a new restaurant had opened.

STYLE TIP

Be sure to place modifiers correctly to show clearly the meaning you intend.

EXAMPLES

Only Mrs. Garza teaches Spanish. [Mrs. Garza, not anybody else, teaches Spanish.]

Mrs. Garza **only** teaches Spanish. [Mrs. Garza teaches Spanish; she does not research Spanish texts.]

Mrs. Garza teaches **only** Spanish. [Mrs. Garza does not teach any other subjects.]

USAGE

Reference Note

For more about **prepositions,** see page 58. For more about **prepositional phrases,** see page 59.

Avoid placing a prepositional phrase so that it seems to modify either of two words. Place the phrase so that it clearly modifies the word you intend it to modify.

MISPLACED | Manuel said in the afternoon he would call Janet.
[Does *in the afternoon* modify *said* or *would call*?]

CLEAR | Manuel said he would call Janet **in the afternoon.**
[The phrase modifies *would call*.]

CLEAR | **In the afternoon** Manuel said he would call Janet.
[The phrase modifies *said*.]

Exercise 4 Revising Sentences with Misplaced Prepositional Phrases

Each of the following sentences contains a misplaced prepositional phrase. Decide where the prepositional phrase belongs; then, revise the sentence.

EXAMPLES
1. In the United States, Zora Neale Hurston grew up in the first self-governed black township.
1. *Zora Neale Hurston grew up in the first self-governed black township in the United States.*

2. The cat toy rolled down the hall with a clatter.
2. *With a clatter, the cat toy rolled down the hall.*

1. Joshua and Reginald heard that there was a destructive hailstorm on the news.
2. The poster caught my eye on the wall.
3. In the tiny bird's nest, we thought there might be eggs.
4. Our teacher said on Monday the class would put on a play.
5. Don't forget to take the box to the store with the empty bottles.
6. We saw José Clemente Orozco's beautiful murals on vacation in Guadalajara.
7. Tranh read that a wasp larva spins a cocoon in the encyclopedia.
8. A beautiful Bolivian weaving hangs on our living room wall from the town of Trinidad.
9. Did you find the kimonos worn by your grandmother in that old trunk?
10. In confusion, they watched with amusement as the puppies scrambled all over each other.

Exercise 5 Placing Prepositional Phrases Correctly

Rewrite each of the following sentences, adding the prepositional phrase given in parentheses.

EXAMPLE 1. Many paintings show strange, fantastical scenes. (*by Marc Chagall*)

1. Many paintings by Marc Chagall show strange, fantastical scenes.

1. Chagall's *The Green Violinist* contains many delightful mysteries and surprises. (*for the eye and mind*)
2. As you can see in the painting, a gigantic violinist sits among the buildings of a small village. (*with a green face and hand*)
3. Dark windows look just like the windows of the houses. (*on the musician's pants*)
4. A man waves to the violinist, and a dog taller than a house seems to smile at the music it hears. (*above the clouds*)
5. As you look at the painting's bright colors, perhaps you can almost hear the enchanting music. (*of the green violinist*)
6. You may be surprised to learn that the fiddler is found in many of Chagall's other works. (*in this painting*)
7. Chagall enjoyed listening to his uncle play the violin. (*during his childhood*)
8. *The Green Violinist* and other paintings of the fiddler are tributes. (*to Chagall's uncle*)
9. In a painting titled *Violinist*, Chagall painted himself standing. (*beside the violinist*)
10. In that unusual painting, Chagall has three heads turned to show enjoyment of the music. (*toward the uncle*)

The Granger Collection, New York

Reference Note

For more information about **participles,** see page 98. For more about **participial phrases,** see page 100.

A dangling modifier often occurs when a sentence is in the passive voice. Rewriting sentences in the active voice not only eliminates many dangling modifiers but also makes your writing more interesting and lively.

The following sentence contains a dangling modifier. Rewrite the sentence in the active voice to remove the dangling modifier.

Having just waxed the car, a trip to the fair was planned.

Reference Note

For more about **active voice and passive voice,** see page 189.

Reference Note

For more information on **using commas with participial phrases,** see pages 299 and 305.

Participial Phrases

A *participial phrase* consists of a present participle or a past participle and its modifiers and complements. A participial phrase is used as an adjective to modify a noun or a pronoun. Like a prepositional phrase, a participial phrase should be placed as close as possible to the word it modifies.

EXAMPLES **Walking to school,** Celia and James found a wallet. [The participial phrase modifies *Celia* and *James.*]

The chair, **built by my grandfather,** is my favorite. [The participial phrase modifies *The chair.*]

A participial phrase that is not placed near the noun or pronoun that it modifies is a *misplaced modifier.*

MISPLACED Stolen from the media center, the deputies found the camera. [Were the deputies stolen from the media center?]

CLEAR The deputies found the camera **stolen from the media center.**

MISPLACED Sleeping on the roof, I saw the neighbor's cat. [Was I sleeping on the roof?]

CLEAR I saw the neighbor's cat **sleeping on the roof.**

MISPLACED We're used to the noise living by the airport. [Is the noise living by the airport?]

CLEAR **Living by the airport,** we're used to the noise.

A participial phrase that does not clearly and logically modify a word in the sentence is a *dangling modifier.*

DANGLING Cleaning the attic, an old trunk was found. [Who was cleaning the attic?]

CLEAR **Cleaning the attic,** we found an old trunk.

Exercise 6   Placing Participial Phrases Correctly

Rewrite each of the following sentences, adding the participial phrases given in parentheses. Be sure to use commas to set off participial phrases that begin or interrupt your sentences.

EXAMPLES 1. Finn and Darcy searched for their younger sister.
          (*scanning the crowd*)

       1. *Scanning the crowd, Finn and Darcy searched for
          their younger sister.*

       2. The sea turtle ducked back into its shell. (*startled by
          the sound of the boat's engine*)

       2. *Startled by the sound of the boat's engine, the sea
          turtle ducked back into its shell.*

HELP

Although some items in Exercise 6 can be revised in more than one way, you need to give only one revision for each.

1. My older sister will be working at the garden center near my house. (*beginning next week*)
2. Our new kitten crawled under the sofa. (*exploring the house*)
3. By mistake, we sat on the swings. (*freshly painted*)
4. Lucy helped her brother find the books. (*lost somewhere in his messy room*)
5. Josie and Fred passed the playground. (*walking through the park*)
6. Ms. Surat told us about Sri Lanka and its people. (*pointing to the map*)
7. The two girls yelled loudly. (*surprised by their little brother*)
8. The horse likes to watch people. (*munching on grass*)
9. Andrea picked up her pencil and waited for the test to begin. (*sharpened moments earlier*)
10. On the beach this morning, the children found a mysterious note. (*folded in a blue bottle*)

Exercise 7 **Revising Sentences to Correct Misplaced
and Dangling Participial Phrases**

Revise all of the sentences that contain misplaced or dangling participial phrases. If a sentence is already correct, write *C*.

HELP

You will need to add, delete, or rearrange some words in your revisions for Exercise 7.

EXAMPLE 1. Made from matzo meal, Rachel cooks tasty
            dumplings.

         1. *Rachel cooks tasty dumplings made from
            matzo meal.*

1. Pacing in its cage, I watched the lion.
2. Talking on the telephone, Amanda did not hear the doorbell ringing.
3. Exploring the cave, a new tunnel was discovered.

4. Wearing a bright orange suit and floppy yellow shoes, the circus featured a clown.
5. Filled with countless daisies, the two young girls walked slowly through the field.
6. Reading his part, the nervousness was hard to overcome.
7. The turkey was large enough for three families stuffed with sage and bread crumbs.
8. Tired from the long walk through the snow, food and rest were welcomed.
9. Checking the shelves, Judy found all the reference books she needed.
10. Selling the old farm, sadness welled up inside.

Adjective Clauses

Reference Note

For more about **adjective clauses,** see page 117.

An *adjective clause* modifies a noun or a pronoun. Most adjective clauses begin with a relative pronoun—*that, which, who, whom,* or *whose.* Like an adjective phrase, an adjective clause should generally be placed directly after the word it modifies.

MISPLACED   The Labor Day picnic in the park that we had was fun. [Did we have the park?]

CLEAR   The Labor Day picnic **that we had** in the park was fun.

MISPLACED   The girls thanked their coach who had won the relay race. [Did the coach win the relay race?]

CLEAR   The girls **who had won the relay race** thanked their coach.

HELP

Be sure to use commas to set off nonessential adjective clauses.

Exercise 8   **Revising Sentences with Misplaced Clause Modifiers**

Revise each of the following sentences by placing the adjective clause near the word it should modify.

EXAMPLE   1. My friend Beverly visited me who lives in Sarasota, Florida.

1. *My friend Beverly, who lives in Sarasota, Florida, visited me.*

Reference Note

For information on using commas to set off **nonessential adjective clauses,** see page 299.

1. The students received an *A* who made the first presentation.
2. The kitten belongs to my neighbor that is on the branch.

3. I showed the colorful cotton fabric to my sister that was made in Kenya.
4. The doctor said that the triplets were quite healthy who examined them.
5. The cleanup program was supported by all of the students that the president of the seventh-grade class suggested.
6. The flight attendant welcomed us aboard the plane whose brother I know.
7. The friend has a broken leg whom I called.
8. Donald's package is from his mother which came in the mail.
9. Quasars fascinate me which many astronomers throughout the world study.
10. The dog barked at the letter carrier that has been running loose in the neighborhood.

Review C Correcting Errors in the Use of Modifiers

Each of the following sentences contains an error in the use, form, or placement of a modifier. Revise each sentence by changing the form of a modifier or by adding, deleting, or rearranging words.

EXAMPLE   1. I have never been more happier in my life.
           1. *I have never been happier in my life.*

1. My stepsister plays both soccer and softball, but she likes soccer best.
2. The waiter brought plates to Terrell and me piled high with spaghetti and meat sauce.
3. Very frustrated, her locker just would not open!
4. Barking and growling loudly, the stranger was frightened by the dogs.
5. The antique German cuckoo clock still runs good after all these years.
6. I didn't do too bad on the geography quiz this morning.
7. Our puppy is much more playfuller than our older dog is.
8. We walked slow past the duck pond to see if any new ducklings had hatched.
9. They never did find no sponsor for their team.
10. The CD is the soundtrack of my favorite movie that we heard.

┌HELP─
Although some sentences in Review C can be correctly revised in more than one way, you need to give only one revision for each sentence.

Each of the following sentences contains an error in the use, form, or placement of a modifier. Revise each sentence by changing the form of a modifier or by adding, deleting, or rearranging words.

EXAMPLE **1.** Of all the important women featured in this book, Dolores S. Atencio is the one I admire more.

1. *Of all the important women featured in this book, Dolores S. Atencio is the one I admire most.*

1. Her mother thought that a law career would offer her daughter the most brightest future.
2. Ms. Atencio always knew she would become a lawyer, but she didn't never expect to be so successful.
3. Looking ahead to college and law school, her grades in high school were excellent.
4. Along with two other Hispanic women, her efforts helped to launch Denver's first bilingual radio station in 1985.
5. Ms. Atencio felt quite proudly about helping to organize Colorado's first minority women lawyers' conference.
6. She decided to run for president of the Hispanic National Bar Association (HNBA) receiving encouragement from a friend.
7. Serving as president of HNBA, the legal rights of Hispanics were her main focus.
8. In 1991, she was named one of the most outstanding Hispanic women in *Hispanic Business Magazine.*
9. She also was given the Outstanding Young Woman Award from the city of Denver, which she received for all the time she had devoted to community service.
10. In addition to enjoying community service, Ms. Atencio feels really well when she is spending time with her family.

USAGE

Chapter Review

A. Using the Correct Modifier

Identify the word in parentheses that will make each sentence correct.

1. I have to admit that this recording sounds (*bad, badly*).

2. Our Irish setter came (*shy, shyly*) toward the new puppy.

3. Yoki was anxious, but she appeared (*calm, calmly*).

4. Must the twins play so (*noisy, noisily*)?

5. We're pleased that you did so (*good, well*).

6. The storm ended as (*sudden, suddenly*) as it began.

7. With a little oil, the engine started (*easy, easily*).

8. Their performance is now (*good, well*) enough for any stage.

9. The kitchen counter looks (*clean, cleanly*).

10. It is (*good, well*) to be alive on a beautiful day like today.

11. Of the five designs, which one do you like (*better, best*)?

12. Coach Ruiz said that we had played (*good, well*).

13. This ring is the (*more, most*) expensive of the two.

14. That striped tie would go (*good, well*) with your green shirt.

15. Choose the (*larger, largest*) of the two poodles.

B. Writing Comparative and Superlative Forms of Modifiers

Write the comparative or superlative form of the italicized adjective or adverb in each of the following sentences.

16. *dry* The towels felt ____ after an afternoon on the clothesline than they had felt coming out of the washer.

17. *grateful* We were ____ for Mr. Chang's advice than we could say.

18. *small* The screwdriver my father used to repair my glasses was the ____ one he had.

19. *proud* After the awards ceremony, Kerry seemed ____ of her son than she ever had before.

20. *slow* The ____ horse of them all finished last in the race.

USAGE

21. *enthusiastically*	Pleased by all the performances, the audience applauded ____ for the dancers.
22. *tasty*	Since Dad started taking cooking classes, each dinner is ____ than the previous one.
23. *loyal*	Tadger is the ____ of our three dogs.
24. *easily*	With more practice, we solved the second puzzle ____ than the first one.
25. *tall*	Which of the five Romine girls do you think is ____?

C. Correcting Double Comparisons and Double Negatives

Rewrite the following sentences to correct errors in the use of modifiers.

26. These Hawaiian shirts don't have no pockets.

27. Pineapple juice tastes more sweeter than orange juice to me.

28. What is the most funniest thing that ever happened to you?

29. I can't hardly take another step.

30. Sakima couldn't barely catch her breath after running so far.

D. Correcting Misplaced and Dangling Modifiers

Each sentence below contains a misplaced or dangling modifier. Rewrite the sentences so that they are clear. You may need to add, delete, or rearrange words.

31. The fruit was marked for quick sale bruised by the storm.

32. Those tapes came from the library that you heard.

33. After leaving India, Singapore was the next destination.

34. Opening a savings account, a form of identification was required.

35. Skateboarding down the street, a large dog chased my brother.

36. Black Hawk was a chief of the Sauk people born in Virginia.

37. Trying to study, the noise from the chainsaw was distracting.

38. These salmon are using fish ladders, which are returning to spawn.

39. Sifting carefully through the sand, an old Spanish coin called a doubloon was found.

40. I saw the gazelles jumping through the binoculars.

Writing Application
Using Comparisons in a Letter

Comparative and Superlative Forms An anonymous donor has given a large sum of money for improvements to your school. Write a letter to the school administrators describing the improvements you would like to see made. Use at least three comparative and two superlative forms of adjectives and adverbs in your writing.

Prewriting What facilities, equipment, or supplies would make your school a better place? List your improvement ideas. You may want to discuss your ideas with a classmate or a teacher before you select the ones to include in your letter. Also, note why the improvements are needed.

Writing As you write your first draft, use your list to help you make clear and accurate comparisons. Keep your audience in mind. The administrators need practical suggestions for how to spend the money, so let them know exactly what improvements your school needs and why.

Revising Read your letter to a parent or other adult to see if your arguments are convincing. Add, delete, or rearrange details to make your letter more interesting and effective.

Publishing Be sure you have used the correct comparative and superlative forms of adjectives and adverbs. Check the form of your letter to make sure it follows the guidelines for business letters. Read through your letter a final time to catch any errors in spelling, grammar, usage, or punctuation. Share your ideas for improving the school with the rest of the class, and make a chart displaying the most popular suggestions.

A Glossary of Usage

Common Usage Problems

1.0 Written and Oral English Language Conventions
Students write and speak with a command of standard English conventions appropriate to this grade level.
1.4 Demonstrate appropriate English usage.

Diagnostic Preview

Correcting Errors in Usage

Each of the following sentences contains an error in the use of formal, standard English. Revise each sentence to correct the error.

EXAMPLE   1. They did they're best to help.
         1. *They did their best to help.*

1. We are already for our trip to Washington, D.C.
2. They divided the crackers equally between the four toddlers.
3. Please take those packages here to me.
4. Elena had a cold, but she is feeling good now.
5. Mr. Chang he is my tai chi instructor.
6. Will you learn me how to play chess?
7. May I borrow that there collection of Cheyenne folk tales?
8. Tara might of come with us, but she had to baby-sit.
9. We use to live in Karachi, Pakistan.
10. She is the woman which owns the Great Dane.
11. I dropped the pictures, but I think they're alright.
12. I read where Mayor Alvarez will visit our school.
13. Their the best players on the team this season.
14. The pipes busted last winter during a hard freeze.
15. We cannot go sailing without we wear life jackets.
16. Her new apartment is bigger then her last one.

17. The group went everywheres together.

18. Lydia acted like she was bored.

19. *Antonyms* are when words are opposite in meaning.

20. I hope that you will except my apology.

About the Glossary

This chapter contains an alphabetical list, or ***glossary,*** of many common problems in English usage. You will notice throughout the chapter that some examples are labeled *nonstandard, standard, formal,* or *informal.* **Nonstandard English** is language that does not follow the rules and guidelines of standard English. **Standard English** is language that is grammatically correct and appropriate in formal and informal situations. **Formal** identifies usage that is appropriate in serious speaking and writing situations (such as in speeches and compositions for school). The label **informal** indicates standard usage common in conversation and in everyday writing, such as personal letters.

The following are examples of formal and informal English.

Formal	Informal
angry	steamed
unpleasant	yucky
agreeable	cool
very impressive	totally awesome

a, an   Use *a* before words beginning with a consonant sound. Use *an* before words beginning with a vowel sound. Keep in mind that the sound, not the actual letter, that a word begins with determines whether *a* or *an* should be used.

EXAMPLES   They are building **a** hospital near our house.

I bought **a** one-way ticket. [Even though *o* is a vowel, the word *one* begins with a consonant sound.]

I would like **an** orange.

We worked for **an** hour. [Although *h* is a consonant, the word *hour* begins with a vowel sound. The *h* is not pronounced.]

Reference Note

For a list of **words often confused,** see page 358.

USAGE

COMPUTER TIP

The spellchecker on a computer will help you catch misspelled words such as *anywheres* and *nowheres.* The grammar checker may help you catch errors such as double negatives. However, in the case of words that are often misused, such as *than* and *then* and *between* and *among,* you will have to check your work yourself for correct usage.

HELP

In doing the exercises in this chapter, be sure to use only standard English.

accept, except *Accept* is a verb; it means "to receive." *Except* may be used as either a verb or a preposition. As a verb, it means "to leave out." As a preposition, *except* means "excluding."

EXAMPLES   Ann **accepted** the gift. [verb]

No one will be **excepted** from writing a research paper. [verb]

All my friends will be there **except** Jorge. [preposition]

ain't Do not use this nonstandard word in formal situations.

all right Used as an adjective, *all right* means "satisfactory" or "unhurt." Used as an adverb, *all right* means "well enough." *All right* should be written as two words.

EXAMPLES   Your science project looks **all right** to me. [adjective]

Judy cut her toe, but she is **all right** now. [adjective]

I did **all right** in the drama club tryouts. [adverb]

a lot *A lot* should be written as two words.

EXAMPLE   I have read **a lot** of American Indian folk tales.

already, all ready *Already* means "previously." *All ready* means "completely prepared."

EXAMPLES   By 5:00 P.M., I had **already** cooked dinner.

The students were **all ready** for the trip.

among See **between, among.**

anyways, anywheres, everywheres, nowheres, somewheres These words should have no final *s.*

EXAMPLE   I looked **everywhere** [not *everywheres*] for it!

as See **like, as.**

as if, as though See **like, as if, as though.**

at Do not use *at* after *where.*

NONSTANDARD   Where are the Persian miniatures at?

STANDARD   Where are the Persian miniatures?

bad, badly *Bad* is an adjective. It modifies nouns and pronouns. *Badly* is an adverb. It modifies verbs, adjectives, and adverbs.

USAGE

STYLE TIP

Many writers overuse *a lot.* Whenever you run across *a lot* as you revise your own writing, try to replace it with a more exact word or phrase.

ACCEPTABLE
Emily Dickinson wrote a lot of poems.

BETTER
Emily Dickinson wrote **hundreds** of poems.

EXAMPLES　The fruit tastes **bad.** [The predicate adjective *bad* modifies *fruit.*]

Don't treat him **badly.** [The adverb *badly* modifies the verb *Do treat.*]

STYLE　　TIP

The expression *feel badly* has become acceptable in informal situations although it is not strictly grammatical English.

INFORMAL
Carl felt badly about losing the race.

FORMAL
Carl felt **bad** about losing the race.

Exercise 1 　Identifying Correct Usage

For each of the following sentences, choose the word or word group in parentheses that is correct according to the rules of formal, standard usage.

EXAMPLE　　1. Navajo people came to the American Southwest from (*somewhere, somewheres*) in the North.

　　　　　　1. *somewhere*

1. One group of Navajos settled in the region where the Pueblo people (*lived, lived at*).
2. The Pueblo people were (*already, all ready*) farming and living in permanent dwellings by the time the Navajos arrived.
3. The Navajos may have (*excepted, accepted*) the practice of sand painting from the Pueblos and adapted it to fit their own customs.
4. When the Navajo artists are (*all ready, already*) to begin a sand painting, they gather in a circle, as shown in the picture here.
5. When creating a sand painting, (*a, an*) artist receives directions from the singer, who leads the ceremony.
6. The painter might make a certain design when things are not (*all right, allright*) in the community.

7. The Navajo sand painter may also use this art to help someone who is injured or feeling (*badly, bad*).
8. Because sand paintings used in healing ceremonies are swept away at the end of each ceremony, the designs are recorded nowhere (*accept, except*) in the artist's imagination.
9. However, the patterns used in sand painting (*ain't, aren't*) limited to this art form.
10. Variations of the sacred designs can be found almost (*anywheres, anywhere*) on items that the Navajos make.

USAGE

between, among   Use *between* when referring to two items at a time, even when they are part of a group consisting of more than two.

EXAMPLES   Who was standing **between** you and Sue?

Between the season's track meets, I trained very hard. [Although there may have been more than two meets, the training occurred between any two of them.]

There isn't much difference **between** these three brands of juice. [Although there are more than two brands, each one is being compared with the others separately.]

Use *among* when referring to a group rather than to separate individuals.

EXAMPLES   We divided the burritos **among** the five of us.

There was much discussion **among** the governors about the new tax plan. [The governors are thought of as a group.]

bring, take   *Bring* means "to come carrying something." *Take* means "to go carrying something." Think of *bring* as related to *come* (*to*), *take* as related to *go* (*from*).

EXAMPLES   Please **bring** that chair here.

Now **take** this one over there.

bust, busted   Avoid using these words as verbs in formal English. Use a form of either *burst* or *break* or *catch* or *arrest*.

EXAMPLES   The pipe **burst** [not *busted*] after the storm.

The Japanese raku vase **broke** [not *busted*] when it fell.

Mom **caught** [not *busted*] our dog Pepper digging in the garden.

Did the police **arrest** [not *bust*] the burglar?

Reference Note

For more about **double negatives,** see page 231.

can't hardly, can't scarcely   The words *hardly* and *scarcely* are negative words. They should not be used with another negative word.

EXAMPLES   I **can** [not *can't*] **hardly** wait to hear your new CD.

We **had** [not *hadn't*] **scarcely** enough food for everyone at the Juneteenth picnic.

could of   Do not write *of* with the helping verb *could*. Write *could have*. Also avoid *ought to of, should of, would of, might of,* and *must of.*

EXAMPLES   Abdullah **could have** [not *could of*] helped us.

You **should have** [not *should of*] hung the piñata higher.

don't, doesn't   See page 162.

everywheres   See **anyways,** etc.

except   See **accept, except.**

fewer, less   *Fewer* is used with plural words. *Less* is used with singular words. *Fewer* tells "how many"; *less* tells "how much."

EXAMPLES   We had expected **fewer** guests.

Please use **less** salt.

good, well   *Good* is an adjective. Do not use *good* to modify a verb; use *well*, which can be used as an adverb.

NONSTANDARD   The steel-drum band played good.
   STANDARD   The steel-drum band played **well.**

Although it is usually used as an adverb, *well* is also used as an adjective to mean "healthy."

EXAMPLE   I did not feel **well** yesterday.

had of   See **of.**

had ought, hadn't ought   The verb *ought* should not be used with *had*.

NONSTANDARD   You had ought to learn to dance the polka.
   You hadn't ought to be late for class.
   STANDARD   You **ought** to learn to dance the polka.
or
   You **should** learn to dance the polka.
   You **oughtn't** to be late for class.
or
   You **shouldn't** be late for class.

┌─ H E L P ─

Feel good and *feel well* mean different things. *Feel good* means "to feel happy or pleased." *Feel well* simply means "to feel healthy."

EXAMPLES
   Helping others makes me feel **good.**

   I went home because I didn't feel **well.**

Reference Note
For more information about **using *good* and *well*,** see page 228.

Exercise 2 **Identifying Correct Usage**

For each of the following sentences, choose the word or word group in parentheses that is correct according to the rules of formal, standard usage.

EXAMPLE **1.** Bike riders (*had ought, ought*) to know some simple rules of safety.

    1. ought

1. Just about (*everywheres, everywhere*) you go these days, you see people riding bikes.

2. Riders who wear helmets have (*fewer, less*) major injuries than riders who don't.

3. When Aunt Shirley came for a visit, she (*brought, took*) her bicycle with her.

4. In choosing clothes, cyclists (*can hardly, can't hardly*) go wrong by wearing bright, easy-to-see colors.

5. On busy streets, groups of cyclists should ride in single file and leave space (*among, between*) their bikes in case of sudden stops.

6. Members of cycling clubs decide (*between, among*) themselves on special communication signals.

7. A cyclist who is involved in an accident should not try to ride home, even if he or she seems to feel (*well, good*).

8. The cyclist should call a family member or friend who can (*bring, take*) both the rider and the bike home.

9. A tire that is punctured can usually be patched, but you may not be able to fix one that has (*burst, busted*).

10. Many of the cycling accidents that have happened over the years (*could of, could have*) been avoided if cyclists and motorists had been more careful.

Review A **Proofreading for Correct Usage**

Each of the following sentences contains an error in formal, standard English usage. Identify each error. Then, write the correct word or words.

EXAMPLE **1.** Don't almonds grow somewheres in Africa?

    1. somewheres—somewhere

1. Check the hoses to see whether a seal has busted.

2. When rainfall is low here, there are less rabbits because there are not as many plants for them to eat.

3. I didn't know you could program computers that good.
4. Except for the spelling errors, you could of gotten an A.
5. Tracy's new hamster has all ready escaped.
6. Even a ten-ton truck can't hardly haul a load this size.
7. That bull ain't likely to appreciate anybody trespassing on his property.
8. Bring a glass of ice water outside to your father.
9. *Chutzpah* is a term applied to people who have alot of nerve.
10. You really had ought to hear Thelonious Monk's music.

he, she, they   Do not use a pronoun along with its antecedent as the subject of a verb. This error is called the *double subject.*

NONSTANDARD   Michael he was named Most Valuable Player.

STANDARD   Michael was named Most Valuable Player.

hisself, theirself, theirselves   These words are non-standard English. Use *himself* and *themselves.*

EXAMPLES   Bob hurt **himself** [not *hisself*] during the game.

They served **themselves** [not *theirselves*] last.

how come   In informal English, *how come* is often used instead of *why.* In formal English, *why* is preferred.

INFORMAL   How come caribou migrate?

FORMAL   **Why** do caribou migrate?

its, it's   *Its* is a personal pronoun in the possessive case. *It's* is a contraction of *it is* or *it has.*

EXAMPLES   The kitten likes **its** new home. [possessive pronoun]

We have Monday off because **it's** Rosh Hashana. [contraction of *it is*]

It's been a long day. [contraction of *It has*]

kind, sort, type   The words *this, that, these,* and *those* should agree in number with the words *kind, sort,* and *type. This* and *that* are singular. *These* and *those* are plural.

EXAMPLES   **That kind** of watch is expensive. [singular]

Those kinds of jokes are silly. [plural]

kind of, sort of   In informal English, *kind of* and *sort of* are often used to mean "somewhat" or "rather." In formal English, *somewhat* or *rather* is preferred.

INFORMAL   I feel kind of tired.

FORMAL   I feel **somewhat** tired.

learn, teach   *Learn* means "to acquire knowledge." *Teach* means "to instruct" or "to show how."

EXAMPLES   My brother is **learning** how to drive.

The driving instructor is **teaching** him.

leave, let   *Leave* means "to go away" or "to depart from." *Let* means "to allow" or "to permit."

NONSTANDARD   Leave her go to the movie.

STANDARD   **Let** her go to the movie.

STANDARD   Let's **leave** on time for the movie.

less   See **fewer, less.**

lie, lay   See page 193.

Reference Note

For more information about **prepositional phrases,** see page 90. For more about **clauses,** see Chapter 6.

like, as   *Like* is used as a preposition to introduce a prepositional phrase. In informal English, *like* is often used before a clause as a conjunction meaning "as." In formal English, *as* is preferred.

EXAMPLES   Your uncle's hat looked **like** a sombrero. [*Like* introduces the phrase *like a sombrero.*]

Marcia trained every day **as** the coach had suggested. [*As the coach had suggested* is a clause and needs the conjunction *as,* not the preposition *like,* to introduce it.]

like, as if, as though   In formal, standard English, *like* should not be used for the subordinating conjunction *as if* or *as though.*

EXAMPLES   The Swedish limpa bread looks **as if** [not *like*] it is ready.

The car looks **as though** [not *like*] it needs to be washed.

might of, must of   See **could of.**

nowheres   See **anyways,** etc.

Exercise 3 Identifying Correct Usage

For each of the following sentences, choose the word or word group in parentheses that is correct according to the rules of formal, standard usage.

EXAMPLE   1. Young rattlesnakes (*learn, teach*) themselves to make a rattling noise by imitating their parents.

    1. *teach*

1. (*Its, It's*) a sound that most people have learned to dread.
2. The snake's rattle consists of "buttons" of flesh at the end of (*its, it's*) tail, which are shaken against rings of loose skin.
3. The rings of skin (*themselves, theirselves*) are fragile.
4. (*Like, As*) zookeepers have discovered, snakes that rattle at visitors all day may damage their rattles.
5. (*This kind, These kind*) of snake delivers a poisonous bite, but rattlesnakes do not attack unless threatened.
6. Not all scientists agree about (*how come, why*) certain snakes have rattles.
7. According to many scientists, rattlesnakes (*they use, use*) the rattling sound to frighten enemies.
8. Some scientists believe that snakes use the rattles (*as, like*) other animals use different sounds—to communicate with each other.
9. Snakes don't have ears; however, they are (*sort of, rather*) sensitive to sound vibrations.
10. When people hear a rattlesnake, they may react (*like, as if*) the situation is an emergency—and it often is.

Review B Proofreading for Correct Usage

Each of the following sentences contains an error in formal, standard English usage. Identify each error. Then, write the correct word or words.

EXAMPLE   1. I should of known that the painting on the next page was done by Grandma Moses.

    1. *should of—should have*

1. My art teacher gave me a assignment to write a report about any artist I chose.
2. Between all the artists that I considered, Grandma Moses appealed to me the most.

Grandma Moses, *Rockabye*. Copyright © 1987, Grandma Moses Properties Co., New York.

3. I went to the library and looked for a quiet place where I could do my research at.
4. I learned that Anna Mary Robertson Moses didn't start painting until she was all ready in her seventies.
5. By then, her children were grown, and she had less responsibilities.
6. Grandma Moses had no art teacher accept herself.
7. As you can see in the self-portrait *Rockabye*, Grandma Moses felt well about her role as a grandmother.
8. You can't hardly help feeling that Grandma Moses really loves these children.
9. My sister Kim likes this painting alot.
10. My report is already for class now, and I can't wait to tell my classmates about Grandma Moses.

of   Do not use *of* with prepositions such as *inside, off,* and *outside*.

EXAMPLES   We waited **outside** [not *outside of*] the theater for the ticket window to open.

The glass fell **off** [not *off of*] the table.

Only Muslims are allowed **inside** [not *inside of*] the city of Mecca in Saudi Arabia.

Of is also unnecessary with the verb *had*.

EXAMPLE   If we **had** [not *had of*] tried harder, we would have won.

ought to of   See **could of**.

real   In informal English, the adjective *real* is often used as an adverb meaning "very" or "extremely." In formal English, *very, extremely,* or another adverb is preferred.

INFORMAL   The new car is real quiet.

FORMAL   The new car is **very** quiet.

rise, raise   See page 191.

she, he, they   See **he,** etc.

should of   See **could of.**

sit, set   See page 190.

some, somewhat   Do not use *some* for the adverb *somewhat.*

NONSTANDARD   I like classical music some.

STANDARD   I like classical music **somewhat.**

somewheres   See **anyways,** etc.

sort   See **kind,** etc.

sort of   See **kind of,** etc.

take   See **bring, take.**

teach   See **learn, teach.**

than, then   *Than* is a subordinating conjunction used in comparisons. *Then* is an adverb meaning "next" or "after that."

EXAMPLES   I sing better **than** I act.

We'll eat first, and **then** we'll ride our bikes.

that   See **who,** etc.

that there   See **this here, that there.**

their, there, they're   *Their* is the possessive form of *they. There* is used to mean "at that place" or to begin a sentence. *They're* is a contraction of *they are.*

EXAMPLES   Do you have **their** CDs?

The lake is over **there.**

There are five movie theaters in town. [*There* begins the sentence but does not add to its meaning.]

They're writing a report on the poet Américo Paredes.

theirself, theirselves   See **hisself,** etc.

them   *Them* should not be used as an adjective. Use *these* or *those.*

EXAMPLE   Where did you put **those** [not *them*] papers?

they   See **he,** etc.

MEETING THE CHALLENGE

A *mnemonic* is a device, often a rhyme or visual aid, used as an aid to remembering. Choose two entries from this chapter (try to pick usage problems that you have trouble with). Create a mnemonic device of your own for each of the entries you picked. See examples of mnemonics in the Tips and Tricks on pages 360, 365, and 367.

Reference Note

For information about **subordinating conjunctions,** see page 121. For more about **adverbs,** see page 54.

USAGE

this here, that there   The words *here* and *there* are not needed after *this* and *that*.

EXAMPLE   I like **this** [not *this here*] Chinese dragon kite, but I like **that** [not *that there*] one better.

this kind, sort, type   See **kind,** etc.

try and   In informal English, *try and* is often used for *try to.* In formal English, *try to* is preferred.

INFORMAL   I will try and be there early.

  FORMAL   I will **try to** be there early.

type   See **kind,** etc.

Exercise 4   Identifying Correct Usage

For each of the following sentences, choose the word or word group in parentheses that is correct according to the rules of formal, standard usage.

EXAMPLE   1. The Amish people (*try and, try to*) maintain a simple, traditional way of life.

    1. *try to*

1. In the early 1700s, the Amish were not allowed to practice (*their, they're, there*) religion in Germany and Switzerland.
2. Hearing that there was more freedom in the Americas (*than, then*) in Europe, the Amish left their homes and settled in North America.
3. Since that time, they have remained (*outside of, outside*) the mainstream of American life.
4. The Amish work (*real, very*) hard at producing organically grown crops.
5. In Amish communities such as (*this, this here*) one, modern conveniences such as telephones, cars, and televisions are not used.
6. The closeness of Amish family life is evident in the way (*these, them*) people build their homes.
7. (*They're, There, Their*) are often three generations—grand-parents, parents, and children—living in a large residence made up of several houses.

USAGE

8. Pictures and photographs are not allowed (*inside of, inside*) Amish homes, but the Amish brighten their plain houses with colorful pillows, quilts, and rugs.
9. If an Amish person gets sick, he or she is almost always cared for by family members rather (*than, then*) by a doctor.
10. The Amish way of life might surprise you (*somewhat, some*), yet Amish communities have thrived in North America for nearly three hundred years.

Oral Practice **Correcting Errors in Usage**

Each of the following sentences contains an error in the use of formal, standard English. Read the sentences aloud, and identify each error. Then, say each sentence again, this time correcting the error.

EXAMPLE   1. It was real cold that spring!
            1. *real—It was extremely cold that spring!*

1. Few people commanded more respect and admiration then Mother Teresa did.
2. Nobody can dance like you do, Ariel.
3. These sort of questions can be found on every standardized test.
4. Oh, no! The baby's gotten oatmeal all over hisself.
5. The structure of molecules like these, it can most easily be understood by building a model.
6. What I want to know is how come we can't go to the concert.
7. Who learned your dog all those tricks?

8. A *howdah* is one of them seats that have a canopy and that sit on a camel or an elephant.

9. The RV campsite is just outside of town.

10. Mrs. Whitfield will try and explain how the European Economic Community is organized.

use to, used to   Don't leave off the *d* when you write *used to.* The same advice applies to *supposed to.*

EXAMPLE   Gail **used to** [not *use to*] be on the softball team.

way, ways   Use *way,* not *ways,* in referring to a distance.

EXAMPLE   Do we have a long **way** [not *ways*] to drive?

well   See **good, well.**

when, where   Do not use *when* or *where* incorrectly to begin a definition.

NONSTANDARD   A *homophone* is when a word sounds like another word but has a different meaning and spelling.

STANDARD   A *homophone* is a word that sounds like another word but has a different meaning and spelling.

where   Do not use *where* for *that.*

EXAMPLE   Did you read in the newsletter **that** [not *where*] the teen center is closing?

who, which, that   The relative pronoun *who* refers to people only. *Which* refers to things only. *That* refers to either people or things.

EXAMPLES   Jolene is the one **who** called. [person]

Here is the salad, **which** is my favorite part of the meal. [thing]

The book **that** you want is here. [thing]

This is the salesperson **that** helped me choose the gift. [person]

who, whom   See page 211.

whose, who's   *Whose* is used as the possessive form of *who* and as an interrogative pronoun. *Who's* is a contraction of *who is* or *who has.*

EXAMPLES   **Whose** book is this? [possessive pronoun]

              Whose is this? [interrogative pronoun]

              Who's the new student? [contraction of *Who is*]

              Who's read "A Walk to the Jetty"? [contraction of *Who has*]

without, unless   Do not use the preposition *without* in place of the conjunction *unless.*

EXAMPLE   I can't go **unless** [not *without*] I ask Dad.

would of   See **could of.**

your, you're   *Your* is the possessive form of *you. You're* is the contraction of *you are.*

EXAMPLES   **Your** Saint Patrick's Day party was great!

              You're a good friend.

> **USAGE**

(Exercise 5) **Identifying Correct Usage**

For each of the following sentences, choose the word or word group in parentheses that is correct according to the rules of formal, standard usage.

EXAMPLE   **1.** Last week I received a letter from Sandra Joyce, (*who's, whose*) a good friend of mine.

        1. who's

1. When I opened the envelope, I saw (*where, that*) she had sent me chopsticks and these instructions.
2. "I thought you'd like (*you're, your*) own pair of chopsticks, with instructions showing how to use them," Sandra wrote.
3. Instructions like the ones Sandra sent me are helpful because chopsticks can be hard to use (*unless, without*) you are shown how.
4. In the letter, Sandra told me (*that, where*) she and her family had been to New York.
5. Because Sandra lives in a small town, she wasn't (*use, used*) to the crowds.

6. She enjoyed visiting her grandparents, (*who's, whose*) home is near Chinatown, on Manhattan Island.
7. While her family was eating in a Chinese restaurant, one of the servers, (*which, who*) was very helpful, showed her how to use chopsticks.
8. "(*Your, You're*) not going to believe this," she wrote, "but by the end of the meal, I was using chopsticks quite well."
9. Etiquette is (*when you use good manners, the use of good manners*); Sandra wondered whether using chopsticks to eat Chinese food was a matter of etiquette or of skill.
10. I'll write Sandra that I have a long (*ways, way*) to go before I'm an expert in using chopsticks.

Review C **Proofreading for Correct Usage**

Each of the following sentences contains an error in the use of formal, standard English. Rewrite each sentence to correct the error.

EXAMPLE   1. If the quarterback can't play, whose the backup?
　　　　　 1. *If the quarterback can't play, who's the backup?*

1. Are you selling you're old bike or one of theirs?
2. If they're not their, you can have their seats.
3. Don't go outside without you wear those galoshes!
4. Is Alfonso García Robles the man which was awarded the 1982 Nobel Peace Prize?
5. "Buzzing the runway" is when a plane flies low and fast over the runway.
6. I read where the word *Nippon* means "where the sun rises."
7. If this hat isn't lucky, then how come every time I wear it, I win?
8. Yes, I use to live in Madrid.
9. Please try and be ready on time tonight.
10. Listen to Lydia's new poem; its dedicated to Queen Liliuokalani.

Chapter Review

A. Identifying Correct Usage

For each of the following sentences, choose the word or word group in parentheses that is correct according to the rules of formal, standard English usage.

1. Helene made (*fewer, less*) mistakes this time.

2. That restaurant looks (*as if, like*) it might be nice.

3. Those (*kind, kinds*) of games are easy to learn.

4. Terrance felt (*badly, bad*) about losing the house key.

5. Leticia practiced an hour every day (*like, as*) her teacher had recommended.

6. Divide the sheet music (*among, between*) the three musicians.

7. We brought the juice, but (*it's, its*) still in the car.

8. Both cars had pinstripes painted on (*their, there*) hoods.

9. The rice will feed more people (*then, than*) the bread will.

10. "(*Your, You're*) a polite young man," Aunt Henrietta told Jason.

11. There's the police officer (*which, who*) helped me yesterday.

12. Did you see in the newspaper (*that, where*) farmers are losing their crops because of the drought?

13. Chika is the woman (*whose, who's*) going to be my math tutor.

14. The child cried out when her balloon (*busted, burst*).

15. Vincent van Gogh did not receive (*a lot, alot*) of recognition during his lifetime.

16. Just do your best, and everything will be (*allright, all right*).

17. Will you (*take, bring*) that *National Geographic* to me?

18. Elyssa must (*of, have*) left her wallet here.

19. Petra likes salsa music (*somewhat, some*).

20. Can your brother (*learn, teach*) me how to play the drums?

21. Let the bread rise for (*a, an*) hour, and then put it in the oven.

22. Is Emily coming to the party, or (*ain't, isn't*) she?

23. (*Leave, Let*) me walk to the concert by myself.

24. We (*should not, hadn't ought to*) let the cat eat whatever it wants.

25. With contacts, I can see (*all right, alright*).

USAGE

B. Proofreading for Correct Usage

Read each sentence below, and decide whether it contains an error in the use of formal, standard English. If the sentence contains an error in usage, rewrite the sentence correctly. If the sentence is already correct, write *C*.

26. Try to be real quiet while you are inside the library.

27. We cannot ride our bikes without it stops raining.

28. Be careful not to knock the lamp off of the table.

29. The cartoon page looks as if it got wet.

30. I told Gretchen to try and keep still.

31. Where's the salt shaker at?

32. Robbie said that the lock on the back door is busted.

33. Andrea thought we should have turned right at the stop sign.

34. Mr. Funicello seems kind of uncomfortable.

35. This here poem would be easier to memorize than that one.

36. Before 1920, farmers use to grow strawberries here.

37. My grandmother she worked in a factory when she was my age.

38. Sakura knows how come the play was canceled.

39. Those game tickets are somewheres in this drawer.

40. Before our trip, we ought to buy a map.

41. Where did Rory put them CDs?

42. Their are two bridges downriver.

43. The tollbooth will except quarters and dimes but not pennies.

44. A pronoun is when a word is used in place of a noun.

45. By noon we had all ready seen Mr. Kerr's film.

46. The class can't hardly wait to go on the field trip to the power plant.

47. The Immerguts have a long ways to drive to visit their grandparents.

48. My older sister is doing very well in law school.

49. In the final seconds of the game, Lee tripped hisself and missed the winning basket.

50. It's true: Mimi doesn't want to come to the New Year's Eve party.

Writing Application
Writing a Speech

Using Formal English   A local television station has started a new program called *Sound-Off.* Each speaker on the program gets five minutes on the air to express an opinion about a community issue. Choose a topic that you think is important, and write a speech to submit to the TV station. Use only formal, standard English in your speech.

Prewriting   First, choose a specific topic that interests you. List important facts and information about the issue. Do you have all the information you need? If not, do some research at your school or local library. Also, be sure to include your own feelings and opinions about your topic. Finally, make a rough outline of what you want to say.

Writing   Use your notes and outline to help you write a draft of your speech. Try to write a lively introduction that will grab your listeners' attention. In your introduction, give a clear statement of opinion. Then, discuss each supporting point in a paragraph or two. Conclude your speech by restating your main point.

Revising   Ask a friend to time you as you read your speech aloud. Then, ask your friend the following questions:

• Is the main idea clear?

• Does the speech give useful information?

Publishing   Proofread your speech for errors in grammar or formal, standard usage. You and your classmates may want to present your speeches to the class. You might also want to investigate whether a local TV or radio program would allow you to give your speeches on the air.

13 Capital Letters
Rules for Capitalization

1.0 Written and Oral English Language Conventions

Students write and speak with a command of standard English conventions appropriate to this grade level.

1.6 Use correct capitalization.

Diagnostic Preview

Proofreading Sentences for Correct Capitalization

Write each word that requires capitalization in the following sentences. If a sentence is already correct, write *C*.

EXAMPLE 1. Next saturday rachel and i will get to watch the taping of our favorite TV show.

1. *Saturday, Rachel, I*

1. The curtiss soap corporation sponsors the television show called *three is two too many*.
2. The show's theme song is "you and i might get by."
3. My favorite actor on the show is joe fontana, jr., who plays the lovable dr. mullins.
4. The female lead, janelle bledsoe, used to go to our junior high school right here in houston, texas.
5. The action is set in the West just after the Civil War.
6. The program is on monday nights, except during the summer.
7. One episode took place at a fourth of july picnic, at which dr. mullins challenged the sheriff to a grapefruit-eating contest.
8. Ms. Bledsoe plays a teacher who is married to Mr. reginald wilson foster II, president of the flintsville National bank.
9. Mrs. foster teaches latin, home economics, and arithmetic I at flintsville's one-room school.

10. One local character, uncle ramón, once played a practical joke on judge grimsby right outside the mayor's office.

11. Some people, including my mother, think that the program is silly, but my father enjoys watching it occasionally.

12. Even i don't think it will receive an emmy from the academy of television arts and sciences.

13. When grandma murray and aunt edna from mobile, alabama, visited us, they watched the program.

14. In that monday night's show, an alien named romax from the planet zarko stayed at the sidewinder hotel.

15. The alien, who looked like president zachary taylor, spoke english perfectly and could read people's minds.

16. He settled a dispute between the union pacific railroad and the flintsville ranchers' association.

17. In another show a united states senator and romax discussed their views of justice.

18. In the silliest show, the people in the next town, longview, thought that a sea monster was living in lake cranberry and reported it to the department of the interior.

19. A week later, mayor murdstone lost the only copy of his secret recipe for irish stew and saw the recipe in the next issue of the *flintsville weekly gazette.*

20. One time a mysterious stranger appeared, claiming he had sailed around cape horn on the ship *the gem of the ocean.*

21. Another time, the wealthy landowner mabel platt hired the law firm of crumbley, lockwood, and starr to sue mayor murdstone and threatened to take the case all the way to the united states supreme court.

22. In the next episode, a buddhist priest who just happened to be traveling through the west on his way back to china stopped off in flintsville.

23. Once, when someone mistakenly thought he had found gold down at cutter's creek, thousands of prospectors flocked to flintsville, including three bank-robbing members of the feared gumley Gang.

24. The programs are taped before a live audience in the metro theater in los angeles, california.

25. You can get tickets to be in the audience by writing to curtiss soap corporation, 151 holly avenue, deerfield, mi 49238.

Using Capital Letters Correctly

Reference Note

For more about using **capital letters in quotations,** see page 323.

13a. Capitalize the first word in every sentence.

EXAMPLES   **M**y dog knows several tricks. **D**oes yours?

The first word of a directly quoted sentence should begin with a capital letter.

EXAMPLE   Mrs. Hernandez said, "**D**on't forget to bring your contributions for the bake sale."

Traditionally, the first word of every line of poetry begins with a capital letter.

EXAMPLE   **I**n the night
The rain comes down.
Yonder at the edge of the earth
There is a sound like cracking,
There is a sound like falling.
Down yonder it goes on slowly rumbling.
It goes on shaking.

A Papago poem, "In the Night"

NOTE   Some modern poets do not follow this style. If you are using a quotation from a poem, be sure to use the capitalization that the poet uses.

Reference Note

For information on using **colons in letters,** see page 312. For information on using **commas in letters,** see page 307.

13b. Capitalize the first word in both the salutation and the closing of a letter.

SALUTATIONS   **D**ear Service Manager:
Dear Emily,

CLOSINGS   **S**incerely,
Yours truly,

13c. Capitalize the pronoun *I.*

EXAMPLE   This week **I** have to write two essays.

13d. Capitalize proper nouns.

Reference Note

For more about **common nouns** and **proper nouns,** see page 26.

A *proper noun* names a particular person, place, thing, or idea. Proper nouns are capitalized. A *common noun* names a kind or type of person, place, thing, or idea. A common noun generally is not capitalized unless it begins a sentence or is part of a title.

MECHANICS

Proper Nouns	Common Nouns
Central **H**igh **S**chool	high school
Saturday	day
Rigoberta **M**enchú	woman
Cambodia	country
USS Nautilus	submarine

Some proper nouns consist of more than one word. In these names, short words such as prepositions (those of fewer than five letters) and articles (*a, an, the*) are generally not capitalized.

EXAMPLES   House **o**f Representatives   Ivan **t**he Terrible

(1) Capitalize the names of persons and animals.
Be sure to capitalize initials in names.

Persons	**M**onica **S**one	**A**aron **N**eville
	Charlayne **H**unter-**G**ault	**M**ohandas **K**. **G**andhi
Animals	**S**hamu	**T**rigger
	Socks	**R**ikki-tikki-tavi

(2) Capitalize geographical names.

Type of Name	Examples	
Continents	**E**urope	**S**outh **A**merica
	Antarctica	**A**sia
Countries	**A**ustralia	**E**gypt
	El **S**alvador	**S**audi **A**rabia
Cities, Towns	**M**iami	**I**ndianapolis
	Los **A**ngeles	**M**anila
States	**T**ennessee	**D**elaware
	Rhode **I**sland	**W**yoming

(continued)

Reference Note

Abbreviations of the names of states are capitalized. See page 291 for more about using and punctuating such abbreviations.

| **STYLE**   **TIP** |

Some names consist of more than one part. The different parts may begin with capital letters only or with a combination of capital and lowercase letters. If you are not sure about the spelling of a name, ask the person with that name or check a reference source.

EXAMPLES
Van **d**en **A**kker, **v**an **G**ogh, **M**c**E**nroe, **L**a **F**ontaine, **d**e **l**a **G**arza, **I**bn **S**aud

| COMPUTER TIP |

If you use a computer, you may be able to use a spellchecker to help you capitalize names correctly. Make a list of the names you write most often. Be sure that you have spelled and capitalized each name correctly. Then, add this list to your computer's dictionary or spellchecker.

MECHANICS

STYLE TIP

A two-letter state abbreviation without periods is used only when it is followed by a ZIP Code. Both letters of the abbreviation are capitalized. No mark of punctuation is used between the abbreviation and the ZIP Code.

EXAMPLES
New Orleans, **LA** 70131-5140

New York, **NY** 10003-6981

Reference Note

In addresses, abbreviations such as *St., Blvd., Ave., Dr.,* and *Ln.* are capitalized. For more about abbreviations, see page 291.

Type of Name	Examples	
Islands	**A**leutian **I**slands **C**rete	**L**ong **I**sland **I**sle of **P**ines
Bodies of Water	**A**mazon **R**iver **C**hesapeake **B**ay **S**uez **C**anal	**L**ake **O**ntario **J**ackson's **P**ond **I**ndian **O**cean
Streets, Highways	**M**ain **S**treet **E**ighth **A**venue	**C**anary **L**ane **H**ighway 71

NOTE In a hyphenated street number, the second part of the number is not capitalized.

EXAMPLE   West Thirty-**f**ourth Street

Type of Name	Examples	
Parks and Forests	**S**herwood **F**orest **B**rechtel **P**ark	**E**verglades **N**ational **P**ark
Mountains	**C**atskills **M**ount **F**uji	**M**ount **E**verest the **A**lps
Regions	the **M**iddle **E**ast **N**ew **E**ngland the **W**est	the **S**outheast **C**orn **B**elt **S**outhern **H**emisphere
Other Geographical Names	**M**ayon **V**olcano **P**ainted **D**esert	**S**inai **P**eninsula **M**eteor **C**rater

NOTE Words such as *east, west, northern,* or *southerly* are not capitalized when the words merely indicate direction. However, they are capitalized when they name a particular region.

EXAMPLES   A car was going **s**outh on Oak Street. [direction]

The **S**outh has produced some of America's great writers. [region of the country]

MECHANICS

Exercise 1 — Writing Proper Nouns

For each common noun given below, write two proper nouns. You may need to use a dictionary and an atlas. Be sure to use capital letters correctly.

EXAMPLE   **1.** country

        1. Canada, Japan

1. lake   **5.** teacher   **8.** ocean
2. continent   **6.** athlete   **9.** city
3. president   **7.** park   **10.** region
4. highway

Exercise 2 — Correcting Errors in Capitalization

Each of the following sentences contains at least one capitalization error. Correct these errors by writing the words that are incorrectly capitalized and either changing capital letters to lowercase letters or changing lowercase letters to capital letters.

EXAMPLE   **1.** The original Settlers of hawaii came from the marquesas islands and tahiti.

        1. settlers, Hawaii, Marquesas Islands, Tahiti

1. our Class is studying hawaii.
2. The Hawaiian islands are located in the pacific ocean, nearly twenty-four hundred miles West of san francisco, california.
3. Hawaii officially became the fiftieth State in the united states in 1959.
4. Our teacher, ms. Jackson, explained that the Capital City is honolulu; she said that it is located on the southeast Coast of oahu island.
5. The largest of the Islands is hawaii.
6. On the southeast shore of hawaii island is hawaii volcanoes national park.
7. Ms. Jackson asked, "can anyone name one of the Volcanoes there?"
8. Since i had been reading about National Parks, i raised my hand.
9. "The Park has two active volcanoes, mauna Loa and kilauea," I answered.

10. "These pictures show how lava from kilauea's eruption threatened everything in its path in 1989," I added.
11. Its crater, halemaumau crater, is the largest active crater in the World.
12. "we'll go into much more detail about volcanoes tomorrow," ms. jackson said.
13. then ms. jackson told us that honolulu is probably the most important business center in the pacific ocean.
14. Ever since captain William Brown sailed into the harbor in 1794, Hawaii has played an increasingly important role in business.
15. It's easy to see why—Hawaii is midway between Continents.
16. hawaii's largest city has a fine seaport; it links japan, china, and even australia with North and south America.
17. Cultural and academic studies thrive there in places such as the university of hawaii and the east-west center.
18. You can even get a look at the iolani palace where the Rulers of hawaii once lived.
19. Perhaps best of all, hawaii offers Tourists a day in the sun at waikiki beach.
20. Suddenly, i blurted out, "wouldn't it be great if we could all go there now!"

(3) Capitalize names of organizations, teams, institutions, and government bodies.

Type of Name	Examples	
Organizations	Clark Drama Club Junior League	Modern Language Association
Teams	Boston Celtics Dallas Cowboys	Los Angeles Dodgers Hutto Hippos
Institutions	Westside Regional Hospital	Roosevelt Junior High School
Government Bodies	United Nations Peace Corps	Congress York City Council

(4) Capitalize the names of historical events and periods, special events, calendar items, and holidays.

Type of Name	Examples	
Historical Events and Periods	Revolutionary War Bronze Age Holocaust	United States Bicentennial Age of Reason
Special Events	Texas State Fair Special Olympics	Super Bowl Festival of States
Calendar Items and Holidays	Monday Memorial Day	February Thanksgiving Day

NOTE Do not capitalize the name of a season unless it is part of a proper name.

EXAMPLES the winter holidays   the Quebec Winter Carnival

(5) Capitalize the names of nationalities, races, and peoples.

EXAMPLES Mexican   Nigerian

African American   Iroquois

HELP

The names of organizations, businesses, and government bodies are often abbreviated to a series of capital letters.

EXAMPLES

National Organization for Women	NOW
American Telephone & Telegraph	AT&T
National Science Foundation	NSF

Usually the letters in such abbreviations are not followed by periods, but always check an up-to-date dictionary or other reliable source to be sure.

STYLE   TIP

The words *black* and *white* may or may not be capitalized when they refer to races. Either way is correct.

EXAMPLE

In the 1960s, both Blacks and Whites [or blacks and whites] worked to end segregation.

Within each piece of writing, be sure to be consistent in your use of capitals or lowercase letters for these words.

MECHANICS

(6) Capitalize the names of businesses and the brand names of business products.

Type of Name	Examples	
Businesses	Sears, Roebuck and Co.	Fields Department Store
	Thrifty Dry Cleaners	First National Bank
Business Products	Schwinn Mesa	Apple Macintosh
	GMC Jimmy	Callaway Big Bertha

NOTE Names of types of products are not capitalized.

EXAMPLES Schwinn bicycle, Apple computer, Callaway golf club

(7) Capitalize the names of ships, trains, aircraft, and spacecraft.

Reference Note
For information on **using italics in names,** see page 320.

Type of Name	Examples	
Ships	*Queen Elizabeth 2*	*Kon Tiki*
Trains	*City of New Orleans*	*Silver Meteor*
Aircraft	*Memphis Belle*	*Spruce Goose*
Spacecraft	*Voyager 2*	*Sputnik*

(8) Capitalize the names of buildings and other structures.

EXAMPLES Sydney Opera House, St. Louis Cathedral, Aswan Dam, Eiffel Tower, Brooklyn Bridge

NOTE Do not capitalize such words as *hotel, theater,* or *high school* unless they are part of the name of a particular building or institution.

EXAMPLES Capital Theater   a theater

Lane Hotel   the hotel

Taft High School   this high school

(9) Capitalize the names of monuments, memorials, and awards.

Type of Name	Examples	
Monuments	Great Sphinx	Stonehenge
	Navajo National Monument	Washington Monument
Memorials	Lincoln Memorial	*The Minute Man*
	the Coronado Memorial	Tomb of the Unknown Soldier
Awards	Emmy Award	Nobel Prize
	Congressional Medal of Honor	Pulitzer Prize

(10) Capitalize the names of religions and their followers, holy days and celebrations, sacred writings, and specific deities.

Type of Name	Examples	
Religions and Followers	Judaism	Christian
	Hinduism	Muslim
Holy Days and Celebrations	Easter	Yom Kippur
	All Saints' Day	Christmas Eve
Sacred Writings	Koran	Dead Sea Scrolls
	Bible	Upanishads
Specific Deities	God	Jehovah
	Allah	Krishna

NOTE The words *god* and *goddess* are not capitalized when they refer to a deity of ancient mythology. However, the names of specific gods and goddesses are capitalized.

EXAMPLES   The king of the Norse gods was Odin.

Athena was the Greek goddess of wisdom and warfare.

The word *earth* is not capitalized unless it is used along with the names of other heavenly bodies that are capitalized. The words *sun* and *moon* are generally not capitalized.

EXAMPLES

Oceans cover three fourths of the **e**arth's surface.

Which is larger—Saturn or **E**arth?

How many **m**oons does **J**upiter have?

(11) Capitalize the names of planets, stars, constellations, and other heavenly bodies.

Type of Name	Examples	
Planets	**M**ercury	**V**enus
Stars	**R**igel	**P**roxima **C**entauri
Constellations	**U**rsa **M**ajor	**A**ndromeda
Other Heavenly Bodies	**M**ilky **W**ay	**C**omet **K**ohoutek

Exercise 3 **Proofreading Sentences for Correct Capitalization**

Supply capital letters wherever they are needed in each of the following sentences.

EXAMPLE   1. Each arbor day the students at franklin junior high school plant a tree.

1. *Arbor Day, Franklin Junior High School*

1. The golden gate bridge spans the entrance of san francisco bay.
2. Our muslim neighbors, the Rashads, fast during the month of ramadan.
3. The peace corps became a government agency by an act of congress.
4. Do you think the henderson hornets will win the playoffs?
5. Thousands of cherokee people live in the Smoky Mountains in and around North Carolina.
6. To stop flooding in the South, the tennessee valley authority, a government agency, built thirty-nine dams on the Tennessee River and the streams that flow into it.
7. Which biographer won the pulitzer prize this year?
8. On new year's day, many fans crowd into football stadiums for annual bowl games such as the rose bowl.
9. Can you see neptune or any of its moons through your telescope?
10. Have you read any myths about apollo, a god once worshiped by the greeks?

Oral Practice **Proofreading Sentences for Correct Capitalization**

Read each of the following sentences aloud. Then, identify the words in each sentence that should be capitalized.

EXAMPLE   **1.** according to my sister, i'm a mall rat.
         1. According to my sister, I'm a mall rat.

1. the branford mall is the largest in melville county.
2. It is on jefferson parkway, two miles north of duck lake state park and the big bridge that crosses duck lake.
3. Across the parkway from the mall is our new local high school with its parking lots, playing fields, and stadium, home of the branford panthers.
4. Near the mall are the american legion hall, bowlarama, and king skating rink.
5. The mall includes two jewelry stores, nicholson's department store, the palace cinema, and thirty-five other businesses.
6. They range from small stationery stores to one of the finest restaurants in the midwest.
7. The restaurant larue is run by marie and jean larue, who are from france.
8. Also in the mall is the american paper box company, which sells boxes for every packaging need.
9. My friends sharon and earl always shop at gene's jeans, which specializes in denim clothing.
10. An outlet store for northwestern leather goods of chicago sells uffizi purses and wallets.

Review A **Correcting Errors in Capitalization**

Each of the following sentences contains errors in capitalization. Correct these errors by changing incorrect capital letters to lower-case letters and incorrect lowercase letters to capital letters.

EXAMPLE   **1.** African americans in massachusetts have played an important part in American history.
         1. Americans, Massachusetts

1. In Boston, the Crispus attucks monument is a memorial to attucks and the other men who died in the boston Massacre.
2. According to many Historians, attucks was a former slave who fought against the british in the american Revolution.

STYLE TIP

Misusing a capital letter or a lowercase letter at the beginning of a word can confuse the meaning of a sentence.

EXAMPLE
I'd like to see inside the **w**hite **h**ouse. [The sentence means I'd like to see inside a particular house that is white.]

I'd like to see inside the **W**hite **H**ouse. [The sentence means I'd like to see inside the home of the president of the United States.]

You may be able to use double meanings effectively in poetry or in other creative writing. In formal writing, though, you should follow the rules of standard capitalization.

Jan Ernst Matzeliger

W.E.B. DuBois

Crispus Attucks

Reference Note

For more about **proper adjectives,** see page 37.

3. The department of the Interior has made the Home of maria baldwin a historic building in cambridge.
4. Baldwin was a Leader in the league for Community Service, an Organization to help the Needy.
5. One of the founders of the National association for the Advancement of colored people, w.e.b. DuBois, was born in great Barrington, Massachusetts.
6. A marker stands on the Spot where DuBois lived.
7. Jan ernst matzeliger, who lived in lynn, invented a machine that made Shoes easier and cheaper to manufacture.
8. The nantucket whaling Museum has information about Peter green, a Sailor on the ship *john Adams.*
9. During a storm at sea, Green saved the Ship and crew.
10. Use the Map of Massachusetts shown above to locate the Towns and Cities in which these notable african Americans lived.

13e. Capitalize proper adjectives.

A ***proper adjective*** is formed from a proper noun and is capitalized.

13
e, f

Proper Noun	Proper Adjective
Greece	**G**reek theater
Mars	**M**artian moons
Darwin	**D**arwinian theory
Japan	**J**apanese tea ceremony

13f. Do not capitalize the names of school subjects, except course names followed by numerals and names of language classes.

EXAMPLES history, typing, algebra, English, Spanish, Latin, History 101, Music III, Art Appreciation I

Exercise 4 **Proofreading Sentences for Correct Capitalization**

Supply capital letters where they are needed in each of the following sentences.

EXAMPLE 1. Rosa said we were eating mexican bread.
         1. *Mexican*

1. The program featured russian ballet dancers.
2. The european Common Market improves international trade.
3. The scandinavian countries include both Norway and Sweden.
4. In geography, we learned about the platypus and the koala, two australian animals.
5. We read several english plays in my literature class.
6. I am planning to take computers I next year.
7. On the floor was a large persian rug.
8. England, France, Scotland, Russia, and the United States played important roles in canadian history.
9. The backyard was decorated with chinese lanterns.
10. Are you taking french or art II?

Review B **Correcting Errors in Capitalization**

Each of the sentences on the following page contains errors in capitalization. Correct these errors by writing the words that are incorrectly capitalized and changing capital letters to lowercase letters or changing lowercase letters to capital letters.

MEETING THE CHALLENGE

Choose a country. Then, write a paragraph giving a short biographical sketch of a current or former leader of that country. In your paragraph, correctly use and capitalize at least five proper nouns and five proper adjectives.

MECHANICS

EXAMPLE   1. "what do you know about Modern architecture at the beginning of the Century, sean?"

1. *What, modern, century, Sean*

1. In Social Studies, i learned about the famous Architect Frank Lloyd Wright.
2. One of wright's best-known works is his house, fallingwater, in bear run, Pennsylvania.
3. "Yes, wright still may be the best-known american architect," Mrs. Lee said.
4. Louis sullivan (1856–1924) was among the first Builders in the united States to use a steel frame.
5. A german architect helped design the Seagram Building, an early Skyscraper in the east.
6. Both architects and the Public wanted new ideas after world war II, according to my architecture 101 teacher.
7. the use of reinforced Concrete made possible large, thin roofs such as the one at the Massachusetts institute of technology.
8. Next tuesday we will see a Film about inventive designs in the brazilian capital.
9. I imagine that brazilian Citizens are proud of the architect Oscar niemeyer.
10. Hear my report on the israeli architect Moshe Safdie during History today.

13g. Capitalize titles.

(1) Capitalize the title of a person when the title comes before a name.

EXAMPLES   **P**resident Lincoln   **M**rs. Oliver Wendell

Mayor Bradley   **C**ommissioner Rodriguez

Generally, a title that is used alone or following a person's name is not capitalized, especially if the title is preceded by *a* or *the.*

EXAMPLES   The **s**ecretary of **d**efense held a news conference.

Lien Fong, our class **s**ecretary, read the minutes.

However, a title used by itself in direct address is usually capitalized.

STYLE   TIP

For special emphasis or clarity, writers sometimes capitalize a title used alone or following a person's name.

EXAMPLES

At the ceremony, the **Q**ueen honored the Royal Navy.

Mr. Biden, the **S**enator from Delaware, called for a committee vote.

EXAMPLES   Is it very serious, **D**octor?

           How do you do, **S**ir [or sir]?

(2) Capitalize a word showing a family relationship when the word is used before or in place of a person's name.

EXAMPLES   We expect **U**ncle Fred and **A**unt Helen soon.

           Both **M**om and **D**ad work at the hospital.

However, do not capitalize a word showing a family relationship when a possessive comes before the word.

EXAMPLE   We asked Pedro's **m**other and his **a**unt Celia to be chaperons.

(3) Capitalize the first and last words and all important words in titles and subtitles.

Unimportant words in titles include

- articles (*a, an, the*)
- coordinating conjunctions (*and, but, for, nor, or, so, yet*)
- prepositions of fewer than five letters (such as *by, for, on, with*)

Type of Name	Examples	
Books	*The Mask of Apollo* *Mules and Men*	*Long Claws: An* *Arctic Adventure*
Chapters and Other Parts of Books	"The Circulatory System" "Language Handbook"	"The Civil War Begins" "Epilogue"
Magazines	*Popular Mechanics* *Ebony*	*Seventeen* *Sports Illustrated*
Newspapers	*The Tennessean* the *Boston Globe*	*The Wall Street Journal*
Poems	"Season at the Shore"	*Evangeline* "Birches"

(continued)

Reference Note

For more information about **articles,** see page 35. For more about **coordinating conjunctions,** see page 62. For more about **prepositions,** see page 58.

Reference Note

For guidelines on **what titles are italicized,** see page 320. For guidelines on **what titles are enclosed in quotation marks,** see page 327.

MECHANICS

(continued)

Type of Name	Examples	
Short Stories	"The Purloined Letter"	"Zlateh the Goat" "Broken Chain"
Plays	*The Three Sisters* *A Midsummer Night's Dream*	*A Doll's House* *I Never Sang for My Father*
Movies and Videos	*Fairy Tale: A True Story* *Babe*	*It's a Wonderful Life* *The Wizard of Oz*
Television Series	*Nova* *Kratt's Creatures*	*Star Trek: The Next Generation*
Cartoons and Comic Strips	*Jump Start* *Cathy*	*Scooby Doo* *Dilbert*
Albums and CDs	*Butterfly* *Falling into You*	*Dos Mundos* *Spirit*
Computer Games and Video Games	*Sonic the Hedgehog* *Math Blaster* *Rockett's New School*	*Logical Journey* *SimCity* *Space Kids*
Works of Art	*Mona Lisa* *David*	*The Night Watch* *Mankind's Struggle*
Musical Compositions	*The Marriage of Figaro*	"America the Beautiful"
Historical Documents	Magna Carta Treaty of Paris	The Declaration of Independence

─HELP─

The official title of a book is found on the title page. The official title of a newspaper or periodical is found on the masthead, which usually appears on the editorial page or the table of contents.

NOTE The article *the* at the beginning of a title is not capitalized unless it is the first word of the official title.

EXAMPLES My father reads *The Wall Street Journal.*

Does she work for the *Texas Review*?

Exercise 5 Correcting Sentences by Capitalizing Words

Most of the following sentences contain at least one word that should be capitalized but is not. Correctly write each incorrect word. If a sentence is already correct, write *C*.

EXAMPLE   **1.** Ms. Chang is meeting with principal Hodges.

         1. Principal

1. Tom Hanks' career really took off after he starred in the movie *big.*
2. In 1998, John Glenn, a former senator, became the oldest person to travel in space.
3. The assignment is to compare and contrast Amy Tan's story "Two kinds" with Bernard Malamud's "The first seven years."
4. Rummaging through the pile of used books, Marcia found a copy of *the Complete Poems of Stephen Crane.*
5. Our English teacher, mrs. Fernandez, has a small sculpture of the globe theatre sitting on her desk.
6. Isn't it a coincidence that your aunt Jenny and my uncle Herbert work for the same company?
7. Which do you prefer, Bob Dylan's CD *Nashville skyline* or his son's *The wallflowers*?
8. Some of my friends claim that *The Empire strikes back* is the best movie of the series.
9. Did you remember to clip that article we read yesterday in *The Washington post*?
10. Mom and dad always chuckle when they read *Hagar the Horrible.*

Review C Proofreading Sentences for Correct Capitalization

Write the sentences on the following page, using capital letters wherever they are needed.

EXAMPLE   **1.** The series *all creatures great and small* is being rerun on public television.

         1. The series All Creatures Great and Small *is being rerun on public television.*

1. While waiting to interview mayor ward, I read an article in *newsweek*.
2. Have you read leslie marmon silko's poem "story from bear country"?
3. You have probably seen a picture of *the thinker*, one of rodin's best-known sculptures.
4. On television last night, we saw the movie *the return of the native*.
5. Every four years voters elect a president and several united states senators.
6. Uncle nick read aloud from francisco jiménez's short story "the circuit."
7. The reporter asked, "Can you tell us, senator inouye, when you plan to announce the committee's final decision?"
8. The main speaker was dr. andrew holt, a former president of the university of tennessee.
9. Besides uncle don, our visitors included aunt pat, aunt jean, both of my grandmothers, and my great-grandfather.
10. The soccer players listened to coach Daly as he outlined defensive strategy.

Review D **Proofreading Sentences for Correct Capitalization**

The following sentences each contain at least one capitalization error. Correctly write the words that require capital letters.

EXAMPLE
1. The waters of the caribbean are pleasantly warm.
   1. Caribbean

1. The greeks believed that zeus, the king of the gods, lived on mount olympus.
2. The *titanic* sank after hitting an iceberg off the coast of newfoundland.
3. My cousin collects scandinavian pottery.
4. Stephanie is taking english, math II, and biology.
5. On friday we were cheered by the thought that monday, memorial day, would be a holiday.
6. My picture is in today's *austin American-Statesman*.
7. The quaker oats company has introduced a new corn cereal.
8. In *roots*, alex haley, a famous author, traces the history of his family.
9. She usually travels to boston on american airlines.

10. I wanted to name my persian cat after one of the justices on the supreme court.

Review E **Proofreading a Paragraph for Correct Capitalization**

Each sentence in the following paragraph contains at least one error in capitalization. Correctly write the words that require capital letters.

EXAMPLE **[1]** Before thanksgiving, i learned some interesting facts about africa in my history II class.

    1. Thanksgiving, I, Africa, History II

    [1] My teacher, mr. davidson, told us about the mighty kingdoms and empires that existed for hundreds of years in africa. **[2]** some of these kingdoms dated back to the time of the roman empire. **[3]** Others rose to power during the period known as the middle ages in europe. **[4]** For many years, the people in the kingdom of cush did ironwork and traded along the nile river. **[5]** Later, the cush were defeated by the people of axum, led by king ezana. **[6]** As you can see in the map below, several kingdoms in africa developed between lake chad and the atlantic ocean. **[7]** Three of these kingdoms were ghana, mali, and songhai. **[8]** These kingdoms established important trade routes across the sahara. **[9]** Tombouctou's famous university attracted egyptian and other arab students. **[10]** I read more about these african kingdoms and empires in our textbook, *world history: people and nations.*

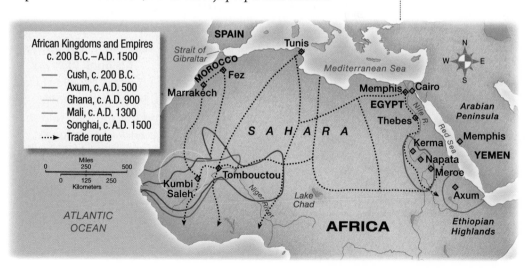

African Kingdoms and Empires
c. 200 B.C.–A.D. 1500

— Cush, c. 200 B.C.
— Axum, c. A.D. 500
- - - Ghana, c. A.D. 900
— Mali, c. A.D. 1300
— Songhai, c. A.D. 1500
····► Trade route

Miles
0   250   500
0   125   250
Kilometers

SPAIN
Strait of Gibraltar
Tunis
MOROCCO
Fez
Marrakech
Mediterranean Sea
Memphis Cairo
EGYPT
Thebes
Nile R.
Arabian Peninsula
Red Sea
Memphis
Kerma
Napata
YEMEN
Meroe
S A H A R A
Tombouctou
Kumbi Saleh
Niger River
Lake Chad
Axum
ATLANTIC OCEAN
AFRICA
Ethiopian Highlands
N W E S

MECHANICS

Correcting Errors in Capitalization

Each of the following sentences contains at least one error in capitalization. Correctly write each incorrect word, changing capital letters to lowercase letters or changing lowercase letters to capital letters.

EXAMPLE
1. On june 25, 1876, sioux and cheyenne warriors defeated general george a. Custer and his Troops.

1. *June, Sioux, Cheyenne, General George A., troops*

1. The Defeat of general custer occurred at the battle of the little bighorn.
2. In december of 1890, many Sioux were killed by Soldiers in a battle at wounded Knee creek in south Dakota.
3. Depicted by artists, writers, and filmmakers, both Battles have become part of american History.
4. In the late nineteenth century, the sioux Artist Kicking bear painted the *Battle Of the little Bighorn.*
5. The painting, done on muslin Cloth, is shown below.
6. Kicking bear, who himself fought in the Battle, painted at the pine Ridge agency in south Dakota, where he lived.
7. soldiers who fought against kicking Bear described him as courageous.
8. The well-known American Poet Stephen vincent benét wrote about the battle of wounded knee in a Poem called "american names."

9. More recently, the author Dee brown wrote about the american indians of the west in his book *bury my Heart at Wounded knee.*
10. In 1970, the movie *Little big Man* told the story of a fictional 121-year-old character who had survived the Battle against general Custer.

Battle of Little Bighorn by Kicking Bear (Sioux), 1898. Courtesy of the Southwest Museum, Los Angeles

MECHANICS

CHAPTER

Chapter Review

A. Correcting Errors in Capitalization

Each of the following sentences contains at least one error in capitalization. Correct the errors either by changing capital letters to lowercase letters or by changing lowercase letters to capital letters.

1. Please pick up a box of Tide Detergent at the store.
2. The "Battle Hymn Of The Republic" was written by Julia ward Howe.
3. Are we going to uncle Ted's house for Thanksgiving again?
4. Charing cross book shop is on Thirty-Second Street.
5. Ms. wong always stays at the Four Seasons hotel when she's in New York city on business.
6. Do you know if professor Ezekiel will be teaching Creative Writing during the spring semester?
7. In what year was the battle of gettysburg fought?
8. Mother Teresa won the Nobel Peace prize in 1979.
9. Every winter my Grandparents travel to the southwest.
10. My Uncle sid read a book about sir Winston Churchill.
11. Mr. Salter often remembers his old house on vine street in McAllen, Texas.
12. Father and mother traveled all over the Earth when they were buying furniture for their antique store.
13. The principal asked me, "how would you like to study Geography next semester?"
14. When Jim went back to New York for Christmas, he left his dog, piper, at the kennel.
15. Sometimes my Mother works at home on friday.
16. Grand Canyon National park was closed this weekend because of heavy snow.
17. Shall we renew our subscription to *national geographic*?
18. This june we plan to welcome a swedish exchange student to our home.

MECHANICS

19. We're going to Washington, D.C., to see the white house.

20. At the Henry Ford Museum in Dearborn, Michigan, you can see a replica of the *spirit of st. louis,* the plane that Charles Lindbergh used to fly solo across the atlantic.

21. At the Crossbay Market, i bought a can of progresso soup.

22. My Aunt Janice visited Petrified Forest National Park.

23. The Rosenbach museum and library in Philadelphia is open Tuesday through Sunday.

24. dear Mr. Boylan:

   I enjoyed your book enormously.

   sincerely yours,

   Jimmy Connolly

25. In History class, we learned about queen Elizabeth I.

B. Proofreading Sentences for Correct Capitalization

Write the following sentences, and correct errors in capitalization either by changing capital letters to lowercase letters or by changing lowercase letters to capital letters.

26. Mars, Venus, and Jupiter were roman gods.

27. *The wind in the willows* is my Mother's favorite book.

28. Davis Housewares emporium has moved to Fifth street.

29. The lozi people in Africa live near the Zambezi river.

30. "Stopping By Woods On a Snowy Evening" is by Robert Frost, a Poet from New England.

31. Do you know when David Souter was appointed to the supreme court?

32. Next Monday is memorial day.

33. When we traveled through the south, we visited the Antietam National Battlefield.

34. Ms. Ling is teaching us about chinese culture.

35. Cayuga lake stretches North from Ithaca, New York.

36. The main religion in Indonesia is islam, but there are also many Indonesian buddhists.

37. My older sister is taking Spanish, Science, Mathematics II, and Art.

38. Carlos and I had turkey sandwiches made with german mustard on french bread.

39. We turned west onto route 95 and stayed on it for five miles.

40. George Copway, who was born in Canada, wrote about his people, the ojibwa.

Writing Application
Using Capital Letters in a Letter

Proper Nouns   Students in your class have become pen pals with students in another country. You have been given the name of someone to write. Write your pen pal a letter introducing yourself and telling about your school and your community. In your letter, be sure to use capitalization correctly.

Prewriting   Note the information you want to give in your letter. You may wish to include information such as your age; a description of yourself; your favorite books, movies, actors, or musicians; some clubs, organizations, or special activities you participate in; some special places, events, or attractions in your community or state.

Writing   As you write your draft, keep in mind that your pen pal may not recognize names of some people, places, and things in the United States. For example, he or she may not recognize the names of your favorite movies or musical groups. Be sure to use correct capitalization to show which names are proper nouns.

Revising   Read through your letter carefully. Have you left out any important information? Are any parts of your letter confusing? If so, you may want to add, cut, or revise some details. Is the tone of your letter friendly? Have you followed the correct form for a personal letter?

Publishing   Read your letter carefully to check for any errors in grammar, spelling, and punctuation. Use the rules in this chapter to help you double-check your capitalization. With your teacher's permission, post a map of the world on the classroom wall and display the letters around the map.

Punctuation
End Marks, Commas, Semicolons, and Colons

1.0 Written and Oral English Language Conventions

Students write and speak with a command of standard English conventions appropriate to this grade level.

1.4 Demonstrate the mechanics of writing (e.g., commas at end of dependent clauses).

1.5 Identify semicolons and use them correctly.

┌HELP┐

All of the punctuation marks that are already in the sentences in the Diagnostic Preview are correct.

Diagnostic Preview

Using End Marks, Commas, Semicolons, and Colons

The following sentences lack necessary periods, question marks, exclamation points, commas, semicolons, and colons. Rewrite each sentence, inserting the correct punctuation.

EXAMPLE   1. Snakes lizards crocodiles and turtles are reptiles
            1. *Snakes, lizards, crocodiles, and turtles are reptiles.*

1. Toads and frogs on the other hand are amphibians
2. Some turtles live on land others live in lakes streams or oceans
3. Turtles have no teeth but you should watch out for their strong hard beaks
4. The words *turtle* and *tortoise* are similar in meaning but *tortoise* usually refers to a land dweller
5. The African pancake tortoise which has a flat flexible shell uses an unusual means of defense
6. Faced with a threat it crawls into a narrow crack in a rock takes a deep breath and wedges itself in tightly
7. Because some species of tortoises are endangered they cannot be sold as pets

8. Three species of tortoises that can be found in the United States are as follows the desert tortoise the gopher tortoise and the Texas tortoise

9. The gopher tortoise lives in the Southeast and the desert tortoise comes from the Southwest

10. Is the Indian star tortoise which is now an endangered species very rare

11. As this kind of tortoise grows older its shell grows larger the number of stars on the shell increases and their pattern becomes more complex

12. The Indian star tortoise requires warmth sunlight and a diet of green vegetables

13. Living in fresh water soft-shelled turtles have long flexible beaks and fleshy lips

14. Their shells are not really soft however but are covered by smooth skin

15. Sea turtles are the fastest turtles the green turtle can swim at speeds of almost twenty miles per hour.

16. Most turtles can pull their head, legs, and tail into their shell however sea turtles cannot do so.

17. Mr Kim my neighbor up the street has several turtles in his backyard pond.

18. Come to my house at 4 30 in the afternoon, and I'll show you our turtle.

19. At 7:00 P M , we can watch that new PBS documentary about sea turtles.

20. Wanda may I introduce you to Pokey my pet turtle

21. Pokey who has been part of our family for years is a red-eared turtle.

22. The book *Turtles A Complete Pet Owner's Manual* has helped me learn how to take care of Pokey.

23. Pokey has been in my family for fifteen years and my parents say that he could easily live to be fifty if he is cared for properly

24. What a great pet Pokey is

25. Don't you agree with me Wanda that a turtle makes a good pet

End Marks

An ***end mark*** is a mark of punctuation placed at the end of a sentence. *Periods, question marks,* and *exclamation points* are end marks.

14a. Use a period at the end of a statement.

EXAMPLE   Tea is grown in Sri Lanka.

14b. Use a question mark at the end of a question.

EXAMPLE   Did you see the exhibit about lightning?

14c. Use an exclamation point at the end of an exclamation.

EXAMPLE   Wow! What a high bridge that was!

14d. Use either a period or an exclamation point at the end of a request or a command.

When an imperative sentence makes a request, it is generally followed by a period. When an imperative sentence expresses a strong command, an exclamation point is generally used.

EXAMPLES   Please call the dog. [a request]
Call the dog! [a command]

> ┌HELP──
> Periods (decimal points) are also used to separate dollars from cents and whole numbers from tenths, hundredths, and so forth.
>
> EXAMPLES
> $10.23 [ten dollars and twenty-three cents]
> 5.7 [five and seven tenths]

Oral Practice   **Adding End Marks to Sentences**

Read each of the following sentences aloud, and indicate which end mark should be added.

EXAMPLE   1. Did you know that a choreographer is a person who creates dance steps

1. Did you know that a choreographer is a person who creates dance steps?

1. Why is Katherine Dunham called the mother of African American dance
2. She studied anthropology in college and won a scholarship to visit the Caribbean
3. How inspiring the dances she saw in Haiti were
4. When Dunham returned to the United States, she toured the country with her own professional dance company
5. How I admire such a talented person
6. Ask me anything about Katherine Dunham

MECHANICS

7. How many honors has Dunham's creativity won her

8. She was named to the Hall of Fame of the National Museum of Dance in Saratoga, New York

9. She was also given the National Medal of Arts for exploring Caribbean and African dance

10. The editors of *Essence* magazine praised Dunham for helping to break down racial barriers

14e. Many abbreviations are followed by a period.

Types of Abbreviations	Examples
Personal Names	A. B. Guthrie W.E.B. DuBois Livie I. Durán
Titles Used with Names	Mr. Mrs. Ms. Jr. Sr. Dr.
Organizations and Companies	Co. Inc. Corp. Assn.

NOTE Abbreviations for government agencies and other widely used abbreviations are written without periods. Each letter of the abbreviation is capitalized.

EXAMPLES FBI NAACP NIH NPR
          PTA TV UN YWCA

Types of Abbreviations	Examples
Addresses	Ave. St. Rd. Blvd. P.O. Box
States	Tex. Penn. Ariz. Wash. N.C.
Times	A.M. (*ante meridiem,* used with times from midnight to noon) P.M. (*post meridiem,* used with times from noon to midnight) B.C. (before Christ) A.D. (*anno Domini,* in the year of the Lord)

STYLE TIP

When writing the initials of someone's name, place a space between two initials (S. E. Hinton). Do not place spaces between three initials (M.F.K. Fisher).

STYLE TIP

An **acronym** is a word formed from the first (or first few) letters of a series of words. Acronyms are written without periods.

EXAMPLES
UNICEF (**U**nited **N**ations **I**nternational **C**hildren's **E**mergency **F**und)

VISTA (**V**olunteers **i**n **S**ervice **t**o **A**merica)

MECHANICS

The abbreviations *A.D.* and *B.C.* need special attention. You should place *A.D.* before the numeral and *B.C.* after the numeral.

EXAMPLES
A.D. 760   54 **B.C.**

However, for centuries expressed in words, place both *A.D.* and *B.C.* after the century.

EXAMPLES
seventh century **B.C.**

fourth century **A.D.**

HELP

If you are not sure whether you should use a period with an abbreviation, look up the abbreviation in a dictionary.

MECHANICS

NOTE A two-letter state abbreviation without periods is used only when it is followed by a ZIP Code. Both letters of such abbreviations are capitalized.

EXAMPLE   Orlando, **FL** 32819

Abbreviations for units of measure are usually written without periods and are not capitalized.

EXAMPLES   mm   kg   dl   oz   lb   ft   yd   mi

However, to avoid confusion with the word *in*, you should use a period with the abbreviation for *inch* (*in.*).

NOTE When an abbreviation with a period ends a sentence, another period is not needed. However, a question mark or an exclamation point is used as needed.

EXAMPLES   We will arrive by 3:00 P.M.
Can you meet us at 3:30 P.M.?
Oh no! It's already 3:30 P.M.!

Exercise 1 Punctuating Abbreviations

Some of the following sentences contain abbreviations that have not been correctly punctuated. Correct each error. If a sentence is already correct, write *C*.

EXAMPLE   **1.** Of course, we watch P.B.S.; we love the science shows it broadcasts.

1. PBS

1. Not everyone knows that WEB DuBois eventually became a Ghanaian citizen.
2. The writing isn't clear, but I think it says *10 ft 6 in* or *10 ft 5 in*.
3. Write me in care of Mrs. Audrey Coppola, 10 Watson Ave..
4. Yes, that's in California—Novato, C.A. 94949.
5. Were those clay statues made as far back as 500 B.C?
6. Send your check or money order to Lester's Low-Cost Computer Chips, Inc, Duluth, Minn, and receive your new chips in two days!
7. Could you be there at 7:00 P.M.?

8. I would never do business with a company whose only address was a PO box.
9. Miss Finch, Dr Bledsoe will see you now.
10. His full name is Marvin French Little Hawk, Jr., but everyone calls him Junior.

Review A **Adding Periods, Question Marks, and Exclamation Points to Sentences**

Rewrite each of the following sentences, adding the necessary periods, question marks, and exclamation points.

EXAMPLE
1. Do you ever think about how electricity is produced
    1. *Do you ever think about how electricity is produced?*

controls

water

turbine

generator

electricity

1. Electricity can come from large hydroelectric power stations
2. Wow, these stations certainly do create a lot of power
3. How do hydroelectric power stations work
4. Look at the diagram to gain a better understanding
5. Falling water from natural falls or artificial dams provides the initial power in the process
6. Have you ever been to Niagara Falls, New York, to see the famous falls
7. From 12:00 AM. to 12:00 AM.—constantly, in other words—the falls are a tremendous power source
8. As you can see, rushing water turns turbines, which then drive generators
9. What exactly are generators, and what do they do
10. J D explained that generators are the machines that turn the motion of the turbines into electricity

MECHANICS

Commas

End marks are used to separate complete thoughts. *Commas,* however, are generally used to separate words or groups of words within a complete thought.

14f. Use commas to separate items in a series.

A *series* is a group of three or more items in a row. Words, phrases, and clauses may appear in a series.

Words in a Series
January, February, and March are all summer months in the Southern Hemisphere. [nouns]
The engine rattled, coughed, and stalled. [verbs]
The baby was happy, alert, playful, and active. [adjectives]

Phrases in a Series
There were fingerprints at the top, on the sides, and on the bottom. [prepositional phrases]
Cut into pieces, aged for a year, and well dried, the wood was ready to burn. [participial phrases]
To pitch in a World Series game, to practice medicine, and to run for mayor are all things I would like to do someday. [infinitive phrases]

Clauses in a Series
We sang, we danced, we ate dinner, and we played trivia games. [short independent clauses]
I knew that we were late, that the ice cream was melting, and that the car was nearly out of gas. [short subordinate clauses]

Reference Note

For information about using **semicolons**, see page 310.

NOTE Only short independent clauses in a series may be separated by commas. A series of independent clauses that are long or that contain commas should be separated by semicolons.

EXAMPLE Yawning, Mother closed the curtains; Father, who had just come in, turned on the porch lights; and my little sister, Christina, put on her pajamas.

MECHANICS

Always be sure that there are at least three items in the series; two items generally do not need a comma between them.

INCORRECT   You will need a pencil, and plenty of paper.

CORRECT   You will need a pencil and plenty of paper.

When all the items in the series are joined by *and* or *or*, do not use commas to separate them.

EXAMPLES   Take water **and** food **and** matches with you.

Stephen will take a class in karate **or** judo **or** aikido next year.

Exercise 2 **Proofreading Sentences for the Correct Use of Commas**

Some of the following sentences need commas; others do not. If a sentence needs any commas, write the word before each missing comma and add the comma. If a sentence is already correct, write *C*.

EXAMPLES   1. Seal the envelope stamp it and mail the letter.

1. *envelope, it,*

2. You should swing the club with your knees bent and your back straight and your elbows tucked.

2. *C*

1. The mountains and valleys of southern Appalachia were once home to the Cherokee people.
2. Cleveland Cincinnati Toledo and Dayton are four large cities in Ohio.
3. The captain entered the cockpit checked the instruments and prepared for takeoff.
4. Luisa bought mangos and papayas and oranges.
5. The speaker took a deep breath and read the report.
6. Rover can roll over walk on his hind feet and catch a tennis ball.
7. The neighbors searched behind the garages in the bushes and along the highway.
8. Rubén Blades is an attorney an actor and a singer.
9. Eleanor Roosevelt's courage her humanity and her service to the nation will always be remembered.
10. Tate dusted I vacuumed and Blair washed the dishes.

STYLE   TIP

In your reading, you will find that some writers omit the comma before the conjunction joining the last two items of a series. Nevertheless, you should form the habit of including this comma. Sometimes a comma is necessary to make your meaning clear. Notice how the comma affects the meaning in the following examples.

EXAMPLES

Mom, Jody and I want to go to the movies. [Mom is being asked for her permission.]

Mom, Jody, and I want to go to the movies. [Three people want to go to the movies.]

MECHANICS

14g. Use a comma to separate two or more adjectives that come before a noun.

EXAMPLES   A white dwarf is a tiny, dense star.

               Venus Williams played a powerful, brilliant game.

Do not place a comma between an adjective and the noun immediately following it.

INCORRECT   My spaniel is a fat, sassy, puppy.

  CORRECT   My spaniel is a fat, sassy puppy.

TIPS & TRICKS

To see whether a comma is needed between two adjectives, insert *and* between the adjectives. If *and* sounds awkward there, do not use a comma.

EXAMPLE
    unshaded electric light

TEST
    unshaded and electric light

ANSWER
    No comma is needed.

    Another test you can use is to switch the order of the adjectives. If the sentence still makes sense when you switch them, use a comma.

EXAMPLE
    tiny, dense star

TEST
    dense, tiny star

ANSWER
    Use a comma.

Sometimes the final adjective in a series is thought of as part of the noun. When the adjective and the noun are linked in such a way, do not use a comma before the final adjective.

EXAMPLES   A huge **horned owl** lives in those woods.
               [not *huge, horned owl*]

               An unshaded **electric light** hung from the ceiling.
               [not *unshaded, electric light*]

NOTE   When an adjective and a noun are closely linked, they may be thought of as a unit. Such a unit is called a **compound noun.**

EXAMPLES   Persian cat   Black Sea   French bread

Review B **Proofreading Sentences for the Correct Use of Commas**

Most of the following sentences need commas. If a sentence needs any commas, write the word before each missing comma and add the comma. If a sentence is already correct, write *C*.

EXAMPLE   1. Chen participated in debate volleyball and drama.

             1. *debate, volleyball,*

1. Carla sneaked in and left a huge gorgeous fragrant bouquet of flowers on the desk.
2. I chose the gift Michael wrapped it and Charley gave it to Gina and Kelly.
3. Smoking is a costly dangerous habit.
4. In the human ear, the hammer anvil and stirrup carry sound waves to the brain.
5. Buffalo Bill was a Pony Express rider a scout and a touring stunt performer.

Reference Note

For more information about **compound nouns,** see page 25.

MECHANICS

6. "The Masque of the Red Death" is a famous horror story by Edgar Allan Poe.
7. According to Greek mythology, the three Fates spin the thread of life measure it and cut it.
8. LeVar Burton played the intelligent likable character Geordi on *Star Trek: The Next Generation*.
9. The fluffy kitten with the brown white and black spots is my favorite.
10. Falstaff begged for mercy in a fight ran away and later bragged about his bravery in battle.

Compound Sentences

14h. Use a comma before *and, but, for, nor, or, so,* or *yet* when it joins independent clauses in a compound sentence.

EXAMPLES   Tamisha offered me a ticket, and I accepted.

They had been working very hard, but they didn't seem especially tired.

The Mullaney twins were excited, for they were going to day care for the first time.

When the independent clauses are very short and there is no chance of misunderstanding, the comma before *and, but,* or *or* is sometimes omitted.

EXAMPLES   It rained and it rained.

Come with us or meet us there.

NOTE   Always use a comma before *for, nor, so,* or *yet* when joining independent clauses.

EXAMPLE   I was tired, yet I stayed.

Do not be misled by a simple sentence that contains a compound verb. A simple sentence has only one independent clause.

SIMPLE SENTENCE WITH COMPOUND VERB   Usually we **study** in the morning and **play** basketball in the afternoon.

COMPOUND SENTENCE   Usually we study in the morning, and we play basketball in the afternoon. [two independent clauses]

STYLE   TIP

The word *so* is often overused. If possible, try to reword a sentence to avoid using *so*.

EXAMPLE
It was late, so we went home.

REVISED
Because it was late, we went home.

Reference Note

For more information about **compound sentences,** see page 131. For more about **simple sentences** with **compound verbs,** see page 15.

MECHANICS

Correcting Compound Sentences by Adding Commas

If a sentence needs a comma, write the word before the missing comma and add the comma. If an existing comma is unnecessary, write the words before and after the comma and omit the comma. If the sentence is already correct, write *C.*

EXAMPLE
1. American Indian artists have a heritage dating back thousands of years and many of them draw on this heritage, to create modern works.

1. *years, heritage to*

1. Today's artists sometimes work with nontraditional materials but they often use traditional techniques.
2. In the photograph below, you can see the work of the Tohono O'odham artist Mary Thomas, and begin to appreciate this basket weaver's skill.
3. The baskets in the photograph are woven in the "friendship design" and show a circle of human figures in a traditional prayer ceremony.
4. Yucca and devil's claw are used to make these baskets and each plant's leaves are a different color.
5. The Navajo artist Danny Randeau Tsosie listened to his grandmother's stories, and learned about his family's heritage.
6. Tsosie's works show her influence but also express his own point of view.
7. Christine Nofchissey McHorse learned the skill of pottery making from her grandmother and now McHorse can make beautiful bowls.
8. McHorse has an unusual style for her designs combine traditional Navajo and Pueblo images.

9. American Indian jewelry makers often use pieces of turquoise and coral found in North America and they also use other stones from around the world.

10. American Indian art often looks very modern yet some of its symbols and patterns are quite old.

Interrupters

14i. Use commas to set off an expression that interrupts a sentence.

Two commas are needed if the expression to be set off comes in the middle of the sentence. One comma is needed if the expression comes first or last.

EXAMPLES   Ann Myers**, our neighbor,** is a fine golfer.

Naturally, we expect to win.

My answer is correct**, I think.**

(1) Use commas to set off nonessential participial phrases and nonessential subordinate clauses.

A *nonessential* (or *nonrestrictive*) phrase or clause adds information that is not needed to understand the basic meaning of the sentence. Such a phrase or clause can be omitted without changing the main idea of the sentence.

NONESSENTIAL PHRASES   My sister**, listening to her radio,** did not hear me.

Paul**, thrilled by the applause,** took a bow.

NONESSENTIAL CLAUSES   *The Wizard of Oz***, which I saw again last week,** is my favorite movie.

I reported on *Secret of the Andes***, which was written by Ann Nolan Clark.**

Each boldface clause or phrase above can be omitted because it is not essential to identify the word or phrase it modifies. Omitting such a clause or phrase will not change the meaning of the sentence.

EXAMPLES   Paul took a bow.

I reported on *Secret of the Andes.*

PEANUTS reprinted by permission of United Feature Syndicate, Inc.

MECHANICS

Reference Note

For more about **phrases,** see Chapter 5. For more about **subordinate clauses,** see page 114.

Do not set off an *essential* (or *restrictive*) phrase or clause. Since such a phrase or clause tells *which one(s)*, it cannot be omitted without changing the basic meaning of the sentence.

ESSENTIAL PHRASES   The people **waiting to see Michael Jordan** whistled and cheered. [Which people?]

A bowl **made by Maria Martínez** is a collector's item. [Which bowl?]

ESSENTIAL CLAUSES   The dress **that I liked** has been sold. [Which dress?]

The man **who tells Navajo folk tales** is Mr. Platero. [Which man?]

Notice how the meaning changes when an essential phrase or clause is omitted.

EXAMPLES   The people whistled and cheered.

A bowl is a collector's item.

The dress has been sold.

The man is Mr. Platero.

NOTE A clause beginning with *that* is usually essential.

EXAMPLE   This is the birdhouse **that I made.**

Exercise 4 **Adding Commas to Sentences with Nonessential Phrases and Clauses**

Some of the following sentences need commas to set off nonessential phrases and clauses. Other sentences are correct without commas. If a sentence needs commas, write the word that comes before each missing comma and add the comma. If the sentence is already correct, write *C*.

EXAMPLE   1. My grandfather's favorite photograph which was taken near Ellis Island shows his family after their arrival from Eastern Europe.

1. *photograph, Island,*

1. Millions of immigrants who came to the United States between about 1892 and 1954 stopped at Ellis Island which is in Upper New York Bay.

2. Families arriving from Europe were interviewed there.

3. The island and its buildings which were closed to the public for many years are now part of the Statue of Liberty National Monument.

4. In 1990, Ellis Island rebuilt as a museum was officially opened to the public.

5. Visitors who wish to see the museum can take a ferry ride from Manhattan Island.

6. The museum's lobby crowded with steamer trunks and other old baggage is the visitors' first sight.

7. One special attraction in the museum consists of audiotapes and videotapes that describe the immigrants' experiences.

The Granger Collection, New York.

8. The Registry Room which is on the second floor sometimes held as many as five thousand people.

9. The immigrants who came from many countries hoped to find freedom and a happier life in America.

10. Immigrants who came to the United States brought with them a strong work ethic and a variety of skills that helped to make our country great.

(2) Use commas to set off nonessential appositives and nonessential appositive phrases.

An **_appositive_** is a noun or a pronoun used to identify or describe another noun or pronoun.

NONESSENTIAL APPOSITIVE	My oldest sister, **Alicia**, will be at basketball practice until 6:00 P.M.
NONESSENTIAL APPOSITIVE PHRASES	Jamaica, **a popular island for tourists**, is in the Caribbean Sea.
	May I introduce you to Vernon, **my cousin from Jamaica**?

Do not use commas to set off an appositive that is essential to the meaning of a sentence.

ESSENTIAL APPOSITIVES

My sister **Alicia** is at basketball practice. [The speaker has more than one sister and must give a name to identify which sister.]

The planet **Mercury** is closer to the Sun than any other planet in our solar system. [The solar system contains more than one planet. The name is needed to identify which planet.]

Exercise 5 **Proofreading for the Correct Use of Commas with Appositives and Appositive Phrases**

Rewrite each of the following sentences, and underline the appositive or appositive phrase. Use commas to set off non-essential appositive phrases.

EXAMPLE
1. Mars one of the planets closest to Earth can be seen without a telescope.

1. Mars, _one of the planets closest to Earth_, can be seen without a telescope.

1. The whole class has read the novel *Old Yeller*.
2. Shana Alexander a former editor of a popular magazine was the main speaker at the conference.
3. The character Sabrina is Josie's favorite.
4. The Galápagos Islands a group of volcanic islands in the Pacific Ocean were named for the Spanish word that means "tortoise."
5. Rubber an elastic substance quickly restores itself to its original size and shape.
6. This bowl is made of clay found on Kilimanjaro the highest mountain in Africa.
7. The North Sea an arm of the Atlantic Ocean is rich in fish, natural gas, and oil.
8. Jamake Highwater a Blackfoot/Eastern Band Cherokee author writes about the history of his people.
9. At Gettysburg a town in Pennsylvania an important battle of the Civil War was fought.
10. My friend Imelda is teaching me how to make empanadas.

MEETING THE CHALLENGE

You can use appositives and appositive phrases to combine sentences.

ORIGINAL
Our old house is on Larchmont Street. That house is my favorite place.

COMBINED
Our old house, my favorite place, is on Larchmont Street.

Use appositive phrases to combine the following sentences.

1. Ms. Blewett asked me to help out after practice. She's our coach.

2. I play halfback. The halfback is the position between the forward and the fullback.

MECHANICS

(3) Use commas to set off words that are used in direct address.

EXAMPLES **Ben,** please answer the doorbell.

Mom needs you, **Francine.**

Would you show me, **ma'am,** where the craft store is?

Exercise 6 **Correcting Sentences by Using Commas with Words of Direct Address**

Identify the words used in direct address in the following sentences. Then, rewrite each sentence, inserting commas before, after, or both before and after the words, as needed.

EXAMPLE 1. Listen folks to this amazing announcement!
1. *folks—Listen, folks, to this amazing announcement!*

1. Andrea when are you leaving for Detroit?
2. Pay attention now class.
3. Let us my sisters and brothers give thanks.
4. Please Dad may I use your computer?
5. Senator please summarize your tax proposal.
6. Help me move this table Marlene.
7. "Tell me both of you what movie you want to see," Jo said.
8. Hurry William and give me the phone number!
9. Mrs. Larson where is Zion National Park?
10. I'm just not sure friends that I agree with you.

(4) Use commas to set off parenthetical expressions.

A *parenthetical expression* is a side remark that adds information or shows a relationship between ideas.

EXAMPLES Carl, **on the contrary,** prefers soccer to baseball.

To tell the truth, Jan is one of my best friends.

Common Parenthetical Expressions		
by the way	in fact	of course
for example	in my opinion	on the contrary
however	I suppose	on the other hand
I believe	nevertheless	to tell the truth

Some of these expressions are not always used parenthetically.

EXAMPLES   **Of course** it is true. [not parenthetical]

That is**,** **of course,** an Indian teakwood screen. [parenthetical]

I suppose we ought to go home now. [not parenthetical]

He'll want a ride**,** **I suppose.** [parenthetical]

Exercise 7 **Correcting Sentences by Using Commas to Set Off Parenthetical Expressions**

The following sentences contain parenthetical expressions that require commas. Write the parenthetical expressions, inserting commas before, after, or both before and after the expressions, as needed.

EXAMPLES   1. Everyone I suppose has heard of the Hubble Space Telescope.

1. *, I suppose,*

2. As a matter of fact even a small refracting telescope gives a good view of Saturn's rings.

2. *As a matter of fact,*

1. You don't need a telescope however to see all the beautiful sights in the night sky.
2. For instance on a summer night you might be able to view Scorpio, Serpens, and the Serpent Bearer.
3. By the way you should not overlook the Milky Way.
4. The Milky Way in fact is more impressive in the summer than at any other time of year.
5. Hercules of course is an interesting constellation.
6. Studying the constellations is in my opinion a most interesting hobby.
7. It takes an active imagination however to spot some constellations.
8. Sagittarius for example is hard to see unless you're familiar with a constellation map.
9. Scorpio on the other hand is quite clearly outlined.
10. Astronomy is a fascinating science I think.

Introductory Words, Phrases, and Clauses

14j. Use a comma after certain introductory elements.

(1) Use a comma after *yes, no,* or any mild exclamation such as *well* or *why* at the beginning of a sentence.

EXAMPLES   **Yes,** you may borrow my bicycle.

           Why, it's Lena!

           Well, I think you are wrong.

(2) Use a comma after an introductory participial phrase.

EXAMPLES   **Beginning a new school year,** Zelda felt somewhat nervous.

           Greeted with applause from the fans, Rashid ran out onto the field.

> **Reference Note**
> For information about **participial phrases,** see page 100.

(3) Use a comma after two or more introductory prepositional phrases.

EXAMPLES   **At the bottom of the hill,** you will see the field.

           Until the end of the song, just keep strumming that chord.

> **Reference Note**
> For information about **prepositional phrases,** see page 90.

Also, use a comma after a single introductory prepositional phrase if the phrase is long. If it is short, a comma may or may not be used. Be sure to use a comma when it is necessary to make the meaning of the sentence clear.

EXAMPLES   In the morning they left. [clear without a comma]

           In the morning, sunlight streamed through the window. [The comma is needed so that the reader does not read "morning sunlight."]

(4) Use a comma after an introductory adverb clause.

EXAMPLES   **After I finish my homework,** I will go to the park.

           When you go to the store, could you please pick up a gallon of milk?

> **Reference Note**
> For information about **adverb clauses,** see page 120.

> **NOTE** An adverb clause that comes at the end of a sentence does not usually need a comma.
>
> EXAMPLE   I will go to the park **after I finish my homework.**

MECHANICS

If a comma is needed in a sentence, write the word before the missing comma and add the comma.

EXAMPLE   1. Walking among the tigers and lions the trainer seemed unafraid.

1. *lions,*

1. Because pemmican remained good to eat for several years it was a practical food for many American Indians.
2. Although Jesse did not win the student council election he raised many important issues.
3. On the desk in the den you will find your book.
4. Yes I enjoyed the fajitas that Ruben made.
5. Walking home from school Rosa saw her brother.
6. When I go to bed late I sometimes have trouble waking up in the morning.
7. Well we can watch television or play checkers.
8. Attracted by the computer games in the store window George decided to go in and buy one.
9. At the stoplight on the corner of the next block they made a right turn.
10. After eating the chickens settled down.

Conventional Situations

14k. Use commas in certain conventional situations.

(1) Use commas to separate items in dates and addresses.

EXAMPLES   She was born on January 26, 1988, in Cheshire, Connecticut.

A letter dated November 26, 1888, was found in the old house at 980 West Street, Davenport, Iowa, yesterday.

┌HELP─

Commas are also used in numbers over 999. Use a comma before every third digit to the left of the decimal point.

EXAMPLE
3,147,425.00

Notice that a comma separates the last item in a date or in an address from the words that follow it. However, a comma does not separate a month from a day (*January 26*) or a house number from a street name (*980 West Street*).

NOTE Use the ZIP Code correctly on every piece of mail you address. The ZIP Code follows the two-letter state abbreviation; no punctuation separates the state abbreviation from the ZIP Code.

EXAMPLE   Fargo, ND 58102-2728

(2) Use a comma after the salutation of a personal letter and after the closing of any letter.

Reference Note

For information about using **colons for salutations in business letters,** see page 312.

EXAMPLES   Dear Dad,   Dear Sharon,

With love,   Yours truly,

Exercise 9   Using Commas Correctly

Rewrite the following sentences, inserting commas wherever they are needed.

EXAMPLE   **1.** I received a package from my friend who lives in Irving Texas.

1. I received a package from my friend who lives in Irving, Texas.

1. On May 25 1935 the runner Jesse Owens tied or broke six world track records.
2. The American Saddle Horse Museum is located at 4093 Iron Works Pike Lexington KY 40511-8462.
3. Marian Anderson was born on February 27 1902 in Philadelphia Pennsylvania.
4. Our new address will be 1808 Jackson Drive Ames IA 50010-4437.
5. Ocean City New Jersey is a popular seaside resort.
6. October 15 2000 is an important date because I was born then.
7. Have you ever been to Paisley Scotland?
8. We adopted our dog, King Barnabus IV, in Lee's Summit Missouri on May 9 1995.
9. The national headquarters of the Environmental Defense Fund is located at 257 Park Avenue South New York NY 10010-7304.
10. Dear Lynn
    I am fine. How are you and your family?

MECHANICS

Review C **Proofreading Sentences for the Correct Use of Commas**

For the following sentences, write each word that should be followed by a comma and add the comma after the word.

EXAMPLE   1. The substitute's name is Mr. Fowler I think.
            1. *Fowler,*

1. What time is your appointment Kevin?
2. My aunt said to forward her mail to 302 Lancelot Drive Simpsonville SC 29681-5749.
3. George Washington Carver a famous scientist had to work hard to afford to go to school.
4. Quick violent flashes of lightning cause an average of 14,300 forest fires a year in the United States.
5. My oldest sister Kim sent a postcard from Ewa Hawaii.
6. A single branch stuck out of the water and the beaver grasped it in its paws.
7. The beaver by the way is a rodent.
8. This hard-working mammal builds dams lodges and canals.
9. Built with their entrances underwater the lodges of American beavers are marvels of engineering.
10. The beaver uses its large tail which is flat to steer.

Review D **Proofreading Sentences for the Correct Use of Commas**

Each of the following sentences contains at least one error in the use of commas. Write each word that should be followed by a comma, and add the comma.

EXAMPLES   1. Kyoto's palaces shrines and temples remind visitors of this city's importance in Japanese history.
             1. *palaces, shrines,*

             2. In Japanese *Kyoto* means "capital city" which is what Emperor Kammu made Kyoto in A.D. 794.
             2. *Japanese, city,*

1. Kyoto a beautiful city was Japan's capital for more than one thousand years.

2. It still may be called the cultural capital of Japan for it contains many Shinto shrines Buddhist temples the Kyoto National Museum, and wonderful gardens.

3. Yes Kyoto which was called Heian-kyo during the ninth century was so important that an entire period of Japanese history, the Heian period, is named for it.

4. Originating from the monasteries outside ancient Kyoto the magnificent mandala paintings feature universal themes.

5. Oh haven't you seen the wonderful *ukiyo-e* paintings of vast mountains and tiny people?

6. Believe it or not readers there are now more than twenty colleges and universities in this treasured city.

7. Its people historic landmarks and art are respected across the globe.

8. With attractions like these it's no surprise that Kyoto is a popular tourist stop.

9. Used in industries around the world the tools of fine crafts are made in Kyoto.

10. Kyoto manufactures silk for the fashion industry copper for artists and electricians and machines for businesses.

11. Fine delicate porcelain from Kyoto graces many tables around the world.

12. The Procession of the Eras celebrated every autumn takes place in Kyoto.

13. The Procession of the Eras festival which celebrates Kyoto's history begins on October 22.

14. The beautiful solemn procession is a remarkable sight.

15. At the beginning of the festival priests offer special prayers.

16. Portable shrines are carried through the streets and thousands of costumed marchers follow.

17. Elaborate headgear and armor for example are worn by marchers dressed as ancient warriors.

18. Because the marchers near the front represent recent history they wear costumes from the nineteenth-century Royal Army Era.

19. Marching at the end of the procession archers wear costumes from the eighth-century Warrior Era.

20. The procession is in fact a rich memorial to Kyoto's long and varied history.

MECHANICS

Semicolons

Semicolons are most effective when they are not overused. Sometimes it is better to separate a compound sentence or a heavily punctuated sentence into two sentences rather than to use a semicolon.

ACCEPTABLE
  Garden visitors include butterflies, bats, and ladybugs; such creatures benefit gardens in various ways, some by adding color, some by controlling pests, and all by pollinating plants.

BETTER
  Garden visitors include butterflies, bats, and ladybugs. Such creatures benefit gardens in various ways, some by adding color, some by controlling pests, and all by pollinating plants.

A *semicolon* looks like a combination of a period and a comma, and that is just what it is. A semicolon can separate complete thoughts much as a period does. A semicolon can also separate items within a sentence much as a comma does.

14l. Use a semicolon between independent clauses if they are not joined by *and, but, for, nor, or, so,* or *yet.*

EXAMPLES   Jimmy took my suitcase upstairs; he left his own travel bag in the car.

After school, I went to band practice; then I studied in the library for an hour.

Use a semicolon to link clauses only if the clauses are closely related in meaning.

INCORRECT   Uncle Ray likes sweet potatoes; Aunt Janie prefers the beach.

CORRECT   Uncle Ray likes sweet potatoes; Aunt Janie prefers peas and carrots.

or

Uncle Ray likes the mountains; Aunt Janie prefers the beach.

14m. Use a semicolon rather than a comma before a coordinating conjunction to join independent clauses that contain commas.

CONFUSING   I wrote to Ann, Ramona, and Mai, and Jean notified Charles, Latoya, and Sue.

CLEAR   I wrote to Ann, Ramona, and Mai; and Jean notified Charles, Latoya, and Sue.

NOTE   Semicolons are also used between items in a series when the items contain commas.

EXAMPLES   They visited Phoenix, Arizona; Santa Fe, New Mexico; and San Antonio, Texas.

Mr. Schultz, my science teacher; Ms. O'Hara, my English teacher; Mrs. Gomez, my math teacher; and Mr. Kim, my social studies teacher, attended the seventh-grade picnic.

MECHANICS

Exercise 10 **Using Semicolons Correctly**

Most of the following sentences have a comma where there should be a semicolon. If the sentence needs a semicolon, write the words before and after the missing semicolon and insert the punctuation mark. If the sentence does not need a semicolon, write *C*.

EXAMPLE   1. Human beings have walked on the moon, they have not yet walked on any planet but earth.

1. *moon; they*

1. Miyoko finished her homework, then she decided to go to Sally's house.
2. Each January some people try to predict the major events of the upcoming year, but their predictions are seldom accurate.
3. Tie these newspapers together with string, put the aluminum cans in a bag.
4. I called Tom, Paul, and Francine, and Fred called Amy, Luis, Carlos, and Brad.
5. Reading is my favorite pastime, I love to begin a new book.
6. In 1991, Wellington Webb was elected mayor of Denver, he was the first African American to hold that office.
7. The two companies merged, and they became the largest consumer goods firm in the nation.
8. Your grades have definitely improved, you will easily pass the course.
9. Paris, France, Cairo, Egypt, and Copenhagen, Denmark, are all places that I would like to visit someday.
10. We haven't seen the movie, for it hasn't come to our town yet.

Colons

14n. Use a colon before a list of items, especially after expressions such as *the following* or *as follows*.

EXAMPLES   You will need these items for map work: a ruler, colored pencils, and tracing paper.

Jack's pocket contained the following items: a key, a note from a friend, a button, and two quarters.

The primary colors are as follows: red, blue, and yellow.

Reference Note

For information about **objects of verbs,** see page 73. For information about **objects of prepositions,** see pages 59 and 90.

Do not use a colon between a verb and its object or between a preposition and its object. Omit the colon, or reword the sentence.

INCORRECT	Your heading should contain: your name, the date, and the title of your essay.
CORRECT	Your heading should contain your name, the date, and the title of your essay.
CORRECT	Your heading should contain the following information: your name, the date, and the title of your essay.

INCORRECT	This marinara sauce is made of: tomatoes, onions, oregano, and garlic.
CORRECT	This marinara sauce is made of tomatoes, onions, oregano, and garlic.
CORRECT	This marinara sauce is made of the following ingredients: tomatoes, onions, oregano, and garlic.

NOTE Colons are also often used before long formal statements or quotations.

EXAMPLE	My opinion of beauty is clearly expressed by Margaret Wolfe Hungerford in *Molly Bawn*: "Beauty is in the eye of the beholder."

Conventional Situations

14o. Use a colon between the hour and the minute.

EXAMPLE	8:30 A.M. 10:00 P.M.

14p. Use a colon after the salutation of a business letter.

EXAMPLES	Dear Sir or Madam:	Dear Mrs. Foster:
	To Whom It May Concern:	Dear Dr. Christiano:

14q. Use a colon between chapter and verse in Biblical references and between all titles and subtitles.

EXAMPLES	I Chronicles 22:6–19
	"Oral Storytelling: Making the Winter Shorter"

S T Y L E   T I P

Use a comma after the salutation of a personal letter.

EXAMPLES
   Dear Kim,
   Dear Uncle Remy,

Exercise 11 Using Colons and Commas Correctly

Make each of the following word groups into a complete sentence by supplying the item called for in the brackets. Insert colons and commas where they are needed.

EXAMPLE   1. The test will begin at *[time]*.
            1. *The test will begin at 9:30* A.M.

1. So far, the class has studied the following topics *[list]*.
2. You will need these supplies for your science-fair experiment *[list]*.
3. If I were writing a book about my friends and me, I would call it *[title and subtitle]*.
4. Meet me at the mall at *[time]*.
5. My classes this year are the following *[list]*.
6. You should begin your business letter with *[salutation]*.
7. The concert begins at *[time]*.
8. I need the following from the hardware store *[list]*.
9. Three countries I would like to visit are *[list]*.
10. The alarm is set to go off at *[time]*.

Review E Using End Marks, Commas, Semicolons, and Colons Correctly

The sentences in the following paragraph lack necessary end marks, commas, semicolons, and colons. Write each sentence, inserting the correct punctuation.

EXAMPLE   [1] What an unusual clever caring way to help animals that is
            1. *What an unusual, clever, caring way to help animals that is!*

[1] Animal lovers have you heard about the Sanctuary for Animals [2] Founded by Leonard and Bunny Brook the sanctuary is a safe home for all kinds of animals [3] Through the years hundreds of stray unwanted and abused animals have found a home at the sanctuary [4] It is located on the Brooks' land in Westtown New York [5] On their two hundred acres the Brooks take care of the following animals dogs cats camels elephants lions and even an Australian kangaroo [6] Of course Mr. and

Mrs. Brook also raise chickens keep horses and look after their other farm animals [7] The Brooks their family and their friends care for animals like this young cougar they also let the animals work for themselves [8] How do the animals work [9] The Brooks formed the Dawn Animal Agency and their animals became actors and models [10] You may have seen a camel or some of the other animals in magazines movies television shows and commercials

Chapter Review

A. Using End Marks, Commas, Semicolons, and Colons Correctly

The following sentences lack necessary periods, question marks, exclamation points, commas, semicolons, and colons. Write each sentence, inserting the correct punctuation.

1. The following students gave reports Carlos Sue and Alan
2. Tanay carved this beautiful soapstone cooking pot
3. Walter this is Ellen who has transferred to our school
4. Calling Simon's name I ran to the door
5. The Wilsons' new address is 3100 DeSoto St New Orleans LA 70119-3251
6. Have you watched that comedian's video Felix
7. Let me know of course if you can't attend
8. Joy our club president will conduct the meeting and Gary our recently elected secretary will take notes
9. Looking at the harsh bright glare Mai closed the blinds
10. Carlos Montoya picked up the guitar positioned his fingers and strummed a few chords of a flamenco song
11. If you hurry you can get home before 9 00
12. Help This is an emergency
13. By the way Rosa have you seen any of Alfred Hitchcock's movies
14. Dave hit a long fly ball but Phil was there to catch it
15. Flooding rapidly the gully quickly became a tremendous torrent
16. *The Grapes of Wrath* which is one of my favorite movies is about a family's struggles during the Great Depression
17. Nicaragua Panama and Honduras are in Central America and Colombia Peru and Chile are in South America
18. One of our cats Gypsy scooted through the door across the room and out the window
19. The Lock Museum of America a fascinating place in Terryville Connecticut has more than twenty thousand locks
20. Could the surprise gift be in-line skates a new football or tickets to a concert

MECHANICS

B. Proofreading a Business Letter

The following business letter lacks periods, commas, semicolons, and colons. Correct each error.

```
Gable Books
387 Monocle Lane
Bozeman, MT  59715
June 28, 2009
```

[21] Dear Mr Gable

[22] Please find enclosed a copy of *Edith Wharton A Biography* a book by R W B Lewis. **[23]** I purchased this book recently at your book shop but I have since discovered that several pages are missing **[24]** I am not happy with the book please send me a new copy.

[25] Sincerely

E. Frome

E. Frome

C. Proofreading for Correct Punctuation

Most of the following sentences lack at least one period, question mark, exclamation point, comma, semicolon, or colon. Correct each error. If a sentence is already correctly punctuated, write *C*.

26. He went shopping, cooked dinner, and washed the dishes.
27. For the good of us all please think before you act next time
28. Mr T E Hawk a friend of my mother's helps me with math.
29. Caroline have your relatives arrived
30. Yes Mario they came just last week.
31. At the center of a map of Texas you will find Brady.
32. Our new address is 72 Maple Ave Rochester NY 14612.
33. Inger designs the clothes her mother sews them
34. We followed the trail it led around the garage.
35. The world record in the long jump was held by Jesse Owens for several years but the record is now held by another outstanding athlete.

MECHANICS

36. On June 15 2003 my father opened his first florist shop.

37. Your use of materials, for example, is very artistic.

38. My hobbies are as follows baseball ballet and magic tricks.

39. After I carry the groceries into the house my sister puts them away.

40. Stop that now Veronica

Writing Application
Using Punctuation in an Announcement

Correct Punctuation   Your class is sponsoring a carwash to raise money for a special project or trip. You have been chosen to write an announcement about the carwash for publication in a community newsletter. Write a brief announcement telling when and where the carwash will be, how much it will cost, what the money will be used for, and any other important details. Be sure to use end marks, commas, semicolons, and colons correctly in your announcement.

Prewriting   List the information that you will include in your announcement. Make sure you have included all the facts people will need to know about the purpose, time, location, and cost of the carwash.

Writing   As you write, remember that the purpose of your announcement is to attract customers. Start with an attention-grabbing first sentence that explains the purpose of the carwash. Be sure to present all your information in clear, complete sentences. Add any important details that you did not list earlier.

Revising   Ask a friend to read your announcement. Is it clear and straightforward? Does it convince your friend that the carwash is for a good cause? If not, revise, rearrange, or add details.

Publishing   As you proofread your announcement, pay special attention to your use of punctuation. Remember to check the placement of colons in expressions of time. You may wish to offer your announcement-writing services to a club or service organization at your school.

Punctuation

Underlining (Italics), Quotation Marks, Apostrophes, Hyphens, Parentheses, Brackets, and Dashes

1.0 Written and Oral English Language Conventions

Students write and speak with a command of standard English conventions appropriate to this grade level.

1.4 Demonstrate the mechanics of writing (e.g., quotation marks).

1.5 Identify hyphens, dashes, and brackets and use them correctly.

┌HELP─

Sentences in the Diagnostic Preview, Part A, may contain more than one error.

Diagnostic Preview

A. Proofreading Sentences for the Correct Use of Underlining (Italics), Quotation Marks, Apostrophes, Hyphens, Parentheses, Brackets, and Dashes

Revise each of the following sentences so that underlining, quotation marks, apostrophes, hyphens, parentheses, brackets, and dashes are used correctly.

EXAMPLE 1. "May I borrow your copy of 'Life' magazine?" Phil asked Alan.

1. *"May I borrow your copy of* Life *magazine?" Phil asked Alan.*

1. Boris Karloff (his real name was William Henry Pratt played the monster in the original movie version of Frankenstein.
2. "Ive never known—do you? what the word *kith* means," Paul said.
3. "It (the new version of the software) corrects that problem," said Steve.
4. I've heard that the parks new basketball court will be completed in June.

5. Anne said that "Norma couldn't understand why twenty two people had voted against having the dance on a Friday night.

6. "A two thirds majority said they didn't want to have it then, Shawn said.

7. Fred said, This magazine article titled Luxury Liners of the Past is interesting."

8. "Does the public library have copies of The Seminole Tribune or any other American Indian newspapers"? Tanya asked.

9. My sisters' enjoy reading folk tales like the stories in Two Ways to Count to Ten by Ruby Dee.

10. The Garcia's cat is I don't think they know living in our garage," Mary said.

B. Punctuating Quotations Correctly

Add quotation marks where they are needed in each of the following sentences.

EXAMPLE   **1.** I wonder why so many people enjoy collecting things, said J. D.

         1. *"I wonder why so many people enjoy collecting things," said J. D.*

11. I know I do! Julia exclaimed.

12. Tomás said, My grandmother said, It's the thrill of the hunt.

13. Do you collect anything as a hobby? Josh asked Marsha.

14. No, Marsha answered, but I know a person who collects old cameras and antique costume jewelry.

15. My aunt collects John McCormack's records, Kevin said. Do you know who he is?

16. I'm not sure, Julia said, but I think that he was an Irish singer.

17. Yes, he sang in the opera; he also sang popular Irish songs such as The Rose of Tralee, Kevin said.

18. My stepbrother has a collection of arrowheads. He hasn't been collecting them very long, Sydney said.

19. You should see Mrs. Kominek's collection of Chinese jade carvings, J. D. said. It's great!

20. Some people—I'm sure you know—have odd collections, Josh said. For instance, my aunt collects old shoelaces.

Underlining (Italics)

COMPUTER TIP

If you use a personal computer, you can probably set words in italics yourself. Most word-processing software and many printers can produce italic type.

Italics are printed letters that lean to the right—*like this*. When you write or type, you show that a word should be italicized by underlining it. If your composition were printed, the typesetter would set the underlined words in italics. For example, if you typed

```
Gary Soto wrote Pacific Crossing.
```

the sentence would be printed like this:

Gary Soto wrote *Pacific Crossing.*

Reference Note

For examples of **titles** that are not italicized but are **enclosed in quotation marks,** see page 327.

15a. Use underlining (italics) for titles and subtitles of books, plays, periodicals, films, television series, works of art, and long musical works.

Type of Name	Examples	
Books	*My Life and Hard Times*	*Life on the Mississippi*
	To Kill a Mockingbird	*Maud Martha*
Plays	*Our Town*	*I Never Sang for My Father*
	Hamlet	
Periodicals	the *Daily News*	*National Geographic*
	Essence	
Films	*The Maltese Falcon*	*Stand and Deliver*
Television Series	*Nova*	*Bill Nye the Science Guy*
	Sesame Street	
Works of Art	*Starry Night*	*The Dream*
	American Gothic	*View of Toledo*
Long Musical Works	*Carmen*	*Don Giovanni*
	An American in Paris	*Music for the Royal Fireworks*

NOTE Underline (italicize) an article at the beginning of a title only if it is the first word of the official title. Check the table of contents or the masthead to find the preferred style for the title.

EXAMPLES   Would you like to subscribe to **the** *San Francisco Chronicle*?

The *Seattle Times* is a daily newspaper.

15b. Use underlining (italics) for the names of ships, trains, aircraft, and spacecraft.

Type of Name	Examples	
Ships	HMS *Titanic*	the USS *Eisenhower*
	the *Pequod*	
Trains	the *City of New Orleans*	the *Orient Express*
		Golden Arrow
Aircraft	the *Silver Dart*	the *Hindenburg*
Spacecraft	*Soyuz XI*	*Atlantis*

15c. Use underlining (italics) for words, letters, and numerals referred to as such.

EXAMPLES   Double the final ***n*** before you add ***–ing*** in words like ***running.***

If your ***Z's*** look like ***2's,*** your reader may see ***200*** when you meant ***zoo.***

Exercise 1 **Using Underlining (Italics) Correctly**

For each of the following sentences, write and underline each word or item that should be italicized.

EXAMPLE   **1.** Does Dave Barry write a humor column for The Miami Herald?

1. *The Miami Herald*

1. The British spell the word humor with a u after the o.
2. In Denmark, you might see the spelling *triatlon* for the word triathlon.

S T Y L E   T I P

Writers sometimes use underlining (italics) for emphasis, especially in written dialogue. Read the following sentences aloud. Notice that by italicizing different words, the writer can change the meaning of the sentence.

EXAMPLES
"Are you going to buy the *green* shirt?" asked Ellen. [Will you buy the green shirt, not the blue one?]

"Are you going to buy the green *shirt*?" asked Ellen. [Will you buy the green shirt, not the green pants?]

"Are *you* going to buy the green shirt?" asked Ellen. [Will you, not your brother, buy it?]

"Are you going to *buy* the green shirt?" asked Ellen. [Will you buy it, or are you just trying it on?]

MECHANICS

3. The current Newsweek has an informative article on the famine in Africa.
4. Our school newspaper, the Norwalk Valley News, is published weekly.
5. Luis Valdez wrote and directed La Bamba, a movie about the life of the singer Ritchie Valens.
6. Mr. Weyer said that the Oceanic is one of the ocean liners that sail to the Caribbean.
7. I think the movie The Sound of Music has some of the most beautiful photography that I have ever seen and some of the most memorable songs.
8. Our local theater group is presenting The Time of Your Life, a comedy by William Saroyan.
9. Charles Lindbergh's Spirit of St. Louis is on display at the museum, along with the Wright brothers' Flyer and NASA's Gemini IV.
10. The best novel that I read during vacation was The Summer of the Swans.

Quotation Marks

15d. Use quotation marks to enclose a *direct quotation*—a person's exact words.

Be sure to place quotation marks both before and after a person's exact words.

EXAMPLES The sonnet containing the words "Give me your tired, your poor, /Your huddled masses/ . . ." is inscribed on the Statue of Liberty.

"When the bell rings," said the teacher, "leave the room quietly."

Do not use quotation marks for an *indirect quotation*—a rewording of a direct quotation.

DIRECT QUOTATION   Tom predicted, "It will be a close game."
[Tom's exact words]

INDIRECT QUOTATION   Tom predicted that it would be a close game.
[not Tom's exact words]

15e. A direct quotation generally begins with a capital letter.

EXAMPLES   Lisa said, **"The** *carne asada* isn't ready yet, but please help yourself to the guacamole.**"**

                While he was in prison, Richard Lovelace wrote a poem containing the well-known line **"S**tone walls do not a prison make.**"**

15f. When an expression identifying the speaker interrupts a quoted sentence, the second part of the quotation begins with a lowercase letter.

EXAMPLE   "Lightning has always awed people," explained Mrs. Worthington, "**a**nd many of us are still quite frightened by it."

A quoted sentence that is divided in this way is called a ***broken quotation.*** Notice that each part of a broken quotation is enclosed in a set of quotation marks.

When the second part of a divided quotation is a complete sentence, it begins with a capital letter.

EXAMPLE   "I can't go today," I said. "**A**sk me tomorrow."

15g. A direct quotation can be set off from the rest of the sentence by one or more commas or by a question mark or an exclamation point, but not by a period.

If a quotation begins a sentence, a comma follows it. If a quotation ends a sentence, a comma comes before it. If a quoted sentence is interrupted, a comma follows the first part and comes before the second part.

EXAMPLES   "I think science is more interesting than history**,**" said Bernie.

                Velma commented**,** "I especially like to do the experiments."

                "Yes**,**" Juan added**,** "Bernie loves experiments, too."

When a quotation at the beginning of a sentence ends with a question mark or an exclamation point, no comma is needed.

EXAMPLES   "Is that a good video game**?**" Jane wanted to know.

                "I'll say it is**!**" Debbie exclaimed.

HELP
To *set off* means "to separate."

MECHANICS

15h. A comma or a period should be placed inside the closing quotation marks.

EXAMPLES   "The Ramses exhibit begins over there**,**" said the museum guide.

             Darnell replied, "I'm ready to see some ancient Egyptian jewelry and artwork**.**"

15i. A question mark or an exclamation point should be placed inside the closing quotation marks when the quotation itself is a question or an exclamation. Otherwise, it should be placed outside.

EXAMPLES   "How far have we come**?**" asked the exhausted man. [The quotation is a question.]

             Who said, "Give me liberty or give me death"**?** [The sentence, not the quotation, is a question.]

             "Jump**!**" ordered the firefighter. [The quotation is an exclamation.]

             I couldn't believe it when he said, "No, thank you"**!** [The sentence, not the quotation, is an exclamation.]

When both the sentence and the quotation at the end of the sentence are questions (or exclamations), only one question mark (or exclamation point) is used. It is placed inside the closing quotation marks.

EXAMPLE   Did Josh really say, "What's Cinco de Mayo**?**"

Exercise 2 Punctuating and Capitalizing Quotations

Use commas, quotation marks, and capital letters where they are needed in each of the following sentences. If a sentence is already correct, write *C*.

EXAMPLE   1. Let's go to a movie this afternoon, said Bob.

             1. *"Let's go to a movie this afternoon," said Bob.*

1. When I shrieked in fear, the usher warned me to be quiet.
2. At the same time, Bob whispered it's only a movie—calm down.
3. He pointed out that the people around us were getting annoyed.

MECHANICS

4. I quietly replied I'm sorry.

5. You shouldn't have screamed, he complained.

6. From now on I said to him I promise I'll try to be quiet.

7. When the lights came on, Bob said "it's time to go."

8. Outside the theater he muttered something about people who shouldn't go to scary movies.

9. I just couldn't help it I explained.

10. You were afraid Bob protested even during the credits!

Exercise 3 **Punctuating and Capitalizing Quotations**

Use capital letters, quotation marks, and other punctuation marks where they are needed in each of the following sentences.

EXAMPLE
   1. Ashley Bryan wore traditional African clothes when he came to our school Elton said.

   1. *"Ashley Bryan wore traditional African clothes when he came to our school," Elton said.*

1. Oh, like the clothes Mr. Johnson showed us in class Janell exclaimed

2. Elton asked have you read any of Ashley Bryan's books about African culture

3. I've read Janell quickly replied the one titled *Beat the Story-Drum, Pum-Pum*

4. I'd like to read that again Elton said those African folk tales are wonderful

5. Mrs. Ray thinks *Walk Together Children* is excellent Janell said

6. Isn't that Elton asked about African American spirituals

7. You're right Janell answered and Bryan wrote that spirituals are America's greatest contribution to world music

8. She added he grew up in New York City and began writing stories and drawing when he was still in kindergarten

9. Did you know Elton asked that he illustrated his own books

10. Bryan made woodcuts to illustrate *Walk Together Children* he added.

Exercise 4 **Creating Direct Quotations**

Revise each of the following sentences by changing the indirect quotation to a direct quotation. Be sure to use capital letters and punctuation wherever necessary.

EXAMPLE   1. I asked my grandmother whether she would like to help us paint our float.

1. "Grandma," I asked, "would you like to help us paint our float?"

1. Mayor Alaniz announced that he would lead the parade this year.
2. Ms. Feldman asked me what my plans for the big parade were.
3. I answered that my brother and I were building a float.
4. She exclaimed that she thought our float would look terrific.
5. Ron remarked that our float probably had something to do with sports.
6. I told Ron that he was exactly right.
7. Alinda asked me what sports will be represented on the float.
8. I replied that the float will salute swimming, soccer, and tennis.
9. Ron said excitedly that he would love to help.
10. Ms. Feldman said that my brother and I would probably be glad to have help.

15j. When you write dialogue (a conversation), begin a new paragraph every time the speaker changes.

EXAMPLE   The young man smiled, and said, "My old master, now let me tell you the truth. My home is not so far away. It is quite near your temple. We have been old neighbors for many years."

The old monk was very surprised. "I don't believe it. You, young man, will have your joke. Where is there another house round here?"

"My master, would I lie to you? I live right beside your temple. The Green Pond is my home."

"You live in the pond?" The old monk was even more astonished.

"That's right. In fact," said Li Aiqi, in a perfectly serious tone, "I'm not a man at all. I am a dragon."

"Green Dragon Pond," a Bai folk tale

MECHANICS

15k. When a quotation consists of several sentences, put quotation marks only at the beginning and the end of the whole quotation.

EXAMPLE   "Mary Elizabeth and I will wait for you at Robertson's Drugstore. Please try to get there as soon as you can. We don't want to be late for the concert," Jerome said.

15l. Use single quotation marks to enclose a quotation within a quotation.

EXAMPLES   Brandon added, "My mom always says, 'Look before you leap.'"

"Did Ms. Neuman really say, 'It's all right to use your books and your notes during the test'?" asked Sakura.

15m. Use quotation marks to enclose the titles of short works such as short stories, poems, songs, episodes of television series, essays, articles, and chapters and other parts of books.

Reference Note

For examples of **titles that are italicized,** see page 320.

Type of Name	Examples
Short Stories	"A Day's Wait" "The Medicine Bag"
Poems	"In Time of Silver Rain" "Birdfoot's Grampa"
Songs	"The Star-Spangled Banner" "Swing Low, Sweet Chariot"
Episodes of Television Series	"This Side of Paradise" "Growing Up Hispanic"
Essays	"Self-Reliance" "The Creative Process"
Articles	"Rooting for the Home Team" "Annie Leibovitz: Behind the Images"
Chapters and Other Parts of Books	"The Natural World" "The Myths of Greece and Rome" "The Double Task of Language"

MEETING THE CHALLENGE

Correctly punctuate each of the following sentences with underlining (italics) and quotation marks.

1. My favorite poem is I Hear America Singing, which I read in the book Leaves of Grass.

2. Today's copy of the San Francisco Chronicle contains the article Moose on the Move.

3. I think the song Don't Touch My Hat is on the CD titled The Road to Ensenada.

NOTE   Titles that are usually set in quotation marks are set in single quotation marks when they appear within a quotation.

EXAMPLE   James said, "We learned 'The Star-Spangled Banner' in music class today."

Exercise 5   Using Quotation Marks

Insert quotation marks where they are needed in each of the following items. If a sentence is already correct, write *C*.

EXAMPLE   1. Let's sing 'The Ballad of Gregorio Cortez,' suggested Jim.

　　　　　1. *"Let's sing 'The Ballad of Gregorio Cortez,'" suggested Jim.*

1. Lani, have you seen my clarinet? asked Rob. It was on this table. I need it for my lesson this afternoon.
2. The most interesting chapter in *The Sea Around Us* is The Birth of an Island.
3. Didn't Benjamin Franklin once say, Time is money? asked Myra impatiently.
4. I believe my favorite Langston Hughes poem is As I Grew Older, said Mom.
5. Lea Evans said, One of the greatest changes in architecture has been in the design of churches. They no longer necessarily follow traditional forms. Churches have been built that are shaped like stars, fish, and ships.
6. The latest issue of *Discover* magazine has a fascinating picture of a shark that swallowed an anchor.
7. Do you know which character asked What's in a name? in *Romeo and Juliet*? I asked.
8. Yes, that was Juliet, answered Li. My mother used to say that to me when I was a little girl. That's how I first heard of Shakespeare.
9. A human hand has more than twenty-seven bones and thirty-five muscles! exclaimed Marcus. No wonder it can do so much.
10. There is an article titled The Customers Always Write in today's newspaper.

Revise the following paragraphs, adding quotation marks and other marks of punctuation wherever necessary. Remember to begin a new paragraph each time the speaker changes. If a sentence is already correct, write *C*.

┌HELP────

The marks of punctuation that are already included in Review A are correct.

EXAMPLES **[1]** Mr. Brown asked Can you baby-sit tonight?

1.   *Mr. Brown asked, "Can you baby-sit tonight?"*

[2] Sure I said I'd be happy to.

2.   *"Sure," I said. "I'd be happy to."*

[**1**] Last night I baby-sat for the Browns, a new family on our block. [**2**] Come in Mrs. Brown greeted me. [**3**] You must be Lisa. [**4**] Hello, Mrs. Brown I replied. [**5**] I'm looking forward to meeting the children. [**6**] First Mrs. Brown explained I want you to meet Ludwig. [**7**] Is he a member of the family I asked. [**8**] In a way replied Mrs. Brown as she led me to the kitchen and pointed to an aging dachshund. [**9**] That is Ludwig. [**10**] He rules this house and everyone in it.

[**11**] Mr. Brown entered the kitchen and introduced himself. [**12**] I see that you've met Ludwig he said. [**13**] Yes Mrs. Brown answered for me. [**14**] Why don't you give Lisa her instructions while I go find the children?

[**15**] If Ludwig whines said Mr. Brown please give him a dog treat. [**16**] Should I take him for a walk I asked. [**17**] No replied Mr. Brown. [**18**] Just let him out into the yard.

[**19**] Mrs. Brown came back into the kitchen with the children. [**20**] Did my husband remind you to cover Ludwig when he falls asleep she asked. [**21**] I'll remember I promised. [**22**] Also, what should I do for the children? [**23**] Don't worry said Mr. Brown. [**24**] They'll behave themselves and go to bed when they're supposed to. [**25**] As I told you laughed Mrs. Brown Ludwig rules this house and everyone in it, even the sitter!

MECHANICS

Apostrophes

Possessive Case

The ***possessive case*** of a noun or a pronoun shows ownership or possession.

EXAMPLES	**Kathleen's** desk	**anybody's** guess
	his bat	an **hour's** time
	their car	those **horses'** manes

15n. To form the possessive case of a singular noun, add an apostrophe and an *s*.

EXAMPLES	a boy's cap	Cleon's pen
	the baby's toy	Charles's opinion

> **NOTE** A proper noun ending in *s* may take only an apostrophe to form the possessive case if the addition of an apostrophe and an *s* would make the name awkward to say.
>
> EXAMPLES the Philippines' government
>
> Ms. Rodgers' cat

Exercise 6 Using Apostrophes for Singular Possessives

Identify the word that needs an apostrophe in each of the following sentences. Then, write that word correctly punctuated.

EXAMPLE
1. The Prado in Madrid, Spain, is one of the worlds greatest museums.
1. worlds—world's

1. Shown on the next page is one of the Prados paintings by Diego Velázquez, *Las Meninas*.
2. Velázquezs painting is known in English as *The Maids of Honor.*
3. In the center of the canvas is Princess Margarita, the royal couples daughter.
4. To the princesss right, a kneeling maid of honor offers her something to drink.

5. To the royal childs left, another maid of honor curtsies.

6. On the far left of the canvas, you can see the artists own image, for he has painted himself!

7. The palaces other important people, such as the chamberlain and a court jester, also appear.

8. The faces of Margaritas parents are reflected in the mirror on the back wall.

9. In the foreground, the royal dog ignores a young guests invitation to play.

10. This paintings fame has grown since it was painted in 1656, and each year millions of people see it when they visit the Prado.

The Granger Collection, New York

MECHANICS

15o. To form the possessive case of a plural noun that does not end in *s*, add an apostrophe and an *s*.

EXAMPLES
mice**'s** tracks	men**'s** hats
children**'s** games	teeth**'s** enamel
women**'s** shoes	Sioux**'s** land

15p. To form the possessive case of a plural noun ending in *s*, add only the apostrophe.

EXAMPLES
| cats**'** basket | four days**'** delay |
| brushes**'** bristles | the Carsons**'** bungalow |

NOTE In general, you should not use an apostrophe to form the plural of a noun.

INCORRECT   Three girl's lost their tickets.
CORRECT   Three **girls** lost their tickets. [plural]
CORRECT   Three **girls'** tickets were lost. [plural possessive]

Reference Note

For information on **using apostrophes to form the plurals of letters, numerals, and symbols and of words used as words,** see page 337.

Writing Possessives

Using the possessive case, rewrite each of the following word groups. Be sure to insert an apostrophe in the correct place.

EXAMPLE   **1.** food for the dog
            1. the dog's food

1. the nominee of the party
2. the clothes of the babies
3. the grades of my sister
4. the name tags of the guests
5. the dish for the cat

6. the yard of Mr. Granger
7. the muscles of my foot
8. the strength of the oxen
9. the computer of James
10. the members of the teams

15q. Do not use an apostrophe with possessive personal pronouns.

EXAMPLES   Is that sticker **yours** or **mine**?

Our cat is friendlier than **theirs**.

His report on Cherokee folk tales was as good as **hers**.

NOTE   Do not confuse the possessive pronoun *its* with the contraction *it's*. The possessive pronoun *its* means *belonging to it*. The expression *it's* is a contraction of the words *it is* or *it has*.

POSSESSIVE PRONOUN   Please give the cat **its** rubber ball.
CONTRACTIONS   **It's** time for the soccer tournament.
                     It's taken three hours.

15r. To form the possessive case of some indefinite pronouns, add an apostrophe and an *s*.

EXAMPLES   neither**'s** homework   somebody**'s** jacket

everyone**'s** choice   anything**'s** cost

Oral Practice **Creating Possessives of Personal and Indefinite Pronouns**

Read each of the following expressions aloud. Then, read it again, changing the expression so that it uses the possessive case. Finally, say whether the revised expression needs an apostrophe when written.

EXAMPLE   **1.** the park for everyone
            1. everyone's park

Reference Note

For more information about **possessive personal pronouns,** see page 30.

Reference Note

For a list of **words that are often confused,** see Chapter 16.

Reference Note

For more information about **indefinite pronouns,** see page 32.

1. the opinion of them
2. the footprints of anyone
3. the fault of nobody
4. the turn of either
5. the stereo that belongs to you

6. the logo of it
7. the idea of neither
8. the backpack of someone
9. the guess of anybody
10. the land owned by no one

Contractions

15s. Use an apostrophe to show where letters, words, or numerals have been omitted (left out) in a contraction.

A *contraction* is a shortened form of a word, a numeral, or a word group. The apostrophe in a contraction shows where letters or numerals have been left out. Contractions are acceptable in informal writing, but in formal writing, you should generally avoid using them.

Common Contractions			
I am	I'm	they had	they'd
1999	'99	where is	where's
let us	let's	we are	we're
of the clock	o'clock	he is	he's
she would	she'd	you will	you'll
we have	we've	what is	what's
they are	they're	I would	I'd

The word *not* can be shortened to *n't* and added to a verb, usually without any change in the spelling of the verb.

EXAMPLES	is not	isn't	has not	hasn't
	are not	aren't	have not	haven't
	does not	doesn't	had not	hadn't
	do not	don't	should not	shouldn't
	was not	wasn't	would not	wouldn't
	were not	weren't	could not	couldn't
EXCEPTIONS	will not	won't	cannot	can't

STYLE **TIP**

In formal writing, avoid using a contraction of a year. In informal writing, if the reader cannot determine the time period from the context of the sentence, it is best to write out the year.

EXAMPLE
The famous tenor toured Europe in '01. [Did the tenor tour in 1801, 1901, or 2001?]

The famous tenor toured Europe in **2001**.

MECHANICS

Be careful not to confuse contractions with possessive pronouns.

Contractions	Possessive Pronouns
It's Friday. [*It is*] **It's** been a pleasure. [*It has*]	**Its** nest is over there.
Who's your server? [*Who is*] **Who's** been practicing the piano? [*Who has*]	**Whose** is this backpack?
They're arriving soon. [*They are*]	**Their** parakeet is friendly.
There's the path. [*There is*]	That rosebush is **theirs.**

─HELP─

Some sentences in Exercise 8 contain more than one error.

MECHANICS

Exercise 8 Using Apostrophes Correctly

Correct each error in the use of possessive forms and contractions in the following sentences. If a sentence is already correct, write *C*.

EXAMPLE 1. Arent you going with us at one oclock?

 1. *Aren't; o'clock*

1. Wed better chain our bicycles to the rack.
2. You're old cars seen better days, hasn't it?
3. She wasnt too happy to see us.
4. Whose ringing the doorbell?
5. We wont forget how helpful youve been.
6. Im certain youll be invited.
7. Whose turn is it to take attendance?
8. Anns an excellent swimmer, but she cant dive.
9. They're turning in their's now.
10. Shes sure theyll show up before its over.

Exercise 9 Punctuating Contractions

For each of the following sentences, identify the word that needs an apostrophe to indicate a contraction. Then, write the word correctly.

EXAMPLE 1. Whats the best route from Lawrenceville, New Jersey, to Newtown, Pennsylvania?

 1. *Whats—What's*

1. Theres one especially pretty route you can take to get there.
2. I think youll enjoy the drive.
3. You shouldnt go due west directly.
4. Youve got to go north or south first.
5. Its easier to go south on Route 206 to Route U.S. 1, cross the Delaware River, and then go north on Route 32 to Yardley.
6. From Yardley, turn left on Route 322, and in a little while Im sure you will find yourself in Newtown.

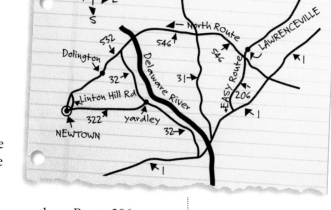

7. If youd prefer a different route, go south on Route 206 to Route 546 and make a right turn to go west.
8. After you cross the Delaware River and the road becomes 532, dont turn until Linton Hill Road.
9. When you turn left onto Linton Hill Road, it wont be long before you arrive in Newtown.
10. Heres a map you can use to help you find your way.

Exercise 10 Writing Contractions

Write a suitable contraction to correctly complete each of the following sentences.

EXAMPLE 1. Do you know _____ for supper?
         1. *what's*

1. _____ my sweater?
2. _____ lying on the beach.
3. We _____ help you right now.
4. _____ dinner ready?
5. They _____ played that game before.
6. She was in the class of _____.
7. _____ go to the museum.
8. I _____ know that game.
9. _____ rather order the salad.
10. Is it nine _____ yet?

Write the contraction of the underlined word or words in each
of the following sentences.

EXAMPLE **1.** If you think it <u>should have</u> been easy to visit the building shown below, guess again!

 1. should've

1. <u>It is</u> the Potala Palace in Lhasa, Tibet, which my parents and
I visited last year.
2. The city of Lhasa is two miles high in the Himalaya
Mountains, and we <u>could not</u> exercise much because the lack
of oxygen made us tired.
3. The Potala Palace is the former residence of the Tibetan
spiritual leader, <u>who has</u> been living in exile in India.
4. Because this palace is a holy shrine, pilgrims <u>do not</u> mind
traveling on foot from all over the country to worship there.

5. After <u>they have</u> bought
yak butter in the city
square, they take it to the
palace as an offering.
6. From the photograph,
you <u>cannot</u> imagine how
steep those stairs on the
right are!
7. Because it <u>would have</u>
taken a long time to
climb them, our bus driv-
er took us directly to the
rear entrance on the left.
8. Once inside, we spent
hours exploring the
palace, but we <u>were not</u>
able to visit most of its
more than one thousand
rooms!

9. <u>I am</u> sure we would never have found our way out without
our guide, who led us to an exit on the right.
10. Walking down the stairs <u>was not</u> too hard, and soon we were
in the beautiful central square in the Himalayan sunshine!

MECHANICS

Plurals

15t. Use an apostrophe and an *s* to form the plurals of letters, numerals, and symbols, and of words referred to as words.

EXAMPLES   Your *o*'**s** look like *a*'**s,** and your *u*'**s** look like *n*'**s.**

There are three *5*'**s** and two *8*'**s** in his telephone number.

Place *$*'**s** before monetary amounts and *¢*'**s** after.

One sign of immature writing is too many *and*'**s.**

STYLE   TIP

In your reading, you may notice that an apostrophe is not always used in forming the kinds of plurals in Rule 15t. Nowadays, many writers leave out the apostrophe if a plural meaning is clear without it. However, to make sure that your writing is clear, you should use an apostrophe.

Review B   **Using Underlining (Italics) and Apostrophes Correctly**

For each of the following sentences, add underlining or apostrophes as necessary. The punctuation already supplied is correct.

EXAMPLE   **1.** One of my oldest brothers college textbooks is History of Art by H. W. Janson.

   1.   brother's; History of Art

1. Whos the painter who inspired the musical play Sunday in the Park with George?
2. Hes Georges Seurat, one of Frances greatest painters.
3. "The young childrens reactions to Jacob Lawrences paintings were surprising," Angie said.
4. Didnt you read the review in Entertainment Weekly of the movie Vincent & Theo?
5. Its about Vincent van Gogh and his brother, who often supported him.
6. "I like Jasper Johns," Rick said, "but I cant tell if that is one of Johnss paintings."
7. Have you ever tried counting all the 2s or 4s in his painting Numbers in Color?
8. On a class trip to Chicago, we saw a bronze statue titled Horse, by Duchamp-Villon.
9. In our group, everybodys favorite painting is Cow's Skull: Red, White and Blue, by Georgia O'Keeffe.
10. "On PBS, Ive seen an American Playhouse program about O'Keeffes life," Joyce said.

MECHANICS

Hyphens

COMPUTER TIP

Some word-processing programs will automatically divide a word at the end of a line and insert a hyphen. Sometimes, such hyphenation will violate one of the rules given here.

Always check a printout of your writing to see how the computer has hyphenated words at the ends of lines. If a hyphen is used incorrectly, revise the line by moving the word or by dividing the word yourself and inserting a "hard" hyphen (one that the computer cannot move).

15u. Use a hyphen to divide a word at the end of a line.

EXAMPLE   Will you and Marguerite help me put the silver-
            ware on the table?

When dividing a word at the end of a line, remember the following rules:

(1) Divide a word only between syllables.

INCORRECT   The tall man in the pinstriped suit sat bes-
              ide the tree, looking bewildered.

CORRECT   The tall man in the pinstriped suit sat be-
              side the tree, looking bewildered.

(2) Do not divide a one-syllable word.

INCORRECT   Exercises like push-ups help to develop stren-
              gth of the arm muscles.

CORRECT   Exercises like push-ups help to develop
              strength of the arm muscles.

(3) Do not divide a word so that one letter stands alone.

INCORRECT   The seating capacity of the new stadium is e-
              normous.

CORRECT   The seating capacity of the new stadium is enor-
              mous.

STYLE   TIP

Hyphens are often used in compound names. In such cases, the hyphen is thought of as part of the name's spelling.

EXAMPLES
  Jackie Joyner-Kersee [person]

  Rikki-tikki-tavi [animal]

  Wilkes-Barre [city]

If you are not sure whether a compound name is hyphenated, ask the person with that name, or look in a reference source.

15v. Use a hyphen with compound numbers from *twenty-one* to *ninety-nine* and with fractions used as modifiers.

EXAMPLES   During a leap year, there are twenty-nine days in
             February.

             Thirty-two species of birds are known to live in the area.

             Did you know that Congress may override a president's
             veto by a two-thirds majority? [*Two-thirds* is an adjective
             that modifies *majority*.]

             The pumpkin pie was so good that only one sixth of it is
             left. [*One sixth* is not used as a modifier. Instead, *sixth* is a
             noun modified by the adjective *one*. Fractions used as
             nouns do not have hyphens.]

MECHANICS

15w. Use a hyphen with the prefixes *ex–, self–, all–, and great–* and with the suffixes *–elect* and *–free.*

EXAMPLES   ex-coach   president-elect   all-star

                great-uncle   self-propelled   fat-free

Exercise 12   Using Hyphens Correctly

Write an expression—using words, not numerals—to replace the blank in each of the following sentences. Use hyphens where they are needed with compound numbers and fractions.

EXAMPLE   **1.** The sum of ten and fifteen is _____.

              1. *twenty-five*

1. January, March, May, July, August, October, and December are the months that have _____ days.
2. _____ of the moon is visible from the earth, but the other half can be seen only from outer space.
3. In twenty years I will be _____ years old.
4. I used _____ cup, which is 25 percent of the original one cup.
5. Our seventh-grade class has _____ students.
6. The train ride is short; the route is only _____ miles long.
7. The doctor said that the heel of my shoe needs to be raised _____ of an inch.
8. Who decided that there should be _____ hours in a day?
9. _____ teaspoon of vanilla is not enough in the cake batter.
10. Only about _____ of the expected people actually attended.

Review C   Punctuating Sentences Correctly

Rewrite the following sentences, correcting any errors in the use of underlining, quotation marks, commas, apostrophes, and hyphens.

EXAMPLE   **1.** For the talent show, Leila is planning to recite Poes poem The Raven.

              1. *For the talent show, Leila is planning to recite Poe's poem "The Raven."*

1. Queen Hatshepsut seized the throne of Egypt in 1503 B.C. and ruled for twenty one years.
2. Whos borrowed my scissors? demanded Jean.
3. Its hard to decide which authors story I should read first.
4. A weeks vacation never seems long enough.

HELP

The prefix *half* often requires a hyphen, as in *half-life, half-moon,* and *half-truth.* However, sometimes it is used without a hyphen, either as a part of a single word (as in *halftone, halfway,* and *halfback*) or as a separate word (as in *half shell, half pint,* and *half note*). If you are not sure how to spell a word containing *half,* look up the word in a dictionary.

HELP

Hyphenate a compound adjective when it comes before the noun it modifies.

EXAMPLE
an event that is well organized

a **well-organized** event

Some compound adjectives are always hyphenated, whether they come before or after the nouns they modify.

EXAMPLE
a **full-scale** model

a model that is **full-scale**

If you are not sure whether a compound adjective is always hyphenated, look it up in an up-to-date dictionary.

MECHANICS

5. After wed eaten supper, we decided to watch an old episode of Star Trek.
6. The driver shouted Move to the rear of the bus!
7. We didnt eat any salmon at all during our visit to Oregon.
8. I wasnt very sorry admitted the clerk to see those three picky customers leave.
9. Very Short on Law and Order is my favorite chapter in Tough Trip Through Paradise.
10. Our phone number has two 6s and two 4s.

Parentheses

15x. Use parentheses to enclose material that is added to a sentence but is not considered of major importance.

EXAMPLES   Emilio Aguinaldo **(**1869–1964**)** was a Filipino statesman.

Mom and Dad bought a kilim **(**pronounced ki • lēm'**)** rug from our Turkish friend Ali.

Material enclosed in parentheses may be as short as a single word or as long as a short sentence. A short sentence in parentheses may stand alone or be contained within another sentence. Notice that a parenthetical sentence within a sentence is not capitalized and has no end mark.

EXAMPLES   Please be quiet during the performance. **(**Take crying babies to the lobby.**)**

Jack Echohawk **(**he's Ben's cousin**)** told us about growing up on a reservation.

Exercise 13 **Correcting Sentences by Adding Parentheses**

Insert parentheses where they are needed in the following sentences.

EXAMPLE   1. My bicycle I've had it for three years is a ten-speed.
1. *My bicycle (I've had it for three years) is a ten-speed.*

1. At the age of fourteen, Martina Hingis began playing tennis my favorite sport professionally.

2. Elijah McCoy 1843–1929 invented a way to oil moving machinery.
3. I bought a new calculator my old one stopped working and a notebook.
4. Charlemagne pronounced shär′lə • mān′ was one of Europe's most famous rulers.
5. Lian Young she's a friend of mine told our class about China.
6. Jojoba pronounced hō•hō′bə is an evergreen desert shrub.
7. Albert Einstein 1879–1955 formulated the theory of relativity.
8. The soloist he's my cousin performed "Memory."
9. I read a book by the author E. M. Forster 1879–1970.
10. The relevant chart shows the election results. See page 88.

Brackets

15y. Use brackets to enclose an explanation added to quoted or parenthetical material.

EXAMPLES Elena said in her acceptance speech, "I am honored by this [the award], and I would like to thank the students who volunteered this year." [The words are enclosed in brackets to show that they have been inserted into the quotation and are not the words of the speaker.]

By a vote of 6 to 1, the council approved the petition to build a nature preserve. (See next page for a map [Diagram A] of the proposed reserve.)

Dashes

A *parenthetical expression* is a word or phrase that breaks into the main thought of a sentence. Parenthetical expressions are usually set off by commas or parentheses.

EXAMPLES Grandma Moses, **for example,** started painting in her seventies.

In the first act of the play, the butler **(Theo Karras)** was the detective's prime suspect.

Some parenthetical elements need stronger emphasis. In such cases, a dash is used.

Reference Note

For more about using **commas with parenthetical expressions,** see page 303. For more about **using parentheses,** see page 340.

MECHANICS

15z. Use a dash to indicate an abrupt break in thought or speech.

EXAMPLES   The right thing to do—I know it'll be hard—is to apologize.

"Do you think Ann will mind—mind very much—if I borrow her sunglasses?" asked Melody.

Exercise 14 **Correcting Sentences by Adding Dashes and Brackets**

Insert dashes or brackets where they are needed in the following sentences.

EXAMPLE   **1.** The school lunchroom it was a dull green has been painted a cheery yellow.

    1. The school lunchroom—it was a dull green—has been painted a cheery yellow.

1. Fireflies I can't remember where I read this make what is called cold light.
2. Roberto has always wanted to be can't you guess? an astronaut.
3. Mark Twain I think his real name was Samuel Clemens is my favorite writer.
4. Do you mind I don't if Jill and Marcus go to the mall with us tomorrow?
5. The best way to learn how to swim that is, after you've learned the basic strokes is to practice.
6. (See page 8 Box A of the school yearbook for a list of the drama club's best performers.)
7. Where is the computer game I've looked everywhere for it that I borrowed from Alex?
8. Please hand me if you don't mind the stack of magazines on the table behind you.
9. The newspaper quoted our principal as saying, "The girls' volleyball team took both the district District 14–5A and regional championships."
10. The class trip to Chicago I've never been there will include a visit to the Art Institute.

Chapter Review

A. Using Underlining (Italics), Quotation Marks, Dashes, Parentheses, and Brackets

The following sentences contain errors in the use of underlining (italics), quotation marks, dashes, parentheses, and brackets. Rewrite the sentences correctly.

1. The song Amazing Grace has been sung for many years.
2. Mr. Peng he is my art teacher has an exhibit at Gallery One.
3. Did you see the article titled Yogamania that appeared in last month's Seventeen magazine?
4. The poet Wallace Stevens 1879–1955 won a Pulitzer Prize.
5. (See the map of Normandy Figure D for the deployment of the German forces on June 6.)
6. The reading list included the novel Great Expectations.
7. Sharon she's my youngest cousin asked me to tell her a story.
8. The bearded man you probably guessed this is really the thief in disguise.
9. He misspelled the word accommodate by leaving out one c.
10. Aunt Rosie the aunt I told you about went to Mexico on the cruise ship Princess.

B. Proofreading for the Correct Use of Punctuation and Capitalization in Quotations

The following sentences contain errors in the use of punctuation and capitalization in quotations. Rewrite the sentences correctly. If a sentence is already correct, write C.

11. "Did you read Robert Hayden's poem "Those Winter Sundays"? asked Jorge.
12. "Who's your favorite baseball player." asked Don?
13. "Meet me at 2:30 sharp," my sister's note read.
14. Why did Ms. Redfeather say, "I need to see a doctor"?
15. Ms. Liu said, Turn to Chapter 7, 'Fractions,' now.
16. "Did you know," Katrina said, "That Robin Williams organizes fund-raisers for the homeless"?

MECHANICS

17. Akeem exclaimed, "Those giant redwoods are more than three hundred feet tall!"
18. "Are the La Vernia Bears playing tomorrow? Lorraine asked Ted.
19. Chang predicted that "it would be a rainy summer."
20. "he can work ten hours a week", said Liang.

┌HELP┐
Some sentences
in Part C may not require
additional punctuation.

C. Writing Dialogue Correctly

Revise the following paragraphs, adding quotation marks and other punctuation marks wherever necessary. Begin a new paragraph each time the speaker changes.

[21] A few of us are starting a reading group said Michael. [22] Would you like to join us? [23] That sounds like fun replied Audra. [24] Who is in the group? [25] Well, I am, of course Michael said and Stephanie, Jeff, and Kerry. [26] I've asked Megan to join, too, but she may be too busy. [27] She's going to let me know tomorrow.

[28] What books are you going to read asked Audra or haven't you decided that yet? [29] I'm going to suggest that we start with The Owl Service, by Alan Garner, said Michael but only if it is everyones choice. [30] I'd love to join! said Audra.

D. Using Apostrophes and Hyphens

The following sentences contain errors in the use of apostrophes and hyphens. Correctly write each incorrectly punctuated word.

31. The test includes twentytwo questions.
32. Its easy to see that you like to use &s instead of writing out the word *and* each time.
33. One fourth of the childrens toys were broken.
34. My two sisters bicycles are sporty, but neithers is as sport-y as mine.
35. Isnt this play often considered one of Shakespeares best wo-rks, Stephanie?
36. Whats the lowest common denominator of these two numbers?
37. Are those lawn chairs our's or the Millers?
38. Theyre drawings of Augusta Savages sculptures.

39. My baby brothers a good sleeper; he should have a mobile made of *Z*s instead of airplanes over his crib.

40. Whos going to help repaint the clubs float for the parade?

Writing Application
Using Quotations in Reports

Direct Quotations   Your social studies class is taking a survey of people's attitudes toward recycling. Interview at least three people from different households in your community. Ask them specific questions to find out whether they think recycling is important; what items, if any, they recycle; and how they think recycling could be made easier for people in the community. Based on the information you gather, write a brief report about recycling in your community. In your report, quote several people's exact words.

Prewriting   First, think of several questions to ask. Next, decide whom you want to interview. Begin each interview by recording the person's name, age, and occupation. When all your interviews are completed, compare your interviewees' responses. What conclusions can you draw about attitudes toward recycling in your community? Jot down some notes to help you organize your information.

Writing   In the first paragraph of your draft, give a statement that sums up the main idea of your report. Then, use your interviewees' answers to support your main idea.

Revising   Re-read your first draft. Does the body of your report support your main idea? If not, you may need to rethink and revise your main idea.

Publishing   As you proofread your report, check your quotations against your notes. Make sure that you have put quotation marks around direct quotations and that you have capitalized and punctuated all quotations correctly. Your class may want to combine the information from all the reports and create a wall chart showing the community's attitudes toward recycling.

Spelling
Improving Your Spelling

1.0 Written and Oral English Language Conventions

Students write and speak with a command of standard English conventions appropriate to this grade level.

1.7 Spell derivatives correctly by applying the spellings of bases and affixes.

Diagnostic Preview

Proofreading Sentences for Correct Spelling

Write correctly all of the misspelled words in the following sentences.

EXAMPLE
   1. Andrew carefuly lifted the massive lid and peekked inside the trunk.

   1. carefully, peeked

1. Do you have any fresh tomatos or strawberrys?
2. Alex rides her bicycle forty miles dayly when she is in trainning.
3. The experienced tour guide lead the students to the base of the trail.
4. My sister made the salad while I layed the spoons and knifes on the table for dinner.
5. Would you please hand me the scissor's?
6. Mr. Escobar's too neices went to the annual family reunion.
7. Icicles formed on the park benchs when the temperature dropped below freezeing.
8. Angela's favorite classes are social studys and swiming.
9. On Wednesday our science class watched *Weavving Ants,* a film about the insect world.
10. Take out a peice of paper, and then prosede with the test.

Good Spelling Habits

Practicing the following techniques can help you spell words correctly.

1. **To learn the spelling of a word, pronounce it, study it, and write it.** Pronounce words carefully. Mispronunciation can lead to misspelling. For instance, if you say *ath•a•lete* instead of *ath•lete*, you will be more likely to spell the word incorrectly.

   - First, make sure that you know how to pronounce the word correctly, and then practice saying it.
   - Second, study the word. Notice especially any parts that might be hard to remember.
   - Third, write the word from memory. Check your spelling.
   - If you misspelled the word, repeat the three steps of this process.

2. **Use a dictionary.** When you find that you have misspelled a word, look it up in a dictionary. Do not guess about the correct spelling.

3. **Spell by syllables.** A *syllable* is a word part that is pronounced as one uninterrupted sound.

   EXAMPLES   **thor•ough** [two syllables]

                   sep•a•rate [three syllables]

   Instead of trying to learn how to pronounce and spell a whole word, break it up into its syllables whenever possible.

Exercise 1   Spelling by Syllables

Look up the following words in a dictionary, and divide each one into syllables. Pronounce each syllable correctly, and learn to spell the word by syllables.

1. legislature	8. definition	15. separate
2. perspire	9. recognize	16. opportunity
3. modern	10. awkward	17. eliminate
4. temperature	11. accept	18. government
5. probably	12. interest	19. business
6. similar	13. temperament	20. appreciation
7. library	14. conscious	

HELP

If you are not sure how to pronounce a word, look it up in an up-to-date dictionary. In the dictionary, you will usually find the pronunciation given in parentheses after the word. The information in parentheses will show you the sounds used, the syllable breaks, and any accented syllables. A guide to the pronunciation symbols is usually found at the front of the dictionary.

STYLE TIP

In some names, marks that show how to pronounce a word are considered part of the spelling.

PEOPLE
Díaz   Rölvaag   Žižka

PLACES
Aswân   Cádiz

Compiègne

If you are not sure about the spelling of a name, ask the person with that name or look it up in a dictionary or other reference source.

MECHANICS

4. **Proofread for careless spelling errors.** Re-read your writing carefully, and correct any mistakes and unclear letters. For example, make sure that your *i*'s are dotted, that your *t*'s are crossed, and that your *g*'s don't look like *q*'s.

5. **Keep a spelling notebook.** Divide each page into four columns:

COLUMN 1   Correctly spell any word you missed. (Never enter a misspelling.)

COLUMN 2   Write the word again, dividing it into syllables and indicating which syllables are accented or stressed.

COLUMN 3   Write the word once more, circling the spot that gives you trouble.

COLUMN 4   Jot down any comments that might help you remember the correct spelling.

Here is an example of how you might make entries for two words that are often misspelled.

Correct Spelling	Syllables and Accents	Trouble Spot	Comments
attendance	at•tend´•ance	attend(a)nce	Think of attending a dance.
unnecessary	un•nec´•es•sar•y	u(nn)ecessary	un + necessary (Study rule 16c.)

Spelling Rules
ie and *ei*

16a. Write *ie* when the sound is long *e*, except after *c*.

EXAMPLES   ch**ie**f, br**ie**f, bel**ie**ve, y**ie**ld, rec**ei**ve, dec**ei**ve

EXCEPTIONS   s**ei**ze, l**ei**sure, **ei**ther, n**ei**ther, prot**ei**n

Write *ei* when the sound is not long *e*, especially when the sound is long *a*.

EXAMPLES   sl**ei**gh, v**ei**l, fr**ei**ght, w**ei**ght, h**ei**ght, for**ei**gn

EXCEPTIONS   fr**ie**nd, misch**ie**f, anc**ie**nt, p**ie**

Exercise 2 **Writing Words with *ie* and *ei***

Rewrite the following words, adding the letters *ie* or *ei*.

EXAMPLE   **1.** conc . . . t

1. *conceit*

1. dec . . . ve
2. n . . . ther
3. rec . . . ve
4. h . . . ght
5. fr . . . nd
6. l . . . sure
7. misch . . . f
8. w . . . ght
9. . . . ght
10. sl . . . gh

11. fr . . . ght
12. n . . . ghbor
13. c . . . ling
14. shr . . . k
15. rec . . . pt
16. p . . . ce
17. r . . . gn
18. th . . . r
19. s . . . ze
20. br . . . f

Exercise 3 **Proofreading Sentences to Correct Spelling Errors**

Most of the following sentences contain a spelling error involving the use of *ie* or *ei*. Write each misspelled word correctly. If a sentence has no spelling error, write *C*.

EXAMPLE   **1.** Last summer I recieved an airline ticket as a birthday gift.

1. *received*

1. I used the ticket to fly to Puerto Rico with my freind Alicia to see my grandmother and other relatives.
2. We flew to San Juan, where my grandmother's nieghbor, Mr. Perez, met us and drove us to my grandmother's house.
3. When we got there, all of my relatives—aunts, uncles, cousins, neices, nephews—came to welcome us.
4. They couldn't believe that niether of us had ever been to Puerto Rico before, so they took us sightseeing the next day.

> ┌ **TIPS** & **TRICKS** ┐
>
> You may find this time-tested verse a help in remembering the *ie* rule.
>
>   *I* before *e*
>   Except after *c*
>   Or when sounded like *a*,
>   As in *neighbor* and *weigh*.
>
> If you use this rhyme, remember that "*i* before *e*" refers only to words in which these two letters are in the same syllable and stand for the sound of long *e*, as in the examples under Rule 16a.

MECHANICS

5. First, we walked through a field in Humacao, which is located on the Caribbean Sea.
6. Then, we drove along the coast to Ponce, the island's cheif city after San Juan.
7. Continuing north from Ponce, we thought that we'd take a liesurely drive on the mountain road *Ruta Panoramica,* which means "Panoramic Road."
8. However, the road turned and twisted so much that I was releived to get back on the main road.
9. After we had a breif rest that afternoon, we explored the western part of the island.
10. Within a week, Puerto Rico no longer seemed foriegn to us.

–cede, –ceed, and –sede

16b. The only English word ending in *–sede* is *supersede.* The only English words ending in *–ceed* are *exceed, proceed,* and *succeed.* Most other words with this sound end in *–cede.*

EXAMPLES   con**cede**   re**cede**

              pre**cede**   se**cede**

Prefixes and Suffixes

A *prefix* is a letter or a group of letters added to the beginning of a word to change its meaning. A *suffix* is a letter or a group of letters added to the end of a word to change its meaning.

16c. When adding a prefix to a word, do not change the spelling of the word itself.

EXAMPLES   il + legal = il**legal**

un + natural = un**natural**

dis + appear = dis**appear**

mis + spent = mis**spent**

16
b–e

┌HELP──
A **derivative** is a word formed by adding one or more prefixes or suffixes to the base form of a word.

EXAMPLES
warmth [*from* warm]
electricity [*from* electric]

Exercise 4   Spelling Words with Prefixes

Spell each of the following words, adding the given prefix.

EXAMPLE   **1.** semi + circle

1. semicircle

1. il + legible   **6.** mis + spell
2. un + necessary   **7.** dis + satisfy
3. im + partial   **8.** dis + approve
4. in + offensive   **9.** mis + understand
5. im + mortal   **10.** over + rule

16d. When adding the suffix –*ness* or –*ly* to a word, do not change the spelling of the word itself.

EXAMPLES   sudden + ness = **sudden**ness

truthful + ly = **truthful**ly

EXCEPTION   For most words that end in *y,* change the *y* to *i* before adding –*ly* or –*ness.*

kindly + ness = kindl**iness**   day + ly = da**ily**

16e. Drop the final silent *e* before adding a suffix beginning with a vowel.

EXAMPLES   nice + est = **nic**est

love + ing = **lov**ing

EXCEPTION   Keep the silent *e* in words ending in *ce* and *ge* before a suffix beginning with *a* or *o.*

notice + able = notic**eable**

courage + ous = courag**eous**

┌HELP──
Vowels are the letters *a, e, i, o, u,* and sometimes *y.* The other letters of the alphabet are consonants.

MECHANICS

FRANK & ERNEST reprinted by permission of Newspaper Enterprise Association, Inc.

16f. Keep the final silent e before adding a suffix that begins with a consonant.

EXAMPLES   care + less = care**less**

plate + ful = plate**ful**

false + hood = fals**ehood**

EXCEPTIONS   argue + ment = argu**ment**

true + ly = tru**ly**

Exercise 5 **Spelling Words with Suffixes**

Spell each of the following words, adding the given suffix.

EXAMPLE   **1.** like + able

    1. *likable*

1. awful + ly   **8.** advance + ment   **15.** value + able
2. care + ful   **9.** true + ly   **16.** hope + ful
3. sincere + ly   **10.** courage + ous   **17.** grateful + ly
4. write + ing   **11.** notice + able   **18.** pleasant + ness
5. desire + able   **12.** brave + est   **19.** sore + est
6. change + able   **13.** accidental + ly   **20.** final + ly
7. cross + ing   **14.** pace + ing

16g. For words ending in *y* preceded by a consonant, change the *y* to *i* before any suffix that does not begin with *i*.

EXAMPLES   beauty + ful = beaut**iful**   mystery + ous = myster**ious**

carry + ing = carr**ying**   envy + able = env**iable**

EXCEPTIONS   dry + ness = dry**ness**   fry + er = fry**er**

Words ending in *y* preceded by a vowel do not change their spelling before a suffix.

MECHANICS

EXAMPLES   key + ed = ke**yed**   buy + er = bu**yer**

pay + ment = pa**yment**   enjoy + ing = enjo**ying**

EXCEPTIONS   lay + ed = la**id**   say + ed = sa**id**   day + ly = da**ily**

16h. Double the final consonant before adding –ing, –ed, –er, or –est to a one-syllable word that ends in a single consonant preceded by a single vowel.

EXAMPLES   sit + ing = si**tt**ing   can + er = ca**nn**er

hop + ed = ho**pp**ed   flat + est = fla**tt**est

EXCEPTIONS   Do not double the final consonant in words ending in w or x.

mow + ed = mo**w**ed   tax + ing = ta**x**ing

For a one-syllable word ending in a single consonant that is not preceded by a single vowel, do not double the consonant before adding –ing, –ed, –er, or –est.

EXAMPLES   reap + ed = rea**p**ed   neat + est = nea**t**est

cold + er = col**d**er   hold + ing = hol**d**ing

In words of more than one syllable, the final consonant is usually not doubled before a suffix beginning with a vowel.

EXAMPLES   final + ist = fina**l**ist   center + ed = cente**r**ed

NOTE   In some cases, the final consonant may or may not be doubled.

EXAMPLES   cancel + ed = cance**l**ed *or* cance**ll**ed

travel + er = trave**l**er *or* trave**ll**er

Most dictionaries list both spellings for each word as correct.

Exercise 6   Spelling Words with Suffixes

Spell each of the twenty words on the following page, adding the given suffix.

EXAMPLE   **1.** beauty + ful
          1. beautiful

HELP
When you are not sure about the spelling of a word, it is best to look it up in an up-to-date dictionary.

MECHANICS

1. bay + ing
2. show + ed
3. drop + ed
4. deny + ing
5. pity + less
6. qualify + er
7. trip + ed
8. employ + ment
9. happy + est
10. hit + ing
11. swim + er
12. tidy + er
13. hurry + ed
14. tap + ing
15. clean + er
16. fold + ed
17. day + ly
18. bounty + ful
19. fix + ing
20. help + ful

Review A **Proofreading Sentences for Correct Spelling**

Most of the following sentences contain a word that has been misspelled. Write each misspelled word correctly. If a sentence is already correct, write *C.*

EXAMPLE
1. Have you seen the beautyful bonsai trees on display in the new garden center?

1. *beautiful*

1. These trees can live to be hundreds of years old, yet you can quickly create one of your own in an afternoon.
2. Simply use these pictures to help you as you procede through the following steps.
3. First, you will need an inxpensive plant (such as a juniper), some soil, some moss, and a shallow bowl.
4. When you are chooseing a plant, try to get one with a trunk that has some of its roots showing above the soil so that your tree will look old.
5. Make a carful study of your plant, and decide how you want the bonsai to look in the bowl.

6. Then, cut or pinch away undesireable branches and leaves until the plant looks like a tree.
7. After triming your plant, remove most of the large roots so that the plant can stand in the bowl.
8. Cover the remaining roots with soil, and if the weather is mild, put your bonsai in a shaded place outside.
9. You don't have to water your plant dayly, but you should keep the soil moist.
10. After your plant has healed, you will have succeded in creating your very own bonsai.

Forming the Plurals of Nouns

16i. Observe the following rules for spelling the plurals of nouns.

(1) To form the plurals of most nouns, add –s.

SINGULAR	girl	breeze	task	oat	banana
PLURAL	girl**s**	breeze**s**	task**s**	oat**s**	banana**s**

> **NOTE** Make sure that you do not confuse the plural form of a noun with its possessive form. Generally, you should not use an apostrophe to form the plural of a word.
>
> INCORRECT   The girl's raced to the stadium for soccer practice.
> CORRECT   The **girls** raced to the stadium for soccer practice. [plural]
> CORRECT   The **girls'** soccer team has practice today. [possessive]

(2) Form the plurals of nouns ending in s, x, z, ch, or sh by adding –es.

SINGULAR	moss	wax	Sanchez	birch	dish
PLURAL	moss**es**	wax**es**	Sanchez**es**	birch**es**	dish**es**

> **NOTE** Some one-syllable words ending in z double the final consonant when forming plurals.
>
> EXAMPLES   quiz   fez
>   qui**zz**es   fe**zz**es

Reference Note
For a discussion of the **possessive forms of nouns,** see page 330. For information about **using an apostrophe and an s to form the plural of a letter, a numeral, a symbol, or a word used as a word,** see page 337.

MECHANICS

Read each of the following nouns aloud. Then, say the plural form of the noun, and say whether the plural form has the –*s* or –*es* ending.

EXAMPLE **1.** match

1. *matches*

1. box	**6.** tax	**11.** mix	**16.** plate
2. crash	**7.** Gómez	**12.** clip	**17.** key
3. sneeze	**8.** ditch	**13.** gym	**18.** pass
4. address	**9.** miss	**14.** coach	**19.** Walsh
5. church	**10.** mask	**15.** dash	**20.** business

(3) Form the plurals of nouns ending in *y* preceded by a consonant by changing the *y* to *i* and adding –*es.*

SINGULAR	lady	hobby	county	strawberry
PLURAL	lad**ies**	hobb**ies**	count**ies**	strawberr**ies**

EXCEPTION With proper nouns, simply add *s.*

the Appleby**s** the Trilby**s**

(4) Form the plurals of nouns ending in *y* preceded by a vowel by adding –*s.*

SINGULAR	toy	journey	highway	Wednesday
PLURAL	toy**s**	journey**s**	highway**s**	Wednesday**s**

┌ **HELP** ─
When you are not sure about how to spell the plural of a noun ending in *f* or *fe,* look up the word in a dictionary.

(5) Form the plurals of most nouns ending in *f* by adding –*s.* The plural form of some nouns ending in *f* or *fe* is formed by changing the *f* to *v* and adding –*es.*

SINGULAR	gulf	belief	knife	loaf	wolf
PLURAL	gulf**s**	belief**s**	kni**ves**	loa**ves**	wol**ves**

(6) Form the plurals of nouns ending in *o* preceded by a vowel by adding –*s.*

SINGULAR	video	ratio	patio	Romeo
PLURAL	video**s**	ratio**s**	patio**s**	Romeo**s**

(7) The plural form of many nouns ending in *o* preceded by a consonant is formed by adding –*es.*

SINGULAR	veto	hero	tomato	potato
PLURAL	veto**es**	hero**es**	tomato**es**	potato**es**

EXCEPTION silo—silo**s**

MECHANICS

With proper nouns, simply add –s.

EXAMPLES   the Sato**s**   the Korolenko**s**

However, you should form the plural of most musical terms ending in *o* preceded by a consonant by adding –*s*.

SINGULAR   piano   alto   solo   trio
  PLURAL   piano**s**   alto**s**   solo**s**   trio**s**

NOTE   To form the plural of some nouns ending in *o* preceded by a consonant, you may add either –*s* or –*es*.

SINGULAR   banjo   mosquito   flamingo
  PLURAL   banjo**s**   mosquito**s**   flamingo**s**
              or   *or*   *or*
            banjo**es**   mosquito**es**   flamingo**es**

The best way to determine the plural forms of words ending in *o* preceded by a consonant is to check their spellings in an up-to-date dictionary.

(8) The plurals of some nouns are formed in irregular ways.

SINGULAR   man   mouse   foot   ox   child
  PLURAL   m**en**   m**ice**   f**eet**   ox**en**   child**ren**

Exercise 7   Spelling the Plurals of Nouns

Spell the plural form of each of the following nouns.

EXAMPLE   **1.** industry
              1. industries

1. turkey   **8.** baby   **15.** bluff
2. studio   **9.** tomato   **16.** radio
3. chief   **10.** echo   **17.** lobby
4. soprano   **11.** ferry   **18.** wife
5. puppy   **12.** joy   **19.** foot
6. self   **13.** life   **20.** Whitby
7. chimney   **14.** hero

Reference Note

For more information on **compound nouns,** see page 25.

(9) For most compound nouns written as one word, form the plural by adding *–s* or *–es.*

SINGULAR	textbook	grandfather	toothbrush
PLURAL	textbook**s**	grandfather**s**	toothbrush**es**

(10) For many compound nouns in which one word is modified by the other word or words, form the plural of the word modified.

SINGULAR	sister-in-law	coat of arms	editor in chief
PLURAL	sister**s**-in-law	coat**s** of arms	editor**s** in chief

(11) Some nouns are the same in the singular and the plural.

SINGULAR AND PLURAL	moose	sheep	salmon
	Sioux	Chinese	spacecraft

(12) Form the plurals of numerals, letters, symbols, and words referred to as words by adding an apostrophe and *s.*

SINGULAR	1800	*B*	*i*	&	*that*
PLURAL	1800**'s**	*B***'s**	*i***'s**	&**'s**	*that***'s**

STYLE TIP

In your reading you may notice that some writers do not use apostrophes to form the plurals of numerals, letters, symbols, and words referred to as words. However, an apostrophe is not wrong, and it may be needed for clarity. Therefore, it is best to use the apostrophe.

Exercise 8 **Spelling the Plurals of Nouns**

Spell the plural form of each of the following nouns.

EXAMPLE   1. push-up
           1. *push-ups*

1. side-wheeler
2. deer
3. mother-in-law
4. *A*
5. *hello*
6. thirteen-year-old
7. aircraft
8. governor-elect
9. *0*
10. commander in chief
11. maid of honor
12. runner-up
13. spoonful
14. vice-president
15. *x*
16. lean-to
17. Swiss
18. *$*
19. Japanese
20. *M*

Words Often Confused

People often confuse the words in each of the following groups. Some of these words are *homonyms*—that is, their pronunciations are the same. However, these words have different meanings and spellings. Other words in the following groups have the same or similar spellings yet have different meanings.

accept	[verb] *to receive; to agree to* The Lanfords would not *accept* our gift.
except	[preposition] *with the exclusion of; but* Everyone *except* Lauren agreed with Selena.
advice	[noun] *a recommendation for action* What is your mother's *advice*?
advise	[verb] *to recommend a course of action* She *advises* me to take the job.
affect	[verb] *to act upon; to change* Does bad weather *affect* your health?
effect	[noun] *result; consequence* What *effect* does the weather have on your health?
already	[adverb] *previously* We have *already* studied the customs of the Navajo people.
all ready	[adjective] *all prepared; in readiness* The crew is *all ready* to set sail.
all right	[adjective] *correct; satisfactory; safe;* [adverb] *adequately* Jesse will be *all right* when his injury heals. We did *all right,* didn't we?

All right is the only acceptable spelling. The spelling *alright* is not generally considered standard usage.

MECHANICS

Exercise 9 **Choosing Between Words Often Confused**

From each pair in parentheses, choose the word or words that make the sentence correct.

EXAMPLE   **1.** All of us (*accept, except*) Josh forgot our tickets.

   1. except

1. By the time Melba arrived, Roscoe had (*already, all ready*) baked the sweet potatoes.
2. One duty of the cabinet is to (*advice, advise*) the president.
3. The soft music had a soothing (*affect, effect*) on the child.
4. The girls were (*already, all ready*) for the sleigh ride.
5. The (*affect, effect*) of Buddhism on Japanese culture was huge.
6. By this time of year, the snow has melted everywhere (*accept, except*) in the mountains.

7. The doctor's (*advice, advise*) was to drink plenty of fluids and get a lot of rest.

8. Sarita was happy to (*accept, except*) the invitation to the party.

9. Reading the newspaper usually (*affects, effects*) my ideas about current events.

10. Do you think it would be (*alright, all right*) to leave before the end of the movie?

Reference Note

In the Glossary of Usage (Chapter 12), you can find many other words that are often confused or mis-used. You can also look up such words in a dictionary.

TIPS & TRICKS

Here is a sentence to help you remember the difference between *capital* and *capitol:* There is a d**o**me on the capit**o**l.

altar	[noun] *a table or stand at which religious rites are performed* There was a bowl of flowers on the *altar.*
alter	[verb] *to change* Another hurricane may *alter* the shoreline near our town.
altogether	[adverb] *entirely* It is *altogether* too cold for swimming.
all together	[adjective] *in the same place;* [adverb] *at the same time* *All together,* the class looked bigger than it was. Sing *all together* now.
brake	[noun] *a device to stop a machine* I used the emergency *brake* to prevent the car from rolling downhill.
break	[verb] *to fracture; to shatter* Don't *break* that mirror!
capital	[noun] *a city; the location of a government* What is the *capital* of this state?
capitol	[noun] *a building; statehouse* The *capitol* is on Congress Avenue.
choose	[verb, rhymes with *lose*] *to select* We *choose* activities today in gym class.
chose	[verb, past tense of *choose*] We *chose* activities yesterday.
cloths	[noun] *pieces of cloth* I need some more cleaning *cloths.*
clothes	[noun] *wearing apparel* I decided to put on warm *clothes.*

Exercise 10 **Choosing Between Words Often Confused**

From each pair in parentheses, choose the word or words that will make the sentence correct.

EXAMPLE   **1.** If it rains, we will (*altar, alter*) our plans.

    1. alter

1. My summer (*cloths, clothes*) are loose and light.
2. In England, you can still see remains of (*altars, alters*) built by ancient peoples.
3. A bicyclist can wear out a set of (*brakes, breaks*) quickly.
4. You should use soft (*cloths, clothes*) to clean silver.
5. The cold weather did not (*altar, alter*) Ling's plans for the Chinese New Year celebration.
6. Accra is the (*capital, capitol*) of Ghana.
7. Keep the pieces of the vase (*altogether, all together*), and I will try to repair it.
8. Did he (*choose, chose*) a partner during class yesterday?
9. On the dome of the (*capital, capitol*) stands a large statue.
10. The audience was (*altogether, all together*) charmed by the mime's performance.

coarse	[adjective] *rough; crude; not fine* The *coarse* sand acts as a filter.
course	[noun] *path of action; series of studies;* [also used in the expression *of course*] What is the best *course* for me to take? You may change your mind, of *course*.
complement	[verb] *to make complete;* [noun] *something that completes* The piano music *complemented* Ardene's violin solo. Red shoes are a good *complement* to that outfit.
compliment	[verb] *to praise someone;* [noun] *praise from someone* Mrs. Katz *complimented* Jean on her persuasive speech. Thank you for the *compliment*.

(continued)

council	[noun] *a group called together to accomplish a job* The mayor's *council* has seven members.
counsel	[noun] *advice;* [verb] *to give advice* He needs legal *counsel* on this matter. His attorney will *counsel* him before the hearing.
councilor	[noun] *a member of a council* The mayor appointed seven *councilors*.
counselor	[noun] *one who advises* Mr. Jackson is the guidance *counselor* for the seventh grade.
desert	[noun, pronounced des'•ert] *a dry, barren, sandy region; a wilderness* This cactus grows only in the *desert*.
desert	[verb, pronounced de•sert'] *to abandon; to leave* A good sport does not *desert* his or her teammates.
dessert	[noun, pronounced de•sert'] *a sweet, final course of a meal* Let's have fresh peaches for *dessert*.

Exercise 11 Choosing Between Words Often Confused

From each pair in parentheses, choose the word that makes the sentence correct.

EXAMPLE   **1.** At the end of dinner, we ate a (*desert, dessert*) made of fresh fruits and berries mixed with frozen yogurt.

     1. dessert

1. The city (*council, counsel*) will not meet unless seven of the ten (*councilors, counselors*) are present.

2. The patient received (*council, counsel*) from the doctor on the best (*coarse, course*) to a speedy recovery.

3. Chutney and yogurt (*complement, compliment*) an Indian meal very well.

4. When we were staying in Cairo last year, we saw the Nile River, of (*coarse, course*).

MECHANICS

5. Edward is preparing the enchiladas, and I'm making empanadas for (*desert, dessert*) tonight.

6. Marilyn made a hand puppet out of (*coarse, course*) burlap, buttons, and felt.

7. We all know the major would not (*desert, dessert*) her regiment for any reason.

8. Please, I am asking for your (*council, counsel*), not your (*complements, compliments*).

9. My mother and father both took part in the (*dessert, desert*) hiking trip last week.

10. What did you think when our camp (*councilor, counselor*) (*complemented, complimented*) us on our endurance?

formally	[adverb] *with dignity; following strict rules or procedures* We must behave *formally* at the reception.
formerly	[adverb] *previously; at an earlier date* *Formerly*, people thought travel to the moon was impossible.
hear	[verb] *to receive sounds through the ears* You can *hear* a whisper through these walls.
here	[adverb] *in this place* How long have you lived *here*?
its	[possessive form of the pronoun *it*] *belonging to it* That book has lost *its* cover.
it's	[contraction of *it is* or *it has*] *It's* [It is] the coldest winter I can remember. *It's* [It has] been a long time.
lead	[verb, rhymes with *feed*] *to go first; to be a leader* Can she *lead* us out of this tunnel?
led	[verb, past tense of *lead*] *went first* Elizabeth Blackwell *led* the movement for hospital reform.
lead	[noun, rhymes with *red*] *a heavy metal; graphite used in a pencil* There is no longer any *lead* in *lead* pencils.

(continued)

MECHANICS

(continued)

loose	[adjective, rhymes with *moose*] *not tight* This belt is too *loose*.
lose	[verb, rhymes with the verb *use*] *to suffer loss* Fran will *lose* the race if she panics.
passed	[verb, past tense of *pass*] *went by* He *passed* us five minutes ago.
past	[noun] *time that has gone by;* [preposition] *beyond;* [adjective] *ended* Good historians make the *past* come alive. We rode *past* your house. That era is *past*.

Exercise 12 **Choosing Between Words Often Confused**

From each pair in parentheses, choose the word that makes the sentence correct.

EXAMPLE 1. Kaya (*lead, led*) us to the ceremonial lodge.

    1. *led*

 1. The woman who (*formally, formerly*) (*lead, led*) the band now teaches music in Alaska.
 2. We do not expect to (*loose, lose*) any of our backfield players this year.
 3. We (*passed, past*) three stalled cars this morning on our way to school.
 4. "Why did you (*lead, led*) us (*hear, here*)?" the bewildered tourist demanded.
 5. Can you (*hear, here*) the difference between the CD and the digital audio file?
 6. The workers removed the (*lead, led*) pipes from the old house and replaced them with copper ones.
 7. Has the (*loose, lose*) bolt lost (*its, it's*) washer and nut?
 8. The guests are to dress (*formally, formerly*) for the governor's inauguration ball.
 9. "I think (*it's, its*) time for a pop spelling quiz," announced Mrs. Ferrari.
10. Has the last school bus of the morning already gone (*passed, past*) our street, Tiffany?

MECHANICS

peace	[noun] *quiet order and security* World *peace* is the goal of the United Nations.
piece	[noun] *a part of something* Lian bought that *piece* of silk in Hong Kong.
plain	[adjective] *unadorned, simple, common;* [noun] *flat area of land* Jeans were part of his *plain* appearance. A broad, treeless *plain* stretched before them.
plane	[noun] *a flat surface; a tool; an airplane* The movers pushed the couch up an inclined *plane* and into the truck. I have just used a carpenter's *plane*. Have you ever flown in a *plane*?
principal	[noun] *the head of a school;* [adjective] *chief, main* Our *principal* spoke of his *principal* duties. I outlined the *principal* ideas.
principle	[noun] *a rule of conduct; a fundamental truth* Action should be guided by *principles*.
quiet	[adjective] *still and peaceful; without noise* The forest was very *quiet*.
quite	[adverb] *wholly or entirely; to a great extent* Some students are already *quite* sure of their career plans.
shone	[verb, past tense of *shine*] *gleamed; glowed* The moon *shone* softly over the grass in the silent meadow.
shown	[verb, past participle of *show*] *revealed; demonstrated* Tamisha has *shown* me how to crochet.

TIPS & TRICKS

Here is a way to remember the difference between *peace* and *piece*. You eat a pie**ce** of **pie**.

TIPS & TRICKS

To remember the spelling of *principal*, use this sentence: The princi**pal** is your **pal.**

MECHANICS

NOTE *Shine* can mean "to direct the light of" or "to polish," but the preferred past tense form for these meanings is *shined,* not *shone.*

EXAMPLES   The firefighters **shined** a light into the attic.

Elton **shined** his shoes before the dance.

Choosing Between Words Often Confused

From each pair in parentheses, choose the word that will make the sentence correct.

EXAMPLE   **1.** Mr. Ramírez used a (*plain, plane*) to smooth the board.

          1. *plane*

1. Each drop of water (*shone, shown*) like crystal.
2. Motor vehicles are one of the (*principal, principle*) sources of air pollution in our cities.
3. If you don't hurry, you will miss your (*plain, plane*).
4. The (*principals, principles*) of justice and trust can lead to world (*peace, piece*).
5. Jan has (*shone, shown*) me how to change a tire.
6. It is clear that Luisa is acting on (*principal, principle*), not from a personal motive.
7. On Christmas Eve we each have a (*peace, piece*) of fruitcake.
8. "The bake sale was (*quiet, quite*) successful," said Gloria.
9. "For once," the (*principal, principle*) announced with a smile, "you do not have to be (*quiet, quite*)."
10. (*Plain, Plane*) fruits and vegetables can be delicious.

┌─HELP─

Some sentences in Review B contain more than one spelling error.

Review B **Proofreading for Words Often Confused**

Identify the incorrect words in the following sentences. Then, give the correct spelling of each word.

EXAMPLE   **1.** Portraits of people do not have to be plane.

          1. *plane—plain*

1. Some portraits have a striking affect.
2. A vivid portrait can often make people from the passed seem alive.
3. The painting on the left is by Rembrandt, one of the principle painters of the seventeenth century.
4. The portrait, probably of a rabbi in the city of Amsterdam, is quiet lovely.
5. It's detail shows why Rembrandt was such a popular portrait artist.
6. The painting illustrates one of Rembrandt's main artistic principals, the strong contrast between light and dark.
7. Light has shown only on the rabbi's face, hands, and a peace of his clothing.

8. The rest of the painting is quiet dark, highlighting these lighted features.
9. The rabbi is shone in a state of piece, and the lack of detail in the painting gives an impression of quite elegance.
10. Rembrandt is excepted as a great artist because of his ability to give life to paintings of the human form.

stationary	[adjective] *in a fixed position* Is that chalkboard *stationary*?
stationery	[noun] *writing paper* Do you have any white *stationery*?
than	[conjunction used in comparisons] Alaska is bigger *than* Texas.
then	[adverb] *at that time* If we meet, we can talk about it *then*.
their	[possessive form of the pronoun *they*] *belonging to them* Can you understand *their* message?
there	[adverb] *at or to that place;* [also used to begin a sentence] Let's meet *there*. *There* are toys hidden inside the piñata.
they're	[contraction of *they are*] *They're* all from Guam.
threw	[verb, past tense of *throw*] *hurled; tossed* Ted *threw* me the mitt.
through	[preposition] *in one side and out the opposite side* I can't see *through* the lens.

MECHANICS

Exercise 14 **Choosing Between Words Often Confused**

From each pair or group in parentheses, choose the word that makes the sentence correct.

EXAMPLE   1. (*Their, They're, There*) first rehearsal is after school.
        1. *Their*

1. The stars appear to be (*stationary, stationery*), but we know that (*their, there, they're*) moving at very high speeds.
2. Thailand is much larger (*than, then*) South Korea.

3. That noise is from a jet plane going (*threw, through*) the sound barrier.
4. The pitcher (*threw, through*) a curveball.
5. A (*stationary, stationery*) store usually sells paper, pencils, and other writing supplies.
6. We started our trip in Barcelona and (*than, then*) traveled west to Madrid.
7. The girls completed (*their, there, they're*) displays for the science fair.
8. Is a moving target much harder to hit (*than, then*) a (*stationary, stationery*) one?
9. Each time Chris got a free throw, he lobbed the ball neatly (*threw, through*) the net to score one point.
10. The children in the back seat kept asking, "When will we get (*their, they're, there*)?"

to	[preposition] *in the direction of; toward* [also used before the base form of a verb] We are going *to* Mexico *to* visit Gabriel.
too	[adverb] *also; more than enough* Audrey is going, *too*. Kazuo used *too* much miso, so the soup was salty.
two	[adjective or noun] *one plus one* We bought *two* sets of chopsticks before we left the restaurant.
waist	[noun] *the midsection of the body* The anchor of the tug-of-war team wrapped the rope around her *waist*.
waste	[verb] *to use foolishly;* [noun] *a needless expense* Try not to *waste* all your film now. Rodney did not agree that golf is a *waste* of time.
weak	[adjective] *feeble; not strong* Melinda's illness has left her very *weak*.
week	[noun] *seven days* We'll wait for at least a *week*.

(continued)

(continued)

weather	[noun] *the condition of the atmosphere* The *weather* seems to be changing.
whether	[conjunction] *if* We do not know *whether* we should expect rain.
who's	[contraction of *who is* or *who has*] *Who's* [Who is] going to the museum? "*Who's* [Who has] been eating my porridge?" asked Papa Bear.
whose	[possessive form of the pronoun *who*] *belonging to whom* *Whose* report was the most original?
your	[possessive form of the pronoun *you*] *belonging to you* What is *your* middle name?
you're	[contraction of *you are*] *You're* my best friend.

MEETING THE CHALLENGE

A **mnemonic** is a device, often a rhyme or visual aid, used as an aid to remembering. The Tips and Tricks features on pages 360, 365, and 367 contain mnemonic devices. Create three mnemonic devices of your own for any of the Words Often Confused that do not already have mnemonics.

MECHANICS

Exercise 15 Choosing Between Words Often Confused

From each pair or group in parentheses, choose the word that makes the sentence correct.

EXAMPLE 1. What are (*your, you're*) plans for celebrating Juneteenth?

1. *your*

1. (*Who's, Whose*) the present secretary of state of the United States, Elaine?
2. My stepsister and I built (*to, too, two*) snow forts on our front lawn yesterday.
3. "(*Your, You're*) late," my friend complained.
4. Would you be able to stand the (*weather, whether*) in Alaska?
5. That sounds like a (*weak, week*) excuse to me.
6. (*Your, You're*) dog is (*to, too, two*) sleepy to learn any new tricks today.
7. "(*Who's, Whose*) boots are these?" Mrs. Allen asked.
8. The pilot must decide very quickly (*weather, whether*) she should parachute to safety or try to land the crippled plane.

9. An obi is a sash that is worn around the (*waist, waste*).

10. My family is going (*to, too, two*) New Orleans.

> **Review C** **Choosing Between Words Often Confused**

From each pair or group in parentheses, choose the word that makes the sentence correct.

EXAMPLE   My parents asked my **[1]** (*advice, advise*) about where we should spend our vacation.

    1. advice

My family could not decide **[1]** (*weather, whether*) to visit Boston or Philadelphia. Finally, we all agreed on Boston, the **[2]** (*capital, capitol*) of Massachusetts. We drove **[3]** (*to, too, two*) the city one week later. Even my parents could not conceal **[4]** (*their, there, they're*) excitement. We did not **[5]** (*loose, lose*) a moment. Boston **[6]** (*formally, formerly*) was "the hub of the universe," and we discovered that **[7]** (*it's, its*) still a truly fascinating city.

Everyone in my family **[8]** (*accept, except*) me had eaten lobster, and I ate it for the first time there in Boston. I was not **[9]** (*altogether, all together*) certain how to eat the lobster, but my doubt did not **[10]** (*affect, effect*) my appetite. My parents insisted that pear yogurt was a strange **[11]** (*desert, dessert*) to follow lobster, but I would not **[12]** (*altar, alter*) my order. After the pear yogurt, I thought about ordering a small **[13]** (*peace, piece*) of pie, but I decided to keep **[14]** (*quiet, quite*).

While in Boston, we walked up and down the streets just to **[15]** (*hear, here*) the Bostonians' accents. **[16]** (*Their, There, They're*) especially noted for **[17]** (*their, there, they're*) pronunciation of *a*'s and *r*'s.

We had been in Boston for only a week or so when the **[18]** (*weather, whether*) bureau predicted a big snowstorm for the area. Since we had not taken the proper **[19]** (*cloths, clothes*) for snow, we decided to return home. On the way back, we were **[20]** (*already, all ready*) making plans for another visit to Boston.

Chapter Review

A. Identifying Misspelled Words

Identify the misspelled word in each of the following groups of words. Then, write the correct spelling of the word.

1. height, weight, cheif
2. succeed, supercede, proceed
3. unecessary, unavailable, unusual
4. happyly, finally, truly
5. said, paid, keyd
6. cleaner, tapping, driped
7. taxes, buzzes, foxs
8. switches, mixs, keys
9. knifes, tomatoes, solos
10. mothers-in-law, father-in-laws, drive-ins
11. achieve, feirce, friend
12. mowwer, followed, staying
13. acquire, arguement, always
14. tired, trys, guesses
15. noticable, yield, daily
16. staying, priceless, easyer
17. halfs, coughs, princesses
18. heating, hiting, trying
19. changable, drinkable, smiling
20. misspell, ilegible, unnoticed

B. Writing the Correct Plural Form

Write the correct plural form of each of the following words.

21. boss
22. thief
23. sheep
24. woman
25. freeway
26. ten-year-old
27. Vietnamese
28. *3*
29. city
30. soprano

MECHANICS

C. Choosing Between Words Often Confused

In each of the following sentences, choose the correct word from the pair in parentheses.

31. Have you (*already, all ready*) adopted a kitten from the animal shelter?

32. Although it's only July, the store already has a display of winter (*cloths, clothes*).

33. "I believe that both candidates for senator have very high (*principals, principles*)," my aunt said.

34. The sophomore (*councilor, counselor*) is working on next year's class schedules.

35. The moon is (*quiet, quite*) bright this evening.

36. Not getting enough exercise can (*effect, affect*) your health.

37. You must (*formally, formerly*) declare your interest in joining the club by filling out the membership card.

38. My (*advise, advice*) is that you buy a mountain bike.

39. (*Its, It's*) hard to believe that the leatherback turtle can grow to be seven feet long!

40. The fabric on the couch in Dr. Alexander's waiting room is (*course, coarse*) and scratchy.

D. Identifying Misused Words

In many of the following sentences, one word has been misused because it has been confused for another word. Write each incorrectly used word. Then, write the word that should have been used. If a sentence is already correct, write *C*.

41. An editor will altar this manuscript.

42. We had fruit and sherbet for desert.

43. I thanked Mr. Chu for the compliment.

44. While you are hear, use this towel.

45. Eventually, winter past and spring arrived.

46. Maria received a box of stationery for her birthday.

47. The blue chair is more comfortable then the green one.

48. The whether report comes on right after the news.

49. Whose the man speaking to Officer Grant?

50. The town voted to except the gift of a new library wing.

Writing Application
Using Correct Spelling in a Review

Spelling Words Correctly   Write a one- or two-paragraph review of your favorite book or movie. Be sure to use at least five of the words listed as Words Often Confused in this chapter.

Prewriting   Pick a favorite book or movie and make a list of the reasons that you prefer it over other books or movies. If you decide to write about a book, for example, you may want to compare it to a film that is based on that book.

Writing   As you write your first draft, be sure to include information about the book or film, such as who wrote it, who directed it, and who stars in it. Remember to use a dictionary to help with correct spelling.

Revising   Evaluate your draft and revise it to improve its content, organization, and style. Add sensory details that make the story come alive for the reader. Replace clichés and worn-out verbs and nouns with fresher, more precise words.

Publishing   Check your paragraph for spelling mistakes. Use a computer spellchecker if one is available, but remember that spellcheckers will not recognize misused words (for example, *piece* for *peace*). Also, pay attention to the spelling of any words in languages other than English, and consult a dictionary if you have any doubt. Exchange your report with a partner, and check each other's spelling.

You and your classmates may want to gather the class's reviews and create a bulletin board display of favorite books and movies.

MECHANICS

Spelling Words

- offshore
  strawberry
  daylight
  seaweed
  wildlife
  grandparents
  moonlight
  chairperson
  killer whale
  watermelon
  headache
  typewrite

- shoot
  mist
  birth
  swayed
  shown
  tied
  pane
  shone
  reel
  berth
  chute
  suede

- gathered
  hammered
  controlling
  bothering
  ruined
  listening
  studying
  swallowed
  permitting
  carrying
  compelled
  groaned

- cafeteria
  alligator
  corral
  vanilla
  mosquito
  stampede
  guitar
  coyote
  jaguar
  chili

cocoa
tortillas

- classical
  conductor
  concert
  instrument
  clarinet
  banjo
  bugle
  harmony
  pianist
  performance
  violin
  rehearsal

- express
  envelope
  extend
  excitement
  exceed
  explode
  enthusiasm
  enclose
  expand
  exclaim
  exclude
  excel

- defeat
  destroyed
  decline
  defects
  disabled
  disappeared
  disappointment
  dependent
  deduction
  disadvantages
  disguised
  dissolved

- Spanish
  Greek
  England
  African
  French
  Spain
  Vietnam

Australia
Japanese
Greece
Australian
Vietnamese

- arrange
  accommodate
  announced
  approaching
  accepted
  appoint
  accompanying
  array
  arrangements
  accomplish
  accelerate
  annoy

- selfish
  marine
  greenish
  awkward
  wholesome
  grayish
  childish
  masculine
  feminine
  reddish
  genuine
  awesome

- temperature
  strength
  length
  vegetable
  arctic
  twelfth
  probably
  jewelry
  literature
  boundary
  reference
  beverage

- machinery
  discovery
  nursery
  dictionary

century
injury
missionary
territory
scenery
revolutionary
treasury
luxury

- barrier
  corridor
  umbrella
  buffalo
  gorilla
  pinnacle
  syllable
  tobacco
  massacre
  opossum
  moccasins
  cinnamon

- muscular
  triangle
  muscle
  circular
  regulation
  particles
  particular
  rectangle
  vehicles
  rectangular
  triangular
  vehicular

- doubtful
  specialist
  misfortune
  fortunate
  unfortunate
  especially
  specific
  specifications
  judicial
  judgment
  prejudice
  undoubtedly

MECHANICS

- organize
  cooperate
  congratulate
  exercise
  calculate
  illustrate
  recognize
  compromise
  memorize
  paralyze
  criticize
  inaugurate

- depositing
  recess
  televised
  revised
  position
  constructing
  composition
  opposite
  structures
  destruction
  vision
  necessary

- existence
  incident
  frequent
  endurance
  balance
  intelligent
  influence
  reluctant
  magnificent
  experience
  confidence
  elegant

- transmission
  contracted
  commitment
  attract
  submit
  references
  offered
  omit
  admits
  distract
  subtraction
  refer

- portrait
  buffet
  ballet
  bouquet
  dialogue
  antique
  unique
  vague
  fatigue
  technique
  plaque
  camouflage

- fantasy
  fantastic
  company
  companion
  editor
  editorial
  colony
  colonial
  strategy
  strategic
  diplomacy
  diplomatic

- hasten
  autumn
  autumnal
  softly
  heritage
  designated
  designed
  reception
  signature
  haste
  sign
  resign

- diameter
  graph
  meters
  astronomer
  barometer
  biography
  astronaut
  kilometers
  astronomy
  photography
  centimeters
  autograph

- trio
  monopoly
  quartet
  tricycle
  decade
  octopus
  decimal
  quarters
  triangles
  binoculars
  triple
  monotonous

- desperate
  lightning
  adjective
  penetrate
  aspirin
  athletes
  identity
  disastrous
  ecstatic
  platinum
  incidentally
  tentatively

- caravan
  luncheon
  champion
  gymnasium
  laboratory
  mathematics
  parachute
  submarine
  teenagers
  memorandum
  limousine
  examination

- logic
  biology
  monologue
  hydrant
  technology
  analogy
  mythology
  apologizing
  periscope
  telescope
  dehydrated
  psychology

- agricultural
  identification
  encyclopedia
  possibility
  exceptionally
  responsibilities
  characteristic
  recommendation
  rehabilitation
  acceleration
  simultaneously
  accumulation

- inspired
  convention
  formula
  adventure
  depends
  uniform
  inventor
  pending
  invention
  transformed
  perform
  suspended

- civilian
  historian
  guardian
  scientist
  biologist
  volunteer
  musician
  engineer
  physician
  technician
  politician
  psychiatrist

Correcting Common Errors

Key Language Skills Review

This chapter reviews key skills and concepts that pose special problems for writers.

- **Sentence Fragments and Run-on Sentences**
- **Subject-Verb and Pronoun-Antecedent Agreement**
- **Verb Forms and Pronoun Forms**
- **Comparison of Modifiers**
- **Misplaced Modifiers**
- **Standard Usage**
- **Capitalization**
- **Punctuation—End Marks, Commas, Semicolons, Colons, Quotation Marks, and Apostrophes**
- **Spelling**

Most of the exercises in this chapter follow the same format as the exercises found throughout the grammar, usage, and mechanics sections of this book. You will notice, however, that two sets of review exercises are presented in standardized test formats. These exercises are designed to provide you with practice not only in solving usage and mechanics problems but also in dealing with these kinds of problems on standardized tests.

Exercise 1 — Finding and Revising Sentence Fragments

Most of the following groups of words are sentence fragments. Revise each fragment by (1) adding a subject, (2) adding a verb, or (3) attaching the fragment to a complete sentence. You may need to change the punctuation and capitalization, too. If the word group is already a complete sentence, write *S*.

Reference Note

For information about **correcting sentence fragments,** see page 414.

EXAMPLE   1. Because she likes Chihuahuas.

             1. *My mother bought a book about dogs because she likes Chihuahuas.*

1. Wanted to study the history of Chihuahuas.
2. Small dogs with big, pointed ears.
3. When my mother's Chihuahuas begin their shrill, high-pitched barking.
4. Chihuahuas lived in ancient Mexico.
5. Ancient stone carvings showing that the Toltecs raised Chihuahuas during the eighth or ninth century A.D.
6. Are related to dogs of the Middle East.
7. Travelers may have brought Chihuahuas to the Americas as companions.
8. That Chihuahuas score poorly on canine intelligence tests.
9. However, can be trained to assist people who have hearing impairments.
10. If you want a Chihuahua.

Exercise 2 — Revising Sentence Fragments

Identify each of the following groups of words as a sentence fragment or a complete sentence. Write *F* if it is a sentence fragment and *S* if it is a sentence. Then, revise each sentence fragment by (1) adding a subject, (2) adding a verb, or (3) attaching the fragment to a complete sentence. You may need to change the punctuation and capitalization, too.

Reference Note

For information about **correcting sentence fragments,** see page 414.

EXAMPLE   1. Juggling a fascinating hobby.

             1. *F—Juggling is a fascinating hobby.*

1. If you would like to be able to juggle.
2. You might start with a good, simple how-to book.
3. Most people can learn the basic moves.
4. Within a fairly short period of time.

COMMON ERRORS

5. While beginners first develop a sense of how to hold one juggling bag.
6. They also practice standing in the proper, relaxed way.
7. Next, must master the ability to toss one bag back and forth.
8. Then learning the right way to throw two bags.
9. Beginners often need to practice juggling with two bags for some time.
10. Before they move up to three bags.

Reference Note

For information about **correcting sentence fragments,** see page 414.

┌─HELP─

Although the example for Exercise 3 shows two possible answers, you need to give only one for each item.

Exercise 3 **Finding and Revising Sentence Fragments**

Some of the following groups of words are sentence fragments. Revise each sentence fragment by (1) adding a subject, (2) adding a verb, or (3) attaching the sentence fragment to a complete sentence. You may need to change the punctuation and capitalization, too. If the word group is already a complete sentence, write *S*.

EXAMPLE
1. Could have been the source of the world's legends of dragons.

1. *Could dinosaur fossils have been the source of the world's legends of dragons?*

or

Large lizards, such as monitors, could have been the source of the world's legends of dragons.

1. Eventually, taking root in the imaginations of many people.
2. Considering this.
3. The word *dinosaur* was first used around one hundred and fifty years ago.
4. That fact surprises many people.
5. Where the first dinosaur eggs were found.
6. For example, magnificent, full skeletons in museums, lifelike animations, television documentaries, and even children's toys and cartoons.
7. Can explain the sudden disappearance of these mighty creatures.
8. The remarkable work of physicists Dr. Luis Alvarez and his son Walter on this mystery.
9. Their theory based on the idea of a meteor hitting the earth.
10. Sending a huge, dark cloud around the earth, killing many plants and destroying the dinosaurs' food sources.

Revising Run-on Sentences

Each of the following items is a run-on sentence. Revise each
sentence by following the italicized instructions in parentheses.
Remember to use correct punctuation and capitalization.

Reference Note

For information about
**correcting run-on
sentences,** see page 416.

EXAMPLE   1. The study of shells is called malacology, shell collections are particularly popular in Japan. (*Make two
sentences.*)

        1. *The study of shells is called malacology. Shell collec-
tions are particularly popular in Japan.*

1. At four feet in diameter, the shell of the giant clam is the
   largest shell today during prehistoric times, the shell of the
   Nautiloidea sometimes grew to eight feet across. (*Make two
   sentences.*)
2. From the Mediterranean to Japan, shells have played an
   important part in everyday life they have functioned as
   money, as decoration, and even as magic charms. (*Make
   two sentences.*)
3. American Indians used wampum, beads cut from shells, as
   money West Africans and Arabs used the cowrie shell in the
   same way. (*Use a comma and a coordinating conjunction.*)
4. Africans prized the shell as jewelry shells are still sold as
   jewelry. (*Use a comma and a coordinating conjunction.*)
5. Jewelry, buttons, figurines, and all kinds of decorative objects
   can be purchased at tourist shops along the coasts, shells are
   plentiful nearby. (*Make two sentences.*)
6. The ancient Greeks boiled mollusks and created a valuable
   purple dye cloth treated with this dye may retain its color for
   hundreds of years. (*Make two sentences.*)
7. Perhaps because of their great beauty, shells have also played
   important parts in religious life they may be found in several
   belief systems. (*Make two sentences.*)
8. Quetzalcoatl, god of the Mayans, Toltecs, and Aztecs, was
   born from a seashell the chank shell is associated with the
   Hindu god Vishnu. (*Make two sentences.*)
9. Shells can be free for the taking their rarity can make them
   quite valuable. (*Use a comma and a coordinating conjunction.*)
10. Shells are regularly exported from the United States to
    Europe, Japan and the United States also ship shells to each
    other. (*Make two sentences.*)

Reference Note

For information about **correcting run-on sentences,** see page 416.

Exercise 5 **Correcting Run-on Sentences**

Correct each of the following run-on sentences by (1) making it into two separate sentences or (2) using a comma and a coordinating conjunction to make a compound sentence. Remember to use correct punctuation and capitalization.

EXAMPLE
1. Anthony uses chopsticks skillfully I have trouble with them.

1. *Anthony uses chopsticks skillfully, but I have trouble with them.*

1. The large crane lifted the ten-ton boxes, it set them on the concrete deck.
2. My dad does not know much about computers he has learned to surf the Internet.
3. Allen Say wrote *The Ink-Keeper's Apprentice* the events in the story are based on his boyhood in Japan.
4. Two robins landed on the ice in the birdbath one of them drank water from around the thawed edges.
5. Egyptian hieroglyphics may be written from left to right or from right to left, they may be written from top to bottom.
6. John is my youngest brother Levy is my oldest brother.
7. The nature preserve was beautiful some people had littered.
8. Grandma believes in keeping a positive attitude, she says that thinking positively is the key to a happy life.
9. Let's see that new movie from Korea I have never seen a Korean movie.
10. All my friends like to shop for bargains at the downtown mall, I do, too.

Exercise 6 **Revising Run-on Sentences**

Revise each of the following run-on sentences by (1) making it into two separate sentences or (2) using a comma and a coordinating conjunction to make a compound sentence. Remember to use correct punctuation and capitalization.

Reference Note

For information about **correcting run-on sentences,** see page 416.

EXAMPLE
1. James Earl Jones is a famous actor he has been in movies and plays.

1. *James Earl Jones is a famous actor. He has been in movies and plays.*

1. You may not remember seeing James Earl Jones, you would probably recognize his voice.
2. Jones provided the voice of Darth Vader in the *Star Wars* movies, Jones's deep voice helped make the character forceful and frightening.
3. Jones has a distinctive voice he has even won a medal for his vocal delivery.
4. The prize was given by the American Academy of Arts and Letters, is that the organization that gives the Academy Awards?
5. Jones's autobiography was published in 1993 it is, quite appropriately, titled *Voices and Silences.*
6. Jones was born in Mississippi in 1931, he was raised by his grandparents on a farm in Michigan.
7. His father was a prizefighter and an actor Jones decided to be an actor, too, and studied in New York City.
8. He portrayed a boxing champion in *The Great White Hope,* he starred in both the Broadway production and the movie version of the play.
9. Jones won a Tony Award for his Broadway performance he was nominated for an Academy Award for his role in the movie.
10. Another of Jones's movies is *The Man,* in that movie he plays the first African American to be elected president of the United States.

Exercise 7 Revising Sentence Fragments and Run-on Sentences

Identify each of the following word groups by writing *F* if it is a sentence fragment, *R* if it is a run-on sentence, and *S* if it is a complete sentence. Revise each fragment to make it into a complete sentence. Revise each run-on to make it into one or more complete sentences. Remember to use correct capitalization and punctuation.

Reference Note

For information on **correcting sentence fragments,** see page 414. For information about **correcting run-on sentences,** see page 416.

EXAMPLE
    1. Because my ancestors were Scandinavian.

    1. *F—I have heard many stories about Vikings because my ancestors were Scandinavian.*

1. The Viking Age lasted three centuries, it started at the end of the eighth century A.D.

2. Vikings from Scandinavian countries known today as Sweden, Denmark, and Norway.

3. Since the Vikings lived along the sea, they often became boatbuilders, sailors, and explorers.

4. The range of influence of the Vikings was enormous the Vikings developed trade routes in western Europe and also in the Middle East.

5. Also were skilled at fishing and farming.

6. All Vikings spoke the language called Old Norse they shared similar religious beliefs.

7. Odin was the chief god of the Vikings, Odin's son Thor was worshiped more widely.

8. After they were converted to Christianity, the Vikings built many wooden churches.

9. Was divided into three main social classes—royal families, free citizens, and slaves.

10. Viking women held several important rights, they could own property and land, for example.

Exercise 8 **Identifying Verbs That Agree in Number with Their Subjects**

For each of the following sentences, choose the form of the verb in parentheses that agrees with the subject.

EXAMPLE   **1.** The band (*play, plays*) mostly reggae.

        1. plays

1. Samantha and Matthew (*take, takes*) art classes at the museum on weekends.

2. The card table or the folding chairs (*belong, belongs*) in that closet by the front door.

3. Earlene (*don't, doesn't*) know the exact time because her watch stopped working last week.

4. Both the stalagmites and the stalactites (*was, were*) casting eerie shadows on the cave walls.

5. Several of the exchange students at our school (*speak, speaks*) Portuguese.

6. Neither an emu nor an ostrich (*lay, lays*) eggs that look like that.

7. The members of the audience always (*clap, claps*) as soon as the star appears onstage.

8. Mike said that either the main herd or the stragglers (*is, are*) in the near canyon.

9. The coaches on the visiting team (*agree, agrees*) with the referee's decision.

10. Some of the fruit baskets (*sell, sells*) for less than three and a half dollars each.

Exercise 9 **Identifying Verbs That Agree in Number with Their Subjects**

For each of the following sentences, choose the form of the verb in parentheses that agrees with the subject.

EXAMPLE **1.** (*Do, Does*) you know what a powwow is?

    1. Do

Reference Note

For information about **subject-verb agreement,** see page 148.

1. Each of us in my class (*has, have*) given a report about powwows, which are ceremonies or gatherings of American Indians.

2. Dancing and feasting (*is, are*) very important activities at powwows.

3. People in my family (*come, comes*) from around the country to attend the Crow Fair, which is held every August in Montana.

4. Many of the people at the powwow (*has, have*) come here from Canada.

5. Everyone here (*know, knows*) that it is the largest powwow in North America.

6. Peoples represented at the fair (*include, includes*) the Crow, Lakota, Ojibwa, Blackfoot, and Cheyenne.

7. Only one of my relatives (*dance, dances*) all four of the main kinds of dances at powwows.

8. Both skill and practice (*go, goes*) into the Traditional, Fancy, Grass, and Jingle-dress dances.

9. Last year, all of the costumes of the Fancy dancers (*was, were*) extremely colorful.

10. Either a row of porcupine quills or a band of beads (*go, goes*) all the way around some of the dancers' headdresses.

COMMON ERRORS

Reference Note

For information about
subject-verb agreement,
see page 148.

Exercise 10 **Correcting Errors in Subject-Verb
Agreement**

Most of the following sentences contain errors in subject-verb
agreement. Identify each error, and give the correct form of the
verb. If a sentence is already correct, write *C*.

EXAMPLE   1. All of us is very excited about our Drama Club's
next play.

1. *is—are*

1. *Six Friends and One Dog* are the title of the play we are
performing this fall.
2. The director and producer of the play are Mark Taylor.
3. Neither our sponsor nor the actors have ever staged a
production like this.
4. Most of the actors was chosen last week.
5. Of course, the cast don't know their lines yet.
6. Many of the costumes is still being made.
7. Either Lauren or Kawanda's older brother is painting the
backdrops.
8. Are five dollars too much for a ticket?
9. My friends and the crew hopes not, because the tickets are
already printed!
10. Channel 6 News have promised to cover our opening night,
so we'll all be famous, at least for a little while.

Reference Note

For information about
**pronoun-antecedent
agreement,** see page 165.

Exercise 11 **Choosing Pronouns That Agree with Their
Antecedents**

Choose the correct pronoun or pronouns in parentheses in each
of the following sentences.

EXAMPLE   1. Tell anyone with an idea to take (*their, his or her*)
suggestion to the vice-principal.

1. *his or her*

1. Everyone on the field trip must bring (*their, his or her*) own
sack lunch.
2. When my sister or mother comes back from the bakery,
(*they, she*) will bring fresh-baked bread.
3. No, neither of the cowboys ever takes off (*their, his*) hat.
4. The United States was proud when (*its, their*) astronauts
landed on the moon.

5. If Doug or Simon is in the clear downfield, pass (*them, him*) the ball.
6. Usually Rosita or Paula plays (*her, their*) guitar at our picnics.
7. If anybody is still in the gym, tell (*them, him or her*) to turn out the lights and shut the door.
8. The colonists and Governor William Bradford depended on Squanto as (*his or her, their*) interpreter.
9. This is a large company, but (*they, it*) treats the employees with respect.
10. Ask Jennie or Sara what (*her, their*) middle name is.

Exercise 12 Proofreading Sentences for Correct Pronoun-Antecedent Agreement

Most of the following sentences contain errors in pronoun-antecedent agreement. Identify each error, and give the correct form of the pronoun. If a sentence is already correct, write *C*.

EXAMPLE   1. Jesse and Michael enjoyed his Kwanzaa activities.
           1. *his—their*

Reference Note

For information about **pronoun-antecedent agreement,** see page 165.

1. During Kwanzaa, which lasts from December 26 through January 1, several of our friends and neighbors celebrate his or her African heritage.
2. African American families affirm traditional values and principles during their Kwanzaa activities.
3. This year, both of my sisters made storybooks as her *zawadi,* or Kwanzaa gifts.
4. Either Uncle Willis or Uncle Roland will bring their candles for the observance.
5. One of them will bring their wooden candleholder, called a *kinara.*
6. The joyful celebration of Kwanzaa has its origins in African harvest festivals.
7. Each of my parents will discuss his or her own individual ideas about Kwanzaa.
8. Either Lily or Charlotte mentioned in their speech that Kwanzaa was created in 1966.
9. Nobody in our family likes to miss their turn to make up dances on the sixth day of Kwanzaa.
10. Jerry and Charles will volunteer his time on the third day of Kwanzaa, when collective work is celebrated.

COMMON ERRORS

Reference Note

For information about **subject-verb agreement,** see page 148. For information about **pronoun-antecedent agreement,** see page 165.

Exercise 13 Proofreading Sentences for Correct Subject-Verb and Pronoun-Antecedent Agreement

Most of the following sentences contain agreement errors. For each error, identify the incorrect verb or pronoun and supply the correct form. If a sentence is already correct, write *C*.

EXAMPLE 1. Every animal, including humans, need water to survive.

1. *need—needs*

1. The human body consist mostly of water.
2. You and I, along with everyone else, is about 65 percent water.
3. Everybody in my family tries to drink at least eight glasses of water a day.
4. "Don't Carlos usually drink more than that?" Janet asked.
5. Either Angie or Ramona said that their family usually drinks bottled water.
6. Evidence shows that drinking water helps our bodies keep its proper temperature.
7. Ian or Calinda have studied the mineral content of our local water supply.
8. Industry and agriculture depend on a good water supply for its success.
9. Most of the world's fresh water is frozen in polar icecaps and glaciers.
10. While more than 70 percent of the earth's surface are covered by water, only 3 percent of that water is not salty.

Exercise 14 Writing the Forms of Regular and Irregular Verbs

Reference Note

For information about **using verbs correctly,** see Chapter 9.

Provide the correct present participle, past, or past participle form of the given verb to complete each of the following sentences.

EXAMPLE 1. *eat* Angela has already _____ her serving of acorn squash.

1. *eaten*

1. *install* The shopping mall has _____ wheelchair ramps at all of the entrances.

2. *send*   We have already _____ for a new crossword-puzzle magazine.

3. *see*   Have you _____ the koalas at the Australian wildlife exhibit?

4. *put*   Marianna is _____ together a colorful mobile.

5. *grow*   My uncle _____ the largest pumpkin in the United States this year.

6. *draw*   Anthony has _____ two different self-portraits.

7. *run*   Both of my stepbrothers have _____ in the Cowtown Marathon.

8. *jump*   Have the cats _____ out of the tree?

9. *write*   Murasaki Shikibu of Japan _____ what may be the world's first novel.

10. *go*   More than half of my friends _____ to the May Day parade.

<hr>

Exercise 15 **Proofreading Sentences for Correct Verb Forms**

Identify any incorrect past or past participle verb forms in the following sentences, and write the correct forms. If a sentence is already correct, write *C*.

EXAMPLE   **1.** Many African American women maked names for themselves during the pioneer days.

    1. made

1. A friend of mine lended me a book called *Black Women of the Old West.*

2. It contains many biographies of African American women who leaded difficult but exciting lives.

3. For example, May B. Mason gone to the Yukon to mine gold during the Klondike Gold Rush.

4. Journalist Era Bell Thompson writed articles about the West for a Chicago newspaper.

5. In *American Daughter* she told about her youth in North Dakota.

6. Our teacher has spoke highly of Dr. Susan McKinney Stewart, a pioneer physician.

7. During the 1800s, Cathy Williams wore men's clothes and served under the name William Cathay as a Buffalo Soldier.

8. I seen a picture of Williams at work on her farm.

For information about **using verbs correctly,** see Chapter 9.

COMMON ERRORS

9. Mary Fields choosed an exciting but sometimes hard life in the West.
10. Nicknamed "Stagecoach Mary," she drived freight wagons and stagecoaches in Montana.

Reference Note

For information about **using verbs correctly,** see Chapter 9.

Exercise 16 Proofreading Sentences for Correct Verb Forms

For each of the following sentences that contains an incorrect past or past participle form of a verb, write the correct form. If a sentence is already correct, write *C*.

EXAMPLE   1. When I was ten, I begun to collect stamps.
            1. *began*

1. Over the years, my collection has growed large enough to fill three binders.
2. I have went to several stamp shows.
3. At nearly every show, I seen many rare and valuable stamps.
4. I told my friend Warren that I aim to own some of those stamps one day.
5. I once saw a picture of a rare two-cent stamp that cost one collector $1.1 million in 1987.
6. As you might imagine, that price setted a world record!
7. Stamps have appear in many shapes.
8. My uncle, a mail carrier, sended me a banana-shaped stamp.
9. He also has give me a book about the history of stamp collecting.
10. It sayed that stamp collecting was already a popular hobby by the 1860s.

Reference Note

For information about using *rise* and *raise, sit* and *set,* and *lie* and *lay,* see page 190.

Exercise 17 Choosing Correct Verb Forms

Choose the correct verb form in parentheses in each of the following sentences.

EXAMPLE   1. (*Set, Sit*) those packages down, and come help me catch these kittens.
            1. *Set*

1. Did Keefe (*rise, raise*) the flag for the ceremony?
2. The crowd roared when Sheila (*sit, set*) a new track record for the fifty-yard dash.
3. A giant lobster was (*laying, lying*) motionless on the seabed.

4. The incoming tide (*rose, raised*) the boat that had been beached on the sandbar.
5. An heirloom quilt (*lays, lies*) neatly folded on the bed.
6. Why is the price of housing (*rising, raising*) in this area?
7. Someone had (*laid, lain*) a row of stones carefully on either side of the path.
8. Freshly washed and brushed, the mare walked out to the corral, (*lay, laid*) down in the dust, and rolled over three or four times.
9. By noon, the fog had (*risen, raised*) and the sun had come out.
10. In the old photograph, five Sioux warriors (*sat, set*) and stared with dignity into the camera.

Exercise 18 Identifying Correct Pronoun Forms

Choose the correct form of the pronoun in parentheses in each of the following sentences.

EXAMPLE   1. Doris and (*me, I*) are planning a trip to Vietnam.
            1. *I*

1. Will you take the first-aid class with (*we, us*)?
2. The principal gave (*he, him*) the key to the trophy case.
3. The minister gave (*they, them*) a wedding present.
4. Ulani and (*he, him*) greeted their guests with "Aloha!"
5. Mr. Galvez saved the comics especially for (*I, me*).
6. (*They, Them*) are learning how to draw with pastels.
7. R. J. asked (*she, her*) for a new CD.
8. Stan's jokes amused Martha and (*I, me*).
9. The person who called you last night was (*I, me*).
10. The captain of the debate team is (*she, her*).

Exercise 19 Identifying Correct Pronoun Forms

Choose the correct form of the pronoun in parentheses in each of the following sentences.

EXAMPLE   1. The guest speaker told (*us, we*) students many facts about Hispanic Americans in the arts.
            1. *us*

1. Mrs. Ramirez picked out some poems by Jimmy Santiago Baca and read (*they, them*) to us.

Reference Note
For information on **using pronouns correctly,** see Chapter 10.

Reference Note
For information on **using pronouns correctly,** see Chapter 10.

COMMON ERRORS

2. Jan and (*he, him*) agree that Barbara Carrasco's murals are outstanding.

3. Between you and (*I, me*), Gaspar Perez de Villagra's account of an early expedition to the American Southwest sounds interesting.

4. (*He, Him*) wrote the first book to have been written in what is now the United States.

5. Our teacher showed (*we, us*) pictures of the work of the Puerto Rican artist Arnaldo Roche.

6. (*Who, Whom*) is your favorite artist?

7. The writings of Christina Garcia appeal to (*we, us*).

8. In Luz's opinion, the best writer is (*she, her*).

9. Tito Puente recorded at least one hundred albums and appeared in several movies; we saw (*he, him*) in *Radio Days.*

10. (*Who, Whom*) did you research for your report?

Exercise 20 **Proofreading for Correct Pronoun Usage**

Most of the following sentences contain errors in pronoun usage. Identify each error, and give the correct pronoun. If a sentence is already correct, write *C.*

EXAMPLE   **1.** Who did the student council appoint?

    1. Who—Whom

1. Let me know whom will be in charge of decorating.

2. Mr. Rodriguez gave Nicole and we shop students a handout on using the jigsaw safely.

3. Waiting for us at the door were Grandma and they.

4. For Ron and myself, geometry is easy.

5. Gina, us girls are going to the park to fly our kites; come along with us!

6. Mr. Chin, his wife, and me are going to the Mayan exhibit at the museum next weekend.

7. The big dog always keeps the bowl of food for hisself, so we feed the little dog on the porch.

8. From who could we borrow a map?

9. Yes, the team did all the planning and production of the video by theirselves.

10. The only ones who can speak French are us boys from Miss LaRouche's class.

For information about **using pronouns correctly,** see Chapter 10.

390   Chapter 17   Correcting Common Errors

Exercise 21 Choosing Correct Forms of Modifiers

Choose the correct form of the modifier in parentheses in each of the following sentences.

Reference Note

For information on **using modifiers correctly,** see Chapter 11.

EXAMPLE   1. Many people think that of all pets, Siamese cats are the (*better, best*).

1. best

1. The boys thought that they were (*stronger, strongest*), but the girls beat them in the tug of war.
2. The (*simplest, simpler*) way to attract birds to a yard is by having water available for them.
3. Jovita is the (*most intelligent, intelligentest*) student in the seventh grade.
4. I worry about my grades (*least often, less often*) now that I do my homework every night.
5. Kim Lee has traveled (*farthest, farther*) on her bicycle than anyone else in our class has.
6. Hasn't this year's quiz-bowl team won (*more, most*) local competitions than last year's team?
7. Grandfather says that this winter is the (*colder, coldest*) one he remembers.
8. Wynton Marsalis was born in the city (*more, most*) associated with jazz—New Orleans.
9. Bicyclists who wear helmets are injured (*least, less*) often than those who do not.
10. Louisiana has (*fewer, fewest*) wetlands than it once had.

Exercise 22 Proofreading for Correct Modifiers

Most of the following sentences contain errors in the use of modifiers. Identify each incorrect modifier, and supply the correct form. If the sentence is already correct, write *C*.

Reference Note

For information on **using modifiers correctly,** see Chapter 11.

EXAMPLE   1. Low, green hills roll gentle in the dawn mist.

1. gentle—gently

1. The tourists looked uncomfortably as they rode the elephant along the beach.
2. An Indian elephant calmly carried a surfboard with its trunk and did the job good, too.
3. The white waves of the Bay of Bengal smell quite well to us.

COMMON ERRORS

4. The island of Sri Lanka was once known as Ceylon, and tea grows good there.
5. At first, I felt bad for the workers up to their waists in mud.
6. I thought they had the worstest job in the world.
7. They were searching for rubies and garnets that might appear sudden in their muddy baskets.
8. I couldn't recognize a raw gem very well; could you?
9. I thought the highlands, especially Sri Pada and World's End, looked beautifully.
10. You can live simple when you are in Sri Lanka.

Reference Note

For information about **double comparisons,** see page 230. For information about **double negatives,** see page 231.

(Exercise 23) **Revising Sentences to Correct Double Comparisons and Double Negatives**

Revise each of the following sentences to correct each double comparison or double negative.

EXAMPLES   1. Of the three games, the first was the least funnest.
1. *Of the three games, the first was the least fun.*

2. There are not hardly any stores near the ranch.
2. *There are hardly any stores near the ranch.*

1. The recycling center is much more busier than it used to be.
2. Sometimes even indoor water pipes freeze if they do not have no insulation around them.
3. I think that our dog Sammy is most happiest when the weather is cold.
4. I haven't received a birthday card from neither of my grandmothers yet.
5. Almost any circle that you draw by hand will be less rounder than one you draw with a compass.
6. Wearing sunscreen with a high sun-protection factor can make being in the sun more safer.
7. My second-oldest cousin, Giovanni, is not like nobody else I know.
8. We never went nowhere during spring vacation this year.
9. That was probably the most cleverest chess move I've ever seen you use, Elise.
10. When I'm old enough to vote, I'm not never going to miss a chance to do so.

Revising Sentences by Correcting the
Placement of Modifiers

The following sentences contain errors in the placement of modifiers. Revise each sentence by adding or rearranging words or by
doing both to correct the placement of each modifier.

Reference Note

For information about
the **correct placement
of modifiers,** see
page 232.

EXAMPLE   1. My grandmother and I saw a horse on the way to
the movie.

1. *On the way to the movie, my grandmother and I
saw a horse.*

1. The party was held in the park celebrating Mary's birthday.
2. With wind-filled sails, I saw a ship approaching the harbor.
3. The tree was struck by lightning that we had pruned.
4. The Yamamotos enjoyed planting the iris that arrived from
their Japanese relatives in a box.
5. The softball team is from my hometown that won the district
championship.
6. Trying to steal home, the catcher tagged the runner.
7. Jaime told Katya about the kitten playing in a happy voice.
8. Painted bright colors, Kamal saw many houses.
9. Hanging from a clothes rack, the drama students finally
found the costumes.
10. Recently picked from the orchard, the bowl was full of fruit.

Exercise 25 Identifying Correct Usage

From the word or words in parentheses in each of the following
sentences, choose the answer that is correct according to the
rules of formal, standard English.

Reference Note

For information on
common usage errors,
see Chapter 12. For
information on **formal,
standard English,** see
page 245.

EXAMPLE   1. The boys carried the new recycling containers
(*themselves, theirselves*).

1. *themselves*

1. This orange marmalade smells (*bad, badly*).
2. In science class last week, we learned (*how come, why*) water
expands when it freezes.
3. The dam (*busted, burst*) because of the rising floodwaters.
4. Mario should plant (*fewer, less*) bulbs in that small flower bed.
5. This button looks (*as if, like*) it will match the material.
6. Let's (*try and, try to*) arrive at the concert early so that we can
get good seats.

COMMON ERRORS

7. The defending champion played (*good, well*) during the chess tournament.

8. Yes, our nearest neighbor lives a long (*way, ways*) from us.

9. Those (*kind, kinds*) of fabrics are made in Madras, India.

10. Did you share the leftover chop suey (*among, between*) the three of you?

Reference Note

For information about **common usage errors,** see Chapter 12. For information about **formal, standard English,** see page 245.

Exercise 26 Identifying Correct Usage

From the word or words in parentheses in each of the following sentences, choose the answer that is correct according to the rules of formal, standard English.

EXAMPLE   **1.** Mrs. Lawrence is (*learning, teaching*) us about the Hohokam culture.

   1. teaching

1. The Hohokam civilization (*might of, might have*) begun around 300 B.C.

2. Where did the Hohokam people (*live, live at*)?

3. The Hohokam (*use to, used to*) live in the American Southwest.

4. Hohokam farmers grew their crops in a climate that was (*real, extremely*) dry.

5. The Hohokam irrigated the land by using (*alot, a lot*) of canals—more than six hundred miles of them!

6. (*Them, These*) canals sometimes changed the courses of rivers.

7. The Hohokam were also skilled artisans (*who's, whose*) work included jewelry, bowls, and figurines.

8. I (*can, can't*) hardly imagine what caused the culture to change so much around A.D. 1450.

9. (*Their, They're*) descendants are the Papago and the Pima peoples.

10. We read (*that, where*) one Hohokam site is known as Snaketown.

Reference Note

For information about **common usage errors,** see Chapter 12. For information about **formal, standard English,** see page 245.

Exercise 27 Proofreading Sentences for Correct Usage

Each of the following sentences contains an error in the use of formal, standard English. Identify each error. Then, write the correct usage.

EXAMPLE   **1.** If that ain't the proper first aid for heat exhaustion, what is?

   1. ain't—isn't

COMMON ERRORS

1. During the track meet last Saturday, we used a American Red Cross guidebook for first aid.
2. Fortunately, their was a handy section about treating heat exhaustion.
3. The day of the meet, the temperature was hotter then it had been all summer.
4. The athletes were all ready hot by the time that the track meet began.
5. Some of the runners should of been drinking more water than they were.
6. Several of the athletes which were not used to running in such high temperatures needed medical treatment for heat exhaustion.
7. We volunteers helped the runners like the first-aid guidebook instructed.
8. They soon felt alright after we led them out of the heat and helped them cool down.
9. The doctor on duty at the meet examined them and checked they're vital signs.
10. According to the doctor, even athletes in good condition must protect theirselves against heat exhaustion and heatstroke.

Grammar and Usage Test: Section 1

DIRECTIONS   Read the paragraph that follows. For each numbered blank, select the word or word group that best completes the sentence.

EXAMPLE   1. The platypus is one of __(1)__ mammals that lays eggs.

     (A) to
     (B) too
     (C) two
     (D) 2

ANSWER   1. (A)   (B)   **(C)**   (D)

    The platypus is __(1)__ very unusual mammal. It __(2)__ external ears, __(3)__ feet are webbed, and it has thick fur. A broad tail and a fleshy bill __(4)__ to the platypus's odd appearance. Platypuses use __(5)__ bills to catch water worms and insects. Besides having a bill like a duck's, a platypus is __(6)__ like a bird than a mammal in another important way. Like a duck, the platypus __(7)__ eggs. The mother deposits __(8)__ in a nest, __(9)__ she has dug in a riverbank. If you get to Australia, you may see a platypus making its nest __(10)__ a burrow.

---

1. (A) an
   (B) a
   (C) the
   (D) some

2. (A) don't have no
   (B) doesn't have no
   (C) has any
   (D) has no

3. (A) its
   (B) it's
   (C) its'
   (D) their

4. (A) adds
   (B) add
   (C) added
   (D) adding

5. (A) its
   (B) it's
   (C) they're
   (D) their

6. (A) more
   (B) most
   (C) mostly
   (D) least

7. (A) lays
   (B) lies
   (C) is lying
   (D) has lain

8. (A) it
   (B) they
   (C) them
   (D) their

9. **(A)** which
   (B) it
   (C) who
   (D) whom

10. **(A)** inside of
    (B) outside of
    (C) a ways from
    (D) inside

Grammar and Usage Test: Section 2

DIRECTIONS   Part or all of each of the following items is underlined. Using the rules of formal, standard English, choose the revision that most clearly expresses the meaning of the item. If there is no error, choose A.

EXAMPLE   1.   The chopsticks that my aunt sent us made of bamboo.

   (A) The chopsticks that my aunt sent us made of bamboo.
   (B) The chopsticks that my aunt sent us are made of bamboo.
   (C) The chopsticks are made of bamboo, that my aunt sent us.
   (D) That my aunt sent us chopsticks made of bamboo.

ANSWER   1.   A   B   C   D

1. Don't buy none of that ripe fruit if you don't plan to eat it soon.
   (A) Don't buy none of that ripe fruit if you don't plan to eat it soon.
   (B) Do buy none of that ripe fruit if you don't plan to eat it soon.
   (C) Don't buy none of that ripe fruit if you do plan to eat it soon.
   (D) Don't buy any of that ripe fruit if you don't plan to eat it soon.

2. The study group meeting in the library on Wednesday?
   (A) The study group meeting in the library on Wednesday?
   (B) The study group that will be meeting in the library on Wednesday?
   (C) Is the study group meeting in the library on Wednesday?
   (D) Will the study group meeting in the library on Wednesday?

3. Some visitors to the park enjoy rock <u>climbing others prefer kayaking</u>.

    (**A**) climbing others prefer kayaking

    (**B**) climbing, others prefer kayaking

    (**C**) climbing, others, who prefer kayaking

    (**D**) climbing, and others prefer kayaking

4. Martin <u>prepares the salad, Justine sets the table</u>.

    (**A**) prepares the salad, Justine sets the table

    (**B**) prepares the salad, and Justine sets the table

    (**C**) prepares the salad Justine sets the table

    (**D**) preparing the salad, and Justine sets the table

5. Many Cherokee now live in Oklahoma, but <u>this area were not their original home</u>.

    (**A**) this area were not their original home

    (**B**) this area was not their original home

    (**C**) this area was not they're original home

    (**D**) this area were not they're original home

6. <u>Pulling weeds in the garden, a tiny toad was discovered by Ernie.</u>

    (**A**) Pulling weeds in the garden, a tiny toad was discovered by Ernie.

    (**B**) A tiny toad was discovered pulling weeds in the garden by Ernie.

    (**C**) While pulling weeds in the garden, a tiny toad was discovered by Ernie.

    (**D**) Pulling weeds in the garden, Ernie discovered a tiny toad.

7. <u>Will rehearse together for the class play.</u>

    (**A**) Will rehearse together for the class play.

    (**B**) Will be rehearsing together for the class play.

    (**C**) We will rehearse together for the class play.

    (**D**) Because we will rehearse together for the class play.

8. Some people are <u>more afraider</u> of snakes than of any other kind of animal.

(A) more afraider

(B) afraid

(C) more afraid

(D) most afraid

9. <u>Several important African kingdoms developed between Lake Chad and the Atlantic Ocean.</u>

(A) Several important African kingdoms developed between Lake Chad and the Atlantic Ocean.

(B) Several important African kingdoms that developed between Lake Chad and the Atlantic Ocean.

(C) Several important African kingdoms between Lake Chad and the Atlantic Ocean.

(D) Several important African kingdoms developing between Lake Chad and the Atlantic Ocean.

10. <u>The singer waved to some people he knew in the audience from the stage.</u>

(A) The singer waved to some people he knew in the audience from the stage.

(B) The singer waved to some people from the stage he knew in the audience.

(C) The singer waved to some people from the stage in the audience he knew.

(D) The singer waved from the stage to some people he knew in the audience.

HELP

Some capital letters in Exercise 28 are already used correctly.

Reference Note

For information on **capital letters,** see Chapter 13.

Reference Note

For information on **capital letters,** see Chapter 13.

Exercise 28 **Correcting Errors in Capitalization**

The following groups of words contain errors in capitalization. Correct the errors either by changing capital letters to lowercase letters or by changing lowercase letters to capital letters.

EXAMPLE   **1.** a buddhist temple

　　　　　　1. a Buddhist temple

1. appalachian state university
2. world history and math 101
3. tuesday, May 1
4. senator williams
5. Summer In texas
6. Thirty-Fifth avenue
7. saturn and the moon
8. a korean Restaurant
9. empire state building
10. will rogers turnpike

Exercise 29 **Proofreading Sentences for Correct Capitalization**

For each of the following sentences, find the words that should be capitalized but are not. Then, write the words correctly.

EXAMPLE   **1.** American indians gave the name Buffalo Soldiers to African American troops who served in the West during the civil war.

　　　　　　1. Indians, Civil War

1. Thirteen Buffalo Soldiers won the congressional medal of honor, which is the highest military award in the United States.
2. *Black frontiers: A history of African american heroes in the Old west,* by Lillian Schlissel, was published in 1995.
3. A chapter about mary fields tells the story of a woman known as Stagecoach Mary who drove freight wagons and stagecoaches in the west.
4. One of the museums listed in the back of the book is the great plains black museum in Omaha, Nebraska.
5. The book also tells about benjamin singleton, who was born into slavery.

6. After the Civil War, he and some others bought land and founded the communities of Nicodemus and dunlap, kansas.
7. The exciting story of the cowboy Nat Love is told in his autobiography, *the life and adventures of Nat Love.*
8. bill pickett, who was of black, white, and American Indian ancestry, was one of the most famous rodeo competitors of all time.
9. Pickett's biography was published by the university of oklahoma press in 1977.
10. The businessman and gold miner Barney Ford became very wealthy and built ford's hotel on fifteenth street in denver, Colorado.

Exercise 30 **Proofreading Sentences for the Correct Use of Commas**

For each of the following sentences, write each word or numeral that should be followed by a comma and then add the comma.

EXAMPLE   1. The colors of the French flag are red white and blue.

　　　　　　1. *red, white,*

1. No the mountain dulcimer is not the same as the hammered dulcimer but both of them are stringed instruments.
2. Abraham Lincoln who was the sixteenth president of the United States died on April 15 1865.
3. If you want to knit a sweater you will need to get knitting needles yarn and a pattern.
4. After oiling the wheels on his sister's wagon Tyrel oiled the wheels on his skates and on his bicycle.
5. Competing in the 10K race Nathan found that he could run faster than his friends.
6. In my opinion a person should be fined if loose trash in the back of his or her pickup truck blows out and litters the road.
7. Lupe please show us how to use the new computer program.
8. Although Cody is afraid of heights he rescued a cat that was stuck high in a tree.
9. I hope that Amy Tan my favorite author will write another book soon.
10. Many people want to conserve resources yet some of these people overlook simple ways to recycle.

Reference Note

For information about **using commas correctly,** see page 294.

COMMON ERRORS

Reference Note

For information about **end marks,** see page 290. For information about **commas,** see page 294.

The following sentences lack necessary periods, question marks, exclamation points, and commas. Write the word before each missing punctuation mark, and insert the correct punctuation.

EXAMPLE 1. When will Anita Luís Martina and Sam be back from the mall

            1. *Anita, Luís, Martina, mall?*

1. Wow look at the size of that alligator
2. Leaning against the mast I could feel the sails catch the wind
3. Won't these new colorful curtains brighten this room
4. By the way that stack of newspapers should be recycled
5. Oil paints whether used for art projects or home improvement should be used only in well-ventilated areas
6. Hidiko watch out for that cactus
7. Was Uncle Jesse born in Cincinnati Ohio or Louisville Kentucky
8. As far as I am concerned the most interesting parts of the lecture were about the life of W E B DuBois
9. Monday Tuesday or Wednesday will be fine for our next meeting
10. Would you like to watch a movie tonight or should I bring over the model-plane kit to work on together

Exercise 32 Using Semicolons and Colons Correctly

Reference Note

For information about **semicolons and colons,** see page 310.

The following sentences lack necessary semicolons and colons. Write the words or numerals that come before and after the needed punctuation, and insert the correct punctuation.

EXAMPLE 1. Elena learned Spanish and English at home she learned French and German at school.

            1. *home; she*

1. They should be here before 9 30 this morning.
2. Our recycling center accepts the following materials glass, newspaper, cardboard, and aluminum cans.
3. The landscape designer planted bushes around the school last fall she will plant flowers this spring.
4. Please be at the station by 2 15 P.M.

5. The children wanted to see bears, lions, and elephants but parrots, snakes, tortoises, and goats were the only animals there.
6. The sermon was based on Isaiah 61 1.
7. To refinish this dresser, we will need some supplies varnish remover, sandpaper, steel wool, wood stain, and a clear polyurethane sealant.
8. Walking is terrific exercise it improves both your stamina and your muscle tone.
9. Many children's books have beautiful illustrations some are worth having just for the art.
10. Many palaces in Europe are spectacular Linderhof in Bavaria is my favorite.

Exercise 33 Punctuating and Capitalizing Quotations and Titles

For each of the following sentences, correct any capitalization errors and add or change quotation marks and other marks of punctuation where needed.

EXAMPLE 1. I learned how to play a new virtual-reality game today Pat said.

1. *"I learned how to play a new virtual-reality game today," Pat said.*

1. The most helpful chapter in my computer manual is "Search Tips" I explained to her.
2. Do Asian cobras look like African cobras Shawn asked.
3. I want to go to the fair after school Ivan said but my trumpet lesson is today.
4. The pilot said we are now beginning our descent into Orlando. Please fasten your seat belts, and return your seats to the upright position.
5. Goodness! what a surprise Taka exclaimed
6. Did some famous person say A smile is contagious
7. Cyclists should always wear helmets said the safety officer
8. Was it he who said a penny saved is a penny earned Troy asked
9. Carlos shouted, look at that dolphin near our boat!
10. During his speech at our school, the mayor said Our children are our future

Reference Note
For information about **punctuating and capitalizing quotations,** see page 322.

COMMON ERRORS

Mechanics **403**

Reference Note

For information about **using quotation marks,** see page 322.

Exercise 34 Punctuating and Capitalizing Quotations and Titles

For each of the following sentences, correct any capitalization errors and add or change quotation marks and other marks of punctuation where needed.

EXAMPLE   1. Mrs. Mendoza asked what can you tell me about Corazon Aquino?

                1. *Mrs. Mendoza asked, "What can you tell me about Corazon Aquino?"*

1. She was the president of the Philippines Ronald said.
2. That's correct. She served as president from 1986 to 1992 explained Mrs. Mendoza.
3. Yes! Sara exclaimed some say she restored democracy to the country.
4. I wrote about her in my paper "Hear Me Roar: Three Asian Women Who Changed the World" Sara said.
5. I bet you mentioned she was *Time* magazine's Woman of the Year in 1987 Chito stated.
6. I did Sara replied As Asia's first female president, she was a real trailblazer.
7. Leo exclaimed wow! I didn't know she was the very first.
8. Didn't she say One must be frank to be relevant inquired Chito.
9. That sounds familiar Sara said I'll have to look back at my research
10. I happen to know said Mrs. Mendoza That Aquino made that statement in a speech to the United Nations.

Reference Note

For information on **using apostrophes,** see page 330.

Exercise 35 Using Apostrophes Correctly

Add, delete, or move apostrophes where needed in the following word groups. If a word group is already correct, write *C*.

EXAMPLE   1. both boys shoes

                1. *boys'*

1. somebodys lunch
2. cant play
3. Neals motorcycle
4. better than theirs
5. womens volleyball
6. too many letter *u*s
7. its engine
8. Betsy Rosss flag
9. no more *if*s
10. the bushes branches

Correcting Spelling Errors

Most of the following words are misspelled. If a word is spelled incorrectly, write the correct spelling. If a word is already spelled correctly, write *C*.

Reference Note

For information on **spelling rules,** see page 348.

EXAMPLE   **1.** succede

        1. succeed

1. taxs	**8.** stathood	**15.** improper
2. neice	**9.** lovelyer	**16.** fancifuly
3. supercede	**10.** clearest	**17.** dryest
4. disallow	**11.** wolfs	**18.** cluless
5. countrys	**12.** sheild	**19.** overjoied
6. emptyness	**13.** preceed	**20.** skiping
7. tracable	**14.** father-in-laws	

Choosing Between Words Often Confused

From each pair in parentheses, choose the word or words that make the sentence correct.

Reference Note

For information on **words often confused,** see page 358.

EXAMPLE   **1.** The school plans to (*except, accept*) the new computer company's offer.

        1. accept

1. Did Coach Jefferson (*advise, advice*) you to take the first-aid course at the community center?

2. My cousins and I are (*all ready, already*) to enter the marathon.

3. Sacramento became the (*capital, capitol*) of California in 1854.

4. When garden hoses (*brake, break*), they sometimes can be mended with waterproof tape.

5. Avoid wearing (*loose, lose*) clothing when operating that equipment.

6. Many people know Mr. Perez, but I think he should be (*formerly, formally*) introduced.

7. My grandfather threw the football (*passed, past*) the trees and over the creek.

8. (*Its, It's*) a good idea to test home smoke detectors frequently to make sure the batteries are still working.

9. One basic (*principle, principal*) of our Constitution is the right to free speech.

10. Some cats are called bobtails because of (*their, there*) very short tails.

COMMON ERRORS

Mechanics Test: Section 1

DIRECTIONS   Each numbered item below consists of an underlined word or word group. Choose the answer that shows the correct capitalization, punctuation, and spelling of the underlined part. If there is no error, choose D (Correct as is).

EXAMPLE   **[1]** 29 South Maple street

      (A) 29 south Maple Street
      (B) 29 South Maple Street
      (C) Twenty Nine South Maple Street
      (D) Correct as is

ANSWER   1.

---

29 South Maple Street
Philadelphia, PA 19107

[1] January 15 2009

Mail-Order Sales Manager
[2] Direct Electronics, Inc.

214-C Billings Boulevard
[3] New Castle, Ken 40050

[4] Dear Sales Manager,

The modem that I ordered from your company arrived today in **[5]** peices. The package was **[6]** open, and appeared not to have been sealed properly. **[7]** In addition I have not yet received the computer game that I also ordered. Please send me a new **[8]** modem the broken modem is enclosed.

I appreciate **[9]** you're prompt attention to both of these matters.

[10] Sincerely yours,

Cameron Scott

Cameron Scott

---

1. **(A)** January 15, 2009
   (B) January, 15 2009
   (C) January 15th 2009
   (D) Correct as is

2. **(A)** direct electronics, inc.
   (B) Direct electronics, inc.
   (C) Direct Electronics, inc.
   (D) Correct as is

3. **(A)** New Castle Ken. 40050
   (B) New Castle, KY 40050
   (C) New Castle KY, 40050
   (D) Correct as is

4. **(A)** Dear sales manager,
   (B) dear sales manager:
   (C) Dear Sales Manager:
   (D) Correct as is

5. **(A)** pieces
   (B) piece's
   (C) peaces
   (D) Correct as is

6. **(A)** open and appeared
   (B) open; and appeared
   (C) open, and, appeared
   (D) Correct as is

7. **(A)** In addition, I
   (B) In addition i
   (C) In addition, i
   (D) Correct as is

8. **(A)** modem, the
   (B) modem; the
   (C) modem: the
   (D) Correct as is

9. **(A)** youre
   (B) your,
   (C) your
   (D) Correct as is

10. **(A)** Sincerely Yours',
    (B) Sincerely your's,
    (C) Sincerely yours:
    (D) Correct as is

Mechanics Test: Section 2

DIRECTIONS   Each of the following sentences contains an underlined word or word group. Choose the answer that shows the correct capitalization, punctuation, and spelling of the underlined part. If there is no error, choose D (Correct as is).

EXAMPLE   1.   Rosie said that her cousin sent her that <u>soft colorful fabric</u> from Kenya.

   (A) soft, colorful, fabric
   (B) soft, colorful fabric
   (C) soft; colorful fabric
   (D) Correct as is

ANSWER   1.

1. The following people have volunteered to make <u>enchiladas, Manuel,</u> Shawn, and Anita.

    (A) enchiladas; Manuel   **(C)** enchiladas: Manuel
    (B) enchiladas. Manuel   **(D)** Correct as is

2. Our school's <u>recycling program which</u> is now three years old, has been quite successful.

    (A) recycling program, which   **(C)** recycling program; which
    (B) Recycling Program, which   **(D)** Correct as is

3. <u>Looking at the astronomical map in my science book</u> I spotted the constellations Orion, Taurus, and Pisces.

    (A) Looking at the astronomical map, in my science book I
    (B) Looking at the astronomical map, in my science book, I
    (C) Looking at the astronomical map in my science book, I
    (D) Correct as is

4. Donna <u>asked, "who</u> plans to work as a baby sitter over the summer?"

    (A) asked, "Who   **(C)** asked, Who
    (B) asked "who   **(D)** Correct as is

5. Angela and Wanda painted the <u>mural, and Jamal</u> attached it to the wall in the gym.

    (A) mural and Jamal   **(C)** mural, and jamal
    (B) mural: and Jamal   **(D)** Correct as is

6. Many television programs have closed captioning for <u>people who cant</u> hear.

    (A) people, who cant   **(C)** people who can't
    (B) people, who can't   **(D)** Correct as is

7. "What a great time we had at the <u>park"! Sandy</u> exclaimed as she got into the car.

    (A) Park"! Sandy   **(C)** park", Sandy
    (B) park!" Sandy   **(D)** Correct as is

8. "<u>Your aunt Helen</u> certainly is a fascinating person," Carla said.

    (A) "Your Aunt Helen   **(C)** Your aunt Helen
    (B) "Your aunt, Helen   **(D)** Correct as is

408   Chapter 17   Correcting Common Errors

9. "Many of us would have gone to the picnic if we had known about <u>it</u>" Alan said.

(A) it",

(B) it,"

(C) it,

(D) Correct as is

10. The Zunigas have a new <u>puppy; its</u> a cocker spaniel.

(A) puppy; Its

(C) puppy, its

(B) puppy; it's

(D) Correct as is

11. The ants <u>carried large leafs</u> across John Henry's backyard.

(A) carryed large leafs

(C) carried large leaves

(B) carryed large leaves

(D) Correct as is

12. Has the guide <u>all ready led</u> the hikers to the top of the mesa?

(A) all ready lead

(C) already led

(B) already lead

(D) Correct as is

13. If Carlos wants to play the role of Eddie in the <u>musical, he'll have too practice</u> the solos.

(A) musical, he'll have to practice

(B) musical; he'll have to practice

(C) musical he'll have too practice

(D) Correct as is

14. <u>Sara said that the big guppy in the class aquarium is going to have babies.</u>

(A) Sara said "That the big guppy in the class aquarium is going to have babies."

(B) Sara said "that the big guppy in the class aquarium is going to have babies."

(C) Sara said "That the big guppy in the class aquarium is going to have babies".

(D) Correct as is

15. On <u>October 1 1960</u> Nigeria became an independent nation.

(A) October, 1 1960

(C) October 1, 1960

(B) October 1, 1960,

(D) Correct as is

PART 2

Sentences

GO TO: go.hrw.com
KEYWORD: HLLA

Writing Effective Sentences

1.0 Written and Oral English Language Conventions
Students write and speak with a command of standard English conventions appropriate to this grade level.
1.3 Identify types and structure of sentences.

Diagnostic Preview

A. Identifying Sentences, Sentence Fragments, and Run-on Sentences

Identify each of the following word groups as a *sentence*, a *sentence fragment*, or a *run-on sentence*. Rewrite each fragment and run-on to make one or more complete sentences.

EXAMPLE   **1.** After we left.

     1. sentence fragment—After we left, I sighed.

1. Like the sound of my pencil on paper.
2. Before we go, please pack the suitcases.
3. Lunch tasted great, we finished everything on our plates.
4. If you think the answer is twenty-two or twenty-four.
5. At sunrise I climbed out of bed then I brushed my teeth.

B. Combining Sentences

Combine the sentences in the following items.

EXAMPLE   **1.** Jon left early. He didn't feel well.

     1. Jon left early because he didn't feel well.

6. I care about the environment. I recycle everything that I can.
7. He collects rocks. He keeps them in a special box.
8. Bees are flying insects that help pollinate flowers. Butterflies are flying insects that help pollinate flowers.

9. She sculpts paper clips into pyramids. The pyramids are tiny.
10. Ms. Merriam sometimes plays piano for our class. She is one of our best teachers.

C. Revising Stringy and Wordy Sentences

Each of the following sentences is stringy, wordy, or both. Revise each sentence to make it simpler and clearer.

EXAMPLE 1. Robbie covered the floor with crackers, but his sitter walked in, and she gasped, and she picked Robbie up.

1. *Robbie covered the floor with crackers. His sitter walked in, gasped, and picked Robbie up.*

11. Felicia and her family visited Carlsbad Caverns, and they spent the whole afternoon inside the cave, but they came out in the evening, and they watched the bats emerge.
12. Felicia's brother wanted to take a picture, but the ranger stopped him, and she told him to put his camera away.
13. He smiled at her, and that was a polite thing for him to have done, but he still really wanted a picture.
14. Due to the fact that he had put his camera away, the ranger told him that she had a poster that she could give him.
15. The ranger walked to her bag, and she took out a poster that was a poster of a bat, and she gave the poster to him.

D. Creating Sentence Variety and Using Transitions

Revise the following paragraph to create sentences of different length and structure, vary sentence beginnings, and improve transitions between thoughts.

EXAMPLE I like to watch storms. I especially like exciting storms.
I especially like to watch exciting storms.

A storm rolled in after sunset last night. Lightning lit the sky. It was on the horizon. The warm wind cooled. The breeze smelled like wet asphalt. The birds were silent. We sat on the porch. The storm got closer. We watched the lightning. It flickered. The thunder rumbled. It shook the porch. It rumbled again. The porch shook again. I grew worried. I imagined that I was a wilted tree. I imagined that I was a patch of dried grass. I felt better about the storm. It looked like a welcome relief.

Writing Complete Sentences

One of the best ways to make your writing clear is to use complete sentences. A **complete sentence**

- has a subject
- has a verb
- expresses a complete thought

┌HELP┐

A word group that has a subject and a verb and that expresses a complete thought is an **independent clause.** All complete sentences contain at least one independent clause.

Reference Note

For more information about **independent clauses,** see page 114.

Reference Note

For more information on **imperative sentences,** see page 18.

| SENTENCES | Trees absorb excess carbon dioxide in the atmosphere. [The subject is *Trees.* The verb is *absorb.*] |
| | Are some species in danger of extinction? [The subject is *species.* The verb is *Are.*] |

The sentences above express complete thoughts. That is, each sentence has a topic (the subject) and tells you something about that topic.

NOTE **Imperative sentences** (sentences that express a command or direct request) have understood subjects. That is, the subject of the sentence is not expressed in the sentence but is understood to be *you.*

| REQUEST | Please tell me more. [The subject is understood to be *you.* The verb is *tell.*] |
| COMMAND | Listen! [The subject is understood to be *you.* The verb is *Listen.*] |

┌TIPS & TRICKS┐

Some words look like verbs but really aren't. These "fake" verbs can fool you into thinking a group of words is a sentence when it is really a fragment. A word that ends in –*ing* cannot stand as a verb unless it has a helping verb (such as *is, are,* or *were*) with it.

FRAGMENT
The children playing on the swings. [Without a helping verb, this is not a complete thought.]

SENTENCE
The children **were playing** on the swings.

Sentence Fragments

Incomplete sentences are called sentence fragments. A **sentence fragment** is a word or word group that looks like a sentence but that has no subject, has no verb, or does not express a complete thought. Because it is incomplete, a sentence fragment can confuse your reader.

FRAGMENT	Went to the grocery store yesterday. [This word group contains no subject. Who went to the grocery store yesterday?]
SENTENCE	**We** went to the grocery store yesterday.
FRAGMENT	The bird nest in the top of the oak tree. [This word group contains no verb. What about the bird nest in the top of the oak tree?]

SENTENCE	The bird nest **is** in the top of the oak tree.

FRAGMENT	Before the ice on the lake melts. [Although this word group contains a subject and a verb, it does not express a complete thought. What will happen before the ice on the lake melts?]
SENTENCE	**We will go skating** before the ice on the lake melts.

FRAGMENT	My friend Larry, who has a good voice. [This word group contains a subject, *friend,* but that subject doesn't have a verb. What about my friend Larry, who has a good voice?]
SENTENCE	My friend Larry, who has a good voice, **is singing.**

As you can see from the examples, you can correct some sentence fragments by adding a subject or a verb. Other fragments need to be attached to an independent clause to make a complete sentence.

┌HELP┐
Remember that a complete sentence meets three requirements: It has a subject, it has a verb, and it expresses a complete thought.

Oral Practice **Identifying Sentence Fragments**

Read each of the following groups of words aloud, and decide whether it is a sentence fragment or a complete sentence.

1. A flying squirrel a squirrel that can gracefully glide through the air.
2. Some Asian flying squirrels three feet long.
3. Skillfully leaps from one tree to another.
4. The squirrel glides downward, then straight, and finally upward.
5. Some flying squirrels more than fifty feet.
6. If they use a higher starting point.
7. Flying squirrels live in the forests of Asia, Europe, and North America.
8. To eat berries, birds' eggs, insects, and nuts.
9. Nesting in the hollows of trees.
10. Notice how this squirrel stretches out its legs to help it glide.

Exercise 1 Finding and Revising Fragments

Some of the following groups of words are sentence fragments.
Revise each fragment so that it contains a subject and a verb and
expresses a complete thought. If an item is already a complete
sentence, write *S*.

EXAMPLE **1.** As soon as we finished eating breakfast.

1. *We left for our camping trip as soon as we finished
    eating breakfast.*

1. As the whole family loaded into the car.
2. We traveled for hours.
3. When we arrived at the campground.
4. My sister and I down to the river.
5. Took our fishing gear with us.
6. We cast our lines the way our aunt had taught us.
7. Caught several trout in a few hours.
8. We headed back to the campsite at sunset.
9. Dad cooking bean soup over the fire.
10. While Mom and my sister pitched the tent.

Run-on Sentences

A *run-on sentence* is a word group made up of two complete sentences that have been run together with no punctuation between
them or with only a comma between them. Run-on sentences make
it hard for the reader to tell where one thought ends and another
begins.

RUN-ON   Mockingbirds are great mimics they can imitate the songs
          of at least twenty other bird species.

CORRECT   Mockingbirds are great mimics**.** **T**hey can imitate the songs
          of at least twenty other bird species.

RUN-ON   People say that life is short, there are some redwoods more
          than 1,500 years old.

CORRECT   People say that life is short**, but** there are some redwoods
          more than 1,500 years old.

NOTE A comma does mark a brief pause in a sentence, but it does
not show the end of a sentence. If you use just a comma between
two sentences and if a coordinating conjunction does not follow the
comma, you create a run-on sentence.

Revising Run-on Sentences

Here are three ways you can revise run-on sentences.

1. You can make two sentences.

RUN-ON   Asteroids are tiny planets they are sometimes called planetoids.

CORRECT   Asteroids are tiny planets**.** **T**hey are sometimes called planetoids.

2. You can use a comma and a coordinating conjunction such as *and, but,* or *or.*

RUN-ON   Some asteroids shine with a steady light, others keep changing in brightness.

CORRECT   Some asteroids shine with a steady light**, but** others keep changing in brightness.

3. You can use a semicolon.

RUN-ON   Asteroids vary greatly in size, they range from about twenty feet across to about 600 miles in diameter.

CORRECT   Asteroids vary greatly in size**;** they range from about twenty feet across to about 600 miles in diameter.

Reference Note

For more information about **coordinating conjunctions,** see page 62. For information about **semicolons;** see page 310.

Exercise 2 Identifying and Revising Run-on Sentences

Decide which of the following groups of words are run-on sentences. Then, revise each run-on in one of the ways shown above. If the group of words is already correct, write *C.*

1. Saturn is a huge planet it is more than nine times larger than Earth.
2. Saturn is covered by clouds, it is circled by bands of color.
3. Some of the clouds are yellow, others are off-white.
4. Saturn has about twenty moons Titan is the largest.
5. Many of Saturn's moons have large craters the crater on Mimas covers one third of its diameter.
6. Saturn's most striking feature is a group of rings that circles the planet.
7. The rings of Saturn are less than two miles thick, they spread out from the planet for a great distance.
8. The rings are made up of billions of tiny particles.
9. Some of the rings are dark, but others are brighter.
10. You can use a telescope to view Saturn, you can visit a planetarium.

Review A **Correcting Sentence Fragments and Run-on Sentences**

Identify the sentence fragments and run-on sentences in the following paragraph. Then, revise each sentence fragment and run-on sentence to make the paragraph clearer.

EXAMPLE   Visited the Mojave Desert.
            I visited the Mojave Desert.

    Many deserts have very little plant
life, some desert regions have a variety of plants. Many plants can survive.
Where the climate is hot and dry.
Cacti, Joshua trees, palm trees, and
wildflowers grow in deserts those
plants do not grow close together. They
are spread out,each plant gets water
and minerals from a large area.

Combining Sentences

Although short sentences can sometimes express your ideas well, using only short sentences will make your writing sound choppy and dull. For example, read the following paragraph, which has only short sentences.

    Thomas Edison invented the phono-
graph. He also experimented with
mechanical toys. Many people do not
know this. Edison created a talking
doll. He created the talking doll in
1894. The doll would recite a nursery
rhyme or poem. It said the words when
a crank in its back was turned. The
talking doll was very popular. Edison
opened a factory. The factory made
five hundred of the dolls every day.

Now read the revised paragraph. Notice how the writer has combined some of the short sentences to make longer, smoother sentences.

```
     Thomas Edison invented the phono-
graph. Many people do not know that
he also experimented with mechanical
toys. Edison created a talking doll
in 1894. When a crank in its back was
turned, the doll would recite a nurs-
ery rhyme or poem. The talking doll
was very popular, and Edison opened a
factory that made five hundred of the
dolls every day.
```

Sentence combining also helps to reduce the number of repeated words and ideas. The revised paragraph is clearer, shorter, and more interesting to read. The following pages contain strategies for combining sentences. Once you learn these strategies, you can apply them to your own writing.

Combining Sentences by Inserting Words

One way to combine short sentences is to take an important word from one sentence and insert it into another sentence. Sometimes you will need to change the form of the word before you can insert it. You can change some words into adjectives by adding an ending such as *–ed, –ing, –ful,* or *–ly.* The adjective can describe another word in the sentence.

Reference Note

For more information about **adjectives,** see page 34.

ORIGINAL Easter lily plants have leaves. The leaves have points.

COMBINED Easter lily plants have **pointed** leaves.

Exercise 3 **Combining Sentences by Inserting Words**

Each of the following items contains two sentences. To combine the two sentences, take the italicized word from the second sentence and insert it into the first sentence. The directions in parentheses will tell you how to change the form of the word if you need to do so.

EXAMPLE **1.** Peanuts are the tiny fruit of the peanut plant. They have a good *taste.* (Change *taste* to *tasty.*)

  1. *Peanuts are the tiny, tasty fruit of the peanut plant.*

1. This picture shows peanuts underground. They *grow* underground. (Add *–ing.*)
2. Peanuts are a crop of many warm regions. They are a *major* crop.
3. Peanuts are a food for snacking. Peanuts are good for your *health.* (Add *–ful.*)
4. The oil from peanuts is used in many dressings. The dressings are for *salad.*
5. Grades of peanut oil are used to make soap and shampoo. The *low* grades are used for these products.
6. Much of the world grows peanuts solely for their oil. This oil is *versatile.*
7. The peanut-producing countries include China, India, and the United States. These countries *lead* the world in peanut production. (Add *–ing.*)
8. Some soils will stain the peanut shells. *Dark* soils are responsible for the stains.
9. After peanuts are harvested, the plants are used for feed. The feed is for *livestock.*
10. Peanuts are a good source of vitamins. Peanuts contain *B* vitamins.

Combining Sentences by Inserting Phrases

A *phrase* is a group of words that acts as a single part of speech and that does not have both a subject and a verb. You can combine sentences by taking a phrase from one sentence and inserting it into another sentence.

ORIGINAL	Arachne is a famous figure. She is a figure in Greek mythology.
COMBINED	Arachne is a famous figure **in Greek mythology.** [The prepositional phrase *in Greek mythology* is inserted into the first sentence.]

ORIGINAL	Arachne was proud. She was proud of her weaving.
COMBINED	Arachne was proud **of her weaving.** [The prepositional phrase *of her weaving* is inserted into the first sentence.]

NOTE Before you insert a phrase into a sentence, ask yourself whether the phrase renames or identifies a noun or pronoun. If it does, it is an **appositive phrase,** and you may need to set it off with one or more commas.

ORIGINAL	Arachne challenged Athena to a weaving contest. Athena was the goddess of wisdom.
COMBINED	Arachne challenged Athena**, the goddess of wisdom,** to a weaving contest. [The appositive phrase in boldface type renames the noun *Athena*.]

Reference Note

For more information and practice on using commas to set off **appositive phrases,** see page 301.

Another way to combine sentences is to change the verb and create a new phrase. Just add *–ing* or *–ed* to the verb, or put the word *to* in front of it. You can then use the new phrase to describe a noun, verb, or pronoun in a related sentence.

ORIGINAL	The name *Inuit* refers to several groups of people. These people live in and near the Arctic.
COMBINED	The name *Inuit* refers to several groups of people **living in and near the Arctic.** [The participial phrase *living in and near the Arctic* describes the noun *people*.]
ORIGINAL	Early Inuit followed a special way of life. They did this so they could survive in a harsh environment.
COMBINED	**To survive in a harsh environment,** early Inuit followed a special way of life. [The infinitive phrase *To survive in a harsh environment* modifies the verb *followed*.]

Reference Note

For more information about **prepositional, participial, infinitive, and appositive phrases,** see pages 89–106.

NOTE When you combine sentences by adding a word or phrase from one sentence to another sentence, the resulting sentence may contain a compound phrase. Be sure to keep the compound elements **parallel,** or matching in form. Otherwise, instead of making your writing smoother, combining may actually make it more awkward.

ORIGINAL	Ana likes to hike. Ana also likes cycling.
NOT PARALLEL	Ana likes to hike and cycling. [*To hike* is an infinitive; *cycling* is a gerund.]
PARALLEL	Ana likes hiking and cycling. [*Hiking* and *cycling* are both gerunds.]

HELP

An **infinitive** is a verb form, often beginning with *to,* that can be used as a noun, an adjective, or an adverb. A **gerund** is a verb form ending in *–ing* that is used as a noun.

Each of the following items contains two sentences. Combine the sentences by taking the italicized word group from the second sentence and inserting it into the first sentence. The hints in parentheses tell you how to change the forms of words if you need to do so. Remember to insert commas where they are needed.

EXAMPLE
1. The Inuit followed their traditional way of life. They followed this way of life *for thousands of years.*

1. The Inuit followed their traditional way of life for thousands of years.

1. The Inuit built winter shelters in a few hours. They *stacked blocks of snow.* (Change *stacked* to *Stacking.*)
2. They used harpoons. This is how they *hunted seals.* (Change *hunted* to *to hunt.*)
3. The Inuit also hunted and ate caribou. Caribou are *a type of deer.*
4. Whalers and fur traders came to the region and affected the Inuit way of life. They arrived *in the 1800s.*
5. The Inuit often moved several times a year. They moved so that they could *find food.* (Change *find* to *to find.*)
6. During the summer, traditional Inuit lived in tents. The tents were *made from animal skin.*
7. In the 1800s, many Inuit began to trap animals. They trapped animals *for European fur traders.*
8. Some Inuit worked on whaling ships. They *needed to find other ways to provide for their families.* (Change *need* to *Needing.*)
9. The Inuit have survived for thousands of years. They have survived *in the harsh Arctic climate.*
10. Most Inuit today follow a modern way of life. They are *like the Canadian Inuit seen in the photo on this page.*

Combining Sentences Using *And, But,* or *Or*

You can also use the coordinating conjunctions *and, but,* and *or* to combine sentences. Doing so is called **coordination.** With these connecting words, you can make a *compound subject,* a *compound verb,* or a *compound sentence.*

Compound Subjects and Verbs

Sometimes two sentences have the same verb with different subjects. You can combine the sentences by linking the two subjects with *and* or *or* to make a **compound subject.**

ORIGINAL   Dolphins look a little like fish. Porpoises look a little like fish.

COMBINED   **Dolphins and porpoises** look a little like fish.

Two sentences can also have the same subject with different verbs. You can use *and, but,* or *or* to connect the two verbs. The result is a **compound verb.**

ORIGINAL   Dolphins live in water like fish. They breathe like other mammals.

COMBINED   Dolphins **live** in water like fish **but breathe** like other mammals.

Exercise 5   Combining Sentences by Creating Compound Subjects and Verbs

Combine each of the following pairs of short, choppy sentences by using *and, but,* or *or.* If the two sentences have the same verb, make a compound subject. If they have the same subject, make a compound verb. Remember to keep the ideas in parallel form.

EXAMPLE   1. Dolphins belong to a group of mammals called cetaceans. Porpoises belong to a group of mammals called cetaceans.

1. *Dolphins and porpoises belong to a group of mammals called cetaceans.*

1. Dolphins are warm-blooded. Porpoises are warm-blooded.
2. Common dolphins live in warm waters. Common dolphins swim in large schools.
3. Porpoises are similar to dolphins. Porpoises generally live in cooler water.

TIPS & TRICKS

When you use the coordinating conjunction *and* to link two subjects, your new compound subject will be a plural subject. Remember to make the verb agree with the subject in number.

ORIGINAL
Zach likes watching the sea mammals. Briana likes watching the sea mammals.

COMBINED
Zach and Briana like watching the sea mammals. [The plural verb *like* is needed with the plural subject *Zach and Briana.*]

For more information on **agreement of subjects and verbs,** see page 148.

HELP

When deciding whether to use *and, but,* or *or,* follow these rules.

- *And* shows equality. Use it if you mean *both.*
  Katie **and** Tyrone are my friends.

- *But* shows contrast. Use it to point out something *different.*
  Katie likes to play tennis, **but** Tyrone does not.

- *Or* shows a choice. Use it if you have *options.*
  Usually either Katie **or** Tyrone waits for me after school.

4. Dolphins have beak-like snouts. Dolphins use sonar to locate objects under water.
5. Dolphins hunt fish. Dolphins eat fish.
6. Dolphins swim by moving their tails up and down. Porpoises swim by moving their tails up and down.
7. Porpoises can swim fast. Dolphins can swim fast.
8. A porpoise could outswim most sharks. A tuna could outswim most sharks.
9. Bottle-nosed dolphins can measure up to fifteen feet in length. Bottle-nosed dolphins can weigh over four hundred pounds.
10. Sharks sometimes attack porpoises. Sharks sometimes kill porpoises.

Compound Sentences

Sometimes you will want to combine two sentences that express equally important ideas. You can connect two closely related, equally important sentences by using a comma plus the coordinating conjunction *and, but,* or *or.* Doing so creates a **compound sentence.**

ORIGINAL   My brother entered the Annual Chili Cook-off. His chili won a prize.

COMBINED   My brother entered the Annual Chili Cook-off**, and** his chili won a prize.

ORIGINAL   I did not help cook. I helped him clean the kitchen.

COMBINED   I did not help cook**, but** I helped him clean the kitchen.

NOTE A compound sentence tells the reader that the two ideas are closely related. If you combine two short sentences that are not closely related, you may confuse your reader.

UNRELATED   Fernando mowed the grass, and I had a broom.

RELATED   Fernando mowed the grass, and I swept the sidewalk.

Exercise 6 Combining Sentences by Forming a Compound Sentence

Each of the following pairs of sentences is closely related. Make each pair into a compound sentence by adding a comma and a coordinating conjunction such as *and* or *but.*

EXAMPLE   1. The Pueblos have lived in the same location for a long time. They have strong ties to their homeland.

   1. *The Pueblos have lived in the same location for a long time, and they have strong ties to their homeland.*

1. Some Pueblos built villages in the valleys. Others settled in desert and mountain areas.
2. Desert surrounded many of the valleys. The people grew crops with the help of irrigation systems.
3. Women gathered berries and other foods. Men hunted game.
4. Their adobe homes had several stories. The people used ladders to reach the upper levels.
5. The Pueblos were generally peaceful. Some Pueblo tribes drove the Spanish from their territories.
6. Today, each Pueblo village has its own government. The Pueblo people still share many customs.
7. Long ago, women helped farm. Now only men cultivate Pueblo lands.
8. Pueblo social life is still centered on the village. Native religion is important.
9. Arts and crafts are part of the Pueblo economy. Pueblos also raise new kinds of crops.
10. The Pueblos share many things with their ancestors. They enjoy much of modern life.

Combining Sentences Using Subordinate Clauses

A **clause** is a group of words that contains a subject and a verb. **Independent clauses** can stand alone as a sentence. **Subordinate** (or **dependent**) **clauses** cannot stand alone because they do not express a complete thought.

INDEPENDENT CLAUSE   Gertrude Ederle swam the English Channel. [This clause can stand alone.]

SUBORDINATE CLAUSE   when she was nineteen years old [This clause cannot stand alone.]

You can combine related sentences by using a subordinate clause. Doing so is called **subordination.** The resulting sentence is called a **complex sentence.** The subordinate clause gives information about a word or idea in the independent clause.

Reference Note

For more information on **independent clauses** and **subordinate clauses,** see page 113.

Reference Note

For more information on **complex sentences,** see page 135.

TWO SIMPLE SENTENCES	Theresa traveled to Rome. She saw the Sistine Chapel.
ONE COMPLEX SENTENCE	Theresa traveled to Rome, **where she saw the Sistine Chapel.**

Making Clauses That Begin with *Who, Which,* or *That*

Reference Note

A clause that begins with *who, which,* or *that* and that modifies a noun or pronoun is an **adjective clause.** For more information on **adjective clauses,** see page 117.

You can often make a short sentence into a subordinate clause by inserting *who, which,* or *that* in place of the subject.

ORIGINAL	The Everglades consist mainly of swamps. The Everglades cover the southern part of Florida.
COMBINED	The Everglades, **which consist mainly of swamps,** cover the southern part of Florida.
ORIGINAL	Everglades National Park is a large area. The area includes about one fifth of the Everglades' original land.
COMBINED	Everglades National Park is a large area **that includes about one fifth of the Everglades' original land.**

Making Clauses with Words of Time or Place

Reference Note

A clause that is used to give information about time and place and that modifies a verb, adjective, or adverb is an **adverb clause.** For more information on **adverb clauses,** see page 120.

Another way to turn a sentence into a subordinate clause is to add a word that tells time or place. Words that begin this type of clause include *after, before, where, wherever, when, whenever,* and *while.* You may need to delete some words to insert the clause into another sentence.

ORIGINAL	The last ice age ended. Water from the melting ice flooded the area.
COMBINED	**After the last ice age ended,** water from the melting ice flooded the area.
ORIGINAL	No humans lived in the Everglades until 1842. In 1842, Seminoles fled to the area.
COMBINED	No humans lived in the Everglades until 1842, **when Seminoles fled to the area.**

Reference Note

For more information on the use of **commas with introductory clauses,** see page 305.

NOTE If you put your time or place clause at the beginning of the sentence, use a comma after the clause.

ORIGINAL	People began draining the swamps to make farmland. The Everglades were in danger.
COMBINED	**When people began draining the swamps to make farmland,** the Everglades were in danger.

Exercise 7 Combining Sentences by Using
Subordinate Clauses

Combine each sentence pair by making one sentence into a subordinate clause and attaching it to the other sentence. You may
need to cut a word or two from the second sentence.

EXAMPLE
1. Mother-of-pearl is a substance made by oysters and
other mollusks. Mother-of-pearl is also called nacre
(pronounced nā'kər). (Use *which*.)

1. *Mother-of-pearl, which is also called nacre
(pronounced nā'kər), is a substance made by
oysters and other mollusks.*

1. The pearl is a gem. It is made by certain kinds of mollusks.
(Use *that*.)
2. The finest pearls are produced by mollusks with special
shells. Their shells are lined with mother-of-pearl. (Use *that*.)
3. Pearls are usually formed around particles of sand or dirt.
The particles get inside the mollusk. (Use *when*.)
4. The mollusk's shell produces cells. The cells attach themselves to a particle. (Use *that*.)
5. A pearl is formed. The cells cover the particle with mother-
of-pearl. (Use *as*.)
6. People culture certain types of pearls. These pearls can be as
beautiful as natural pearls. (Use *that*.)
7. The first cultured pearls were grown in China. Chinese pearl
divers discovered that they could put bits of mud, wood,
bone, or metal inside a living mollusk. (Use *after*.)
8. Seed pearls form. It takes about three years for them to grow
into full pearls. (Use *Once*.)
9. Cultured pearls often are grown on boats. Young oysters are
raised in barrels. (Use *where*.)
10. A pearl producer puts spheres of polished mother-of-pearl
inside the oysters. The oysters are ready to begin forming
beautiful new gems. (Use *when*.)

Review B Revising a Paragraph by Combining
Sentences

The following paragraph sounds choppy because it has too many
short sentences. Use the methods you have learned in this section
to combine sentences in the paragraph.

EXAMPLE   Basketball is an exciting team sport. It
           is also a popular form of recreation.
           Basketball is an exciting team sport as well as a popular
           form of recreation.

Dr. James Naismith invented the game
of basketball over one hundred years ago.
He probably never guessed the sport would
become so popular. He just wanted a new
game that could be played indoors. The
original basketball teams started in
1891. They had nine players instead
of five. The first basket was a peach
basket. A player had to climb up and
retrieve the ball after each score. Some
parts of the game have stayed the same.
Players still cannot hold the ball while
they run. They must dribble. Thousands
of teams across the world now play
Dr. Naismith's game.

Improving Sentence Style

In addition to combining some sentences, you can also make your
writing more effective by revising *stringy* and *wordy sentences* to
make them shorter and clearer.

Revising Stringy Sentences

A **stringy sentence** is made up of several complete thoughts
strung together with words like *and* or *but.* Stringy sentences just
ramble on and on. They don't give the reader a chance to pause
before new ideas.

To fix a stringy sentence, you can

- break the sentence into two or more sentences
- turn some of the complete thoughts into phrases or
  subordinate clauses

STRINGY   Martina climbed the stairs of the haunted house, and she
           knocked on the door several times, but no one answered, and
           she braced herself, and then she opened the door.

REVISED Martina climbed the stairs of the haunted house. She knocked on the door several times, but no one answered. Bracing herself, she opened the door.

NOTE When you revise a stringy sentence, you may decide to keep *and* or *but* between two closely related independent clauses. If you do this, be sure to use a comma before the *and* or *but*.

EXAMPLE She knocked on the door**, but** no one answered.

Reference Note

For more information on **punctuating compound sentences,** see page 131.

Exercise 8 **Revising Stringy Sentences**

Some of the following sentences are stringy and need to be improved. First, identify the stringy sentences. Then, revise them by (1) breaking each sentence into two or more sentences or (2) turning some of the complete thoughts into phrases or subordinate clauses. If the sentence is effective and does not need to be improved, write *C* for *correct*.

EXAMPLE 1. I have a hero; and her name is Mercedes O. Cubría, and she had an interesting career.

　　　　 1. *My hero, Mercedes O. Cubría, had an interesting career.*

1. Mercedes O. Cubría was born in Cuba, but her mother died, and she moved to the United States, and she moved with her two sisters.
2. She worked as a nurse, and then she joined the Women's Army Corps, and she soon became an officer in the army.
3. Cubría was the first Cuban-born woman to become an officer in the U.S. Army.
4. Her job during World War II was to translate important government papers into a secret code.
5. The war ended, and she was promoted to captain, and later her official rank rose to major.
6. Then there was the Korean War, and she worked as an intelligence officer, and she studied information about the enemy.
7. Cubría retired from the army in 1953 but was called to duty again in 1962.
8. After the Castro revolution, thousands of Cubans fled to the United States, and Cubría interviewed many of these refugees, and she also prepared reports on Cuba.

HELP

As you revise these sentences, keep in mind that there is often more than one correct way to revise a sentence.

9. In her spare time, she helped people from Cuba find jobs and housing.
10. She retired again in 1973, and she settled in Miami, Florida, and she was surrounded by friends and family there.

Revising Wordy Sentences

Sometimes you use more words in a sentence than you really need. Extra words do not make writing sound better, and, in fact, they can even interfere with your message. Revise *wordy sentences* in these three ways.

1. Replace a group of words with one word.

WORDY	In a state of exhaustion, Tony slumped across the bus seat and fell asleep.
REVISED	**Exhausted,** Tony slumped across the bus seat and fell asleep.

WORDY	As a result of what happened when the tire went flat, we were late.
REVISED	**Because** the tire went flat, we were late.

2. Take out *who is, which is,* or *that is.*

WORDY	Yesterday I went for a long hike with Sonya, who is my best friend.
REVISED	Yesterday I went for a long hike with Sonya, **my best friend.**

WORDY	Afterward, we drank some apple juice, which is a good thirst quencher.
REVISED	Afterward, we drank some apple juice, **a good thirst quencher.**

3. Take out a whole group of unnecessary words.

WORDY	I spent a lot of time writing this report because I really want people to learn about manatees so they can know all about them.
REVISED	I spent a lot of time writing this report because I want people to learn about manatees.

Exercise 9 **Revising Wordy Sentences**

Some of the following sentences are wordy and need improvement. To revise wordy sentences, you can (1) replace a group of words with one word, (2) take out *who is* or *which is,* or (3) take out a whole group of unnecessary words. If a sentence is effective as it is, write *C* for *correct.*

EXAMPLE   **1.** In order to be able to see the starfish better, I leaned toward the aquarium.

   1. To see the starfish better, I leaned toward the aquarium.

1. Our science class has been learning about the starfish, which is a strange and beautiful animal.
2. What I want to say is that starfish are fascinating creatures.
3. A starfish has little feet tipped with suction cups that are powerful.
4. At the end of each arm is a sensitive eyespot.
5. In spite of the fact that the eyespot cannot really see things, it can tell light from dark.
6. The starfish's mouth is in the middle of its body.
7. When it uses its arms, it can pull at the shells of clams.
8. At the point at which the clam's shell opens, the starfish can feed on the clam.
9. Starfish come in a variety of colors, shapes, and sizes, and some are bigger than others.
10. This photograph shows a blue sea star that is holding onto a soft coral.

Beyond Sentence Style

To make your writing the best it can be, you'll need to look at how your sentences go together. Good writers use a variety of sentence beginnings and a variety of sentence structures to keep readers interested. Good writers also use transitions to show the connections between ideas in a paragraph or other composition.

Varying Sentence Beginnings

Basic English sentences begin with a subject followed by a verb, perhaps with a few adjectives and adverbs included. If you use too many basic sentences in a row, your sentences will sound too much the same, and you very likely will bore your reader—even if each separate sentence is itself interesting. Notice how dull the following paragraph sounds.

STYLE ✏ **TIP**

When planning your own writing assignments, save time to edit your composition for style. Many writers revise first for content and organization; then they look at style elements like sentence variety.

> Long-distance bicycle tours can be fun. Bicycle tours combine two sports, camping and cycling, into one. Cyclists study maps. The cyclists decide where to go and what to see. They choose to visit places new to them. They load their bicycles with food and equipment. Then they ride off down the highways and back roads. They meet interesting people. Cyclists on bicycle tours may see wildlife such as deer, birds, and even bears!

One good way to avoid boring your reader is to vary sentence beginnings. Instead of starting most sentences with the subject, you can begin some with one-word modifiers, with introductory phrases, or with subordinate clauses.

> As with many other adventures, long-distance bicycle tours can be fun. Bicycle tours combine two sports, camping and cycling, into one. To decide where to go and what to see, cyclists study maps. Often, they choose to visit places new to them. Happy with their choices, they load their bicycles with food and equipment and ride off down the highways and back roads. On many occasions, they meet interesting people. If they are especially lucky, they see wildlife such as deer, birds, and even bears!

Varying Sentence Beginnings

One-Word Modifiers	**Suddenly,** a noise woke Gwen. [adverb] **Rustling,** some creature was in the underbrush of the woods. [adjective]
Phrases	**After a few minutes,** Gwen went back to sleep. [prepositional phrase] **Trotting away,** a raccoon left the campground with Gwen's favorite cap. [participial phrase] **To keep our caps safe,** we should zip them into our packs. [infinitive phrase]
Subordinate Clauses	**Since the raccoon took her cap,** Gwen thought she would have to buy a new one. [adverb clause] **When she went hiking the next day,** she found the cap in a nearby creek. [adverb clause]

TIPS & TRICKS

To check your writing for varied sentence beginnings, put parentheses around the first five words of each of your sentences. If most of your subjects and verbs fall within the parentheses, you need to begin more of your sentences with single-word modifiers, phrases, or subordinate clauses.

SENTENCES

Exercise 10 **Revising a Paragraph to Vary Sentence Beginnings**

Rewrite the following paragraph to vary sentence beginnings so that the paragraph is more interesting. You can use one-word modifiers, introductory phrases, or subordinate clauses to begin the sentences, and you can rearrange other words as necessary.

EXAMPLE   I enjoy reading. I go to the library often to borrow books.

Because I enjoy reading, I go to the library often to borrow books.

    Good books are full of great characters. Those characters are really just words on a page, but they certainly seem to be more than that. They can be wonderful friends. These characters are people who entertain us when we are bored. They show us exciting things that we might do with our time. They warn us about the foolish activities we should avoid. They say

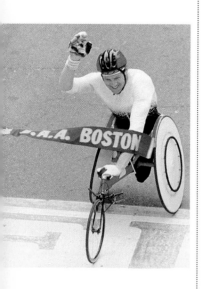

and do things with which we might disagree. They say and do things that we
respect. We can get angry with them.
We can laugh with them. They share
all of the qualities of a good friend.
Characters in books sometimes help us
know that we are never really alone.

Varying Sentence Structure

An important way to keep your readers' attention is to mix
sentences of different lengths and structures. Think like a movie
director. If you were making a movie, you would include long,
complex scenes; but you would mix those scenes with shorter,
simpler scenes to keep your audience's attention. A movie made
up entirely of long scenes or short scenes would be difficult for
your audience to follow. Apply the same ideas to your writing.

For example, the writer of the following paragraph uses
only short, simple sentences.

> Jim Knaub lost the use of his legs
> in a motorcycle accident. He did not
> let that slow him down. He started
> racing wheelchairs. All the other
> racers were using standard wheel-
> chairs. Those wheelchairs were not
> fast enough for Jim. He began to
> design his own. Soon, his light-
> weight, ultrafast wheelchair was
> winning races. He became a well-known
> wheelchair-racing champion. Jim now
> designs wheelchairs for others.

Now read the revised paragraph. Notice how the writer
has varied the sentence structure to include different sentence
lengths and a mixture of simple, compound, and complex
sentences.

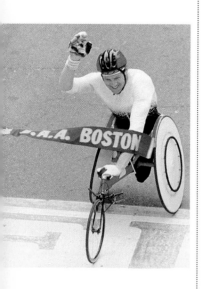

SENTENCES

When Jim Knaub lost the use of his legs in a motorcycle accident, he did not let that slow him down. He started racing wheelchairs. All the other racers were using standard wheelchairs, but those wheelchairs were not fast enough for Jim. He began to design his own. Soon, his lightweight, ultrafast wheelchair was winning races. He became a well-known wheelchair-racing champion and began to design wheelchairs for others.

HELP

When adding variety to sentences in a paragraph, first look for words that are repeated. Sentences with repeated words can often be combined or rewritten to improve the paragraph.

Below is a chart that shows you the four sentence structures. Using a balance of these four structures will help you keep your reader interested in what you have to say.

Reference Note

For more help **identifying sentence structures,** see page 130.

Sentence Structure	Example
simple sentence contains one independent clause	Estivation is somewhat like hibernation.
compound sentence contains two or more independent clauses	Some animals hibernate to protect themselves during cold weather, and others estivate to protect themselves during hot, dry weather.
complex sentence contains one independent clause and at least one subordinate clause	When an animal estivates, its breathing and heartbeat slow down.
compound-complex sentence contains two or more independent clauses and at least one subordinate clause	Some animals, such as salamanders, form cocoons before they enter estivation; the cocoons help protect them from dehydration.

Exercise 11 **Adding Variety to Sentences**

The following paragraph is uninteresting because it includes only compound sentences. Rewrite the paragraph to include a variety of sentence structures. Mix short, simple sentences; compound sentences; and longer sentences with subordinate clauses in your version. Use variety to keep your audience involved.

EXAMPLE   I have an idea, and I think it's a
             good one.
             I have a good idea.

    My friends and I have been talking, and
we have made a decision. We would like
a day off, and we could go on a class
picnic. We could do it right before winter
break, or we could go near the end of the
school year. We could each bring a sack
lunch, or we could each bring something to
share with the rest of the class. The park
near the school has picnic tables, and it
has playing fields and a pool. It might
seem bad to take a free day, but we work
hard the rest of the year. We would enjoy
the picnic, and we would have a fun day.
We would return to school, and we would
have smiles on our faces.

Review C **Revising a Paragraph by Improving
Sentence Style**

The following paragraph is hard to read because it contains stringy and wordy sentences. Use the methods you have learned to revise them. Try to use a mix of simple, compound, and complex sentences in your improved version.

EXAMPLE   One thing I would like to say is that I
             saw the movie *Anastasia*, and I very much
             enjoyed it.
             I saw the movie Anastasia, *which I very much enjoyed.*

The movie *Anastasia* is based on a real story about a real girl from history. Her name was Anastasia Romanov and she was born in 1901 and lived in Russia. The movie is about some historical events in Russia's history, and many things in the movie are not true. For example, the movie says that Anastasia was eight years old when the revolutionaries came to overthrow and defeat her father, who was the czar, but the real Anastasia was a teenager in real life. The movie shows Anastasia and her grandmother, who was the Grand Duchess Marie, escaping together, but in reality her grandmother was already safely in Denmark when the family was seized and captured. Unlike the character in the movie, the real Anastasia did not get away, her remains were found with her family's remains when they were found in 1991. Although *Anastasia* is an interesting movie, people who see it should also know the real story that happened.

Using Transitions

Imagine that you are reading a passage that is full of clear, complete sentences. Each sentence is itself interesting, and the writer has used a variety of sentence beginnings and a variety of kinds of sentences. However, you can't tell how the sentences are related to each other. You find yourself re-reading the passage and trying to puzzle out the connections between thoughts. What could be wrong? Chances are, the writer failed to include transitions. *Transitional words and phrases* help connect ideas. Acting as signposts, they lead readers along, pointing out the relationships between thoughts.

Transitional Words and Phrases		
also	first	meanwhile
another	for example	moreover
as a result	for instance	on the other hand
at last	furthermore	soon
besides	however	then
consequently	in fact	therefore
eventually	last	though
finally	mainly	thus

Read the following passage, which includes underlined transitional words and phrases. As you read, stop when you get to each underlined transition. Before you read the rest of the sentence, predict what kind of information will be in that sentence. For instance, will the sentence support the one before it? Will it present a contrast? Watch for transitional "signposts" that tell you that the passage is going to keep going straight and for those that tell you the writer is changing direction.

> Ed and I set out to hike to the peak of the highest ridge. <u>Soon, though</u>, I realized that the blister on my left heel was getting worse. <u>Furthermore</u>, we had waited until afternoon, and the highest ridge was almost two miles away. <u>However</u>, my uncle had told me that the view from the peak was spectacular. I would be leaving on Saturday and might not have this chance again. <u>In fact</u>, Uncle Alex was planning to sell his house and move inland, away from the rocky shore. I decided, <u>therefore</u>, to put a moleskin bandage on my heel and hurry on.

Notice how the transitional words and phrases tell the reader what kind of ideas to expect. When you write, you should include words and phrases like these to guide your reader. Doing so will help you express your ideas more clearly and help you keep the interest of your reader.

Exercise 12 Identifying Transitional Words and Phrases

The transitional words and phrases in the following paragraph show how the ideas are related to one another. Make a list of the transitions in the paragraph.

EXAMPLE   I found something that I thought was a
fossil. Soon, though, I found out that it
was just a rock with an unusual shape.
Soon, though

Sometimes we can be fooled by the way
things look. For instance, earlier in this
century, Charles Dawson found a few fos-
silized fragments of bone inside a gravel
formation. The fragments seemed important.
Consequently, Dawson took his discovery
to a museum. Soon, a museum scientist
announced that the fragments might be from
a "missing link" between apes and people.
As a result of his announcement, other
scientists quickly believed that the missing link had been found. In fact, they
even gave the new creature a fancy name,
Eoanthropus dawsoni. However, they had
been taken in by a hoax.

Exercise 13 Revising a Paragraph to Show Transitions

The sentences in the following paragraph do not clearly show how one idea is related to another. Rewrite the paragraph, adding appropriate transitions to show how the ideas are related.

EXAMPLE   Eager for exciting discoveries, people
can be taken in. Experts can be fooled.
***Eager for exciting discoveries, people can be taken in.
In fact, even experts can be fooled.***

Scientists discovered that the bones
could not be as old as they seemed. Someone
had stained the bones to make them look
older than they were. People doubted
whether a missing link had been found.
Scientists discovered that the jaw
and some of the teeth were those of an
orangutan. One tooth was from a

chimpanzee. Someone had filed the teeth to make them look human. No one knows who planned the hoax and hid the bones in the gravel. We do know that almost anyone may be fooled by the way things look.

Review D   Revising a Passage to Improve Style

Rewrite the following passage to make it clearer and to improve its style.

EXAMPLE   Carlie and Monica listened to the wind howl, and they wondered whether the storm would let up soon.

Wondering whether the storm would let up soon, Carlie and Monica listened to the wind howl.

The girls had been staying in the old house for nearly a week. They decided to explore some of the rooms. The rooms were ones that Carlie and Monica hadn't explored yet. These rooms were in the west wing. They were closed up. No one used them. The rooms were not empty. They contained very old furniture, which was ornate and old-fashioned. The day was dreary, and it had been raining since dawn, and sometimes lightning flashed and thunder cracked, and the rooms seemed spooky. The girls had a flashlight with them, and it was good that they did because the power went out when they were about to enter the big, dark study that was at the end of the hall. The room seemed very mysterious and also to be neglected. Due to the fact that the power was out and the room was dark, Carlie and Monica were nervous. They stood in the hallway and looked inside. The storm outside grew more fierce. Lightning flared and lit up the room. Thunder roared. The wind rattled the windows. It also made a howling sound. The girls looked at each other. They each took a deep breath. They stepped into the room.

Chapter Review

A. Identifying Sentences, Sentence Fragments, and Run-ons

Identify each of the following word groups as a *sentence*, a *sentence fragment*, or a *run-on sentence*. If a word group is a sentence fragment, rewrite it to make a complete sentence. If a word group is a run-on sentence, rewrite it to make it one or more complete sentences.

1. The morning spent at the dentist.
2. Since sometime near the beginning of last week.
3. I should stay home and help with the yard work.
4. Turn left at the convenience store the library will be on your left.
5. Said not to worry about the change to the schedule.
6. The goat standing on top of John's car and chewing on your hat.
7. Because I want you to meet my cousin Ari.
8. The boat sailed at noon, however, the first mate was not aboard.
9. My computer was not working well, so I restarted it.
10. We cleaned the house, we raked the yard.

B. Combining Sentences

Each of the following items contains two complete sentences. Combine these sentences to make a single sentence that is clear and interesting. To combine the sentences, you can add or delete words, insert words or phrases, or use compound or complex sentences.

11. I will send Terry a thank-you note. I appreciated her help last weekend.
12. The roses need to be pruned. They are overgrown and scraggly.
13. Aunt Sally is my father's oldest sister. She visited us last September.

14. Dr. Severson bought a bouquet of daisies. They are for his wife.

15. The horse that she was riding can run like the wind. It can also leap over fences and hedges.

C. Revising a Passage to Correct Errors and Improve Style

Using the skills you have learned throughout this chapter, revise the following paragraph. Be sure to correct sentence fragments and run-ons, to combine sentences where appropriate, to improve stringy and wordy sentences, and to vary your sentences.

> We know about hockey and ice-skating. Even about ice-fishing. They are fun. There are other sports people can play on ice these sports are just as enjoyable. There is the game of curling. Curling is played on frozen lakes or on ice rinks. It is a little bit like lawn bowling, and there are two teams, and each team has four players. There is a large circle on the ice and it is called the "house" and there is a mark in the middle of the circle and it is called the "tee." The players slide round stones across the ice the stones have slightly curved bottoms and handles. The object of the game is for players to slide their stones into the house. Close to the tee. A player on each team slides two stones toward the tee. Only one of the stones is worth a point, it is the stone closest to the tee. The next players on the two teams slide their stones toward the tee. The stone that is closest to the tee is worth one point. Players can use their stones

to block their opponents from scoring.
Because they can slide stones in front of
the tee. They also use brushes or brooms
in order to sweep away particles of ice
or snow in the path of an oncoming stone
and also so that the stone can slide
across the ice more easily.

SENTENCES

CHAPTER

Sentence Diagramming

1.0 Written and Oral English Language Conventions
Students write and speak with a command of standard English conventions appropriate to this grade level.
1.3 Identify all parts of speech and types and structure of sentences.

The Sentence Diagram

A *sentence diagram* is a picture of how the parts of a sentence fit together. It shows how the words in the sentence are related.

Subjects and Verbs

Reference Note

For information on **subjects and verbs,** see page 5.

To diagram a sentence, first find the simple subject and the simple predicate, or verb, and write them on a horizontal line. Then, separate the subject and verb with a vertical line. Keep the capital letters, but leave out the punctuation marks, except in cases such as *Mr.* and *July 1, 1999.*

EXAMPLE   Horses gallop.

Horses	gallop

Questions

Reference Note

For information on **questions,** see page 19.

To diagram a question, first make the question into a statement. Then, diagram the sentence. Remember that in a diagram the subject always comes first, even if it does not come first in the sentence.

EXAMPLE   Are you going?

you	Are going

444   Chapter 19   Sentence Diagramming

The previous examples are easy because each sentence contains only a simple subject and a verb. Now, look at a longer sentence.

EXAMPLE   One quiet, always popular pet is the goldfish.

To diagram the simple subject and verb of this sentence, follow these steps.

Step 1:   Separate the complete subject from the complete predicate.

complete subject	complete predicate
One quiet, always popular pet	is the goldfish.

Step 2:   Find the simple subject and the verb.

simple subject	verb
pet	is

Step 3:   Draw the diagram.

pet	is

Understood Subjects

To diagram an imperative sentence, place the understood subject *you* in parentheses on the horizontal line.

EXAMPLE   Clean your room.

(you)	Clean

Reference Note

For information on **understood subjects,** see page 19.

Exercise 1 Diagramming Simple Subjects and Verbs

Diagram only the simple subject and verb in each of the following sentences.

EXAMPLE   **1.** Gwendolyn Brooks was the poet laureate of Illinois.

1. | Gwendolyn Brooks | was |
|---|---|

┌HELP┐

Remember that simple subjects and verbs may consist of more than one word.

1. Angela just returned from Puerto Rico.
2. She was studying Spanish in San Juan.
3. Listen to her stories about her host family.

4. She really enjoyed the year.

5. Have you ever been to Puerto Rico?

Compound Subjects

Reference Note

For information on **compound subjects,** see page 13. For information on **conjunctions,** see page 62.

To diagram a compound subject, put the subjects on parallel lines. Then, put the connecting word (the conjunction) on a dotted line that joins the subject lines.

EXAMPLE   **Sharks** and **eels** can be dangerous.

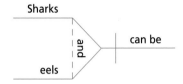

Compound Verbs

Reference Note

For information on **compound verbs,** see page 15.

To diagram a compound verb, put the two verbs on parallel lines. Then, put the connecting word (the conjunction) on a dotted line that joins the verb lines.

EXAMPLE   The cowboy **swung** into the saddle and **rode** away.

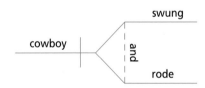

This is how a compound verb is diagrammed when it has a helping verb that is not repeated.

EXAMPLE   Ray Bradbury **has written** many books and **received** several prizes for them.

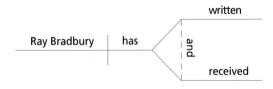

SENTENCES

Compound Subjects and Compound Verbs

A sentence with both a compound subject and a compound verb combines the patterns for each.

EXAMPLE **Rosa Parks** and **Dr. Martin Luther King, Jr., saw** a problem and **did** something about it.

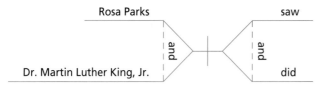

Sometimes parts of a compound subject or a compound verb are joined by correlative conjunctions, such as *both . . . and.* Correlatives are diagrammed like this:

EXAMPLE **Both** Luisa **and** Miguel can sing.

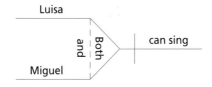

Reference Note

For information on **using compound subjects with compound verbs,** see page 15.

SENTENCES

Exercise 2 Diagramming Compound Subjects and Compound Verbs

Diagram the simple subjects and the verbs in the following sentences. Include the conjunctions that join the compound subjects or the compound verbs.

EXAMPLE **1.** Both LeAnn Rimes and Clint Black are going on tour and cutting new albums.

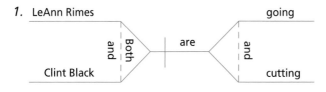

1. Everyone knows and likes Mr. Karras.
2. Hurricanes and tornadoes occur most often during the summer.
3. Julio and Rosa were cutting paper and tying string for the kites.

PEANUTS reprinted by permission of United Feature Syndicate, Inc.

4. Both Jade Snow Wong and Amy Tan have written books about their childhoods in San Francisco's Chinatown.
5. Elena and I grabbed our jackets and took the bus to the mall.

Adjectives and Adverbs

Reference Note

For information on **possessive pronouns,** see page 30.

Adjectives and adverbs are written on slanted lines connected to the words they modify. Notice that possessive pronouns are diagrammed in the same way adjectives are.

Adjectives

Reference Note

For information on **adjectives,** see page 34.

EXAMPLES   **dark** room   **a lively** fish   **my best** friend

```
    room              fish              friend
      \ dark           \ a  \ lively      \ my  \ best
```

> **Exercise 3** Diagramming Sentences with Adjectives

Diagram the subjects, the verbs, and the adjectives that modify the subjects in the following sentences.

EXAMPLE   **1.** A huge silver spaceship landed in the field.

```
1.      spaceship | landed
          \ A  \ huge  \ silver
```

1. The action movie will soon begin.
2. The soft, silky kitten played with a shoelace.
3. A tall, redheaded woman walked into the room.
4. A talkative horse starred in that popular TV show.
5. A weird green light shone under the door.

Adverbs

Reference Note

For information on **adverbs,** see page 54.

EXAMPLES   walks **briskly**   arrived **here late**

```
    walks              arrived
      \ briskly          \ here  \ late
```

When an adverb modifies an adjective or another adverb, it is placed on a line connected to the word it modifies.

EXAMPLES   a **very** happy child   drove **rather slowly**

This **extremely** rare record will **almost certainly** cost a great deal.

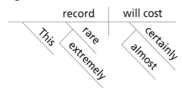

Conjunctions and Modifiers

When a modifier applies to only one part of a compound subject or compound verb, it is diagrammed like this:

EXAMPLE   Benjamin Davis, Sr., and **his** son worked **hard** and rose **quickly** through the military.

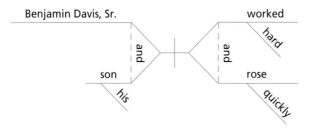

A conjunction joining two modifiers is diagrammed like this:

EXAMPLE   The **English and American** musicians played **slowly and** quite **beautifully.**

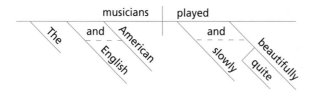

Reference Note

For information on **conjunctions,** see page 62. For information on **modifiers,** see Chapter 11.

SENTENCES

Diagram the subjects, verbs, adjectives, adverbs, and conjunctions in the following sentences.

EXAMPLE **1.** A relatively unknown candidate won the election
easily and rather cheaply.

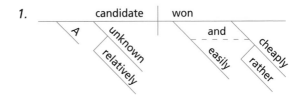

1. The determined young Frederick Douglass certainly
worked hard.
2. The talented actress spoke loudly and clearly.
3. Mei-Ling and her younger sister will arrive early tomorrow.
4. The best musicians always play here.
5. That glue does not work very well.

Reference Note

For information on
objects, see Chapter 4.

Reference Note

For information on
direct objects, see
page 74.

Objects

Direct Objects

A direct object is diagrammed on the horizontal line with the
subject and verb. A vertical line separates the direct object from
the verb. Notice that this vertical line does not cross the horizontal line.

EXAMPLES We like **pizza.**

The robin caught a **worm.**

Compound Direct Objects

EXAMPLE   Lizards eat **flies** and **earthworms.**

Reference Note

For information on **compound direct objects,** see page 75.

Indirect Objects

An indirect object is diagrammed on a horizontal line beneath the verb. The verb and the indirect object are joined by a slanting line that extends past the lower horizontal line.

EXAMPLE   Marisol brought **me** a piñata.

Reference Note

For information on **indirect objects,** see page 76.

Compound Indirect Objects

EXAMPLE   Tanya gave the **singer** and the **dancer** cues.

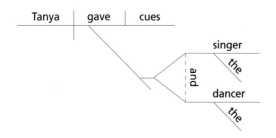

Reference Note

For information on **compound indirect objects,** see page 77.

Exercise 5   **Diagramming Direct and Indirect Objects**

Diagram the following sentences.

EXAMPLE   **1.** I gave the clerk a dollar.

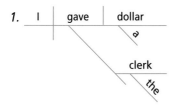

SENTENCES

1. Kim drew a quick sketch.
2. He sent the American Red Cross and Goodwill Industries his extra clothes.
3. My aunt knitted Violet and me sweaters.
4. Gerardo and Wendie are organizing the play and the refreshments.
5. Several businesses bought our school new computers.

Subject Complements

Reference Note

For information on **subject complements,** see page 79.

A subject complement is diagrammed on the horizontal line with the subject and the verb. It comes after the verb. A line slanting toward the verb separates the subject complement from the verb.

Predicate Nominatives

Reference Note

For information on **predicate nominatives,** see page 79.

EXAMPLES   Mariah Carey is a famous **singer.**

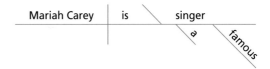

That bird is a female **cardinal.**

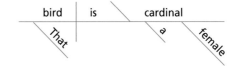

Compound Predicate Nominatives

EXAMPLE   Clara is a **student** and a volunteer **nurse.**

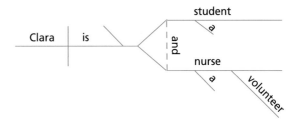

Predicate Adjectives

EXAMPLES   She was extremely **nice**.

This juice tastes **great**.

Compound Predicate Adjectives

EXAMPLE   We were **tired** but very **happy**.

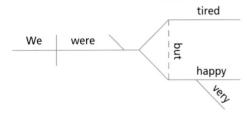

Reference Note

For information on **predicate adjectives,** see page 81.

SENTENCES

> **Exercise 6   Diagramming Sentences**

Diagram the following sentences.

EXAMPLE   **1.** The snake is large and shiny.

1.

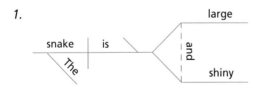

1. Turtles are reptiles.
2. Their tough beaks look sharp and strong.
3. Turtles may grow very old.
4. The alligator snapper is the largest freshwater turtle.
5. Few turtles are dangerous.

Phrases

Prepositional Phrases

A prepositional phrase is diagrammed below the word it modifies. Write the preposition on a slanting line below the modified word. Then, write the object of the preposition on a horizontal line connected to the slanting line.

Reference Note

For information on **prepositional phrases,** see page 90.

Adjective Phrases

Reference Note

For information on **adjective phrases,** see page 92.

EXAMPLES   traditions **of the Sioux**

gifts **from Nadine and Chip**

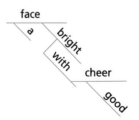

Adverb Phrases

Reference Note

For information on **adverb phrases,** see page 94.

EXAMPLES   a face bright **with good cheer**

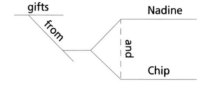

search **for the gerbil and the hamster**

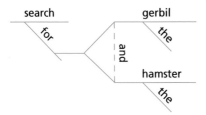

Two prepositional phrases may modify the same word.

EXAMPLE   The tour extends **across the country** and **around the world.**

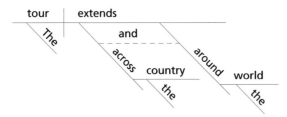

When a prepositional phrase modifies the object of another preposition, the diagram looks like this:

EXAMPLE   Richard Wright wrote one **of the books on that subject.**

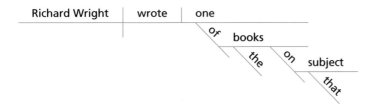

Exercise 7) **Diagramming Sentences with Prepositional Phrases**

Diagram the following sentences.

EXAMPLE   **1.** Our team practices **in the afternoon.**

1. team | practices
    Our   in afternoon
                    the

.

1. The scientist worked into the night.
2. A play about Cleopatra will be performed tonight.
3. Leroy practices with his band and by himself.
4. Garth Brooks has written songs about love and freedom.
5. The director of that movie about the Civil War was chosen for an Academy Award.

Verbals and Verbal Phrases

Participles and Participial Phrases

Reference Note

For information on **verbals** and **verbal phrases,** see page 98.

Participles are diagrammed much as other adjectives are, but the participle curves onto a horizontal line.

EXAMPLE   Juan helped the **wailing** child.

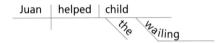

Reference Note

For information on **participles** and **participial phrases,** see pages 98 and 100.

Participial phrases are diagrammed as follows:

EXAMPLE   **Seeing the new employee,** Sandy waved.

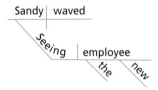

Notice that the participle has a direct object (*the new employee*), which is diagrammed in the same way that the direct object of a verb is.

Infinitives and Infinitive Phrases

EXAMPLES   **To act** is her dream. [infinitive used as subject]

He was the first one **to finish the race.** [infinitive phrase used as adjective]

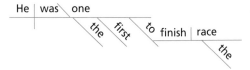

Would you like **to leave early**? [infinitive phrase used as direct object]

He hurried **to help us.** [infinitive phrase used as adverb]

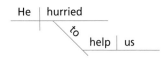

Appositives and Appositive Phrases

To diagram an appositive or appositive phrase, write the appositive in parentheses after the word it identifies.

EXAMPLES My brother **Dan** is an accountant.

Samuel Johnson, **the British writer,** wrote an English dictionary.

Reference Note

For information on **appositives** and **appositive phrases,** see page 106.

Exercise 8 **Diagramming Sentences That Contain Verbal and Appositive Phrases**

Diagram the following sentences.

SENTENCES

EXAMPLE   **1.** She saw them riding bicycles.

1.
| She | saw | them |

riding | bicycles

1. To win was Reginald's goal.
2. The drifting snow blocked the road.
3. The person to ask is Lecia.
4. Hearing the announcement, I looked up.
5. Kris, my good friend, will help.

Subordinate Clauses

Adjective Clauses

Diagram an adjective clause by connecting it with a broken line to the word it modifies. Draw the broken line between the relative pronoun and the word to which it relates.

NOTE The words *who, whom, whose, which,* and *that* are relative pronouns.

An adjective clause is diagrammed below the independent clause.

EXAMPLE   The students **whose projects are selected** will attend the regional contest.

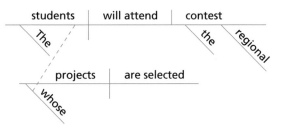

Adverb Clauses

Diagram an adverb clause by using a broken line to connect the adverb clause to the word it modifies. Place the subordinating conjunction that introduces the adverb clause on the broken line.

Reference Note
For information on **subordinate clauses,** see page 114.

Reference Note
For information on **adjective clauses,** see page 117.

Reference Note
For information on **relative pronouns,** see page 118.

Reference Note
For information on **adverb clauses,** see page 120.

SENTENCES

The adverb clause is diagrammed below the independent clause.

Reference Note

For information on **subordinating conjunctions,** see page 121.

EXAMPLE **If I study for two more hours,** I will finish my home-work.

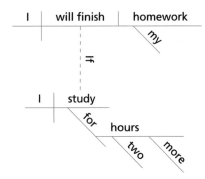

Exercise 9 Diagramming Sentences with Adjective Clauses and Adverb Clauses

Diagram the following sentences.

EXAMPLE **1.** Will you stop by my house after you go to the library?

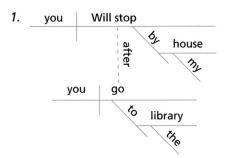

1. Most proverbs are sayings that give advice.
2. Because the day was very hot, the cool water felt good.
3. If it does not rain tomorrow, we will visit Crater Lake.
4. Janice and Linda found some empty seats as the movie started.
5. The problem that worries us now is the pollution of underground sources of water.

SENTENCES

Reference Note

For information on the **kinds of sentence structure,** see Chapter 7.

Reference Note

For information on **simple sentences,** see page 130.

Reference Note

For information on **compound sentences,** see page 131.

The Kinds of Sentence Structure

Simple Sentences

EXAMPLE   Ray showed us his new bike. [one independent clause]

Compound Sentences

The second independent clause in a compound sentence is diagrammed below the first and usually is joined to it by a coordinating conjunction. A dotted line joins the clauses. The line is drawn between the verbs of the two clauses, and the conjunction is written on a solid horizontal line connecting the two parts of the dotted line.

EXAMPLE   Ossie Davis wrote the play, and Ruby Dee starred in it.
            [two independent clauses]

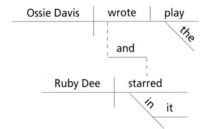

Exercise 10 Diagramming Compound Sentences

Diagram the following compound sentences.

EXAMPLE   **1.** Lucas likes that new CD, but I have not heard it.

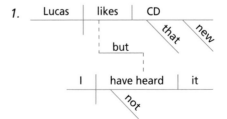

1. We went to the mall, and everyone had a good time.
2. Do you like basketball, or do you prefer hockey?

3. Luis Alvarez was an atomic scientist, but his son became a geologist.

4. Miriam celebrates Hanukkah, and she told our class about the holiday.

5. Baseball is my favorite sport, but my sister prefers football.

Complex Sentences

EXAMPLE   Cheryl has a carving **that was made in Nigeria.**
            [one independent clause and one subordinate clause]

Reference Note

For information on **complex sentences,** see page 135.

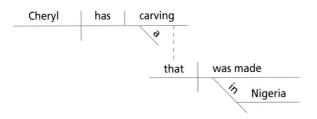

Exercise **11**   **Diagramming Complex Sentences**

Diagram the following complex sentences.

EXAMPLE   **1.** If you see Lola, you can give her this book.

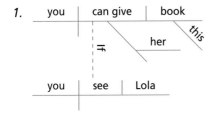

1. Valentina Tereshkova was the first woman who flew in space.

2. Because my cousins live in Toledo, they took a plane to the wedding.

3. Although Wilma Rudolph had been a very sick child, she became a top Olympic athlete.

4. All three of the children screamed as the roller coaster began its descent.

5. The amusement park that we like best offers two free rides to frequent customers.

Compound-Complex Sentences

Reference Note

For information on **compound-complex sentences,** see page 137.

EXAMPLES   Soon-Yee, whose father is a sculptor, studies art, but Mi-Kyung prefers the violin. [two independent clauses and one subordinate clause]

After the raccoon had fallen from the tree, it looked injured, so we called the Humane Society.

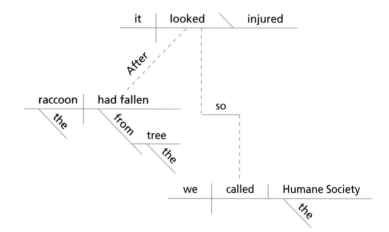

Exercise 12 **Diagramming Compound-Complex Sentences**

Diagram the following compound-complex sentences.

EXAMPLES 1. I smiled when I saw Wendell, and Mike waved.

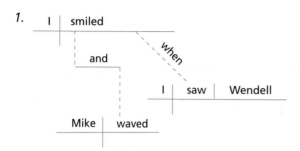

2. The room that Carla painted had been white, but she changed the color.

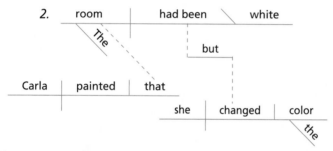

1. We have a game that we bought in Korea, but we do not understand the instructions.
2. Mariella wanted frozen yogurt after she won the tennis match, but Hector and I wanted sandwiches and milk.
3. When I returned to the store, the blue backpack had been sold, so I bought the green one.
4. The restaurant that we like best serves excellent seafood, and the chef has won many awards.
5. Before we conduct the experiment, we should ask for permission from the principal, and we should prepare the science lab.

PART 3

3

Resources

The History of English

Test Smarts

Grammar at a Glance

GO TO: go.hrw.com
KEYWORD: HLLA

The History of English

Origins and Uses

A Changing Language

No one knows exactly when or how English got started. We do know that English and many other modern-day languages come from an early language that was spoken thousands of years ago. The related languages still resemble that parent language. For example, notice how similar the words for *mother* are in the following modern-day languages.

ENGLISH mother   FRENCH mère
SPANISH madre   ITALIAN madre
SWEDISH moder

Over 1,500 years ago, a few small tribes of people invaded the island that is now Britain. These tribes, called the Angles and Saxons, spoke the earliest known form of English, called **Old English.** Old English was very different from the English we speak. English continued to evolve through a form known as **Middle English.** While the English language has always changed and grown,

some of its most basic words have been around since the very beginning.

EARLY WORD
hand   dohtor   andswaru   hleapan
PRESENT-DAY WORD
hand   daughter   answer   leap

Changes in Meaning   It may be hard to believe that the word *bead* once meant "prayer." Many English words have changed meaning over time. Some of these changes have been slight. Others have been more obvious. Below are a few examples of words that have changed their meanings.

naughty—In the 1300s, *naughty* meant "poor or needy." In the 1600s, the meaning changed to "poorly behaved."

lunch—In the 1500s, a *lunch* was a large chunk of something, such as bread or meat.

caboose—*Caboose* entered the English language in the 1700s when it meant "the kitchen of a ship."

Even today the meanings of words may vary depending on where they are used. For example, in the United States a *boot* is a type of shoe, but in Great Britain, a *boot* may refer to the trunk of a car.

Changes in Pronunciation and Spelling

If you traveled back in time a few hundred years, you would probably have a hard time understanding spoken and written English.

■ **Changes in pronunciation** English words used to be pronounced differently from the way they are pronounced today. For example, in the 1200s, people pronounced *bite* like *beet* and *feet* like *fate*. They also pronounced the vowel sound in the word *load* like the word *awe*.

You may have wondered why English words are not always spelled as they sound. Changes in pronunciation help account for many strange spellings in English. For example, the *w* that starts the word *write* was not always silent. Even after the *w* sound that started the word *write* was dropped, the spelling stayed the same. The *g* in *gnat* and the *k* in *knee* were once part of the pronunciations of the words, too.

■ **Changes in spelling** The spellings of many words have changed over time. Some changes in spelling have been accidental. For example, *apron* used to be spelled *napron*. People mistakenly attached the *n* to the article *a*, and *a napron* became *an apron*. Here are some more examples of present-day English words and their early spellings.

EARLY SPELLING

jaile	locian	slæp	tima

PRESENT-DAY SPELLING

jail	look	sleep	time

■ **British vs. American spelling and pronunciation** Pronunciations and spellings still vary today. For instance, the English used in Great Britain differs from the English used in the United States. In Great Britain, people pronounce *bath* with the vowel sound of *father* instead of the vowel sound of *cat*. The British also tend to drop the *r* sound at the end of words like *copper*. In addition, the British spell some words differently from the way people in the United States do.

AMERICAN SPELLING

theater	pajamas	labor

BRITISH SPELLING

theatre	pyjamas	labour

Word Origins

English grows and changes along with the people who use it. New words must be created for new inventions, places, or ideas. Sometimes, people borrow words from other languages to create a new English word. Other times, people use the names of people or places as new words.

■ **Borrowed words** As English-speaking people came into contact with people from other cultures and lands, they began to borrow words. English has borrowed hundreds of thousands of words from French, Hindi, Spanish, African languages, and many other languages spoken around the world. In many cases, the borrowed words have taken new forms.

| FRENCH ange | HINDI champo |
| ENGLISH angel | ENGLISH shampoo |

| KIMBUNDU mbanza | SPANISH patata |
| ENGLISH banjo | ENGLISH potato |

■ **Words from names**   Many things get their names from the names of people or places. For example, in the 1920s, someone in Bridgeport, Connecticut, discovered a new use for the pie plates from the Frisbie Bakery. He turned one upside down and sent it floating through the air. The new game sparked the idea for the flying disk of today.

Dialects of American English

You probably know some people who speak English differently from the way you do. Different groups of people use different varieties of English. The kind of English we speak sounds most normal to us even though it may sound unusual to someone else. The form of English a particular group of people speaks is called a *dialect.* Everyone uses a dialect, and no dialect is better or worse than another.

Ethnic Dialects   Your cultural background can make a difference in the way you speak. A dialect shared by people from the same cultural group is called an *ethnic dialect.* Because Americans come from many cultures, American English includes many ethnic dialects. One of the largest ethnic dialects is the Black English spoken by many African Americans. Another is the Hispanic English of many people whose families come from places such as Mexico, Central America, or Cuba.

Regional Dialects   Do you *make* the bed or *make up* the bed? Would you order a *sub* with the *woiks* or a *hero* with the *werks*? In the evening, do you eat *supper* or *dinner*? How you answer these questions is probably influenced by where you live. A dialect shared by people from the same area is called a *regional dialect.* Your regional dialect helps determine what words you use, how you pronounce words, and how you put words together.

Not everyone from a particular group speaks that group's dialect. Also, an ethnic or regional dialect may vary depending on the speaker's individual background and place of origin.

Standard American English

Every dialect is useful and helps keep the English language colorful and interesting. However, sometimes it is confusing to try to communicate using two different dialects. Therefore, it is important to be familiar with *standard American English.* Standard English is the most commonly understood variety of English. You can find some of the rules for using standard English in this textbook. Language that does not follow these rules and guidelines is called *nonstandard English.* Nonstandard English is considered inappropriate in many formal situations.

NONSTANDARD   I don't want no more spinach.

STANDARD   I don't want **any** more spinach.

NONSTANDARD   Jimmy was fixing to go hiking with us.

STANDARD   Jimmy was **about** to go hiking with us.

Formal and Informal   Read the following sentences.

Many of my friends are excited about the game.

A bunch of my friends are psyched about the game.

Both sentences mean the same thing, but they have different effects. The first sentence is an example of *formal English,* and the second sentence is an example of *informal English.*

Formal and informal English are each appropriate for different situations. For instance, you would probably use the formal example if you were talking to a teacher about the game. If you were talking to a friend, however, the second sentence might sound natural. Formal English is frequently used in news reports and in schools and businesses.

■ **Colloquialisms**   Informal English includes many words and expressions that are not appropriate in more formal situations. The most widely used informal expressions are *colloquialisms.* *Colloquialisms* are colorful words and phrases of everyday conversation. Many colloquialisms have meanings that are different from the basic meanings of words.

EXAMPLES

I wish Gerald would *get off my case.*
Don't get *all bent out of shape* about it.
We were about to *bust* with laughter.

■ **Slang**   *Slang* words are made-up words or old words used in new ways. Slang is highly informal language. It is usually created by a particular group of people, such as students or people who hold a particular job, like computer technicians or artists. Often, slang is familiar only to the groups that invent it.

Sometimes slang words become a lasting part of the English language. Usually, though, slang falls out of style quickly. The slang words in the sentences below will probably seem out of date to you.

That was a really *far-out flick.*
Those are some *groovy duds* you're wearing.
I don't have enough *dough* to buy a movie ticket.

Test Smarts
Taking Standardized Tests in Grammar, Usage, and Mechanics

Becoming "Test-Smart"

Standardized achievement tests, like other tests, measure your skills in specific areas. Standardized achievement tests also compare your performance to the performance of other students at your age or grade level. Some language arts standardized tests measure your skill in using correct capitalization, punctuation, sentence structure, and spelling. Such tests sometimes also measure your ability to evaluate sentence style.

The most important part of preparing for any test, including standardized tests, is learning the content on which you will be tested. To do this, you must

■ listen in class

■ complete homework assignments

■ study to master the concepts and skills presented by your teacher

In addition, you also need to use effective strategies for taking a standardized test. The following pages will teach you how to become test-smart.

General Strategies for Taking Tests

1. **Understand how the test is scored.** If no points will be taken off for wrong answers, plan to answer every question. If wrong answers count against you, plan to answer only questions you know the answer to or questions you can answer with an educated guess.

2. **Stay focused.** Expect to be a little nervous, but focus your attention on doing the best job possible. Try not to be distracted with thoughts that aren't about the test questions.

3. **Get an overview.** Quickly skim the entire test to get an idea of how long the test is and what is on it.

4. **Pace yourself.** Based on your overview, figure out how much time to allow for each section of the test. If time limits are stated for each section, decide how much time to allow for each item. Pace yourself, and check every five to ten minutes to see if you need to work faster. Try to leave a few minutes at the end of the testing period to check your work.

5. **Read all instructions.** Read the instructions for each part of the test carefully. Also, answer the sample questions to be sure you understand how to answer the test questions.

6. **Read all answer choices.** Carefully read *all* of the possible answers before you choose an answer. Note how each possible answer differs from the others. You may want to make an *x* next to each answer choice that you rule out.

7. **Make educated guesses.** If you do not know the answer to a question, see if you can rule out one or more answers and make an educated guess. Don't spend too much time on any one item, though. If you want to think longer about a difficult item, make a light pencil mark next to the item number. You can go back to that question later.

8. **Mark your answers.** Mark the answer sheet carefully and completely. If you plan to go back to an item later, be sure to skip that number on the answer sheet.

9. **Check your work.** If you have time at the end of the test, go back to check your answers. This is also the time to try to answer any questions you skipped. Make sure your marks are complete, and erase any stray marks on the answer sheet.

Strategies for Answering Grammar, Usage, and Mechanics Questions

The questions in standardized tests can take different forms, but the most common form is the multiple-choice question. Here are some strategies for answering that kind of test question.

Correcting parts of sentences

One kind of question contains a sentence with an underlined part. The answer choices show several revised versions of that part. Your job is to decide which revised version makes the sentence correct or whether the underlined part is already correct. First, look at each answer carefully. Immediately rule out any answer in which you notice a grammatical error. If you are still unsure of the correct answer, try approaching the question in one of these two ways.

- **Think how you would rewrite the underlined part.** Look at the answer choices for one that matches your revision. Carefully read each possible answer before you make your final choice. Often, only tiny differences exist between the answers, and you want to choose the *best* answer.

- **Look carefully at the underlined part and at each answer choice, looking for one particular type of error, such as an error in capitalization or spelling.** The best way to look for a particular error is to compare the answer choices to see how they differ both from each other and from the underlined part of the question. For example, if there are differences in capitalization, look at each choice for capitalization errors.

After ruling out incorrect answers, choose the answer with no errors. If there are errors in each of the choices but no errors in the underlined part, your answer will be the "no error" or "correct as is" choice.

RESOURCES

EXAMPLE

Directions: Choose the answer that is the **best** revision of the underlined words.

1. My neighbor is painting his <u>house and my brother helped him.</u>

   A. house; and my brother is helping him.
   B. house, and my brother had helped him.
   C. house, and my brother is helping him.
   D. Correct as is

Explanation: In the example above, the possible answers contain differences in punctuation and in verb tense. Therefore, you should check each possible answer for errors in punctuation and verb tense.

   A. You can rule out this choice because it has incorrect punctuation.
   B. This choice creates inconsistent verb tenses, so you can rule out this answer.
   C. This choice has correct punctuation and creates consistent verb tenses.
   D. You can rule out this choice because the original sentence lacks correct punctuation between the clauses.

Answer: Choice C is the only one that contains no errors, so the oval for that answer choice is darkened.

Correcting whole sentences

This type of question is similar to the kind of question previously described. However, here you are looking for mistakes in the entire sentence instead of just an underlined part. The strategies for approaching this type of question are the same as for the other kind of sentence-correction questions. If you don't see the correct answer right away, compare the answer choices to see how they differ. When you find differences, check each choice for errors relating to that difference. Rule out choices with errors. Repeat the process until you find the correct answer.

EXAMPLE

Directions: Choose the answer that is the **best** revision of the following sentences.

1. After Brad mowed the lawn, he swept the sidewalk and driveway, then he took a shower. And washed his hair.

   A. After Brad mowed the lawn, he swept the sidewalk and driveway. Then he took a shower and washed his hair.
   B. After Brad mowed the lawn, he swept the sidewalk and driveway. Then he took a shower, and washed his hair.
   C. After Brad mowed the lawn. He swept the sidewalk and driveway; then he took a shower and washed his hair.
   D. Correct as is

Explanation: The original word groups and answer choices have differences in sentence structure and punctuation, so you should check each answer choice for errors in sentence structure and punctuation.

    A. This choice contains two complete sentences and correct punctuation.

    B. This choice contains two complete sentences and incorrect punctuation.

    C. This choice begins with a sentence fragment, so you can rule it out.

    D. You can rule out this choice because the original version contains a sentence fragment.

Answer: Choice A is the only one that contains no errors, so the oval for that answer choice is darkened.

Identifying kinds of errors

This type of question has at least one under-lined part. Your job is to determine which part, if any, contains an error. Sometimes, you also may have to decide what type of error (capitalization, punctuation, or spelling) exists. The strategy is the same whether the question has one or several underlined parts. Try to identify an error, and check the answer choices for that type of error. If the original version is correct as written, choose "no error" or "correct as is."

EXAMPLE

Directions: Read the following sentences and decide which type of error, if any, is in the underlined part.

1. Marcia, Jim, and Leroy are participating in <u>Saturday's charity marathon. they</u> are hoping to raise one hundred dollars for the new children's museum.

    A. Spelling error

    B. Capitalization error

    C. Punctuation error

    D. Correct as is

Explanation: If you cannot tell right away what kind of error (if any) is in the original version, go through each answer choice in turn.

    A. All the words are spelled correctly.

    B. The sentences contain a capitalization error. The second sentence incorrectly begins with a lowercase letter.

    C. The sentences are punctuated correctly.

    D. The sentences contain a capitalization error, so you can rule out this choice.

Answer: Because the passage contains a capitalization error, the oval for answer choice B is darkened.

Revising sentence structure

Errors covered by this kind of question include sentence fragments, run-on sentences, repetitive wording, misplaced modifiers, and awkward construction. If you don't immediately spot the error, examine the question and each answer choice for specific types of errors, one type at a time. If you cannot find an error in the original version and if all of the other answer choices have errors, then choose "no error" or "correct as is."

EXAMPLE

Directions: Read the following word groups. If there is an error in sentence structure, choose the answer that best revises the word groups.

1. Mary Lou arranged the mozzarella cheese and fresh tomatoes. On a platter covered with lettuce leaves.

A. Mary Lou arranged the mozzarella cheese and fresh tomatoes on a platter covered with lettuce leaves.

B. Mary Lou arranged the mozzarella cheese and fresh tomatoes, on a platter covered with lettuce leaves.

C. Mary Lou arranged the mozzarella cheese and fresh tomatoes; on a platter covered with lettuce leaves.

D. Correct as is

Explanation: The original sentence and answer choices have differences in sentence structure and punctuation.

A. This choice is correctly punctuated and contains a correct, complete sentence.

B. This choice contains an incorrect comma, so you can rule it out.

C. This choice contains an incorrect semicolon, so you can rule it out.

D. The original word groups contain a sentence fragment, so D cannot be correct.

Answer: Choice A is the only one that contains no errors, so the oval for that answer choice is darkened.

Questions about sentence style

These questions are often not about grammar, usage, or mechanics but about content and organization. They may ask about tone, purpose, topic sentences, supporting sentences, audience, sentence combining, appropriateness of content, or transitions. The questions may ask you which is the *best* way to revise the passage,

or they may ask you to identify the *main* purpose of the passage. When you see words such as *best*, *main*, and *most likely* or *least likely*, you are not being asked to correct errors; you are being asked to make a judgment about style or meaning.

If the question asks for a particular kind of revision (for example, "What *transition* is needed between sentence 4 and sentence 5?"), analyze each answer choice to see how well it makes that particular revision. Many questions ask for a general revision (for example, "Which is the *best* way to revise the last sentence?"). In such situations, check each answer choice and rule out any choices that have mistakes in grammar, usage, or mechanics. Then, read each choice and use what you have learned in class to judge whether the revision improves the original sentence. If you are combining sentences, be sure to choose the answer that includes all important information, that demonstrates good style, *and* that is grammatically correct.

EXAMPLE

Directions: Choose the answer that shows the **best** way to combine the following sentences.

1. Jacques Cousteau was a filmmaker and author. Jacques Cousteau explored the ocean as a diver and marine scientist.

A. Jacques Cousteau was a filmmaker and author; Jacques Cousteau explored the ocean as a marine scientist.

B. Jacques Cousteau was a filmmaker and author, he explored the ocean as a diver and marine scientist.

C. Jacques Cousteau was a filmmaker

and author who explored the ocean as a diver and marine scientist.

D. Jacques Cousteau was a filmmaker, author, diver, and scientist.

Explanation:

A. Answer choice A is grammatically correct but unnecessarily repeats the subject *Jacques Cousteau* and leaves out some information.

B. Choice B is a run-on sentence, so it cannot be the correct answer.

C. Choice C is grammatically correct, and it demonstrates effective sentence combining.

D. Choice D is grammatically correct but leaves out some information.

Answer: Because answer choice C shows the best way to combine the sentences, the oval for choice C is darkened.

Fill-in-the-blanks

This type of question tests your ability to fill in blanks in sentences, giving answers that are logical and grammatically correct. A question of this kind might ask you to choose a verb in the appropriate tense. A different question might require a combination of adverbs (*first, next*) to show how parts of the sentence relate. Another question might require a vocabulary word to complete the sentence.

To approach a sentence-completion question, first look for clue words in the sentence. *But, however,* and *though* indicate a contrast; *therefore* and *as a result* indicate cause and effect. Using sentence clues, rule out obviously

incorrect answer choices. Then, try filling in the blanks with the remaining choices to determine which answer choice makes the most sense. Finally, check to be sure your choice is grammatically correct.

EXAMPLE

Directions: Choose the words that **best** complete the sentence.

1. When Jack _____ the dog, the dog _____ water everywhere.

A. washes, splashed

B. washed, will be splashing

C. will have washed, has splashed

D. washed, splashed

Explanation:

A. The verb tenses (present and past) are inconsistent.

B. The verb tenses (past and future) are inconsistent.

C. The verb tenses (future perfect and present perfect) are inconsistent.

D. The verb tenses (past and past) are consistent.

Answer: The oval for choice D is darkened.

Using Your Test Smarts

Remember: Success on standardized tests comes partly from knowing strategies for taking such tests—from being test-smart. Knowing these strategies can help you approach standardized achievement tests more confidently. Do your best to learn your classroom subjects, take practice tests if they are available, and use the strategies outlined in this section. Good luck!

RESOURCES

Grammar at a Glance

abbreviation An abbreviation is a shortened form of a word or a phrase.

■ **capitalization of** (see page 267.)

TITLES USED WITH NAMES	**M**rs.	**C**apt.	**S**r.	**M.D.**
KINDS OF ORGANIZATIONS	**A**ssn.	**I**nc.	**D**ept.	**C**orp.
PARTS OF ADDRESSES	**A**ve.	**S**t.	**B**lvd.	**P.O. B**ox

NAMES OF STATES	[without ZIP Codes]	**V**a.	**A**rk.
			Mass.	**N. M**ex.
	[with ZIP Codes]	**VA**	**AR**
		MA	**NM**

TIMES	**A.M.**	**P.M.**	**B.C.**	**A.D.**

■ **punctuation of** (See page 291.)

WITH PERIODS	(See preceding examples.)
WITHOUT PERIODS	CD-ROM NBC UFO FBI
	DC (D.C. without ZIP Code)
	mg qt tbsp cm yd
	[Exception: inch = in.]

action verb An action verb expresses physical or mental activity. (See page 45.)

EXAMPLE   Uncle Jim **drives** a school bus.

active voice Active voice is the voice a verb is in when it expresses an action done by its subject. (See page 189. See also **voice.**)

EXAMPLE   The dog **chased** the squirrel across the yard.

adjective An adjective modifies a noun or a pronoun. (See page 34.)

EXAMPLE   Do you see **that beautiful, old wood** house over there?

adjective clause An adjective clause is a subordinate clause that modifies a noun or a pronoun. (See page 117.)

EXAMPLE   We saw an advertisement for a car **that has aluminum wheels.** [The adjective clause modifies the noun *car.*]

adjective phrase A prepositional phrase that modifies a noun or a pronoun is called an adjective phrase. (See page 92.)

EXAMPLE   Dana prefers the backpack **with large pockets.** [The adjective phrase modifies the noun *backpack.*]

adverb An adverb modifies a verb, an adjective, or another adverb. (See page 54.)

EXAMPLE   Mom and Dad **often** drive us to the lake on weekends. [The adverb modifies the verb *drive.*]

adverb clause An adverb clause is a subordinate clause that modifies a verb, an adjective, or an adverb. (See page 120.)

EXAMPLE   Trudy's grades have improved **since she cut back her TV viewing.** [The adverb clause modifies the verb *have improved.*]

adverb phrase A prepositional phrase that modifies a verb, an adjective, or an adverb is called an adverb phrase. (See page 94.)

EXAMPLE   **After dark,** the carol singers went from house to house. [The adverb phrase modifies the verb *went.*]

affix An affix is a word part that is added before or after a base word or root. (See page 350. See also **prefix** and **suffix.**)

EXAMPLES   de + code = **de**code

            im + polite = **im**polite

            feel + ing = feel**ing**

            serious + ly = serious**ly**

agreement Agreement is the correspondence, or match, between grammatical forms. Grammatical forms agree when they have the same number and gender.

■ **of pronouns and antecedents** (See page 165.)

SINGULAR	**Desmond** often rides **his** bicycle to school.
PLURAL	Desmond's **classmates** ride **their** bicycles to school.

SINGULAR	Has **everyone** in the club paid **his** or **her** dues?
PLURAL	Have **all** of the club members paid **their** dues?

SINGULAR	**Neither Darleen nor Clarissa** was pleased with **her** audition.
PLURAL	**Darleen and Clarissa** were not pleased with **their** auditions.

■ **of subjects and verbs** (See page 148.)

SINGULAR	The music **teacher is composing** an opera.
	The music **teacher,** with the help of her students, **is composing** an opera.
PLURAL	The music **students are composing** an opera.
	The music **students,** with the help of their teacher, **are composing** an opera.

SINGULAR	**Each** of the students **is looking** forward to seeing the dinosaur exhibit.
PLURAL	**All** of the students **are looking** forward to seeing the dinosaur exhibit.

SINGULAR	**Neither Kevin nor I was** able to go to band camp last summer.
PLURAL	Needless to say, both **Kevin and I were** disappointed.

SINGULAR	Here **is** a **list** of topics from which you can choose.
PLURAL	Here **are** the **topics** from which you can choose.

SINGULAR	The social studies **class is watching** a video about the space program.
PLURAL	The social studies **class are writing** their essays on the space program.

SINGULAR	**Six dollars is** the price of the kite.
PLURAL	From this stack of bills, **six dollars are** missing.

RESOURCES

SINGULAR	*Parallel Journeys* **was written** by Eleanor Ayer.
PLURAL	Early **journeys** to North America **were** risky.

SINGULAR	**Is gymnastics** an Olympic sport?
PLURAL	**Are** the **scissors** in your sewing basket?

antecedent
An antecedent is the word or words that a pronoun stands for. (See page 30.)

EXAMPLE **Tim** doesn't know how long his essay will be.
[*His* refers to *Tim*.]

apostrophe

■ **to form contractions** (See page 333.)
EXAMPLES wouldn't   I'll   o'clock   '99

■ **to form plurals of letters, numerals, and words used as words** (See page 337.)
EXAMPLES *A*'s and *B*'s   *and*'s instead of *&*'s   5's and 10's

■ **to show possession** (See page 330.)
EXAMPLES player's uniform

players' uniforms

children's literature

someone's backpack

Steven Spielberg's and George Lucas's movies

Batman and Robin's first adventure

appositive
An appositive is a noun or a pronoun placed beside another noun or pronoun to identify or describe it. (See page 106.)

EXAMPLE My friend **Désirée** recently moved to a new house.
[*Désirée* identifies *friend*.]

appositive phrase
An appositive phrase consists of an appositive and its modifiers. (See page 106.)

EXAMPLE The first taxi in the line was driven by Stavros, **a gray-haired man with a mustache.**

article The articles, *a, an,* and *the,* are the most frequently used adjectives. (See page 35.)

EXAMPLES **a** football   **a** uniform

an antelope   **an** honor

the answer   **the** farmhouse

bad, badly (See page 246.)

NONSTANDARD   This green apple tastes badly.

STANDARD   This green apple tastes **bad.**

base A base is a word that can stand alone or combine with other word parts. Prefixes and suffixes can be added to a base to create many different words. (See also **root.**)

EXAMPLES **cycle**   re**cycle**   **graph**   **graph**ic

base form The base form, or infinitive, is one of the four principal parts of a verb. (See page 175.)

EXAMPLE   Can you help me to **find** this address?

brackets (See page 341.)

EXAMPLES   The movie critic wrote, "This actor's performance is a tour de force **[**an unusually skillful performance**]**."

Many of the Iroquois legends we know today might have been lost without the efforts of Kaiiontwa'ko (perhaps better known as Cornplanter **[**his Iroquois name means "by what one plants"**]**).

capitalization

  ▪ **of abbreviations** (See **abbreviation.**)

  ▪ **of first words** (See page 266.)

EXAMPLES   **M**y brother has started taking cello lessons.

Nick asked, "**W**hat does the French phrase *déjà vu* mean?"

Dear Ms. Neruda:

Yours truly,

■ **of proper nouns and proper adjectives** (See pages 266 and 276.)

Proper Noun	Common Noun
North America	continent
El Salvador	country
Staten Island	island
Chautauqua Lake	body of water
Jurassic Period	historical period
Mother's Day	holiday
Blue Ridge Mountains	mountain chain
Saguaro National Park	park
Bernheim Arboretum and Research Forest	forest
Mammoth Cave	cave
Kings Canyon	canyon
Southeast	region
Thirty-second Street	street
National Urban League	organization
San Diego Padres	team
Bowling Green State University	institution
Democratic Party (*or* party)	political party
Roth's Optical	business firm
Super Bowl	special event
February, May, August, November	calendar items
Yavapai-Apache	people
Christianity	religion
Buddhist	religious follower
God (*but* the god Zeus)	deity
Passover	holy day
Torah	sacred writing
Jupiter	planet
Alpha Centauri	star
Ursa Major	constellation
Andrea Doria	ship

(continued)

(continued)

Proper Noun	Common Noun
*E*nola *G*ay	aircraft
*A*tlantis	spacecraft
*B*iology I (*but* *b*iology)	school subject
*M*andarin	language
*M*ount *R*ushmore *N*ational *M*emorial	monument
*W*orld *T*rade *C*enter	building
Heisman *T*rophy	award

■ **of titles** (See page 278.)

EXAMPLES **S**enator Feinstein [preceding a name]

Feinstein, a **s**enator from California [following a name]

Thank you, **S**enator. [direct address]

Uncle Alphonse (*but* my **u**ncle Alphonse)

*A*nasazi: *A*ncient *P*eople of the *R*ock [book]

*M*ythic *W*arriors: *G*uardians of the *L*egend [TV program]

*A*rrangement in *B*lack and *G*ray: *T*he *A*rtist's *M*other [work of art]

*R*hapsody in *B*lue [musical composition]

"**T**he **F**rog **W**ho **W**anted to **B**e a **S**inger" [short story]

"**I A**m of the **E**arth" [poem]

*R*eader's *D*igest [magazine]

the *O*rlando *S*entinel [newspaper]

*F*amily *C*ircus [comic strip]

*B*ack to *T*itanic [audiotape or CD]

case of pronouns Case is the form a pronoun takes to show how it is used in a sentence. (See page 201.)

NOMINATIVE **She** and **I** are taking tae kwon do lessons.

Two of the award winners are Erica and **he**.

Neither baby sitter, Brigitte nor **she,** is available this evening.

We students presented historical skits.

Is David Alfaro Siqueiros the artist **who** painted this?

We don't know **who** she is.

OBJECTIVE   Did you see Jamaal and **her** at the Juneteenth festival?

Kristen invited **him** and **me** to the concert.

Are you going with **them** to the video arcade?

The Earth Day festivities are being organized by two teachers, Mr. Zapata and **her.**

Our guide gave **us** spelunkers a map of the cave we would explore.

Ms. Jennings, **whom** everyone at school admires, will retire this year.

One of the candidates **whom** I will vote for is Tamisha.

POSSESSIVE   **Their** understanding of the rules differs from **ours.**

Her making the jump shot in the final seconds sent the game into overtime.

clause A clause is a group of words that contains a subject and a verb and is used as part of a sentence. (See page 113. See also **independent clause** and **subordinate clause.**)

EXAMPLES   she arrives at work on time [independent clause]
unless the bus is late [subordinate clause]

She arrives at work on time unless the bus is late.

clear reference Clear reference occurs when a pronoun clearly refers to its antecedent. (See page 216.)

EXAMPLES   After **Ben** finished his homework, **he** walked to the library and checked out three books. [*He* refers to *Ben.*]

Although **Avery** and **Becca** arrived at the theater late, **they** were still able to find good seats. [*They* refers to *Avery* and *Becca.*]

colon (See page 311.)

■ **before lists**

EXAMPLES   To assemble the bookcase, you will need the following tools: a crescent wrench, a small hammer, and a Phillips screwdriver.

The Bookends Club is featuring books by these
authors: A. A. Milne, Laura Ingalls Wilder, and
Judy Blume.

■ **in conventional situations**

EXAMPLES   7:30 P.M.

Exodus 20:3–17

The Whole Internet: User's Guide & Catalog

Dear Sir:

comma (See page 294.)

■ **in a series**

EXAMPLES   Shandra, Seth, and I spent the summer working
at the animal shelter.

Alonzo's hobbies include making wind chimes,
working jigsaw puzzles, and writing short stories and
poems.

■ **in compound sentences**

EXAMPLES   We seventh graders performed three plays this year,
but my favorite was *Androcles and the Lion* by
Bernard Shaw.

My friend Albert portrayed Androcles, and I played
the part of the lion.

■ **with nonessential phrases and clauses**

EXAMPLES   Yu the Great, a mythical Chinese king, possessed
superhuman powers. [nonessential phrase]

Yu the Great, who possessed superhuman powers,
could transform himself into different animals.
[nonessential clause]

■ **with introductory elements**

EXAMPLES   Sitting around the campfire, we sang songs and told
silly stories.

If you like to read books in which animals are the
main characters, you may enjoy *The Long Patrol*.

In one of the store windows, I saw an unusual silver
trinket.

■ with interrupters

EXAMPLES   The Gila monster, for example, is a poisonous lizard.
Most other lizards, however, are harmless.

■ in conventional situations

EXAMPLES   On Friday, July 17, 2006, we flew from Baltimore,
Maryland, to Raleigh, North Carolina, to attend my
brother's graduation.

Isn't your address 728 Lakewood Boulevard, Grand
Rapids, MI 49501-0827?

comma splice A comma splice is a run-on sentence in which only a comma separates two complete sentences. (See **run-on sentence.**)

COMMA SPLICE   In 1962, John H. Glenn, Jr., became the first American
to orbit the earth, then in 1998, at the age of 77,
Glenn made history again by becoming the oldest
person to travel in space.

REVISED   In 1962, John H. Glenn, Jr., became the first American
to orbit the earth, **and** then in 1998, at the age of
77, Glenn made history again by becoming the oldest
person to travel in space.

REVISED   In 1962, John H. Glenn, Jr., became the first American
to orbit the earth; then in 1998, at the age of 77,
Glenn made history again by becoming the oldest
person to travel in space.

comparison of modifiers (See page 224.)

■ comparison of adjectives and adverbs

Positive	Comparative	Superlative
short	short**er**	short**est**
heavy	heav**ier**	heav**iest**
generous	**more (less)** generous	**most (least)** generous
slowly	**more (less)** slowly	**most (least)** slowly
bad/ill	**worse**	**worst**

■ **comparing two**

EXAMPLES   Of Mars and Venus, which planet is **closer** to Earth?

In the balloon, we flew **higher** and **farther** than we had thought we would.

China is **more populous** than **any other** country.

■ **comparing more than two**

EXAMPLES   Lake Superior is the **largest** of the five Great Lakes.

Of all of the figure skaters in the competition, I think that Michelle Kwan performed **most gracefully.**

complement A complement is a word or word group that completes the meaning of a verb. (See page 73. See also **direct object, indirect object, subject complement, predicate nominative,** and **predicate adjective.**)

EXAMPLES   All of Ms. Lozano's students admire **her.**

Bring **us** the map, please.

Do you feel **thirsty**?

Angela, this is **Ramona.**

complex sentence A complex sentence has one independent clause and at least one subordinate clause. (See page 135.)

EXAMPLES   My favorite animated film was *Cinderella* [independent clause] until I saw *The Jungle Book* [subordinate clause].

When my little sister wrote a letter to Santa Claus [subordinate clause], she used the address North Pole, AK 99705 [independent clause], which, by the way, is the correct address. [subordinate clause]

compound-complex sentence A compound-complex sentence has two or more independent clauses and at least one subordinate clause. (See page 137.)

EXAMPLES   The Taj Mahal, which is located near Agra, India [subordinate clause], is a beautiful structure made almost entirely of white marble [independent clause]; it was built in the seventeenth century by Shah Jahan as a tomb for his wife [independent clause].

When they publish their works [subordinate clause], some writers use pseudonyms, or pen names, instead of their real names [independent clause]; for example, Theodor Geisel published most of his books for children under the pen name Dr. Seuss [independent clause].

The sweater that I bought last week [subordinate clause] was on sale [independent clause], and it fits well, too [independent clause].

compound sentence A compound sentence has two or more independent clauses but no subordinate clauses. (See page 131.)

EXAMPLES   Two of the kittens are gray [independent clause], but the third one is orange [independent clause].

Yuri was born on February 29 [independent clause]; consequently, each year, except in a leap year, he celebrates his birthday on February 28 [independent clause].

Last night, Dad and I made pizza primavera [independent clause]; he prepared the dough and the Parmesan-cheese sauce [independent clause], and I diced the green onions, red peppers, carrots, and broccoli [independent clause].

compound subject A compound subject is made up of two or more subjects that are connected by a conjunction and that have the same verb. (See page 13.)

EXAMPLES   **Leaves** and **branches** littered the yard after the hailstorm.

Apples, plums, and **blackberries** grow in my grandmother's orchard.

compound verb A compound verb consists of two or more verbs that are joined by a conjunction and that have the same subject. (See page 15.)

EXAMPLES   At the last track meet, Trevor **ran** the mile relay, **threw** the discus, and **participated** in the high jump.

Lauren **attended** soccer practice yesterday but **missed** today's game.

conjunction A conjunction joins words or groups of words. (See page 62.)

COORDINATING	fish **or** fowl
CORRELATIVE	**not only** fair **but also** firm
SUBORDINATING	**Although** Boris had a cold, he insisted on performing.

contraction A contraction is a shortened form of a word, a numeral, or a group of words. Apostrophes in contractions indicate where letters or numerals have been omitted. (See page 333. See also **apostrophe.**)

EXAMPLES

you**'**re [you are]	there**'**s [there is *or* there has]
who**'**s [who is *or* who has]	they**'**re [they are]
aren**'**t [are not]	it**'**s [it is *or* it has]
'14–**'**18 war [1914–1918 war]	o**'**clock [of the clock]

coordinating conjunction (See **conjunction.**)

coordination Coordination is the use of a conjunction to link ideas of approximately equal importance. (See page 423. See also **conjunction.**)

EXAMPLES   Kim **and** Ted volunteered to help. [*And* joins two nouns.]
The bird is in the tree **or** on the telephone wire. [*Or* joins two phrases.]
I enjoy the outdoors, **but** I have never liked camping. [*But* joins two clauses.]

correlative conjunction (See **conjunction.**)

dangling modifier A dangling modifier is a modifying word, phrase, or clause that does not clearly and sensibly modify a word or a word group in a sentence. (See page 233.)

DANGLING   Digging a well near Xi'an, China, in 1974, thousands of ancient terra-cotta sculptures of warriors, horses, and chariots were uncovered. [Were thousands of sculptures digging a well?]

REVISED   Digging a well near Xi'an, China, in 1974, **workers** uncovered thousands of ancient terra-cotta sculptures of warriors, horses, and chariots.

dash (See page 341.)

EXAMPLE   The marine biologist spent several days—ten, I think—recording the movements of the manatee and her calf.

declarative sentence A declarative sentence makes a statement and is followed by a period. (See page 18.)

EXAMPLE   Edinburgh is the capital of Scotland.

dependent clause (See **subordinate clause**.)

derivative Derivatives are words derived from other words.

EXAMPLES   earthling [from *earth*]

union [from the Latin word *unus*, meaning "one"]

direct object A direct object is a word or word group that receives the action of the verb or shows the result of the action. A direct object answers the question *Whom?* or *What?* after a transitive verb. (See page 74.)

EXAMPLE   Rashmi visited **them** Tuesday afternoon.

double comparison A double comparison is the nonstandard use of two comparative forms (usually *more* and *–er*) or two superlative forms (usually *most* and *–est*) to express comparison. In standard usage, the single comparative form is correct. (See page 230.)

NONSTANDARD   Olympus Mons, a volcano on Mars, is the most highest mountain in our solar system.

STANDARD   Olympus Mons, a volcano on Mars, is the **highest** mountain in our solar system.

double negative A double negative is the nonstandard use of two negative words when one is enough. (See page 231.)

NONSTANDARD   Alonzo is so very sleepy that he can't hardly keep his eyes open.

STANDARD   Alonzo is so very sleepy that he **can hardly** keep his eyes open.

NONSTANDARD	I haven't never ridden in an airplane.
STANDARD	I **have never** ridden in an airplane.
STANDARD	I **haven't ever** ridden in an airplane.

double subject A double subject occurs when an unnecessary pronoun is used after the subject of a sentence. (See page 251.)

| NONSTANDARD | Abner Doubleday, contrary to popular belief, he did not create the game of baseball. |
| STANDARD | Abner Doubleday, contrary to popular belief, did not create the game of baseball. |

end marks

▪ with sentences (See page 290.)

EXAMPLES   In 2008, I read more books than my sister.
[declarative sentence]

How many books did you read in 2008?
[interrogative sentence]

Wow! [interjection] You read 32 books!
[exclamatory sentence]

Don't forget that in 2008 your sister also read a lot of books. [imperative sentence]

▪ with abbreviations (See page 291. See also **abbreviation**.)

EXAMPLES   In 1964, the Nobel Peace Prize was awarded to Dr. Martin Luther King, Jr.

In 1964, was the Nobel Peace Prize awarded to Dr. Martin Luther King, Jr.?

essential clause/essential phrase An essential, or restrictive, clause or phrase is necessary to the meaning of a sentence and is not set off by commas. (See page 300.)

EXAMPLES   The woman **who gives the lectures on Romanian art** is Ms. Antonescu. [essential clause]

The animals **drinking at the water hole** gave the elephants a wide berth. [essential phrase]

exclamation point (See **end marks**.)

RESOURCES

exclamatory sentence An exclamatory sentence expresses strong feeling and is followed by an exclamation point. (See page 19.)

EXAMPLE   What a surprise this is**!**

fragment (See **sentence fragment.**)

fused sentence A fused sentence is a run-on sentence in which no punctuation separates complete sentences. (See **run-on sentence.**)

FUSED   Most totems, or images, carved into a totem pole are symbolic usually the totem at the top of the pole represents the family's guardian spirit.

REVISED   Most totems, or images, carved into a totem pole are symbolic**;** usually the totem at the top of the pole represents the family's guardian spirit.

REVISED   Most totems, or images, carved into a totem pole are symbolic**.** **U**sually the totem at the top of the pole represents the family's guardian spirit.

future perfect tense (See **tense of verbs.**)

future tense (See **tense of verbs.**)

good, well (See page 228.)

EXAMPLES   For a beginner, Julian is a **good** golfer.

Yes, for a beginner, Julian plays golf extremely **well** [*not* good].

hyphen (See page 338.)

■ **to divide words**

EXAMPLE   The Ecology Club at our school recently organ**-** ized a recycling campaign.

■ **in compound numbers**

EXAMPLE   The Ecology Club has ninety**-**seven members.

■ **with prefixes**

EXAMPLE   The Ecology Club began a recycling campaign in mid**-**September.

imperative sentence An imperative sentence gives a command or makes a request and is followed by either a period or an exclamation point. (See page 18.)

EXAMPLES   Please turn the TV off. [request]
           Turn that TV off! [command]

indefinite pronoun An indefinite pronoun does not refer to a definite person, place, thing, or idea. (See page 32.)

EXAMPLES   I have **many,** but he has **few.**
           Is **someone** calling for you?
           Both of the children wanted a drink of water.

independent clause An independent clause (also called a *main clause*) expresses a complete thought and can stand by itself as a sentence. (See page 114.)

EXAMPLE   Because Dad never has any spare time, **he hired a contractor to build the deck.**

indirect object An indirect object is a word or word group that often comes between a transitive verb and its direct object and tells to whom or to what or for whom or for what the action of the verb is done. (See page 76.)

EXAMPLE   Kathleen gave the **dog** a rubber toy. [The direct object is *toy.*]

infinitive An infinitive is a verb form, usually preceded by *to,* that is used as a noun, an adjective, or an adverb. (See page 102.)

EXAMPLE   We all wanted **to swim,** so Mom took us to the pool.

infinitive phrase An infinitive phrase consists of an infinitive and its modifiers and complements. (See page 103.)

EXAMPLE   **To help one's fellow human beings** is an admirable goal, Ronny.

interjection An interjection expresses emotion and has no grammatical relation to the rest of the sentence. (See page 65.)

EXAMPLE   **Wow!** Look at those fireworks!

interrogative sentence An interrogative sentence asks a question and is followed by a question mark. (See page 19.)

EXAMPLE   Have you ever seen the Rockies**?**

intransitive verb An intransitive verb is a verb that does not take an object. (See page 52.)

EXAMPLE   The wind **howls** fiercely.

irregular verb An irregular verb is a verb that forms its past and past participle in some way other than by adding *–d* or *–ed* to the base form. (See page 178. See also **regular verb.**)

Base Form	Present Participle	Past	Past Participle
be	[is] being	was, were	[have] been
bring	[is] bringing	brought	[have] brought
choose	[is] choosing	chose	[have] chosen
cost	[is] costing	cost	[have] cost
eat	[is] eating	ate	[have] eaten
grow	[is] growing	grew	[have] grown
pay	[is] paying	paid	[have] paid
spread	[is] spreading	spread	[have] spread

italics (See **underlining [italics].**)

its, it's (See page 251.)

EXAMPLES   **It's** [It is] your turn to clean **its** [the gerbil's] cage.
It's [It has] been a long time since **it's** [it has] been cleaned.

lie, lay (See page 193.)

EXAMPLES   "You look tired, Mom. Perhaps you should **lay** your work aside and **lie** down for a while," I suggested.
Agreeing with me, Mom **laid** her reading glasses on her desk and **lay** down on the sofa.

linking verb A linking verb connects the subject with a word that identifies or describes the subject. (See page 46.)

EXAMPLE   Starlings **are** determined nest-builders.

misplaced modifier A misplaced modifier is a word, phrase, or clause that seems to modify the wrong word or words in a sentence. (See page 233.)

MISPLACED   The pod of humpback whales entertained the passengers aboard the tour boat, leaping gracefully out of the gentle ocean waves. [Was the tour boat leaping gracefully?]

REVISED   **Leaping gracefully out of the gentle ocean waves,** the pod of humpback whales entertained the passengers aboard the tour boat.

modifier A modifier is a word or word group that makes the meaning of another word or word group more specific. (See page 223.)

EXAMPLES   Harriet is **happy.**

Laughing excitedly, the children burst the balloon.

nonessential clause/nonessential phrase A nonessential, or nonrestrictive, clause or phrase adds information not necessary to the main idea in the sentence and is set off by commas. (See page 299.)

EXAMPLES   Diana discussed her trip to Florida**, which took place last month.** [nonessential clause]

The twins**, sitting quietly for a change,** posed for the picture. [nonessential phrase]

noun A noun names a person, a place, a thing, or an idea. (See page 25.)

EXAMPLES   Elizabeth Peña   Paris   mountain   knowledge

number Number is the form a word takes to indicate whether the word is singular or plural. (See page 147.)

SINGULAR	child	man	leaf	town
PLURAL	children	men	leaves	towns

object of a preposition An object of a preposition is the noun or pronoun that ends a prepositional phrase. (See page 59.)

EXAMPLE   She heard a composition on the **radio** by her **music teacher.** [*On the radio* and *by her music teacher* are prepositional phrases.]

parallelism Parallelism is the repetition of sentence patterns or of other grammatical structures. (See page 421.)

NOT PARALLEL   Mark is a friendly person and kind. [a noun and an adjective]

PARALLEL   Mark is **friendly** and **kind.** [two adjectives]

NOT PARALLEL   He is in a hurry, anxious, and has run out of patience. [prepositional phrase, adjective, and predicate]

PARALLEL   He is **hurried, anxious,** and **impatient.** [three adjectives]

parentheses (See page 340.)

EXAMPLES   A praying mantis **(**see Illustration C**)** is the only insect that can turn its head from side to side.

A praying mantis is the only insect that can turn its head from side to side. **(**See Illustration C.**)**

participial phrase A participial phrase consists of a participle and any complements and modifiers it has. (See page 100.)

EXAMPLE   **Admired for his courage,** my cousin George is an impressive young man.

participle A participle is a verb form that can be used as an adjective. (See page 98.)

EXAMPLE   **Blushing,** Tina accepted the award.

passive voice The passive voice is the voice a verb is in when it expresses an action done to its subject. (See page 189. See also **voice.**)

EXAMPLE   The treasurer **was re-elected** with 60 percent of the vote.

past perfect tense (See **tense of verbs.**)

past tense (See **tense of verbs.**)

period (See **end marks.**)

phrase A phrase is a group of related words that does not contain both a verb and its subject and that is used as a single part of speech. (See page 89.)

EXAMPLES   Steve, **our champion swimmer,** will represent King Junior High **at the meet in Kansas City.** [*Our champion swimmer* is an appositive phrase. *At the meet* and *in Kansas City* are prepositional phrases.]

To make her own quilt is Maya's goal. [*To make her own quilt* is an infinitive phrase.]

The leaves, **pressed thoroughly and laminated,** will make beautiful coasters. [*Pressed thoroughly and laminated* is a participial phrase.]

predicate The predicate is the part of a sentence that says something about the subject. (See page 8.)

EXAMPLES   **Will** she **perform a solo**?

Horace **may be responsible for that solution.**

predicate adjective A predicate adjective is an adjective that completes the meaning of a linking verb and modifies the subject of the verb. (See page 81.)

EXAMPLES   The trees looked **red** in the evening light.

This rose smells **beautiful.**

predicate nominative A predicate nominative is a noun or pronoun that completes the meaning of a linking verb and identifies or refers to the subject of the verb. (See page 79.)

EXAMPLES   A lizard is a **reptile.**

My sister will be a **lawyer** soon.

prefix A prefix is a word part that cannot stand alone and that is added before a base word or root to form a new word. (See page 350.)

EXAMPLES   un + fair = **un**fair   il + legal = **il**legal

re + new = **re**new   pre + historic = **pre**historic

self + esteem =   ex + governor =
   self-esteem   **ex**-governor

mid + April =   post + Holocaust =
   mid-April   **post**-Holocaust

preposition A preposition shows the relationship of a noun or a pronoun to some other word in a sentence. (See page 58.)

EXAMPLE   Berlin, the capital **of** Germany, is located **in** the east.

prepositional phrase A prepositional phrase is a group of words beginning with a preposition and ending with its object. (See page 59. See also **object of a preposition.**)

EXAMPLE   **Before work,** Dan always feeds the birds.

present perfect tense (See **tense of verbs.**)

present tense (See **tense of verbs.**)

pronoun A pronoun is used in place of one or more nouns or pronouns. (See page 30.)

EXAMPLES   **His** muscles ached, **she** was sunburned, and **their** feet were sore, but all in all **they** had had a wonderful day.

All of the guests helped **themselves** to **more** of the spinach salad.

question mark (See **end marks.**)

quotation marks (See page 322.)

■ **for direct quotations**

EXAMPLE   "Learning a few simple rules," said the teacher, "will help you avoid many common spelling errors."

■ **with other marks of punctuation** (See also preceding example.)

EXAMPLES "Through which South American countries does the Amazon River flow?" asked Enrique.

Which poem begins with the line "The wind was a torrent of darkness among the gusty trees"?

Cynthia asked, "Did Amy Tan write the short story 'Fish Cheeks'?"

■ **for titles**

EXAMPLES "Song of the Trees" [short story]

"Mama Is a Sunrise" [short poem]

"Many Rivers to Cross" [song]

regular verb A regular verb is a verb that forms its past and past participle by adding *–d* or *–ed* to the base form. (See page 176. See also **irregular verb.**)

Base Form	Present Participle	Past	Past Participle
ask	[is] asking	asked	[have] asked
attack	[is] attacking	attacked	[have] attacked
drown	[is] drowning	drowned	[have] drowned
suppose	[is] supposing	supposed	[have] supposed
use	[is] using	used	[have] used

rise, raise (See page 191.)

EXAMPLES The river **rose** rapidly.

The lieutenant **raised** a white flag to signal surrender.

root A root is a word part that cannot stand alone. It combines with other word parts to form words. Prefixes and suffixes can be added to a root to create new words. (See also **base.**)

EXAMPLES   *–loq–*   *–dict–*   *–lith–*

          e**loq**uent   pre**dict**   mono**lith**

run-on sentence A run-on sentence is two or more complete sentences run together as one. (See page 416. See also **comma splice** and **fused sentence.**)

RUN-ON	We were so impressed by the story that we said nothing he grew a little impatient.
REVISED	We were so impressed by the story that we said nothing. **H**e grew a little impatient.
REVISED	We were so impressed by the story that we said nothing; he grew a little impatient.

semicolon (See page 310.)

■ **in compound sentences with no conjunction**

EXAMPLE   My sister plays violin in her school's symphony orchestra; her goal is to become first chair.

■ **in compound sentences with conjunctive adverbs**

EXAMPLE   I play that movie's soundtrack nearly every day; consequently, I know the lyrics of all of its songs.

■ **between items in a series when the items contain commas**

EXAMPLE   The band's cross-country tour includes concerts in Seattle, Washington; Albuquerque, New Mexico; Cincinnati, Ohio; and Miami, Florida.

sentence A sentence is a group of words that contains a subject and a verb and expresses a complete thought. (See page 4.)

$$\text{S} \qquad \text{V}$$
EXAMPLE   Mr. Holland will give his presentation in the auditorium.

sentence fragment A sentence fragment is a group of words that is punctuated as if it were a complete sentence but that does not contain both a subject and a verb or that does not express a complete thought. (See pages 4 and 414.)

FRAGMENT	In 2002, the Winter Olympic Games in Salt Lake City.
SENTENCE	In 2002, the Winter Olympic Games were held in Salt Lake City.
FRAGMENT	To find more information about the Zapotec culture.
SENTENCE	To find more information about the Zapotec culture, we searched the Internet.

RESOURCES

simple sentence A simple sentence has one independent clause and no subordinate clauses. (See page 130.)

EXAMPLES   Both the cheetah and the chimpanzee are endangered species.

How many other species of mammals are endangered?

sit, set (See page 190.)

EXAMPLES   The science students **sat** quietly, watching the televised launch of the space shuttle *Atlantis*.

On top of the television, the science teacher **set** her model of the space shuttle *Atlantis*.

stringy sentence A stringy sentence is a sentence that has too many independent clauses. Usually, the clauses are strung together with coordinating conjunctions like *and* or *but*. (See page 428.)

STRINGY   I remember that the first time I looked through binoculars at the night sky I was surprised that I could clearly see the craters of the moon and the satellites of Jupiter, but what amazed me most was a bright object shimmering with many different colors near the horizon, and I, of course, immediately thought that I had spotted a UFO, but I learned later that the colorful object was not a UFO but the planet Venus.

REVISED   I remember the first time I looked through binoculars at the night sky**.** I was surprised that I could clearly see the craters of the moon and the satellites of Jupiter**. W**hat amazed me most, however, was a bright object shimmering with many different colors near the horizon**. I,** of course, immediately thought that I had spotted a UFO**. I** learned later, though, that the colorful object was not a UFO but the planet Venus.

subject The subject tells whom or what a sentence is about. (See page 5.)

EXAMPLE   Finally, **the train** entered the station.

subject complement A subject complement is a word or word group that completes the meaning of a linking verb and identifies or describes the subject. (See page 79.)

EXAMPLE   Linus was **impressive** in the play last night.

subordinate clause A subordinate clause (also called a *dependent clause*) does not express a complete thought and cannot stand alone as a sentence. (See page 114. See also **adjective clause** and **adverb clause.**)

EXAMPLE   Margaret and Melanie are two six-year-old girls **who live in San Marcos, Texas.**

subordinating conjunction (See **conjunction.**)

subordination Subordination is the use of a subordinate clause to show that an idea is not as important as the idea in an independent clause. (See page 425. See also **conjunction.**)

EXAMPLES   Until you called, I didn't know of your return. [*Until* connects the subordinate clause *Until you called* to the independent clause *I didn't know of your return.*]

Is the painting that Laura did on display? [*That* connects the subordinate clause *that Laura did* to the independent clause *Is the painting on display?*]

suffix A suffix is a word part that is added after a base word or root. (See page 350.)

EXAMPLES   safe + ly =safe**ly**   fair + ness =fair**ness**

busy + ly =busi**ly**   enjoy + ing = enjoy**ing**

active + ity = activ**ity**   knowledge + able = knowledge**able**

swim + er = swimm**er**   teach + er = teach**er**

syllable A syllable is a word part that can be pronounced as one uninterrupted sound. (See page 347.)

EXAMPLES   stretch [one syllable]

per • plex [two syllables]

un • der • stand [three syllables]

tense of verbs The tense of verbs indicates the time of the action or state of being expressed by the verb. (See page 186.)

Present

I write	we write
you write	you write
he, she, it writes	they write

Past

I wrote	we wrote
you wrote	you wrote
he, she, it wrote	they wrote

Future

I will (shall) write	we will (shall) write
you will (shall) write	you will (shall) write
he, she, it will (shall) write	they will (shall) write

Present Perfect

I have written	we have written
you have written	you have written
he, she, it has written	they have written

Past Perfect

I had written	we had written
you had written	you had written
he, she, it had written	they had written

Future Perfect

I will (shall) have written	we will (shall) have written
you will (shall) have written	you will (shall) have written
he, she, it will (shall) have written	they will (shall) have written

their, there, they're (See page 255.)

EXAMPLES   Did Mr. and Mrs. Wilson invite us to **their** Fourth of July party? [*Their* tells whose party.]

I hung the calendar **there** on the kitchen wall. [*There* tells where the calendar was hung.]

There is not much vegetable soup left. [*There* begins the sentence but does not add to the sentence's meaning.]

They're playing a new computer game. [*They're* is a contraction of *They are*.]

transitions Transitions are words or word groups that show how ideas are related. (See page 437.)

EXAMPLES Sara and Adrian waded in the river; **however,** they decided not to swim.

Afterward, they had a picnic and **then** walked home.

transitive verb A transitive verb is an action verb that takes an object. (See page 52.)

EXAMPLE Marcia **washed** her minivan yesterday.

underlining (italics) (See page 320.)

■ **for titles**

EXAMPLES *Thurgood Marshall: American Revolutionary* [book]

Sports Illustrated for Kids [periodical]

American Gothic [work of art]

The Water Carrier [long musical composition]

■ **for words, letters, and symbols used as such and for foreign words**

EXAMPLES Notice that the word *Mississippi* has four *i*'s, four *s*'s, and two *p*'s.

A *fait accompli* is anything that is done that cannot be undone.

verb A verb expresses an action or a state of being. (See page 45.)

EXAMPLES We **walked** slowly down the steep hill.

The grasshopper **is** near the fence.

verbal A verbal is a form of a verb used as a noun, an adjective, or an adverb. (See page 98. See also **participle** and **infinitive**.)

EXAMPLES The children were amazed by the **leaping** lemurs.

To leave was hard.

verbal phrase A verbal phrase consists of a verbal and any modifiers and complements it has. (See page 98. See also **participial phrase** and **infinitive phrase.**)

EXAMPLES   **Running fast,** the squirrel reached the safety of the tree.

           I don't want **to say goodbye.**

verb phrase A verb phrase consists of a main verb and at least one helping verb. (See page 11.)

EXAMPLES   **Have** you **seen** Rich today?

           I **would be going** tomorrow, otherwise.

voice Voice is the form a transitive verb takes to indicate whether the subject of the verb performs or receives the action. (See page 189.)

ACTIVE VOICE   Patricia MacLachlan **wrote** the book *Sarah, Plain and Tall.*

PASSIVE VOICE   The book *Sarah, Plain and Tall* **was written** by Patricia MacLachlan.

well (See *good, well.*)

who, whom (See page 211.)

EXAMPLES   For two weeks last summer, I visited my pen pal Émile, **who** lives in Montreal, Quebec.

           My pen pal Émile, **whom** I have known for five years, has taught me much about French Canadian traditions.

wordiness Wordiness is the use of more words than necessary or the use of fancy words where simple ones will do. (See page 430.)

WORDY   In the event that it rains, we will not cancel the party that we have planned in celebration of Cinco de Mayo but instead, as an alternative, will hold the party indoors, not outdoors.

REVISED   If it rains, we will hold our Cinco de Mayo party indoors.

state of being and, 46
subject complements and, 79
Loose, lose, 364
Lose, loose, 364
Lose, **principal parts of,** 181
–ly **ending,** 55, 223
–ly **or** *–ness,* **spelling rules for,** 351

Main verbs, 49–50
Make, **principal parts of,** 178, 181
Many, **comparison of,** 227
Masculine pronouns, 165
Meet, **principal parts of,** 181
Middle English, 466
Might of, must of, 249
Misplaced modifiers, 233, 234, 236, 494
Mnemonic devices, 255, 369
Modifiers
    adjective clauses as, 238
    adjective phrases as, 92
    adjectives as, 34–37, 223
    adverb phrases as, 94–95
    adverbs as, 223–24
    clauses as, 224
    comparative degree, 225–27
    comparison of adjectives and adverbs, 224–27
    compound number used as, 338
    dangling modifiers, 233, 236
    decreasing comparison of, 226–27
    definition of, 223, 494
    degrees of comparison of, 224–27
    diagramming and, 449
    double comparisons and, 230
    double negatives and, 231
    fractions used as, 338
    irregular comparison, 227
    misplaced modifiers, 233, 234, 494
    one-word modifiers, 223–24, 433
    participial phrases as, 236
    phrases as, 224
    placement of, 232–38
    positive degree, 225–27
    in prepositional phrases, 90
    prepositional phrases as, 233–34
    problems with, 228–30
    regular comparison, 225–27
    superlative degree, 225–27
More, most, 226
Much, **comparison of,** 227
Must of, might of, 249

Negative words, 231
–ness, –ly, **spelling rules for,** 351
Neuter pronouns, 165
Newspapers, 320, 328
Nominative case, 201, 202, 203–204, 482–483
Nonessential appositive phrases, 301
Nonessential phrases and clauses, 299, 494
Nonrestrictive phrases and clauses, 299
Nonstandard English, 245, 468–69
Nor, 297
    antecedents joined by, 166
    subjects joined by, 156
Not
    as adverb, 12, 55
    contractions and, 333
Not, never, 12
Noun(s)
    abstract nouns, 28
    capitalization of nouns used as adjectives, 37
    case form, 201
    collective nouns, 29, 158–59, 167
    common nouns, 26
    compound nouns, 25, 296, 358
    concrete nouns, 28
    definition of, 25, 494
    as indirect objects, 76–77
    infinitives used as, 102
    irregular formation of plurals, 357
    plural nouns, 331, 355–58
    plural possessive case, 331
    possessive case, 201
    possessive form of, 330–31
    proper nouns, 26
    used as adjectives, 35, 37, 39
Nowheres, anyways, anywheres, everywheres,
    somewheres, 246
Number (grammar), definition of, 147, 494
Numbers (numerals)
    forming plurals of, 337, 358
    hyphens with compound numbers, 338
    underlining (italics) and, 321

Objective case, 201, 202, 206–209, 483
Object of preposition, 59–60, 90, 207, 209
    definition of, 495
Of, 254
Off of, 254
Often, **comparison of,** 227
Old English, 466

apostrophes and, 330, 332
contractions distinguished from, 332, 334
Powerful, comparison of, 226
Predicate(s)
  complete predicate, 10–11
  definition of, 8, 496
  placement of, 8–9
  simple predicate, 10–11
Predicate adjectives
  definition of, 81, 496
  diagramming and, 453
  linking verbs and, 229
Predicate nominatives
  choosing correct form of pronoun and, 204
  completing linking verbs, 80
  compound predicate nominatives, 80
  definition of, 79, 204, 496
  diagramming and, 452
  direct objects distinguished from, 80
  nominative case pronouns and, 204
  placement of, 80
  pronouns as, 204
Prefixes
  definition of, 350, 497
  hyphens with, 339, 491, 497
  spelling and, 350–51
Preposition(s)
  adverbs distinguished from, 61
  capitalization and, 279
  definition of, 58, 497
  for as, 62
  list of, 58
Prepositional phrases, 209
  as adjective phrases, 92, 95
  as adjectives, 233
  as adverb phrases, 94, 95
  as adverbs, 233
  definition of, 59, 90, 497
  diagramming and, 454–55
  direct object and, 74
  example of, 89
  indirect object and, 77
  infinitives distinguished from, 60, 91, 102
  as modifiers, 233–34
  modifiers in, 90
  placement of, 233–34
  punctuation of, 305
  subject-verb agreement and, 153
Present participles
  definition of, 98
  helping verbs and, 175
  of irregular verbs, 178–82
  as principal part of verbs, 175
  of regular verbs, 176
Present perfect tense, 186, 187
Present tense, 186, 187
Principal, principle, 365

Principal parts of verbs
  base form, 175
  definition of, 175
  dictionary and, 178
  irregular verbs, 178–82
  past participle, 175
  past tense, 175
  present participle, 175
  regular verbs, 176
Progressive form, 188
Pronoun-antecedent agreement. *See* Agreement
  (pronoun-antecedent).
Pronouns
  as adjectives, 36, 39
  antecedents and, 30, 216–17, 479
  apostrophes and, 330, 332
  appositives and, 106, 213
  case form of, 201–209, 482–83
  clear reference and, 216–17, 483
  as compound object, 207
  definition of, 30, 497
  demonstrative pronouns, 31, 36
  as direct object, 74
  feminine pronouns, 165
  gender and, 165
  himself, hisself, 214
  indefinite pronouns, 32
  intensive pronouns, 31
  interrogative pronouns, 32
  masculine pronouns, 165
  neuter pronouns, 165
  nominative case, 201, 202, 203–204, 482–83
  number and, 165–68
  objective case, 201, 202, 206–209, 483
  as object of prepositions, 209
  personal pronouns, 30, 202
  possessive case, 201, 202, 483
  possessive pronouns, 330, 332
  as predicate nominative, 204
  problems with, 211–17
  reflexive pronouns, 31, 214
  relative pronouns, 32, 118
  theirselves, themselves, 214
  types of, 30–32
  uses of, 201–14
  who, whom, 211–12
Pronunciation, spelling and, 347
Proper adjectives
  capitalization of, 276–77
  definition of, 37, 276
Proper nouns
  abbreviation of, 291
  apostrophes and, 330
  capitalization of, 266–74
  definition of, 26, 266
  used as adjectives, 37
Punctuation